WHITE PROPERTY, BLACK TRESPASS

RELIGION AND SOCIAL TRANSFORMATION

General Editors: Anthony B. Pinn and Stacey M. Floyd-Thomas

Prophetic Activism: Progressive Religious Justice Movements in Contemporary America
Helene Slessarev-Jamir

All You That Labor: Religion and Ethics in the Living Wage Movement
C. Melissa Snarr

Blacks and Whites in Christian America: How Racial Discrimination Shapes Religious Convictions
James E. Shelton and Michael O. Emerson

Pillars of Cloud and Fire: The Politics of Exodus in African American Biblical Interpretation
Herbert Robinson Marbury

American Secularism: Cultural Contours of Nonreligious Belief Systems
Joseph O. Baker and Buster G. Smith

Religion and Progressive Activism: New Stories About Faith and Politics
Edited by Ruth Braunstein, Todd Nicholas Fuist, and Rhys H. Williams

"Jesus Saved an Ex-Con": Political Activism and Redemption after Incarceration
Edward Orozco Flores

Solidarity and Defiant Spirituality: Africana Lessons on Religion, Racism, and Ending Gender Violence
Traci C. West

After the Protests Are Heard: Enacting Civic Engagement and Social Transformation
Sharon D. Welch

Ecopiety: Green Media and the Dilemma of Environmental Virtue
Sarah McFarland Taylor

Catholic Activism Today: Individual Transformation and the Struggle for Social Justice
Maureen K. Day

Religion, Race, and Covid-19: Confronting White Supremacy in the Pandemic
Edited by Stacey M. Floyd-Thomas

Networking the Black Church: Digital Black Christians and Hip Hop
Erika D. Gault

The Contemporary Black Church: The New Dynamics of African American Religion
Jason E. Shelton

White Property, Black Trespass: Racial Capitalism and the Religious Function of Mass Criminalization
Andrew Krinks

White Property, Black Trespass

*Racial Capitalism and the Religious Function
of Mass Criminalization*

Andrew Krinks

NEW YORK UNIVERSITY PRESS
New York

NEW YORK UNIVERSITY PRESS
New York
www.nyupress.org

© 2024 by New York University
All rights reserved

Library of Congress Cataloging-in-Publication Data
Names: Krinks, Andrew, author.
Title: White property, Black trespass : racial capitalism and the religious function of mass criminalization / Andrew Krinks.
Description: New York : New York University Press, 2024. |
Series: Religion and social transformation |
Includes bibliographical references and index.
Identifiers: LCCN 2023040769 (print) | LCCN 2023040770 (ebook) |
ISBN 9781479823840 (hardback) | ISBN 9781479823857 (paperback) |
ISBN 9781479823871 (ebook) | ISBN 9781479823895 (ebook other)
Subjects: LCSH: Discrimination in justice administration—United States. | Police power—United States. | Christian conservatism—United States. | Capitalism—United States. | White nationalism—United States. | Racism—United States. | African Americans—Social conditions.
Classification: LCC HV9950 .K75 2024 (print) | LCC HV9950 (ebook) | DDC 364.3/496073—dc23/eng/20240317
LC record available at https://lccn.loc.gov/2023040769
LC ebook record available at https://lccn.loc.gov/2023040770

This book is printed on acid-free paper, and its binding materials are chosen for strength and durability. We strive to use environmentally responsible suppliers and materials to the greatest extent possible in publishing our books.

Manufactured in the United States of America

10 9 8 7 6 5 4 3 2 1

Also available as an ebook

For Lindsey,

for all who have endured criminalization,

and for all who are building a world beyond it

CONTENTS

Preface ix

Introduction: The Religion of Mass Criminalization 1

1. Patriarchal Whiteness and Private Property 33

2. "Ownership of the Earth Forever and Ever, Amen!" 69

3. The Mortal God of Police Power 113

4. Criminalization and Deification 141

5. Measuring Salvation in "Chains and Corpses" 181

Conclusion: The Religion of Abolition 235

Acknowledgments 243

Notes 247

Index 303

About the Author 313

PREFACE

There is a photograph of me as a little boy—five or six years old, early 1990s—wearing a plastic riot-police helmet, decked out in camouflage, surrounded by a squadron of little green army men and GI Joes, aiming a plastic toy gun at the camera. As a white kid born into a loving upper-middle-class Protestant Christian household in a semirural New Jersey suburb of Philadelphia, I understood cops and soldiers as the good guys who protected me from a world filled with the dangerous people I saw on the news we watched every night from our living room. The youngest of three by seven years, I spent a lot of time playing basketball by myself in the driveway. Once, a teenager who lived down the street drove by and cursed at me from his open car window. For years after that, I would run toward the house anytime a car came down our rural suburban road. When I was in high school, someone broke into our house while no one was home and stole change from my dresser and jewelry from my parents'. It jarred me deeply—indeed, it still occasionally appears in my dreams to this day. Though I was already aware of and somewhat invested in antiracism by that time, despite never seeing the suspect's face, before I ever had time to think about it, in the white imaginary I inherited, a dark face had already appeared.

When I was growing up, we went to church three times a week: Sunday morning, Sunday night, and Wednesday night. That community raised and shaped me nearly as much as my own family did. Most of that shaping was born of love, but I also inherited an innate sense of fear, not only of the sinful world itself but of hell. After the mother of a kid on my basketball team died when a deer ran into her car at night, I finally put off delaying the only thing I knew would keep me safe from hell if I, too, were to die in a car accident: baptism. Though my baptism means something different—and perhaps more—to me today than it did then, in retrospect, I see now that my fear of hell was deeply intertwined with my fear of strangers and my fear of the dark criminality portrayed on the evening news out of Philly. Likewise, the fear being born in that white kid decked out in toy police and military gear was in some sense the same fear that later drove him under water to avoid the fires of hell. I was in high school when the US invaded Afghanistan and Iraq, which led to an existential crisis of faith: my agnostic punk friends at school opposed the war like I did, but my church family proclaimed its holiness from the pulpit and the pews. Stuck in a new uncertainty about who I was in a world of religiously justified violence, the objects of my fear shifted and the seeds of a new kind of faith were born in me as I marched alongside half a million strangers in the streets of Washington, DC, shouting opposition to the war and global police machine.

A year later, I moved to Tennessee, where, as a college student, I began a new journey of theological and political education that delivered me into solidarity with people long rendered the objects of fear by the white, propertied carceral imaginary I inherited as a young person. After graduating and marrying my best friend, with whom I shared—and still share—a religious and political commitment to solidarity and collective liberation, I began working as a street newspaper editor, where I listened for five years to the accounts of unhoused folks who endured criminalization at the hands of police for acts of survival in a world that deemed them disposable. Around the same time, a former professor and friend invited me into a new community—of which I am still a part—with men behind the razor-wire fences and walls of Riverbend Maximum Security Institution in Nashville. Encountering the world anew from its carceral underside has forever changed how I see everything.

My theological and political education continued from 2010 to 2019 as a master's and doctoral student in theology at Vanderbilt University. Outside of the classrooms where I studied liberation and political theologies, social ethics, critical race theory, materialist biblical criticism, and the religion of social movements, and outside of the coffee shops and home office where I wrote my dissertation, I continued to experience the world in deeply radicalizing ways through relationship with criminalized and incarcerated peoples and through participation in the movements for economic and racial justice and against anti-Black criminalization that thrived during those years in my own city and beyond.

One experience in particular crystallized some of the core questions that catalyzed this book and the dissertation that preceded it. In October 2014, I was invited to speak about the criminalization of unhoused people at a gathering of social service providers working with unhoused people in Nashville. My copanelist was the Central Precinct commander of the Metro Nashville Police Department. I spoke first. After I had detailed with statistics and stories how Metro officers target and criminalize unhoused people in the city and how these unjust actions harm people already struggling to survive, it was the commander's turn to speak. Stepping up to the podium, he smiled, thanked me for my words, said that he agreed with virtually everything I said, and then proceeded to identify and praise, in quite explicit terms, the philosophy of broken windows policing, which he dared to suggest benefited people living on the street.[1] Either he did not make the connection, or he was trying to pull one over on a room full of service providers working with people experiencing broken windows criminalization every day. The commander completely avoided the content of my critiques about how police victimize unhoused people, shifting focus instead to the ways in which people experiencing homelessness endure victimization at the hands of others living on the street.

When the commander and I continued our conversation outside the meeting hall, I tried to press the issue by getting more specific. I told him about Anthony, an unhoused Black man in his forties with a disability that required him to use a motorized scooter. Police cited Anthony for Obstructing a Passageway at 4:09 a.m. on February 15, 2013, at the corner of Seventh and Commerce in downtown Nashville. As the arresting officer describes in the affidavit, Anthony and others were on a heating grate—it was a freezing-cold night—which blocked the sidewalk, forcing a pedestrian to step off the sidewalk in order to get around them. Anthony pled guilty and was fined $259.33 in court costs. The commander stopped me before I could go any further, telling me that it is impossible that Anthony was cited for merely sitting on the sidewalk, suggesting that he must have been intoxicated; otherwise the officer would not have cited him. But the charge was not for public intoxication, and the affidavit mentioned nothing of the sort; the charge was for obstructing a passageway. The commander did not believe me. So I told him about William, a white, unhoused seventy-three-year-old man who was arrested for criminal trespass while seeking shelter during a rainstorm under the overhang of an unused property downtown.

For trespassing while seeking shelter during a storm, William spent a night in jail and owed the court $365.65. "Who was William hurting when he sat under that overhang during a rainstorm?" I asked. Quick to correct what he took to be the misguided premise of my question, the commander fired back. "You have to remember, there's no crime without a victim," he said. "When that man trespassed on that property, he turned the owner of that property into a victim of crime." The commander suggested that by trying to stay dry during a rainstorm, William—a white propertyless man—assaulted a property owner who was not even present and, by extension, the state that exists to secure that property. Why is it that states of precarity that the state makes inevitable also register to the state as states of criminality? This question haunted and guided me as I prepared to write and then eventually wrote my dissertation.

Shortly before I began writing, I coordinated and helped research and write a collaborative report criticizing the Metro Nashville Police Department for its mass criminalization of Black drivers in Nashville. The police chief responded by calling those of us who wrote it "morally disingenuous." Less than a year later, as I started work on the dissertation, Nashville cops murdered Jocques Clemmons and, just over a year later, Daniel Hambrick, two Black men who were running for their lives after traffic stops. Their deaths at the hands of white agents of the state, and participation in the movements that responded to their deaths, brought a level of clarity and urgency to my own calling as a scholar, educator, and movement builder, as well as to this project, that I would not have experienced otherwise. A few months after defending my dissertation in May 2019, I cofounded the Nashville People's Budget Coalition, an anticapitalist and abolitionist organization working to build safe and thriving communities beyond cops and cages in Nashville. As we built and launched that organization, the state killed George Floyd in Minnesota, Breonna Taylor in Kentucky, and many others, in response to which uprisings emerged across the US, including in Nashville. As a result of the decades—centuries—of organizing that preceded the summer of 2020, the concept and politics of "abolition" entered the consciousness and vocabulary of millions for the first time. Between nonstop late-night meetings, protests, and budget hearings, and with the support of loved ones, fellow scholars, and comrades, I wrote the book you hold in your hands.

Today, I am catalyzed less by a fear of hell and more by a desire to transform the carceral and capitalist hells around us into places where all people have what they need to be well. This book is but one small manifestation of that desire: it is an attempt to better understand—in order to help dismantle and build a world beyond—the interlocking eurochristian colonial, racial capitalist, and carceral systems against which an ever-growing number of us struggle daily.[2] I also write as an inheritor and beneficiary of the powers that this book interrogates. Indeed, the fearful kid in the plastic cop helmet could never have imagined writing what follows. And yet, I did. Having come to believe that the imperative to cling to my own racial, gender, and class inheritances as a means of salvation is in fact an invitation to spiritual death, I am convinced, as Fannie Lou Hamer and other Black radical feminists have insisted over the course of the past century, that nobody is free until everybody is free. I wrote this book and organize for a world beyond cops and cages, then, not only for the Black people, Indigenous people, other people of color, and propertyless peoples of all races who are most vulnerable to the state's organized abandonment and violence but for that white kid in the cop helmet, too.[3] I have never endured state violence in its most direct or brutal forms; indeed, I have in some sense benefited from such violence, whether I wanted to or not. And yet, as Hamer and others invite me to understand, salvation that requires chains and corpses is no salvation at all. The death-making pseudo-safety of cops and cages will not serve, protect, or save me. The safety that I most desire is the authentic, inherently collective, and perhaps even salvific safety that comes about when all people have what they need to thrive and we have learned to navigate conflict and harm in ways that bring about life-giving accountability, transformation, and repair.

May it be so.

Introduction

The Religion of Mass Criminalization

Why do we have police and prisons?

It's a question few ever ask, perhaps because the answer, for most people, seems so self-evident that it hardly warrants reflection: we have police and prisons because there are a lot of bad people out there and we need someone to catch them and somewhere to keep them in order for us to be safe. For many people in the United States, police and prisons just *are*—a fact of life as natural as the air we breathe. Many people—white people especially—are habituated into accepting the legitimacy of cops and human cages from an early age, sometimes before we even learn to communicate.[1] As a parent of young children, I can attest to the alarming regularity with which young people are introduced to the trope of dangerous bad guys on the loose and the armed, badged, and uniformed good guys who save the day by capturing and putting them away. In a world where cops and cages are means of *saving* from danger, which is to say, means of a kind of *salvation*, even posing the question "why" to police and prisons risks offending popular sensibilities for which the "thin blue line"—the line that allegedly protects good from evil—is sacred. Who would dare question those who keep us safe and who risk their lives doing so?

Yet thanks to decades of organized struggle and writing from Black radical, Black feminist, Marxist, anarchist, Indigenous, anticolonial, critical race, critical criminologist, and abolitionist practitioners and theorists, it is becoming abundantly clear to a growing number of people that police and prisons do not, in fact, provide the safety that we all deserve but in fact compromise our collective safety and indeed actively endanger us.[2] As prison industrial complex abolitionists and survivors of violence Mariame Kaba and Andrea Ritchie write, police prevent safety "by actively perpetrating violence, by failing to offer protection, by diminishing life chances through criminalization, by looting resources from the things we need to generate more genuine and long-term safety for more people, and by sowing fear and capturing our imaginations to prevent anything new from emerging."[3] One does not have to self-identify as an abolitionist, however, to understand that police do not make safety. David Bayley, the late twentieth-century political scientist who believed in the legitimacy of police and who devoted his entire scholarly career to researching and understanding police work, begins his most widely read book with a surprising assertion: "The police do not prevent crime. This is one of the best kept secrets of modern life. Experts know it, the police know it, but the public does not know it. Yet the police pretend that they are society's best defense against crime and continually argue that if they are given more resources, especially personnel, they will be able to protect communities against crime. This is a myth."[4] The same can be said of the cages into which cops and prosecutors have disposed of a staggering number of people on a daily basis for the past half century. To paraphrase restorative justice practitioner Danielle Sered, if police, jails, and prisons produced safety, the nation that captures and cages more people than any nation in all of human history—the United States—would be the safest nation in all of human history.[5] As we know, the US is not the safest nation in all of human history, and as Kaba and Ritchie help us to understand, it is so unsafe precisely *because* we are more invested in cops and cages than in the resources and responses that actually create safe and thriving communities.

If cops and cages do not exist to keep us all safe, then why *do* they exist, and why do they continue to exist so abundantly? This is a question not just of the origins or daily operation of police and prisons but of their larger *function*. It is a question, in other words, not just of what and who police and prisons are *against* but what and who they are *for*: What do they create and preserve, whom do they empower and save, why do they exist? One of the most powerful forms this question has taken has been the question that anticapitalist and abolitionist demonstrators have shouted at cops in the streets for decades: *Who do you serve? Who do you protect?* As we know, cops and prosecutors and wardens tell us that their purpose is to serve and protect all of us from the threat of violence and crime.[6] But as systems theorist Stafford Beer argues, the true purpose of a system is not what it claims to do but what it actually does.[7] Extensive research shows us that cops and cages do not create the safety that they say they do.⁸ So, what *do* police and prisons do? Modern police and prisons emerged over the course of the eighteenth and nineteenth centuries primarily as means of producing and maintaining colonial racial capitalist order by controlling Black, Indigenous, and other dispossessed peoples whom the state and ruling classes defined as sources of intolerable social disorder.⁹ Even as police and prisons have evolved over time, this core function—social control of racialized and dispossessed peoples defined as criminal threats—has remained central.¹⁰ In the early 1970s, the revanchist state response to the people power gained through decades of radical social movements gave birth to the state abandonment and violence of neoliberal racial capitalism, seeding the beginning of what would come to be known as mass incarceration, or, as I prefer, mass criminalization.¹¹ Less a break from than a terrifying expansion of the powers of criminalization that preceded it, mass criminalization has created entire generations of people made "vulnerable to premature death" in ways that we will still be reckoning with and enduring the impacts of for decades to come.¹²

One of the reasons it is so important to understand the *why* behind police and prisons is that our understanding of their purpose and function inevitably shapes how we interpret and respond to the harms they perpetuate. The widely held premise that police and prisons are, most fundamentally, "public safety" institutions originally intended for the well-being of all leads many people to conclude that, if these systems are hurting people or acting with prejudice, then they must be broken, which is to say that whatever violence they enact must be an aberration from the norm. And aberrations need fixing, some intervention that corrects course so that the system can resume functioning as intended. When we understand, however, that police and prisons were created not to serve or protect all people but to secure the hierarchies that constitute colonial racial capitalist order by eliminating those who seem to threaten them, it becomes clear that these institutions are not broken but are working exactly as designed.¹³ And when we understand that cops and cages are working exactly as designed—that their violence is intentional, not accidental, that their failure to keep all people safe is inherent, not aberrational—then we realize that genuine safety requires the society-transforming work of replacing the systems that prevent safety with social arrangements, relationships, and institutions that make safety and thriving a reality for us all.

While establishing that police and prisons do not make us all safe is a critical place to start, it does not yet answer the question of what *does* keep us all safe and whether we really have to get rid of the system we already have in order to make that shared safety possible. It is important to be honest about the fact that doing away with and ultimately replacing the institutions that claim to keep us safe is a terrifying prospect for most people. This is probably the case because most people prefer the certainty of the familiar—even if it is not entirely good or effective—to the uncertainty of the unfamiliar.[14] Thus, one might legitimately ask, Even if police and prisons enact harmful white supremacist, capitalist, and patriarchal values, don't they also capture and contain people who have in fact committed serious, sometimes mortal harm against others? Do we really have to get rid of the whole system if part of the system is in fact protecting us from dangerous people? These questions are entirely understandable, especially in a society that is indeed quite dangerous, that is governed by a political class that proliferates and capitalizes on fear of mortal danger, and that has thereby made the work of capturing and caging so many people seem so necessary. In the end, the question is not whether many of those who are caged inside prisons and jails have in fact harmed other people—many, though by no means all, have. The real question is *which* acts of harm and *whose* acts of harm are the target of police and carceral power in a racial capitalist society and which and whose are not. Not all acts of harm and violence are criminalized: the acts of harm and violence that white people of wealth commit are frequently disregarded or normalized, while the same or even less harmful acts, when committed by nonwhite and economically dispossessed people, are frequently punished in life-altering or even life-eradicating ways. In the rare case that the same acts are criminalized both for dispossessed folks and for white folks of wealth, white folks of wealth have the means to afford devoted and effective legal representation that increases their chance of avoiding caging, whereas dispossessed peoples do not. The outcome of this dynamic is that the state captures and punishes Black people, Indigenous people, other people of color, and economically dispossessed people of all races at rates far higher than white people of wealth.¹⁵ This is the case not merely because individual cops, prosecutors, judges, corrections officers, and wardens are racist, classist, or sexist, though many certainly are. This is the case because the systems that these individuals operate quite literally originated as means of establishing and defending the hierarchies of racial capitalist patriarchal order. We cannot adequately understand the work of cops and cages if we do not understand their work at a systemic level.

When it comes to the question of how we would effectively deal with harm and violence in the absence of our current system, the first thing to recognize is that our system is already doing very little or nothing about—and in some cases is actively defending—significant amounts of harm and violence, both interpersonal and systemic.¹⁶ It is also important to recognize that harm and violence do not emerge in a vacuum: many of the actions that the police power of the racial capitalist state defines and targets as "criminal" are themselves outcomes of the systemic dispossession and deprivation on which racial capitalism is premised—and not just acts of theft, as we might expect, but acts of violence as well. As Danielle Sered points out, what research shows to be the main drivers of individual acts of violence—"shame, isolation, exposure to violence, and an inability to meet one's economic needs"—are also "the core features of imprisonment."¹⁷ Racial capitalism runs on systemic violence that generates conditions of desperation that in turn generate interpersonal violence, to which racial capitalism responds the only way it knows how: with more violence. Criminalizing the very desperation and harm that it makes inevitable, racial capitalism ignores, legitimates, and even sacralizes the far greater systemic and individual acts of theft and violence that its managers carry out every day.¹⁸ Police and prisons rarely stop harmful things from happening: when they *do* respond to genuinely harmful behavior, they most frequently intervene *after* the harm has already occurred, meaning they do not so much prevent harmful action as occasionally respond—with more violence—after the damage has already been done and in ways that utterly fail to disrupt the cycles that generated the harm in the first place.

The widely held premise that our current criminal punishment system is, despite its "faults," worth salvaging because it still protects us from *some* dangerous people and thereby provides at least a modicum of safety, while understandable, ultimately makes us less safe in the long run. Here's why. To begin with, this idea presumes that the system we have inherited is the only possible way to respond to conflict, harm, and violence—that nothing else whatsoever is possible or effective. This kind of carceral and capitalist realism "arrests our imaginations," chaining us to conditions that do not support life for all—in the name of life for all.[19] The reality is that, despite widespread devotion to capture and captivity as solutions to the state-generated social problems we face, people are already creating genuine safety without—and in spite of—police, jails, and prisons, in a multitude of ways.[20] The notion that cops and cages are salvageable institutions even despite their shortcomings is also premised on the idea, derived from a fusion of European Christian, colonial, capitalist, and carceral rationales, that some people may have to be sacrificed in order for the rest of us to thrive, a premise that transforms the natural human desire for safety into a dangerous and indeed genocidal aspiration. The tangible outcome of these rationales is that even when agents of the state concern themselves with protecting people from genuinely harmful or violent situations, they inescapably do so by selectively criminalizing the actions of those who are already dispossessed or targeted for dispossession by the state. As Alex Vitale writes, "Today's police are clearly concerned with matters of public safety and crime control, however misguided their methods are. [Their crime control] techniques are in fact designed to address serious crime problems, and significant resources go into these efforts. But this crime-fighting orientation is itself a form of social control. . . . What counts as crime and what gets targeted for control is shaped by concerns about race and class inequality and the potential for social and political upheaval."[21] Crime control *is* social control.[22] Partial security for a few *is* criminalization for many. Derived as police and prisons are from colonial racial capitalism, they share with colonial racial capitalism the core operating principles of disposability and control. As such, even when real harm takes place in society—harm that in most cases is catalyzed by conditions of fabricated scarcity— police and prisons only know how to respond with the same logic of disposability and control that guides the order from which they emerge. Indeed, pursuing safety by means of violence quite literally expands the cycle of harm and makes genuine safety unattainable. Violence that begets violence and then responds to that violence with more violence cannot, by definition, stop violence. Disposing of people cannot prevent harm or help people heal from it.

If the managers, beneficiaries, and devotees of racial capitalist order really wanted safety for all, they would have already tried something more likely to produce it. Racial capitalist order does not seek safety for all; it seeks absolute security for itself, no matter the cost to people or planet. Some people benefit from this pursuit of security—at least in part, for now, before it all collapses—but most do not. At the end of the day, genuine safety for all is a matter not of negation—of eliminating problems by disposing of those who seem to cause them—but of creation. To put it another way, just as genuine peace is not simply the mere absence of conflict but the presence of justice, as Martin Luther King Jr. argued, so safety is not simply the mere absence of people who have inflicted harm but is, in fact, the presence of abundance for all, including an abundance of opportunities to take real, transformative accountability for one's actions.[23] As such, genuine safety begins not at the point of harm but well before it ever occurs. As Danielle Sered puts it,

> Safety is produced by resources, by connection, by equity, and by reciprocal accountability among neighbors. The vision of a society that does not rely on policing or on prisons as its primary response to harm is not mostly a vision of less, but a vision of *more*. . . . This vision of safety, to be fully realized, includes and requires the redistribution of resources from the criminal penal methods to more productive, reliable measures of producing safety: investments in health care, in education, in housing, in living wages, in violence interrupters and intergenerational interventions that draw on the moral authority of those most respected by their neighbors, in conflict resolution and restorative and transformative justice, and in a social service infrastructure and safety net that in time will render enforcement not just less dominant, but obsolete.[24]

While meeting all people's needs will not eliminate all harm or violence, it would reduce them immensely. When real harm does inevitably still occur, it can only be dealt with and disrupted if the social, political, economic, and interpersonal dynamics that made it possible are addressed head-on. Restorative and transformative justice practices—practices that directly address the social and communal sources of harm, invite active accountability for that harm, and pursue actual pathways to healing, repair, or recompense—take harm, accountability, and the need for safety and healing far more seriously than our current criminal punishment system ever could. Such practices have long been carried out in a multitude of ways, and they continue to be deployed in more places and by more people than ever.[25] By seeking to transform the conditions that give rise to harm and to make life more livable for those who are impacted by it, noncarceral modes of accountability like transformative and restorative justice take into consideration the full array of human complexity of all those involved in a situation of harm or violence. Such responses to harm refuse to eliminate people who have hurt others, recognizing that everyone who hurts someone in a significant, life-altering way are themselves survivors of some significant harm. In the end, the argument for pursuing noncarceral means of making safety is far more than a matter of promoting selfless compassion for people who have seriously violated our personhood. Indeed, restorative and transformative justice do not require reconciliation or forgiveness between those who have harmed and those who have been harmed. As Sered points out, the predominant narrative, forged by lawmakers capitalizing on people's pain, that all survivors want the harshest punishment for the people who have hurt them, is a lie—but not necessarily for the reasons that most people might expect. As she and her colleagues at Common Justice, a New York City–based restorative justice diversion program for violent offenses, have found, when given the opportunity, the vast majority of people impacted by violent crime choose a restorative process rather than the traditional criminal punishment process precisely because it better serves *them* too.[26]

For these reasons, to critique the so-called public safety institutions of police, jails, and prisons, as I do in this book, is not to critique the premise that all people deserve to be safe. Quite the opposite. Indeed, the critique of mass criminalization I undertake in this book is rooted in a desire for a world in which millions of nonwhite and dispossessed people have what they need to thrive and are no longer subject to state violence, a world in which fewer people commit and experience serious harm, and in which all those who do commit and experience harm are given the opportunity to make and experience some semblance of repair. In other words, the struggle for a world beyond cops and cages—the struggle for abolition—is a struggle for more safety, not less. As abolitionist lawyer Erin Miles Cloud puts it, "Everyone cares about someone's safety, somewhere, some of the time. Abolitionists care about everyone's safety, everywhere, all of the time."[27] Faced with the idea of a world beyond police and prisons, many people will ask, "If we get rid of police and prisons, what would we replace them with?" The answer is, many different kinds of things. No single response to harm is a panacea. Indeed, the pretension that police and prisons *alone* can solve all of our problems is itself part of the problem. As Mariame Kaba argues, there is no such thing as a single replacement for the criminal punishment system; instead, we need a million experiments to make a safer world.[28] If we really want a safer world, we should invest in meeting all people's most basic needs and in developing the many kinds of nonpolice, noncarceral response to crisis and harm that we already know are more likely to keep us safe. Police and prisons do not and cannot create, are not interested in creating, and actively prevent the creation of a genuinely safer world.

Today, more people than ever before are finding the vision of a world of safety and abundance beyond cops and cages irresistible. Indeed, since 2014, millions of people across the US and beyond have taken to the streets to demand such a world, with many joining organized efforts to actualize it long after the protests conclude. With so much opposition to our present carceral reality and so much desire for something different, one would think that the power of cops and cages would be steadily diminishing. Why, then, despite so much organized opposition, do cops and cages seem stronger than ever, enjoying steady support among many Americans even as a growing number of people push for a world without them? Why, even after the greatest crisis of legitimacy they have ever faced, do cops and cages—and the violence they perpetrate—still persist and grow? Part of the answer lies in the fact that the colonial-capitalist-carceral state responds to crises of legitimacy by expanding its violence as a means of eliciting consent and preventing the kind of upheaval that would destabilize its power. Part of the answer also lies in the fact that the state, together with corporate-owned media, responds to crises of legitimacy by proliferating "copaganda" that convinces a majority of people that the world would go to hell if not for police and prisons.

In the end, it is precisely such a sentiment—that the world would go to hell without cops and cages—that invites us to discern in popular conceptions of police and prisons far more than the mundane secular work of serving and protecting. By all accounts, a majority of people in the US do in fact believe that the absence of police and prisons would result in the triumph of evil. This is no mere rhetorical flourish either. For many people, the preservation of police and prisons is a matter of ultimacy, of life and death. Indeed, the work of coming to their defense is, for many people, a manifestation of the work of making ultimate meaning of our shared existence. Understanding that police and prisons are sites of profound meaning-making for so many people invites us to consider more seriously the existential, mythological, and deeply religious function that police and prisons fulfill for those who benefit or seem to benefit from their violence, a function apart from which they would not continue to exist. The radical, largely materialist accounts of police and prisons that deeply inform this book are indispensable for better understanding why we have police and prisons. And yet, when such accounts consider the religious, and they seldom do, they tend to interpret it as a happenstantial factor, at best a long-abandoned feature of police and prisons in their earliest form that bears little to no impact on their present-day function.

This book takes a different approach, arguing that mass criminalization is best understood, in itself, as a religious phenomenon. Mass criminalization is religious not only in the sense that European Christian theological ideas and practices played a crucial role in the formation of modern carceral systems in western Europe and the United States, which they did. At a more fundamental level, mass criminalization is religious because it is a manifestation of the godlike power to create, redeem, and sustain a racial capitalist and settler colonial social order that is, for its managers and beneficiaries, sacred. Racial capitalist settler colonial order is functionally sacred not because it manifests real divine presence—it does not—but because it is a means by which its white propertied managers and beneficiaries get to be as powerful as gods over both people and planet. Saving sacred order from the mortal threat embodied by those who refuse proper subjection to the gods of whiteness and property, criminalization makes heaven for a few by exiling many to carceral hell. In so doing, the ordained violence of police power elicits mass devotion from the managers of order and even from many of its exploited subjects, who put their faith in the pseudo-divine power of cops and cages to make safe, which is to say, to *save*, in the midst of the existentially threatening disorder that colonial racial capitalism itself creates. The managers of carceral, capitalist, and colonial order tell us that cops and cages are natural phenomena, that they are necessary, and that without them we will all descend into chaos and death. The reality, as we will see, is that cops and cages and the functionally sacred order they protect requires making many people vulnerable to death and dispossession in order for a few to live in heavenly abundance. Cops and cages make life for some by sacrificing others.

The fact that death in exchange for life is taken as a given, that it is, for many, a natural, perhaps even divinely derived fact of life necessary for survival, means that our critical interventions must explore the existential, mythological, and religious functions that criminalization fulfills for so many people and for the social order itself. Indeed, if we fail to grapple with the religion of criminalization and mass devotion to the police power at its core—if we only consider the raw materiality of social forces at play in the capturing and caging of masses of dispossessed peoples—then our interventions will be insufficient to prepare the ground for something new to emerge. Building a world on the other side of state capture and caging requires that we understand the indispensable, life-preserving, and thus sacred work that police and prisons perform in the social imaginary of hundreds of millions of people. Such insights promise to sharpen not only our understanding of police and prisons but also our organizing interventions in pursuit of a world of safety and abundance beyond them. It is also crucial to recognize, as I explore further in the book's conclusion, that criminalization's status as a religious or mythological phenomenon does not mean that religion or myth are themselves necessarily carceral or violent. On the contrary, if we want to build a world of genuine safety and thriving beyond cops and cages, we will need to uncover and elaborate on the intellectual and practical resources that will nourish that world into being, resources that already circulate within an array of religious and spiritual traditions broadly conceived.

But in order to build what could be, we must more fully understand what is.

Conceptual Cornerstones

Four conceptual cornerstones anchor the foundation on which this book's argument takes shape. Most of them are found in the book's full title: *White Property, Black Trespass: Racial Capitalism and the Religious Function of Mass Criminalization*. In order to set up the book's argument and to give some initial signals as to what I have in mind when I use these terms, I briefly introduce the book's key concepts and terms in this section. The nature of language and writing are such that it is impossible to encapsulate all that might be signified by a word the first time one uses it—or even the hundredth time, for that matter. Meanings unfold and reveal themselves with repetition and elaboration and continue to unfold well after the final punctuation mark. Thus, what I offer in what follows is not the final word on the possible meanings contained in the concepts under consideration but rather a means of nudging these terms into their unfurling, a process that will take place more fully over the course of the entire book and hopefully beyond it.

Religion

In order to dig more deeply into the *why* beneath criminalization, I deploy the interpretive tools of religious study and political theology alongside the radical analyses that emerge from centuries of struggle against the forces under consideration. Most scholars of religion agree that there can be no final agreement on a single, all-encompassing definition of "religion."[29] Most scholars also agree that we should continue deploying, interrogating, and elaborating on "religion" anyway. "Religion" is a word with relatively recent modern and complex European Christian, colonial, and imperial origins.[30] And yet, at this point in its usage, "religion" continues to signify something widely accepted as integral to much of human experience. Even for those who do not affiliate with any religious tradition, whether they realize it or not, religious thought and practice nevertheless shape the contours of their experience by shaping both the social formations and institutions with which they interact and the interpretive frames through which they perceive and engage the world. Religion means many things in many ways. Foremost among its predominant significations are formally recognized "religions" or religious traditions. Christianity, and what Native American theologian Tink Tinker calls the "eurochristian" tradition in particular, is indeed central to the "religion," "religious," and "religiosity" with which this book is concerned—not because Christianity is a superior religious tradition but because religious and political authorities in the European colonial and American Protestant world have long situated it as superior in ways that have deeply shaped the social and carceral realities that this book explores. More than a matter of individual religious affiliation, this book is about how particular forms of religious thought and practice fuse with particular political rationales and practices in ways that shape some of the central conceptualities and institutions that order life in the United States and in other places as well.

Including but also exceeding the particularities of eurochristian thought and practice, "religion" as I understand and think with it in this book has to do primarily with the human work of navigating how and what it means to be mortal together, a task that often—though not always—takes place in relation to that which is understood to transcend mortality. Though I do not venture a fixed definition, I understand religion primarily as a set of practices and orientations by which humans transcend, transform, and/or make ultimate meaning of the conditions of finitude.[31] More than abstract belief alone, religion is about what Charles Long calls "orientation in the ultimate sense," the ways of being, knowing, and doing by which individuals and communities arrange their embodied and psychic lives in accordance with some shared interpretation of that which undergirds or shapes reality itself.[32] Even when the work of meaningfully navigating the conditions of finitude incorporates some sense of that which is beyond finitude—God, the divine, spirit, heaven, hell—it nevertheless does so from the concreteness and materiality of embodied, mortal, finite life. Religion, in other words, is a fundamentally human endeavor, and as a human endeavor, religion, like humans, is fundamentally material, social, and even political, which is to say, concerned with the arrangement of material life, resources, and relationships here and now.

Additionally, because religion is a means of meaningfully navigating—interpreting, understanding, traveling through, shaping—the conditions of finitude, it often entails the work of delineation, of organizing aspects of reality into a navigable sense of order. And where there is order there is often conceptual partition of one kind or another and, in many cases, dichotomies, oppositionalities through which meaning and value are assigned differentially, including across seemingly distinct peoples, places, and things. One of the most predominant oppositionalities that operates within religion broadly conceived, and within eurochristian religion in particular, is that between the sacred and the profane, between that which embodies the divine or ultimate and that which opposes the divine or ultimate. More than a mere abstraction, the idea of the sacred and the profane and other religious oppositionalities—good and evil, moral and immoral, pure and impure, orderly and disorderly—help forge real-life partitions that structure our shared existence, from the minutiae of everyday life to institutional practices that give life to some people and take it away from others.

One need not be a scholar or practitioner of religion in order to understand or think with this book. Indeed, I hope that people who study and practice matters other than religion will find that this book opens space for perceiving anew, perhaps with greater depth, some of the central forces that structure life in the United States and beyond. As a practice of inherently complex human beings, religion itself is neither exclusively good nor exclusively bad. While much of this book consists of critique of certain manifestations and deployments of religion—namely, eurochristian religion—this book does not reduce religion as a whole to a manifestation of absolute irrationality, illusion, superstition, or violence. Marxist, Freudian, and other critiques of religion are important and even inform aspects of this book's core arguments.[33] And yet, critically interrogating particular manifestations of religion is not inherently the same thing as delegitimizing or dismissing religion altogether. Thus, while this book analyzes religion as a force that shapes the colonial racial capitalist conditions of finitude in the United States and beyond, it also contends that abolition can and should be understood as a religious practice and orientation by which people transcend and transform—build a new world beyond, in the ashes of—the conditions of the colonial racial capitalist present. The invitation to interpret abolition as a religious practice is not necessarily an invitation to join a church, a synagogue, a mosque, or any other traditionally religious community and start evangelizing about the eradication of prisons and police, though that would be a perfectly good and fruitful thing to do. Rather, it is an invitation to discern the deep structural resonances between religion, spirituality, and abolition and to understand, in strategic terms, that if cops and cages fulfill a meaningful function on which people's sense of reality depends, then abolition must do the same: it must engage people not just at the material surface but at the depths of their experience and perception of reality.

White Property

Much popular commentary on matters of race and gender takes the categories themselves for granted as natural and neutral: they seem to refer to aspects of human difference so simply and directly that most people assume that the categories have always been with us and that they do no more than objectively describe the way things already happen to be. The reality, however, is that the categories of race and gender themselves, as well as the realities that have been tethered to them, have a history, a point of origin, which means they only seem natural today because they have undergone multiple processes of naturalization at the hands of ruling classes wherein their conceptual and material construction have been largely erased and/or forgotten.[34] The fact that these categories are constructed does not, however, mean that they are socially insignificant: while the categories of race and gender may be constructed—made up, fabricated—their effects are all too real in shaping people's lives and social relationships.[35]

Far from a mere descriptor of difference, race in particular is best understood as a political strategy, what Robin D. G. Kelley calls "a means of structuring power through difference."[36] While notions of group differentiation understood in some sense as "racial" existed prior to the emergence of European capitalism and colonialism, it was in and through the world-rearranging, paradigm-shifting processes of capitalism and colonialism that racial differentiation eventually took on new, more rigid, and absolutized meanings organized around the supremacy of European identity or, as it would eventually come to be known in the early eighteenth century, whiteness. As a manifestation of European colonialism, capitalism, and Christianity, whiteness came into being in and through what propertied European men understood to be divinely ordained acts of violent dispossession against non-European and propertyless peoples throughout Europe, Africa, Southeast Asia, and the Americas. Indeed, when European identity eventually solidified into "whiteness," it did so precisely by casting Europeanness as a positionality in superior moral opposition to non-European peoples—and people of African descent in particular—whom Europeans defined as uncivilized, unintelligent, and immoral. As such, it is important to understand whiteness as an inherently violent, destructive, and even deadly phenomenon, not only for those who dwell outside its boundaries but eventually for those who inhabit and possess it as well.[37] Having emerged through the world-possessing pretensions of eurochristian colonialism and capitalism, whiteness is best understood as a manifestation of the aspiration to godlike transcendence and power, a means of exercising near total control over people and planet, of controlling the world from beyond the world's vulnerabilities. More than just a god that people worship, whiteness is a means by which those who inhabit and possess it get to be as powerful as gods.[38]

Whiteness, W. E. B. Du Bois writes, is the godlike power to possess the world without limitations of time or space: "ownership of the earth forever and ever, Amen!"[39] Whiteness is a modality of world-encompassing ownership because whiteness entered the world alongside colonial and capitalist regimes of absolutely exclusive private ownership. As critical race theorist Cheryl Harris shows, whiteness and property have, from their beginnings, been bound together, both conceptually and materially. Harris's groundbreaking 1994 essay "Whiteness as Property" played an integral role in the development of this book's arguments, as highlighted in the first two words of its title: *White Property*.[40] "White property" is perhaps the most concise description of the world that eurochristian colonialism and racial capitalism creates, a world in which police and carceral power play a central organizing role. As a manifestation of European men's aspiration to godlike possession of the Earth, whiteness in all its forms is inherently patriarchal and possessive. Thus, in addition to "whiteness," I frequently use the terms "patriarchal whiteness" and "possessive whiteness" as more descriptive ways of referring to the same thing. Likewise, when I use the more concise term "whiteness," I am using it, in every instance, as shorthand for "patriarchal and possessive whiteness." Alternating between the terms, as I do throughout this book, conveys the multidimensionality of whiteness and allows me to emphasize its particular dynamics as needed.

When I refer to "property," in almost every case, except where clearly noted otherwise, I am referring to the regime of what I call "absolutely exclusive private property" that emerged together with whiteness via eurochristian colonial-capitalist thought and practice in the early modern period. Absolutely exclusive private property is a radical expansion of the notion of relatively "private" property that had existed since at least the ancient Greeks. Because the term "absolutely exclusive private property" is somewhat less concise, I mostly use "private property" and in some cases just "property" as a shorthand way of referring to it. "Private property" in its modern usage typically refers to privately owned land, a phenomenon central to the development of colonial racial capitalism. I use the term "property" with this material, landed quality in mind, and engage and deploy it more than "capital," precisely because it is the partitioning and privatization of land that makes capital possible in the first place, a process I explore further in chapter 1. Where I explore property in this more tangible form, I do so more generally, in a way that includes both rural and urban forms. Some examples in the book focus on property in the context of early agricultural forms of capitalism, while others are implicitly concerned with property in its more urban and neoliberal capitalist iterations. While there are important distinctions between these different forms of property across time and space, my intervention treats property generally, focusing on the continuities between its various forms. I also focus primarily on property rather than capital in this book because the term "property"—and "trespass" along with it—connotes a spatiality that is fundamental to the place-making and dis-placing dynamic at the heart of eurochristian colonial-capitalist order. At the same time, while I use the term "property" with this landed, spatial quality in mind, my exploration of private property is not strictly limited to privately owned land or other material phenomena. Beyond the materiality of that which is possessed, I also explore property ownership as a mode of relation, one derived from religious and political conceptualities that give shape to the white propertied world and the police and carceral power that help make and defend it.

Black Trespass

Whiteness and property, together, are oppositional forces that require the dispossession and elimination of people in relation to whom they assert their godlike superiority. As such, all that falls outside their sacred partitions inevitably appears, to those who depend on those partitions for their transcendent security, as attempts to destroy them. And all that seemingly attempts to destroy that which is of God, God—or humans claiming to act on God's behalf—must destroy. Eurochristian colonial and capitalist order is order based on what Patrick Wolfe calls the "logic of elimination," according to which all who stand in the way of the infinite expansion of white possession must be disposed of, or at least brought under control, hence the innate connection between the colonial, the capitalist, and the carceral. Structured as it is by a dynamic of opposition, a world in which whiteness is sacred property is a world in which Blackness is trespass. The term "trespass" conveys multiple meanings that reflect the intertwining of the religious and the political at the heart of eurochristian order: trespass as sin against a divine sovereign and trespass as offense against the sacredness of whiteness, property, and their possessors. The term "trespass" also conveys the out-of-place-ness that many forms of religion interpret as a disorderly disruption of the sacred.[41]

For the world that eurochristian colonialism and racial capitalism create, there is whiteness, and there is everything and everyone that is not white. Or, in Du Bois's terms, there is the "white world" and the "dark world," divided by the well-reinforced boundary of the "color line."[42] Throughout this book, I occasionally use the term "nonwhite" as a functional descriptor of this implicitly genocidal dynamic that emerged through European thought and practice. As I use it, the term "nonwhite" is more about the violent oppositionality that animates whiteness—the primary positionality I interrogate throughout the book—than it is about Black, Indigenous, Latinx, Arab, Asian, or other racial and ethnic subject positions. I thus use the term "nonwhite" not to collapse diverse racial identities into one monolithic whole but to be consistently specific about the fact that whiteness invents and empowers itself by violently setting itself over against those whom it constructs as monolithic, inferior, and threatening to its godlike power.

While the world as whiteness arranges it boils down to white and nonwhite, for people of European descent, the original, most threatening, and disorderly manifestation of the "dark world" is Blackness. It was primarily in violent relation to people of African descent that Europeans deified themselves, and it is primarily in relation to Blackness that the possessors of whiteness continue to deploy violence in pursuit of their own transcendent security and power. While the Black-white binary reflected in the title of this book does not capture the full range of racialization that undergirds the eurochristian project, it is, particularly in the North American context, the central dyad of modern race in relation to which patriarchal and possessive whiteness asserts its pseudo-divinity and through which it deploys its police power.

In addition to people racialized as Black, the nonwhite peoples whom whiteness fears and disdains most are Indigenous peoples. Cast, much like African peoples, as ungodly, savage, violent impediments to God-ordained white settler expansion, Indigenous peoples register, like Black people, as fundamentally out of place, despite the fact that if anyone has a rightful claim to the *place* of North America, where this book largely focuses, it is Native Americans. The white world that demonizes Black and Indigenous people also demonizes other nonwhite people, including Asian and Arab people and other nonwhite migrants—including people identified as Latinx—crossing into predominantly white territories. The white world even demonizes white people who fail to live up to the white norms of patriarchy and possession. As patriarchal, whiteness is also particularly violent against queer, transgender, and gender-nonconforming people, particularly Black and other queer, trans, and gender-nonconforming people of color. Finally, intertwined as it is with capitalism, colonialism, and the normativities that they establish and police, whiteness also defines itself over and against people with disabilities who register to the possessors of whiteness as manifestations of abnormality that can only fail to serve—and thereby impede—racial capitalist accumulation.[43] While this book focuses primarily on Black and propertyless peoples, I understand capitalist, colonial, and carceral violence as a violence that ultimately antagonizes all nonwhite people, propertyless people, and people defined in opposition to patriarchal, white, and propertied normativity.

It is important to understand that patriarchal and possessive whiteness does not just recklessly antagonize; it empowers and indeed deifies itself through functionally religious violence against the dangerous inhabitants of the "dark," propertyless, and nonnormative world, violence that it then erases from its memory, as if the states of dispossession that characterize the present are simply reflections of the way things always have been and always will be. And yet, while Black people, Indigenous people, other people of color, migrants, propertyless peoples, queer and trans people, and disabled people register to the managers and beneficiaries of the white propertied world as embodiments of trespass, they are also agents who exercise their will to make new worlds in which it is possible to survive and thrive. Indeed, the organized struggles of those who manage to collectively survive the violence of capitalist, colonial, and carceral systems have forged ways of knowing, being, and doing that deeply inform the core insights of this book.

Criminalization

Whiteness and property cannot exist without first displacing those who stand in the path of their ever-expanding territoriality. Displacement—physically separating people from a place—is an act of dispossession, and dispossession requires violence. Once established, white property depends on ongoing violence to defend itself against dispossessed peoples' acts of trespass that jeopardize its perceived security and purity. The hedges, fences, gates, and walls that partition white property over against the wild disorder it imagines beyond its boundaries can be understood as manifestations of a kind of inanimate or static police power, possessive and carceral means of forcibly inhibiting the presence of nonwhite, propertyless, and nonnormative peoples. When inanimate partitions alone are not enough, the living partition of police power—the thin blue line—carries out the same task.

One of the foremost names by which the state defines those whom it constructs as embodiments of profane opposition to sacred social order is "criminal." The etymological roots of the English term "crime" most likely originate with the Latin *cernere*, meaning to decide or sift, in the sense of discriminating between or separating things. Beginning in the mid-thirteenth century, the term entered the English language to denote sinfulness in the sense of an "infraction" against "the laws of God" and, shortly thereafter, as an offense that "the law punishes in the name of the state," a state widely understood at that time to be a channel of divine power in the world. As such, "crime" and "criminal" reflect the godlike power of the state to determine who has offended against God's law and to separate them—conceptually and physically—from those who have not. As a manifestation of the oppositionality inherent to many aspects of the eurochristian religiosity from which it emerges, the modern state is itself inherently oppositional in the sense that its very existence depends on its enemies, which are, by extension, the enemies of God. And foremost among the enemies of the sacred modern racial capitalist state and the order it upholds is the "criminal." "The State creates the Criminal," James Baldwin writes, "because the State cannot operate without the criminal."[44] Without a demonized other, a monstrous figure who threatens to destroy sacred order, the capitalist-colonial state as we know it could not exist. Why? Because the capitalist-colonial state is a manifestation of the human aspiration to hierarchical, godlike power, and such power is impossible—unintelligible—without someone over whom to exercise it. The "criminal," therefore, should be understood as one whose personhood or actions the state defines as a moral, political, and legal offense—a trespass—against sacred social order and the law that upholds it. "Criminalization," then, is the work of determining who and what constitutes a threat to sacred social order and of capturing, separating, and/or eliminating those whose behaviors, understood as a manifestation of their corrupted personhood, embody that threat.[45]

The power to identify and eliminate threats—the power to criminalize—is the power of *police*, broadly conceived. Before the early nineteenth-century advent of badged, armed, salaried, uniformed agents of the state called "police," managers of hierarchical order understood the police power and function of the state as a central means by which the state made and maintained social order more broadly. Police power, in short, was the power to institute and maintain the *policies* that constitute order; indeed, the managers of order called this work of order-making "police science."[46] Out of the broader state task of making and maintaining order came "police" as we know them today: agents of the state who deploy violence or the threat thereof to make and maintain an order that is, for its managers and beneficiaries, natural, necessary, sacred, ultimate, of God. While professional police eventually came to be known as "law enforcement" officials of the state, their first task has always been the making and maintenance of order, which the law exists to serve. Order does not serve law; law serves order. And police power is the power to make and maintain both. Notice, once again, that this historical description of the emergence of police power has nothing to do with safety in the sense of the general well-being of people living in a society. As noted earlier, police—and the cages into which they throw many of those whom they capture—do not exist to create safety and in fact inhibit it in multiple ways. The only safety with which racial capitalist settler colonial order is concerned is the safety, the security—the salvation—of hierarchical order itself and, by extension, those who manage and benefit from it. Ironically, as we will see, the salvation of order requires a kind of "salvation" through subjection for those who are criminalized. For an inherently hierarchical order to exist, and to exist securely, many people must be made subject, which is to say, vulnerable to premature death.

In the end, the fundamentally oppositional act of making and maintaining capitalist-colonial order is an act of war against those alleged enemies of God who stand in the path of or directly oppose it. Police, from their origins to the present, are frontline soldiers in the sacred racial class war to forge heaven for a few by eliminating and exiling many to hell, a war they wage by identifying and eliminating enemy threats to order, which is to say, by criminalization. Without the godlike work of judging, capturing, and separating peoples, there would be no such thing as the capitalist-colonial state. This is what it means to say that police power is a godlike power: it *creates*, *saves* from threat, and *sustains* a functionally sacred colonial racial capitalist order into the future, "forever and ever, Amen."[47]

Criminalization, as I understand it, is a police power in the broadest sense, which means that it includes not only the moment that a cop confronts or captures someone but also the work of identifying, surveilling, and pursuing people whose behaviors constitute what the state considers criminal and of separating, caging, and containing them in the millions of traditional prisons and jails that populate the US landscape, as well as those open-air prisons of dispossession and exile in which millions live before and after state captivity. Thus, what begins in the work of defining criminality ends in the concreteness of capture and caging and the long processes of dispossession and death that capture and caging put into motion. Criminalization includes the state violence work of identification, capture, containment, and dispossession, but it also includes the discursive and symbolic work—such as that carried out by mainstream, corporate-owned media—of constructing the figure of the criminal in the popular imagination and of inducing fear of the threats they seem to pose, threats, the state tells us, that can only be neutralized by cops and cages.

In addition to the term "criminalization," I also use the term "carceral" throughout this book. "Carceral" is a term that derives from the notion of an enclosed space, including a prison or jail. Thus, the carceral, or carcerality, is a matter of the work of containment, captivity, confinement, and control, both in the quite concrete sense of a prison or jail cell and in the broader sense of landscapes arranged through partitions that contain and control the movement of entire populations. On the most fundamental level, carcerality and the enclosures that pave the way for private property are bound together as interrelated means of distributing power by partitioning life. The captivity of confinement is also a deeply religious phenomenon with a theological lineage that still shapes the present. Carcerality is a continuum composed of many forms, and in a functionally sacred capitalist-colonial society that requires forcibly controlling those who might inhibit its own infinite expansion, the work of criminalization—identifying and eliminating threats—is central among them.

At the end of the day, the main focus of this book is the police work of criminalization, from its early modern origins to the present-day, neoliberal racial capitalist era of "mass criminalization." As I endeavor to show, mass criminalization, and all the forms of criminalization that precede it, is a manifestation of the religious dynamic captured in the oppositionality between "white property" and "Black trespass." From Muslim ministers to Public Enemy, Black folks have been saying for a long time that "white man's heaven is a Black man's hell."[48] And it is the police power of criminalization that makes it so. In form and function alike, criminalization constitutes a religion.

Chapter Outline

As noted earlier, a central premise of this book is that understanding the *why* of the centuries-long criminalization of Black people, Indigenous people, other people of color, and economically dispossessed peoples of all races in the United States requires understanding criminalization as a religious phenomenon. And in order to understand criminalization as a religious phenomenon, we must first understand not only whom criminalization is *against* but what and whom criminalization is *for*, what function it fulfills for those who benefit or seem to benefit from it. More than some senseless system of randomly occurring cruelty, the police power to criminalize and cage is a self-preserving manifestation of the fundamentally hierarchical social order through which it arises. As such, the book begins, in chapter 1, where the story of criminalization begins, in the deeply intertwined histories of patriarchal whiteness and absolutely exclusive private property that emerged together through the confluence of eurochristian settler colonialism and racial capitalism. In the early modern European context out of which colonialism and capitalism emerged, the religious and the political were not separable in the way they seem to be today. Indeed, the formation of colonial-capitalist order and the enactment of mass dispossession and enslavement that are central to it were thoroughly religious processes that depended on and incorporated eurochristian ideas and practices at nearly every turn. Fundamentally oppositional in nature, patriarchal whiteness and private property hinge on the displacement, exploitation, and elimination of all who fall outside their functionally sacred boundaries. In a world arranged according to the sacred supremacy of those who possess whiteness and property, to be nonwhite and/or propertyless is to pose the existential threat of moral and political trespass, a threat that ultimately necessitates police power as a means of securing—of *saving*—the social order from those whom it dispossesses. My account of mass criminalization develops over the course of the book as I explore how the core concepts and realities under consideration—race, property, gender, religion, criminalization—relate to one another. While I do not argue that they are, each and every one, tethered together in all places and at all times, I do argue that it is impossible to fully understand them without attending to their multiple intertwinings across space and time.

Building on the account of the formation of whiteness and property developed in chapter 1, chapter 2 argues that patriarchal whiteness and absolutely exclusive private property do not merely derive from religious sources but are, in their very structure, religious phenomena, manifestations of the oppositionality between sacred and profane, and means by which people seek to transcend, transform, and make meaning of the conditions of finitude. Anchored by W. E. B. Du Bois's definition of whiteness—"ownership of the earth forever and ever, Amen!"—chapter 2 theorizes patriarchal whiteness and private property as aspirations to godlike power, transcendence, and invulnerability maintained at the expense of those whom they dispossess, who in turn register as existential threats against them. Treating the vulnerabilities of finitude as threats to be avoided, patriarchal whiteness and private property are means of transforming those whom they dispossess into a ladder on which to escape the world into a transcendent, paranoid, and ultimately illusory safety. In seeking to escape finitude, patriarchal and possessive whiteness steals life not only from others but, by rejecting the forms of relation necessary for life, from its possessors as well. As manifestations of the pretension to godlike power over the Earth and its peoples, patriarchal whiteness and private property isolate themselves as the sacred center of the social order that revolves around them, an order that must therefore be protected at any cost, including through the use of violence against those who seem to threaten it. Indeed, the deification of whiteness and property demands the destruction of those who are, by nature or by action, out of place—socially, spatially, and hierarchically. Securing heavenly safety for a few requires exiling the enemies of God and order to carceral hell.

In the end, it is one thing to aspire to godlike power and invulnerability but another to secure and possess it. After tracing the foundational contours of the world of which cops and cages are an integral part, chapter 3 shows that the functionally sacred colonial racial capitalist order that makes heaven for a few at the expense of many depends for its very existence on the vigilant management and elimination of all who threaten to desecrate it. Capitalist colonial order only exists—and only exists as sacred—in other words, because the functionally divine violence work of police maintains the hierarchies on which sacred social order depends. Since at least the first century CE, up through the medieval and modern eras and into the present, theologians, philosophers, and members of the ruling class have posited political power and the law by which it governs as a derivation of divine will, nature, or both. At the beginning of the modern era and the formation of the modern liberal nation-state, Thomas Hobbes borrowed from biblical mythology to narrate the birth of civil order as a story of the state imposing order and peace through the taming of chaotic disorder that prevails without a subjecting force. Figured as a "mortal God" that partially embodies the power of the "immortal God," Hobbes thus imagines the state as an extension of the divine power to create and maintain order through a social contract based on subjection and obedience. As theorists of police power show, the patriarchal state power to create and maintain order by eliminating threats to it is in fact a definition of the police power, a concept and practice that, while it originates in the ancient world, eventually takes formal institutional shape in the modern era through the emergence of "police" officers deployed by the state to use violence to produce and maintain the hierarchies central to colonial racial capitalist order. Hobbes's vision of the state is thus a vision of the state power of police, the mortal God that, partially mimicking the immortal God of the Christian tradition, creates, saves, and sustains the functionally sacred social order that grants near transcendent power to a few by criminalizing and dispossessing many. Just as the racial capitalist settler colonial order that revolves around whiteness and property is, for its managers and beneficiaries, sacred, so the police work of creating that order, saving it from threats, and sustaining it into the future amounts to divine power in our midst.

Mirroring the work of the immortal God, the mortal gods of police and carceral power maintain sacred social order through what I identify in chapter 3 as a soteriology of subjection. Developed over the course of more than a thousand years of Christian theologizing—particularly through the work of Augustine, Anselm, and Calvin—the soteriology of subjection is an account of sin and salvation according to which sin consists of a corrupted ontology that leads to a refusal to be properly subject to a sovereign and benevolent God. This rebellious refusal to be subject, to be in one's proper place, establishes as an allegedly natural consequence a relation of obligated indebtedness and a state of condemnation or guilt. As such, the condition of sin is a condition of confinement—

both to sin and to the penal and debt consequence of sin. Importantly, because it is human disobedience that leads to its seemingly natural consequence of captivity, captivity is said to be a condition that humans effectively will for themselves. For the God of carceral soteriology, the primary problem with the refusal to be subject to God is that it disrupts the divine-human hierarchy on which cosmic and social order depend, which in turn creates disorder, cosmic and social alike. The only way to resolve the disorder that the debt-making, guilt-producing refusal to be subject creates, then, is through acts that restore the order of divine-human hierarchy by reestablishing proper life-giving subjection to divine and divinely derived power. For theologians working within this framework, the primary means of restoring proper subjection, of returning rebellious humans to their proper place within cosmic and social order, is through the satisfactory payment of debt and/or the meting out of punishment that a just God and order require. Recompense and punishment are satisfactory, in short, because they reestablish that God is God and humans are not, an arrangement on which cosmic and social order depends.[49]

Chapter 3 concludes by beginning to consider how carceral soteriology relates to carceral practice: just as a corrupted ontology leads to a refusal to be subject that establishes indebtedness and condemnation, a condition resolved through recompense or punishment that in turn restores divine-human hierarchy, so the allegedly inherent criminality of dispossessed peoples manifests itself as a disorder-generating refusal to be properly subject to divinely derived political authority, a refusal that finds its resolution in a forced return to subjection to the godlike power of the state and those who manage and benefit from it. In terms of the nature of the relationship between carceral soteriology and carceral practice, my argument is that carceral soteriology makes possible and is thus homologous to—sharing family origins and thus core conceptualities with—carceral practice, which means that carceral practice not only resembles but channels and embodies core aspects of carceral soteriology.[50] When we discern the work of cops and cages in terms of a kind of salvific subjection, we begin to understand the larger mythological and indeed religious function that they fulfill in a racial capitalist settler colonial order that is, for those who manage and benefit from it, sacred.

Building on the framework established in the chapters that precede it, chapter 4 explores in greater depth how the criminalization of Black and other dispossessed and propertyless peoples is itself a means by which the state deifies patriarchal whiteness and sacralizes private property. The history of the modern emergence of institutionalized police power and carceral captivity is a history of the oppositional dynamic between criminalization and deification: racial capitalist settler colonial order deploys police power to enact dispossession that in turn creates the conditions for the acts of trespass that it subsequently criminalizes as a means of reproducing the godlike power of its managers and beneficiaries. The clearest points of origin of modern police power are the enclosure of the commons that displaced masses of people from land across Europe and the implementation of vagrancy laws that criminalized those so dispossessed. Centuries of ruling-class legislation and political commentary clarify that central to the problem of the so-called masterless people that vagrancy laws and proto-police forces targeted was the allegedly immoral refusal to labor to produce other people's wealth, which is to say, the refusal to be properly subject to the sacred power of capital. Following the early modern proliferation of vagrancy laws, the covenantal criminalization facilitated by the Puritans and the mortifying salvation facilitated by the penitentiary gave new shape to the idea that criminals are those who fail to be subject to divine and political authority and that salvation—both for those who are captured and those who are rid of their presence—demands a return to allegedly benevolent subjection.

The formal institutionalization of police power in the late eighteenth and early nineteenth centuries in England and the northern United States similarly emerged out of the idea that the dispossessed whose labor makes capitalism possible constitute a "dangerous" class whose inherent immorality, evil dispositions, and polluting presence requires subjection as a means of maintaining order. In a similar way, the late eighteenth-century advent of policing in the US South emerged out of the work of keeping the imagined depravity of Blackness in its proper subjected place by granting godlike power—including the mortal God of police power—to the possessors of whiteness. At the same time and often in the same place that eurochristian colonial-capitalist police powers criminalized Blackness and deified whiteness, they also criminalized trespass in ways that reproduced the sacrality of absolutely exclusive private property as a fundamentally white possession. In a world ordered according to the expansive boundaries of patriarchal whiteness and private property, police exist to criminalize the disorder of trespass—matter and people out of place—and to reproduce and reinforce the sacred partitions that constitute it. The divine violence work of police makes white propertied men divine.

Chapter 5 brings the modern history of criminalization into the present as it brings the book's account of the religion of mass criminalization to its completion. In an open letter to Angela Davis, published in 1970, at the precipice of the rise of mass criminalization, James Baldwin reflected on the meaning of the ongoing reality of "chains on black flesh." Against his hope that Americans would at last find such chains intolerable, Baldwin bemoans that Americans continue to "measure their safety in chains and corpses" through a system that binds Black people, "both soul and body," in "hell."[51] For white propertied folks to enjoy paradise on Earth, Black folks, along with Indigenous people, other people of color, and propertyless people of all races, must be damned to hell. In the theocarceral imaginary, the work of making heaven for a few is the work of safety, which is to say, *salvation*. Etymologically, to save is to "make safe," which is why the pseudo-divine police power to "make safe" is also the pseudo-divine power to *save*: the safety that cops and cages supposedly create is in fact a kind of what I call *save*-ty. Who and what do police and carceral power save? Police and carceral power save—make safe—sacred social order and its managers from those who refuse to be properly subject to them, which they do by forcibly returning the rebellious and disobedient to their proper subjected place in social and divine hierarchy, which is to say, by violently "saving" them.

The salvific dynamic at the heart of criminalization is evident not only in the distant past but in the present as well. Beginning in the early 1970s, in the wake of the long Black freedom movement and other movements for liberation across the US and beyond, the racial capitalist state sought to reclaim the ground it lost through the victories of those movements by expanding the sphere of privatization and austerity, divesting from public goods that supported the livelihoods of dispossessed peoples, and increasing funding for the organized violence of cops and cages to manage the disorderly outcomes of mass divestment. The name of this era, which continues into the present, is neoliberalism, or neoliberal racial capitalism. Undergirded by political theologies that mystified and even deified the market and by eurochristian politics that racially demonized those victimized by state-sponsored dispossession, neoliberal order is, for those who manage and benefit from it, no less sacred than the stages of capitalism that preceded it. The same can be said of the police power that reproduces and maintains it. Building on the long history that precedes it, professional police power during the past half century has continued to articulate itself in deeply mythological and religious terms. Through "broken windows" and other related modes of contemporary order-maintenance policing, the narrative goes, cops do the "Lord's work" of restoring "civilization" by "cleaning" the streets of the "scum" and "waste," the beasts, monsters, and demons embodied by Black, Indigenous, unhoused, and other dispossessed peoples. By eliminating the sources of moral and social disorder, cops save and maintain racial capitalist order from the existential threats that racial capitalism itself generates.

Inextricable as the pseudo-divine power of police is from whiteness and property, it is ultimately the power to rearrange the world into geographies of salvation and damnation, of sovereignty and subjection, partitioned by the so-called thin blue line that embodies, reproduces, and extends the color line and the property line throughout the spaces of our lives. Derived from the war metaphor of the thin red line, according to police mythology, the thin blue line that police embody protects sacred order from the existential threat posed by the disorderly, demonic, hellish jungle of criminality that lingers just outside the gate. The racial capitalist state's theological-political claim that cops and cages save us from evil soothes so deeply that it elicits mass devotion anchored in the belief that our very lives depend on them. The reality, however, is that cops and cages not only fail to protect but in fact proliferate violence and harm on a massive scale, not only by directly perpetrating it but by inhibiting our collective ability to resource the public goods that actually create safe and thriving communities. Faith in the saving power of cops and cages, then, is faith in the illusory power of safety for a few by means of the premature death of many. Mass criminalization brings about salvation through chains and corpses.

If the story ended with chains and corpses, we would be left with nothing but despair. But the story does not end there. The presumption that criminalization and the social order that it makes, saves, and maintains are natural, inevitable, and permanent is an illusion that has long shaped the predominant—white, propertied, patriarchal—American imaginary. The reality is that cops and cages have not always been with us and will not always be. In the book's conclusion, I argue that the proclamation embraced by an entire generation of radical social movements that "another world is possible" may be understood as a proclamation of faith—not in the sense of doctrinal assent but in the sense of embodied belief in the possibility of material life beyond the present order of things. "Abolition" names one such movement of radical faith in the realizability of a world beyond our own—a world of safety and abundance in which cops and cages have become obsolete. As leading prison industrial complex abolitionists such as Angela Davis and Ruth Wilson Gilmore suggest, abolition is less about negation than it is about creation—the making of a world in which all people's basic human needs are met and we learn to navigate conflict and harm in ways that bring life rather than death. If religion is a meaning-making means by which humans transcend and/or transform the conditions of finitude, then abolition may be understood as a simultaneously religious and political set of practices that mediate the felt emergence of another world at the intersices of our own, even if those who pursue it do not identify as people of faith in the traditional sense. Building a world beyond mass criminalization requires understanding how criminalization fulfills a religious, salvific function for those who benefit from or imagine that they benefit from it. But it also requires us to embody new modes of collective transcendence and transformation, which is to say, new mythologies, religiosities, and spiritualities that elaborate and build on old mythologies, religiosities, and spiritualities. If mass criminalization fulfills a religious function for those who are existentially invested in it, abolition must offer an even more irresistible means of transcendence and transformation on the way to a world made new.

1

Patriarchal Whiteness and Private Property

Building a world beyond the mass criminalization of Black people, Indigenous people, other people of color, and propertyless peoples of all races in the United States requires that we attend to the religiosity at the heart of criminalization. In order to understand criminalization as a manifestation of religion, however, we must first understand what and who it is that criminalization defends. What and whom, exactly, do police—the primary agents and enactors of criminalization—serve and protect when they surveil, pursue, stop, search, harass, cite, capture, wound, cage, control, and kill Black people and other dispossessed peoples on a daily basis across the US and beyond? Contrary to popular presumption, police did not come into existence for the purpose of keeping all people safe by enforcing the law. Rather, police came into existence to help create and maintain a racial capitalist settler colonial social order that makes power and wealth for a few by dispossessing many and that in turn depends for its continued existence on the power to control or eliminate those whom it dispossesses. If police are concerned with "safety," then, it is the safety of the social order itself, which is to say, security for a few at the expense of many. As a tool deployed to maintain the security and supremacy of a few by dispossessing, caging, and disappearing many, the police power to criminalize and cage is not an anomaly within but a manifestation of the fundamentally hierarchical order through which it arises. Thus, to understand the nature and function of police power, we begin where the story of criminalization begins, in the conjoined histories and mythologies of patriarchal whiteness and private property: world-ordering, landscape-shifting forces of the modern West that emerged together through the historical confluence of European colonialism, racial capitalism, and Christianity.

Eurochristian Colonialism and Racial Capitalism

In contrast to the present-day tendency to conceptualize the political and the religious in absolute distinction from each other, the predominant conceptual frame and practical orientation of the late medieval and early modern era out of which European colonialism and racial capitalism emerged treated the political and the religious as two dimensions of a single way of understanding, navigating, and arranging the conditions of finitude. European colonialism, like the racial capitalism with which it is deeply intertwined, is a centuries-long social, political, economic, and cultural project of capturing, controlling, and exploiting land and peoples as a means of empowering and enriching European nations and peoples. Built from its beginnings on a fusion of Christian theological and political rationales, European colonialism is a eurochristian project of perceiving and arranging the world and its peoples.[1] Ecclesiastically sanctioned and theologically conceived, European colonial conquest beginning as early as the fifteenth century constituted a theological way of viewing, ordering, and exercising power over the world from what theologian Willie Jennings calls "the commanding heights."[2] Colonialism consists in acts of displacement that rearrange "space and bodies, land and identity" according to a racial "scale of existence" organized around Europeanness, which would eventually come to be recognized as whiteness.[3] This racial and spatial reconfiguration constitutes a "theological operation," Jennings argues, because it was carried out through a synthesis of ecclesial and political power that did its work according to a theological vision that claimed the pseudo-godlike ability to discern salvific potential in peoples and places conceived racially. Standing between people and land, the eurochristian colonizer "adjudicates, identifies, and determines" peoples and places according to the superiority of European ways of thinking and doing over against non-European ones. By separating peoples from places, and transforming those places into "raw, untamed land," Jennings writes, eurochristian colonizers over the course of centuries deployed a "distorted vision of creation" that situated place-transcending Europeanness—whiteness—at its center.[4]

From the theological meaning-making of Prince Henry of Portugal's fifteenth-century royal chronicler Gomes Eanes de Azurara to the royal religiosity of the journals of the fifteenth-century Italian genocidal "explorer" Christopher Columbus to the fifteenth-century papal bull that established the so-called doctrine of discovery to the anti-Black theological-colonial proclamations of sixteenth-century Jesuit missionaries like José de Acosta Porres of Spain and Alessandro Valignano of Italy to the theological-political rationales permeating the Virginia Charter signed in 1606 by England's King James I to the nineteenth-century British imperial slogan "Christianity, Commerce, and Civilization" to the religiously imbued nineteenth- and twentieth-century manifest destiny practices of mass dispossession in North America, there is no such thing as European colonialism apart from European Christianity. "Colonialism is Christianity. Christianity is colonialism," Tink Tinker writes. "They go hand in hand.... The violence of colonialism is the violence of Christianity."[5]

Where there is European colonialism there is also racial capitalism. Much like colonialism, capitalism is, at its most basic level, a system of hierarchical social relations that generates wealth for a few through the dispossession and exploitation of many, including the Earth itself. When capitalism emerged in Europe over the course of the fifteenth, sixteenth, and seventeenth centuries out of the feudal order that preceded it, it did so in and through the forced displacement of masses of people from land and thus from their means of subsistence, as lords and other landholders enclosed, combined, and privatized common lands in order to expand their wealth. At its most elementary level, the premise and purpose of capitalism is the narrow accumulation of greater and greater wealth, and increasing wealth, by definition, requires dispossession and exploitation: without the private possession of land and other means of production and without a class of propertyless people who survive by producing wealth for others in exchange for a wage, there is no capitalism. Early architects and proponents of capitalism make this fact plain. As the Scottish merchant and theorist of political economy and police power Patrick Colquhoun wrote in the early nineteenth century, "Poverty is... a most necessary and indispensable ingredient of society, without which nations and communities could not exist in a state of civilization. It is the lot of man—it is the source of wealth, since without labour there would be no riches, no refinement, no comfort, and no benefit to those who may be possessed of wealth."[6] The nineteenth-century English social reformer Edwin Chadwick put it even more concisely: "Banish poverty, you banish wealth."[7] Private possession necessitates dispossession, and wealth necessitates poverty. Capitalism hinges on inequality.

Like eurochristian colonialism, capitalism operates on the basis of mythologies that naturalize and eternalize the present order as the way things always have been and always will be. The necessary inequity at the heart of capitalism legitimizes itself on the basis of the premise that the hyperproductive wealth generation of capitalism is natural and even divinely ordained and that it ultimately benefits more people than do more common or equitable distributions of wealth and property. The implication is that capitalism is not a forced condition or set of relations but one that emerges naturally and that corresponds with already existing differences between people.[8] This premise would eventually be taken to its logical conclusion in the work of nineteenth-century Social Darwinists like William Graham Sumner, who argued that the seeming scarcity of nature's resources requires that humans labor in competition with one another for their accumulation, which inevitably—naturally—results in social and economic inequality. Arranging society according to what he deemed a forced equality, Sumner argued, would contradict the natural law of competition and thereby require an unfreedom that "carries society downwards and favors all its worst members." Conceptualizing capitalism in such terms, Sumner understood the private property on which capitalism was founded as "a feature of society organized in accordance with the natural conditions of the struggle for existence," which is why absolutely exclusive private property is—and can only be—an inherently unequal relation.[9] Capitalism, its proponents argue, reflects the world as it really is, which is why they propose it as the model of political economy that, despite its inherent inequities, most promises to benefit all in the end. The mythology that capitalism is a natural outgrowth of the way the world happens to be is part of what gives it such staying power. Indeed, the apparent unquestionability of the arrangements inherent in capitalist political economy functions as a well-reinforced boundary that keeps most people from imagining a world arranged any other way. But capitalism has not always been with us and need not always be.

Emerging in tandem with modern liberal, individualistic conceptions of personhood, capitalism hinges on the idea of freedom *from* state interference in economy, which in turn enables freedom *for* the unfettered disposal of oneself and one's property. The reality, however, is that the "freedom" of capitalism both depends on and proliferates unfreedom on a massive scale. Contrary to capitalism's mythological origin story, capitalism came into the world not through a natural evolution in the division of labor, or through the ingenuity of wealthy people, but through the violence of conquest, displacement, enslavement, and exploitation. The transition to capitalism was not inevitable and thus was far from peaceful.[10] Transforming the Earth into a means of capital accumulation, separating people from the land, and leaving them no choice for survival but to submit to exploitative wage-labor relations inevitably summons resistance, the defeat of which requires force and a state prepared to deploy that force as needed. As I outline in chapters 3 and 4, the capitalist imperative to funnel masses of dispossessed peoples into wage labor helped catalyze the formation of modern police power in some of its earliest forms. Massive disparities in wealth, along with massive, organized resistance to such disparities in practically all capitalist societies over the past four hundred years, is evidence that capitalism does not benefit everyone and indeed that freedom and abundance for a few not only creates but depends on unfreedom and scarcity for many.[11]

While capitalism partitions populations into "owning" and "working" classes—the few and the many—capitalism cannot be reduced to a matter of purely economic "class" alone, in isolation from other forms of social differentiation. As scholars in the Black radical tradition make clear, the violent history of capitalist "accumulation by dispossession" is a racial history, which is to say that capitalism is always already "racial capitalism."[12] Cedric Robinson, the political theorist who first developed the idea of racial capitalism into a general theory, argues that value-laden social differentiations—what he calls "racialism"—were inherent to European civilization prior to capitalism's emergence, which is why, when capitalism did emerge, it "pursued essentially racial directions."[13] Like Robinson, abolitionist geographer Ruth Wilson Gilmore argues that capitalism was "never not racial," including in early modern rural England and across Europe, where "hierarchies among people whose descendants might all have become white depended for their structure on group-differentiated vulnerability to premature death."[14] The hierarchies inherent to capitalism—hierarchies that empower and enrich a few by dispossessing many—are the hierarchies inherent to racial order. As Gilmore puts it, "Capitalism requires inequality and racism enshrines it."[15] In addition to the inter-European "racialism" that preceded and shaped the emergence of capitalism, the "racial" in racial capitalism can also be understood in its more modern sense as a mark of essential—as opposed to merely incidental, cultural, or geographical—difference that ruling classes use to determine value and distribute power hierarchically. Through their emergence as fundamental features of social order in the West, eurochristian colonialism and enslavement capitalism absolutized, essentialized, and thereby *reproduced* and deepened the power of racial categorization. In the process, the "racialism" that first took root within Europe ultimately expanded beyond it, giving racial differentiation new, more absolute, all-encompassing, and world-transforming meaning and power that continue into the present.

Racial capitalism, like eurochristian colonialism, consists of the theft of lands inhabited by others, the extraction of resources from those lands, and the profitable exploitation of displaced and captured peoples. Also like eurochristian colonialism, the acts of possession and dispossession through which racial capitalism entered and continues to structure the world amount to acts of religion, in multiple ways. To begin with, the enclosure of common lands that catalyzed capital accumulation for a few at the expense of many was a process first legitimized and defended on the basis of a political theology of private ownership articulated by John Locke and other political philosophers of the early modern era. According to this theology of primitive accumulation, outlined in greater depth later in this chapter and in chapter 2, God commands European peoples to subdue and take private possession of the Earth over against the godless commoners and uncivilized Indigenous peoples whose communal mode of habitation allegedly constitutes an offense against God. A few decades before Locke, Thomas Hobbes mythologized the origins of liberal order in terms that borrowed heavily from biblical myths and Christian theology: the chaos that precedes social order derives from the sin of pride, which leads to disobedience and rebellion, while order comes about through the "mortal God" of the state, the Leviathan, who, in the book of Job, inspires fear and commands obedience.[16] While Hobbes stopped short of advocating a theocratic order, his liberal, proto-capitalist theory depends so heavily on biblical and theological frames of reference that it amounts to a "secularized theology" that deifies what would soon become the capitalist state.[17] Building on the work of Hobbes, Locke, and others, theorists of capitalist political economy, including Adam Smith, mythologized the origins of capitalist order by way of biblical myth and theological concepts, including the idea that the market functions according to the godlike power of an "invisible hand" that mystically and naturally guides political economy toward ends that supposedly benefit all.[18]

As noted earlier, for the early modern European world within which colonialism and capitalism emerged, religion and politics were not wholly separable in the way most people presume them to be today. More specifically, it is not just that religion is a source from which secular political economy draws but that capitalism would not have developed in the way that it did apart from the fused religious and political rationales circulating around the point of its emergence.[19] As Walter Benjamin argues, capitalism is not merely "a religiously conditioned construction . . . but an essentially religious phenomenon."[20] As such, Benjamin writes, the Protestant Reformation did not simply "encourage the emergence of capitalism, but rather changed itself into capitalism."[21] There is no capitalism without Christianity. More specifically, there is no racial capitalism without eurochristianity, as the religiosity of capitalism manifests itself not just through the dynamics of political economy but through the dynamics of racial ordering. Modern liberal political order, which transforms Christian conceptualities into political realities, hinges on group-differentiated hierarchies of value and power, which is to say, racial hierarchies. Derived from eurochristian thought and practice, Cedric Robinson argues, modern liberal racial order can be understood as a modality through which eurochristian notions of salvation and redemption are lived.[22] Colonial racial capitalist order is eurochristian order, and eurochristian order is colonial racial capitalist order. Deriving from European political economy and religion, racial capitalist settler colonial order is, for those who manage and benefit from it, sacred and thus worthy of vigilant defense no matter the cost. As will become clearer in what follows, it is the existential need to vigilantly defend and maintain colonial-capitalist order that gives rise to the emergence of police and carceral power as we know them today.

The intertwining of eurochristian colonial and capitalist order is most readily discernible in the acts of dispossession and capture that constitute African enslavement and settler colonization in the Americas, acts that continue, in evolved form, into the present. The practice of enslaving human beings is nearly as old as human civilization itself, but it was Europe, and later Europe's Atlantic and American colonies, that expanded slavery into a global phenomenon that forged European and European-American political and economic power through mass subjection, suffering, and death.[23] The European nation of Portugal began capturing and forcibly enslaving Africans in the middle of the fifteenth century. By the early sixteenth century, Portugal and Spain began colonizing the lands of Indigenous peoples beyond European boundaries, including in the so-called New World of the Americas, by way of the forced labor of the African peoples they captured and shipped there as human cargo. Starting in the late sixteenth and early seventeenth centuries, Dutch, French, and English colonizers entered the trade of enslaved African peoples in pursuit of their own land-theft expansions across the globe.[24] European powers kidnapped African peoples as indentured servants and slaves and shipped them to colonial territories on the stolen lands of Indigenous peoples because colony building required labor cheap enough to yield the kind of profit that colonial power—which, by the seventeenth century, became capitalist power—demanded. Based on the enrichment of European elites, the Atlantic slave trade at the heart of European colonialism was essential to the global proliferation of racial capitalism more broadly: the sugar and cotton plantations of the US South and the factories of the US North and England were inextricably linked in a web of global capital accumulation built on the mass exploitation and dispossession of multiple populations across multiple continents.[25]

The English colonization of what came to be known as North America was a fundamentally "settler" form of colonialism in that it aimed not just to funnel wealth forged through captive African labor back to England but to inhabit and claim ownership of lands on which Indigenous peoples had dwelled for centuries. Taking possession of other people's lands requires displacing people from that land, which requires violence. As historian Patrick Wolfe posits, settler colonialism is premised on a "logic of elimination" that "destroys" in order to "replace."[26] Through violence both immediate and protracted, violence exacted on bodies as well as on land, cultures, and ways of life, the destructions that constituted European settler colonialism constitute genocide.[27] The bloody history of Indigenous elimination and the deadly brutality of chattel slavery that took place on the lands of Indigenous peoples constitute the foundation on which the United States came into existence and continues to exist.

As a cornerstone of European colonialism and racial capitalism, the Atlantic slave trade and the slaveholding agents of plantation capitalism conceptualized and maintained the institution of chattel slavery in and through eurochristian theological and biblical reasoning. Rationalized from an Aristotelian and Thomist framework on the nature and telos of different kinds of human beings, many slave-owning elites in the eighteenth century justified their capture and expropriation of African life and labor by proclaiming as self-evident that African peoples were inherently disposed to servitude because they were allegedly incapable of the rational, self-possessing freedom that characterized European peoples. Being literally incapable of freedom, defined in individualist and liberal European terms, colonial elites argued, African peoples pose a threat to civilized social order when left unrestrained. As such, they contended, it was in the best interest not only of European peoples but of African peoples themselves to be held in bondage, as freedom would not suit their natural, God-given dispositions.[28] Slave owners and advocates of chattel slavery further legitimated the practice of owning and enslaving Africans and expropriating their forced labor by leaning on the authority of Christian scripture that seemingly commands slaves to "obey their masters" and that requires all people to submit to God-ordained governing authorities—governing authorities that, in the eighteenth and nineteenth centuries, established the legality of owning African peoples as chattel slaves.[29] Since, as the eighteenth-century Baptist minister and educator Richard Furman put it, "the right of holding slaves is clearly established in the Holy Scriptures," chattel slavery, many people believed, must be a manifestation of God's will.[30]

In an effort to forge docile, profit-yielding subjects out of people of African descent kidnapped from their native lands, some slave owners developed Christian catechisms specifically for the people they enslaved.[31] One such catechism used in European-American Episcopal churches for enslaved Africans began by establishing the alleged historical naturalness of African slavery by marking the God-cursed biblical figure Cain as Black and by explicitly claiming that "the Southern slave

[came] from him."³² Citing Abraham's God-fearing, obedient slaves, Jesus's relative silence (as recorded in scripture) on slavery, and Paul's moral encouragement to the runaway slave Onesimus to return to his owner, Philemon, the catechism established the order of chattel slavery as a biblically and divinely ordained feature of the natural order of things. In so doing, European-made slave catechisms helped forge what would soon become whiteness as a religious subjectivity naturally proximate to God and contrasted against Blackness as a religious subjectivity naturally distant from God. The Episcopal slave catechism makes the allegedly inherent sinfulness of enslaved Africans clear:

Q. Did Adam and Eve have to work?
A. Yes, they were to keep the garden.
Q. Was it hard to keep that garden?
A. No, it was very easy.
Q. What makes the crops so hard to grow now?
A. Sin makes it.
Q. What makes you lazy?
A. My own wicked heart.
Q. How do you know your heart is wicked?
A. I feel it every day.
Q. What teaches you so many wicked things?
A. The Devil.³³

Establishing the moral and anthropological inferiority of enslaved African peoples as a reflection of the divine and natural order of things, the catechism renders African peoples' forced servitude to racial capital a naturally occurring phenomenon—the way things always have been and always should be.³⁴

The same eurochristian powers that captured and confined African peoples and eliminated Indigenous peoples in the Americas also entrapped and exploited dispossessed peoples of European descent. Before England and its colonies transitioned fully to a system of chattel slavery as their primary source of labor, they utilized a system of indentured servitude, importing many of its laborers from within Europe itself. Among the European indentured servants shipped across the Atlantic were English commoners dispossessed by religiously legitimated capitalist enclosure who, having been displaced from their lands, were subsequently criminalized by labor and vagrancy laws and caged in the first prisons and workhouses throughout England.[35] In 1606, English investors formed the Virginia Company, which was, in the words of its chief chronicler, "primarily a business organization with large sums of capital invested by adventurers whose chief interest lay in the returns expected from their investment."[36] Advocates of the company successfully sold its cause to the leaders and people of England by casting the proposed Virginia colony as an opportunity for fulfilling both the religious obligation to convert "savages" and the national duty to expand English dominion.[37] Tethered to these purposes, colonial advocates argued that Virginia would help solve England's growing social problems by ridding the nation of the burden of what Richard Hakluyt, a foremost advocate for English colonization, called the "swarmes of idle persons"—vagrants and commoners dispossessed by enclosure and then criminalized for their state of forced dispossession. As the Virginia Company put it in its appeal to authorities and business leaders in London, its venture would "ease the city and suburbs of a swarme of unnecessary inmates, as a contynual cause of death and famine, and the very orginall cause of all the plagues that happen in this kingdome."[38] In accordance with the growing consensus of elites, forced labor in the colonies was sold as a remedy, like workhouses and houses of correction, for punishing, disciplining, and correcting allegedly criminally disposed working-class and underclass populations. As Hakluyt argued, colonial plantations like Virginia would function as a "prison without walls."[39] Sending these "unnecessary" populations overseas would serve as a remedy not only for those who were shipped but for those who were finally rid of their presence back at home in England. More importantly, shipping England's surplus poor to the American colonies was an opportunity to transform what Hakluyt called "waste people" into a means of profit by using them to harvest the idle "waste land" unharvested by Indigenous peoples in the Americas. As historian Nancy Isenberg puts it, "The land and the poor could be harvested together, to add to . . . the nation's wealth."[40] Using the forced labor of England's expendable peoples—peoples rendered expendable through a synthesis of religious and political rationales—in service of Christian colonial expansion, its advocates and investors reasoned, was a win-win for all involved.

As the plantation model proliferated in colonial America over the course of the seventeenth century, so did the need for a greater supply of cheap labor to maintain it. Racial capitalism by its very nature must grow or else cease to exist. Indentured servitude, the primary means of labor in colonial America up to that point, could no longer satisfy the needs of colonial racial capitalism. The reason was essentially twofold. On the one hand, according to indentured servitude's design, after a period of only a few years, laborers completed their terms of service and either became or expected to become upwardly mobile landowners, thereby ceasing to supply the cheap labor needed to render the profits necessary for further colonial expansion.[41] In addition to the problem of completed terms of service, widespread solidarity and resistance among indentured servants of both European and African descent, as well as enslaved Africans and poor wage laborers of European descent, jeopardized indentured servitude's role in creating planters' wealth.[42] Resistance to English colonial expropriation began before some of the vessels carrying dispossessed peoples ever reached Virginia's shores: the dispossessed and criminalized working-class and underclass "hands" that steered the Virginia Company across the Atlantic, though coming from different places and backgrounds, unified in multiple acts of defiance against their overlords, rejecting poor wages and dehumanizing treatment. In response to these acts of rebellion, colonizers developed legislation that sanctioned terror and death as a means of controlling laborers disposed to a freedom that contradicted the terms of their service.[43]

In addition to these and many other transatlantic rebellions, during the early years of the American colonies, including in Virginia, indentured servants of European and African descent, enslaved Africans, and poor bond laborers of European descent banded together on more than one occasion to reject their shared state of exploitation and servitude, most famously in Bacon's Rebellion in 1675–1676.[44] After burning and looting parts of Jamestown and the estates of Governor Berkeley and his supporters, authorities ultimately put down the rebellion in early 1677. Many rebels were falsely promised freedom only to be reenslaved, while others met their end on the gallows.[45] Though the rebellion was ultimately defeated, it inspired a series of similar rebellions across the colonies in the years that followed.[46] The blow that these rebellions dealt to the plantation system, however, led planters to accelerate the transition from reliance on European and African indentured servitude as their primary source of cheap labor to the forced enslavement of Africans by way of the Atlantic slave trade. Utilizing forced African slavery as the primary labor source, it was thought, would circumvent the threats of coalitional rebellions like Bacon's by socially separating Africans from Europeans and giving even poor Europeans a basis for identification with their exploiters instead of with the exploited African servants and slaves with whom they had much more in common. Moreover, a shift away from indentured servitude and toward the all-encompassing violence of lifelong African enslavement would supply a reproductively self-renewing labor force that would enable planters to grow their wealth more freely and rapidly.

Toward these ends, planters in colonies like Virginia developed and passed legislation in the late seventeenth century that retained limits on servitude for people of European descent but eliminated them for people of African descent, even going so far as to deem that any child born of a woman of African descent was, by definition, born into the status of slavery, thereby rendering African women's reproductive labor—often a result of slave owners' sexual violence against them—a means of capital accumulation.[47] By the early eighteenth century, roughly thirty years after Bacon's Rebellion, colonies including Virginia, South Carolina, and Maryland had transitioned almost entirely from indentured servitude to a system of African slavery.[48] By the 1770s, one hundred years after the rebellion and before American independence from British colonial rule, African slavery predominated throughout all the American colonies, thereby forging a new social order based entirely on the mass exploitation, suffering, social death, and premature biological death of people of African descent.[49]

Patriarchal Whiteness

It was in religious pursuit of legitimating, legalizing, implementing, and then maintaining lifelong African enslavement that eurochristian planter elites in North America contributed to the development of new and more absolute notions of race. Prior to the eighteenth century, discourse on "race" presupposed a meaning somewhat different from what people understood the term to mean by the middle of the eighteenth century and what most in the United States understand the term to signify today.[50] According to philosopher Ladelle McWhorter, predominant ideas of race in the seventeenth century referred not to physical or biological difference—to traits of embodiment—but rather to "language, tradition, and custom," to "lineage" or "cultural heritage."[51] Faced with the threat of "a general uprising and a destabilization of the colonial economy" through coalitional working-class and underclass rebellions, along with the upward mobility of former servants, the ruling European-American colonial class of the early eighteenth century pursued the security of the plantation system by legally defining and separating peoples according to "bodily marks" that planters and lawmakers defined as signifiers of "the essence of racial membership."[52] In other words, whereas race before the eighteenth century referred to general differences in language and culture, European colonialism and capitalism helped facilitate the transformation of "race" into what Wolfe defines as a "classificatory concept" whose function was to distribute value hierarchically by linking "physical characteristics" to "cognitive, cultural, and moral" essences.[53]

What this means is that absolute racial differentiation, from its eighteenth-century origins, is not a matter of neutral, objective identification of naturally occurring human difference but is, rather, a "Eurocolonial" strategy for coming into profitable possession of the world and its peoples, a strategy that powers like England carried out by claiming land and displacing Indigenous peoples from it, on the one hand, and by expropriating the labor of captured African peoples to produce profit on that land, on the other.[54] By absolutizing, essentializing, and systematizing already-existing racial or proto-racial differentiations in pursuit of political and economic power over the world, eurochristian elites ensured that Western social order would remain a racial order for centuries to come.

The new, more absolute notions of racial difference forged within eurochristian colonial capitalism ultimately hinged not on an abstract conceptualization of race in general but on the forging of what would come to be known as whiteness in particular. Before the middle of the eighteenth century, there existed identities rooted in citizenship or belonging to specific European nations and cultures, but there was not yet a coherent global, all-encompassing concept of "white" identity as such. Indentured servants and wage laborers of European descent in the American colonies throughout the seventeenth through nineteenth centuries had more in common with indentured servants and enslaved people of African descent than they did with the European-American plantation owners who exercised power over them all. And yet, planters helped to fracture the possibility of further European-African solidarity by giving laborers of European descent a sense of "racial" belonging tethered to morphological distinctions constructed as signs of absolute difference that would ultimately eclipse any sense of shared interest with other oppressed peoples, a sense of belonging that Du Bois called a "public and psychological wage."[55] Planters helped to concretize this sense of belonging during the eighteenth and nineteenth centuries by limiting enslaved, formerly enslaved, and even free Africans' ability to do practically anything outside European-American supervision and surveillance, in part by granting some European-American laborers supervisory policing powers over enslaved Africans, as well as through legal protections, economic privileges, and political power that they systematically withheld from African peoples. Through these deliberately inequitable distributions of power, whiteness became, both de jure and de facto, an inherently valuable identity and power in relation to which non-European peoples—African and Indigenous peoples in particular— were racially defined and disempowered.

Thus, while "racial" distinction broadly construed did not begin with Christian Europe's colonial and capitalist encounter with the rest of the world, it was in and through such encounters that it took hold in a new way, making race—and whiteness specifically—a tool for possession and dispossession, a means of obtaining social, political, economic, and cultural dominance over non-European peoples, as well as economically dispossessed, propertyless peoples of European descent. Racial differentiation ordered around whiteness is not an accidental by-product of colonial and capitalist political economies, then, but is an inherent dimension of the logic of colonial acquisition and capital accumulation itself.[56]

Deriving from eurochristian colonialism and capitalism, the formation of modern race, and whiteness in particular, was a deeply religious and specifically Christian theological process. For early American settler colonizers and founders, American identity was Anglo-Saxon identity, and Anglo-Saxon identity was a resolutely religious identity.[57] Indeed, well before people of European descent in the British-American colonies ever recognized themselves as "white," the title by which they were most commonly named was simply "Christian."[58] From the origination of whiteness to the present, it has been widely conceived as an inherently "moral attribute" that only people of European descent can fully possess.[59] In the context of chattel slavery, the Protestant Christian faith of its European-American managers was not peripheral but integral to the process of forging the anthropological fiction of moral, godlike, valued whiteness and immoral, demonic, devalued Blackness.[60] Indeed, the constructed moral supremacy of whiteness and the constructed moral inferiority of Blackness and other forms of nonwhiteness, at their points of origin and beyond, are mutually dependent—two sides of the same coin: one requires the other. "The valorizing of whiteness," philosopher Robert Birt writes, "entails the devaluation of blackness."[61] The free, white, male propertied citizen and his noncitizen, nonpropertied Black and Indigenous "others" were, in historian David Roediger's words, "fashioned together."[62] By forging this psychological sense and material fact of racial (and citizenship) belonging and exclusion, rooted first in morphology and later in doctrines of biology, eurochristian colonizers and capitalists of the eighteenth and nineteenth centuries gave the racial differentiations that revolve around whiteness a near transcendent power that persists to this day.

The eurochristianity at the heart of colonial racial capitalism generated whiteness as the crux of social, economic, and political value and power in the modern world. As such, whiteness should be understood as more than simply a social construct or a manifestation of purely political and economic forces. Nor is whiteness simply a secular social phenomenon that subsequently gets theologized as a way of justifying colonialism and plantation capitalism; rather, the history of its emergence shows that whiteness comes into existence as a theological category and thus a religious phenomenon in itself.[63] Whiteness is a force forged in the fires of eurochristian theological, colonial, and capitalist reasoning and practice.

In addition to Christian theological-political rationales, modern forms of racial differentiation further evolved with the help of discourses that utilized pseudoscientific forms of reasoning to defend the institution of chattel slavery and the racial oppression inherent in it.[64] Subsequent to the articulation of race as a matter of physicality, which arose out of the white racial capitalist pursuits of planter elites, the advent and development of the branch of the sciences called natural history gave the category of race an air of scientific legitimacy by articulating and situating race—as a matter of "skin color, hair texture, facial structure"— within systems of racial classification in the same way that science classifies animals, species, plants, and so on.[65] The most famous natural historian was Carolus Linnaeus, whose *Systema Naturae*, revised and republished many times throughout his life, set out to classify all of the natural world in accordance with the order established by the creator God. For Linnaeus, "nature is continuous, without gaps," which, in turn, means that "species have real essences that are immutable," essences, finally, that are observable in nature and in humans, according to their various forms.[66] Linnaeus articulated four human varieties: Americanus, Europaeus, Asiaticus, and Africanus, which he accounts for by way of observable physical differences made by differences in geography and climate. Linnaeus's scientific racialism would inform generations of other racial—and racist—scientists after him.

In the wake of discourses that tabulated racial essences according to morphology—distinctions in physical form—race came to be understood in terms not just of surface-level physicality but of biology. Whereas morphological conceptions of race fix race as something essentially real in the "physical structure" of bodies—literally, in facial shapes, hair texture, skin color, and so on—with biological racism, McWhorter argues, race comes to be conceived in terms of "development." Tethering race to biological notions of development helped to transform race into a phenomenon marked by different ways of behaving in the world "characterized by normality, deviance, or pathology."[67] As McWhorter writes, "race came to be a matter of function, not structure per se: differently raced bodies *behaved* differently."[68] By defining physical, moral, and cultural normativity in terms of the traits and capacities associated with people of European descent and abnormality in terms of the traits and capacities associated with nonwhite peoples, anthropologists and scientists in the nineteenth century contributed to the idea that racial difference marks the "relative success or failure in a biological march toward social and moral as well as physical perfection."[69]

If nonwhite people, and Black people in particular, behaved differently—because they have biologically limited moral capacities—then social and political institutions that kept nonwhite people in their proper place were essential to the smooth functioning and survival not just of society but of the species as a whole. In the early nineteenth century, the doctor, anthropologist, and scientist Samuel George Morton developed a theory that allegedly showed that the characteristics that constitute racial difference—the degenerate savagery of Blackness, the evolved civility of whiteness—are inherent and unchangeable. Morton eagerly deployed his research for the sake of the proslavery movement, research that white supremacist officials like South Carolina senator John C. Calhoun deployed to argue that white civilized society's only hope for survival and prosperity was the physical and economic subordination of naturally inferior populations.[70] Another purveyor of pseudoscientific racism was Dr. Samuel Cartwright, a physician, slaveholder, and professor at the University of Louisiana. In the process of tabulating the allegedly natural biological characteristics of African peoples, Cartwright developed a theory of two major "pathologies" that he argued beset the people he enslaved, pathologies that ultimately hurt his bottom line: *drapetomania*, a "disease causing negroes to run away," and *dysaesthesia Aethiopica*, which was when one was "half-asleep" when one should be laboring. As both a physician and enslaver, Cartwright proposed religiously imbued remedies for these fictional pathologies, including "preventively ... whipping the devil" out of enslaved people who show signs of the "pathological" desire to run away.[71] Together with religious and cultural justifications that established the superiority of whiteness and the inferiority of nonwhiteness in all its forms, and Blackness in particular, scientific racism contributed concretely to securing racial slavery and thus the broader racial capitalist order it buttressed, often as a direct response to increasingly widespread challenges to it.[72] By the early twentieth century, scientific racism gave rise to eugenics, forced sterilization, and other practices premised on the idea that race is a biological status and that mixing nonwhite with white—both reproductively and socially—threatens the species as a whole.[73]

With a biological focus on racial purity and reproduction, the development of racial science clarifies that modern racialization, throughout all its stages, is itself a manifestation of patriarchal power, as the conquests of early and late European-American colonialism and capitalism that forged modern race also required, exploited, and helped solidify differentiations based on gender and sexuality.[74] The patriarchal structure of capitalism from its earliest stages meant that women were essential for capital accumulation while their contributions to others' wealth and well-being remained unrecognized and inadequately compensated, leaving them not only dependent on men and employers but transformed into exploitable resources themselves.[75] In the context of the United States, the combination of racial and gender oppression at the heart of the settler colonial plantation capitalist project is most evident in the experiences of enslaved African women. As the property of white slave owners, kidnapped African men and women alike were instruments at the complete disposal of planters who extracted wealth from their labor and bodies. To be of African descent *and* woman, however, was—and still is—to be subject to multiple forms of oppression at once.[76] Subjected to physical violence in the master's fields and sexual violence in the master's domestic spaces, Black enslaved women's exploitation was all-encompassing.[77]

It was not race alone, then, but a combination of race and gender—as modalities through which class is lived—that determined states of freedom and subjection during more than two centuries of American chattel slavery.[78] This violent synthesis is perhaps most discernible in the 1662 law in Virginia, noted earlier, that declared "that all children borne in this country shalbe held bond or free only according to the condition of the mother."[79] As David Roediger points out, the fact that "'white' women could only give birth to free children" and that enslaved African women "could only legally give birth to property" meant that "the master's sexual violence against slave women potentially increased his property."[80] Such laws would become the norm throughout the American colonies and states for two full centuries, tethering race and gender to the reproductive requirements and properties of eurochristian colonial racial capitalism in fundamental ways.[81] The violent sexual-economic exploitation of Black women carried out by white propertied men was legitimated in significant part on the basis of the fabricated idea that women in general, and Black women in particular, are, in their essence, irrational, sensual, and hypersexual, which, by extension, would mean that, from white men's point of view, sexual violence against Black women is not violence at all but a natural act that corresponds with the natural distinctions in power and personhood between white men and Black women, a premise rooted in the deeply violent white patriarchal myth that Black women are inherently "unrapeable."[82]

It is not simply that race and gender "intersect." More fundamentally, at the level of the original formation of absolutized forms of modern race itself, eurochristian colonial racial capitalism reproduced race in and through differentiations of gender and sexuality that it weaponized in service of dispossession. In gazing on a world deemed ready for the taking beyond Europe's borders, European colonizers regularly observed, tabulated, and racially defined non-European otherness through explicitly gendered and sexual notions of European normativity. Indeed, European colonial and cultural descriptions of African women's gendered physical traits and alleged sexual habits were a primary means by which Europeans defined and captured African women as both an exploitable resource and a monstrous threat to norms of European social and political order. According to historian Jennifer Morgan, these gendered and sexualized descriptions did not simply classify aspects of African peoples' gender and sexuality alone but served as an "index of racial difference" more broadly: "Confronted with an Africa they needed to exploit, European writers turned to Black women as evidence of a cultural inferiority that ultimately became encoded as racial difference."[83] By the time of the emergence of more distinctly modern "racial" notions of difference in the mid-seventeenth century, when Europeans invoked the sexual and reproductive "savagery" of African women, Morgan argues, they conjured "a gendered and racialized figure that marked the boundaries of English civility" at the same time that it "naturalized the subjugation of Africans and their descendants in the Americas."[84] In the process of describing and categorizing Europe's non-European others, early eurochristian colonizers helped solidify a European self-understanding within which whiteness took shape as a fundamentally patriarchal phenomenon.

Later, on the heels of English colonization of the Americas, during the early republic period of the United States, a newly constructed sense of fraternity emerged at the nexus of whiteness, masculinity, and civic identity. Building on the thought and work of the colonizers who preceded and paved the way for white property-owning men of the eighteenth and nineteenth centuries, this imagined sense of what historian Dana Nelson calls "white national manhood" first manifested itself through the shared positionality of people with an allegedly natural capacity to scientifically recognize, diagnose, and manage the "difference" of all who were not white men.[85] It is not just that white men's gaze was a means of control over all who were not white men but that the very act of gazing on and controlling others gathered various forms of European manhood into a coherent and eminently powerful positionality.

Whiteness, from its origins, has always been patriarchal whiteness. And patriarchal whiteness, as Indigenous scholar Aileen Moreton-Robinson argues, is always inherently possessive, a manifestation of the patriarchal and white presumption to exploitative ownership of places, people, capital, and state power.[86] Indeed, the formation of patriarchal whiteness was itself a manifestation of the presumed capacity to possess both people and places. The rhetoric of white settlers and other propertied men of the modern era shows that, for white men of property, the possession of land and the possession of women were two aspects of the same natural capacity to own. Writings by white propertied men of the seventeenth and eighteenth centuries in the American colonies are full of metaphors that conceptualize possession of land in terms of possession of women: unhusbanded land was, like the ideal woman, fertile for reproduction that yields wealth. Some colonists who obtained new plots of land even spoke of entering into a kind of "marriage contract" that, as with an actual marriage contract, is structured according to ideas of the natural patriarchal right of possession. As Nancy Isenberg puts it, for the patriarchal facilitators of eurochristian colonial expansion, "women and land were for the use and benefit of man."[87] Whiteness has always been patriarchal, and patriarchal whiteness has always been possessive.

The intertwined dynamic of race and gender in the context of the colonial and capitalist appropriation of land and exploitation of peoples clarifies, among other things, that modern categories of race and gender are not neutral means of classification but are coconstitutive means by which colonial racial capitalism reproduces, absolutizes, and exploits human difference in pursuit of immense profit and power.[88] The racial differentiations that colonial capitalism helped produce and reproduce may seem to many people today, far removed from the time of their formation and crystallization, to be natural, neutrally descriptive, and original, but they are in fact anything but. Modern race emerged not as a value-free or "prepolitical" descriptor of difference but as a "strategic" political tool for differentiating and distributing power among peoples.[89] It is not the case, in other words, that "race" first exists as a natural, neutral, or objective fact and that "racism" subsequently deploys that neutral fact for ill. On the contrary, counterintuitive as it may seem, the very category of race in modernity is already premised on "rac*ism*," which is why, as Wolfe argues, "racism" is actually redundant: the category of race itself "already is an 'ism,'" what Robin Kelley calls "a means of structuring power through difference."[90] Structuring power hierarchically through difference requires a dynamic of oppositionality in which one's power depends on the disempowerment of others. Under eurochristian colonial racial capitalism, possession requires dispossession, wealth requires poverty, and valorized whiteness requires dehumanized Blackness, Indigeneity, and other modes of nonwhiteness. Patriarchal whiteness, then, is quite literally born and sustained through violence that dehumanizes and then eliminates others in pursuit of its own power.

Produced in and through religiously articulated eurochristian quests for power over the world, the modern category of race, in Michael Omi and Howard Winant's words, "is a way of 'making up people'" in service of particular political ends.[91] Or, as James Baldwin put it, "Color is not a human or a personal reality; it is a political reality."[92] The fact that race is not an objective, naturally occurring human reality does not, however, mean that it can be dismissed as illusory and thus inconsequential. Race as a marker of absolute and essential difference may be a fabrication, but the effects of defining people racially are all too real, impacting and shaping people's lives and the world as we know it in quite concrete ways. For these reasons, the scope of white supremacy and anti-Black racism cannot be grasped simply as a matter of individual, interpersonal bias or prejudice alone. Because the racial categories that European quests for unlimited power produce are not naturally occurring realities but rather "means of structuring power through difference," racism must be understood not just as personal bias but as structural and systemic ways of distributing and withholding power, including to the point of death. As Ruth Wilson Gilmore summarizes, racism is "the state-sanctioned or extralegal production and exploitation of group-differentiated vulnerability to premature death."[93]

Moreover, if race in its more absolute, modern form comes into existence not as a neutral descriptor of different kinds of people but as a means of structuring power through difference, then race in general and patriarchal whiteness in particular cannot be adequately understood today exclusively by reference to differences in individual or collective identity, or as matters of phenotype or pigmentation alone, in isolation from the maintenance of settler colonial, capitalist political economy and the anthropological differentiations they require and exploit. In other words, whiteness certainly includes but ultimately encapsulates—both conceptually and materially, both in its origins and today—more than "skin color" and "white people" as such.[94] Indeed, whiteness is best understood not only as an individual, physically marked, agential subject position but as an individually, collectively, and institutionally embodied mode of exclusive possession so powerful that it has produced "a new social order."[95] Patriarchal whiteness is a means of arranging the world from beyond the world's limitations in a way that enables life for some by making life a living—and dying—hell for others.

Modern racialization was and is an immensely violent process whereby people of European descent define and dehumanize their non-European others as inherently inferior and made for subjection while defining themselves as superior and made for authority. In so doing, however, European peoples ultimately dehumanize themselves as well. Subjected to these violent realities, those who are racialized in antagonism to whiteness have also repurposed the racialization violently imposed on them into a means of collective survival and liberation. Blackness, in particular, despite first designating European projections of inferiority, has also long been a powerful symbolic and embodied means of kinship and solidarity between peoples of African descent, as well as a means of collective power and defiance in the face of the violence of white supremacy in all its forms. "For Europeans," theorist Saidiya Hartman writes, "race established a hierarchy of human life, determined which persons were expendable, and selected the bodies that could be transformed into commodities." And yet, for those who were torn from their kin and homeland and racialized as Black, collectively embracing and embodying the "wound" of racialization and enslavement was also a way of attempting to heal it. "For those chained in the lower decks of a slave ship," Hartman writes, "race was both a death sentence and the language of solidarity."[96] Derived from European terror but reclaimed as a site of dignity and self-determination, Blackness, as both concept and living reality, retains its multidimensionality into the present: in the hands of patriarchal whiteness, Blackness is a mode of proximity to death, while in the hands of those who embody it together, Blackness is a transcendent means of life in the face of death.

Absolutely Exclusive Private Property

Eurochristian colonial capitalist order merges not only the religious and the racial but the religious, the racial, and the spatial. The modern formation of patriarchal whiteness as a world-possessing power is thus a story not just of colonial and capitalist order in general but of the formation of absolutely exclusive private property in particular. Indeed, while patriarchal whiteness and private property are not wholly reducible to each other, they share a common history and come into existence by way of each other such that it is difficult to adequately understand one apart from the other.

What are we talking about when we talk about "property"? Earliest uses of the term point to natures or qualities possessed by a person or thing, for example, the "properties" of a substance found in nature or even the "properties" of God.[97] In addition to referring to a quality and the person or thing that possesses it, "property" also refers to the dynamic relationship between persons and things and, by extension, the relationship between persons and persons.[98] Etymologically, "property" derives in part from the Latin *proprietas*, which in old English law referred to "that which is one's own," and thus ownership.[99] The relationship between persons and things—"that which is one's own"—can take many forms, including claims to things, rights to use and dispose of things how we see fit, possession of things, and so on. These claims, rights, and modes of possession can also subsequently manifest themselves in multiple forms: communal possession, individual possession, exclusive possession, corporate or state possession, or even a mixture of multiple forms of possession.[100] Because property is in significant part a question of the relationship between persons and things, any understanding of that relationship also entails a conception of what a person is, on the one hand, and what the world is, on the other. A theory of property, in other words, is also a theory of the nature or constitution of persons who relate to it and to one another—an anthropology—as well as an understanding of the origins, nature, purpose, and ends of the world itself, which is to say, a cosmology of some kind, such as a theology of creation. As property also implies a set of social relations, claims to property necessarily lead to conflict among various and sometimes competing claims. As such, questions of property and its justification also entail questions of political order and the guiding conceptions of power, authority, and sociality that accompany it. Moreover, because questions of property and its justification necessarily entail questions about the nature of power and authority, considerations of property also entail questions about the theological concepts on which many justifications of property are built.[101] Talking about modern notions of property, then, is best served by reflecting on the fusion of theological and political ideas about persons, the world, and God on which property stands.

The general idea of a right to property held in relative privacy has existed since the ancient world. From that time up to today, we can observe two predominant and distinct views on privately possessed property, each containing multiple variations.[102] On the one hand are those throughout Western history who argue that finite, sinful, self-centered humanity needs privately possessed property because human finitude and/or sinfulness are such that commonly possessed property can only lead to perpetual conflict and chaos. As such, the argument goes, private property, while not what nature or God originally intended, is understood to serve the divine, natural, or universally necessary purpose of protecting humankind from the violence and chaos that are inevitable when fundamentally finite, sinful humans try to share. On the other hand are those who argue that property privately possessed is not a safeguard against the conflict and chaos that emerge from finitude and sin but is itself a fundamental manifestation of human selfishness or sinfulness because it claims for oneself alone what, by God's intention or nature's provision, actually belongs to all. In this view, private property is understood to be not an expression but a disruption of the natural order or God's will for the world and a forfeiting of the natural or God-given capacity of humans to live in accordance with that nature or divine will. Both, then, are based on interpretations of human finitude and/or sin but in opposing ways: one holds that finitude and/or sin produce an inability to possess property in any way other than privately, while the other holds that possessing property privately is itself an inherent manifestation of sin or disruption of natural order that proliferates further sin, evil, or chaos in the world.

While "property" has described aspects of the relationship between humans and between humans and the material world for millennia, property possessed to the absolute exclusion of others, without any responsibility to the needs of a broader community—a modern manifestation of the former view on property just mentioned—is only a few hundred years old. Absolutely exclusive private property emerges from the same confluence of forces that patriarchal whiteness does, namely, eurochristian colonialism and racial capitalism, which is why understanding how we came to a world so privatized requires attending to the theological-political rationales and practices that helped facilitate and proliferate absolute privatization in early modern Europe and the Americas and ultimately across the globe.

Before the seventeenth century, the legal and cultural right to private property was still relatively limited: such rights were never absolute and were never claimed without some degree of regard for the well-being of the larger community in which one lived. The notion of absolute individual private property rights emerged in the seventeenth century, on the one hand, from the idea that human finitude and sin make common property untenable and, on the other, from the idea that citizens should have the right to defend themselves and their belongings against overreaching and tyrannical political and ecclesial authority. With the work of John Locke in the late seventeenth century, predominant understandings of the meaning and scope of private property underwent a radical shift that opened the door to a world in which not just "private" but relatively unlimited, absolutely exclusive private property would become the norm throughout the European colonial world. An English philosopher, colonialist, and investor in the then-burgeoning transatlantic slave trade, Locke by no means invented private property as we know it today, but his writing on property solidified a tradition of thinking on the issue that was already moving toward privileging and naturalizing absolutely exclusive private possession as the mode of relating to the material world that most aligned with divine and natural law.[103] Whether he intended it or not, Locke's political philosophy and theology of property was subsequently used to rationalize and build the foundations of the order of absolutely exclusive private property that structures much of our world today.[104]

Locke's work helped catalyze what would become a number of significant shifts in predominant understandings of the right to private property in the modern era. Liberal political and economic thought starting in the seventeenth century centered around the right to life, liberty, and property. While some early liberal formulations conceived "liberty" primarily as a right of freedom against tyrannical power, with and after Locke, the right to liberty became primarily a matter of the security of property, particularly that belonging to wealthy men of European descent.[105] In addition to influencing English colonizers in their pursuit of the possession of Indigenous lands in the Americas, Locke's thought also informed the work of liberal theorists of capitalism like Adam Smith, who, like Locke, argued that government exists "for the security of property," as well as English jurists including William Blackstone, who, like both Locke and Smith, established the centrality of security, liberty, and private property in law in England and in the American colonies, where the founding fathers would soon articulate the rights of white men there in the same way.[106]

Additionally, Locke largely follows the trajectory of thinking on private property that presumes that, based on human finitude and sin, private property is necessary to uphold order and guard against chaos. What changes with Locke—who synthesizes and elaborates the thought that preceded him, as opposed to inventing something entirely new—is that privately held property shifts from being understood as a necessary evil to being understood as a natural and positive feature of the order that God created.[107] Instead of a regrettable but necessary mechanism for guarding against chaos, private property transformed into an original and enduring feature of the world as God always intended it. Finally, with Locke, the right to private property transforms from a mere natural *right* to a natural, God-ordained *mandate*. As noted earlier, Locke's theory of property doubles as a theology of creation that understands humans to be not merely invited but required to use their labor to "subdue," make industrious use of, and privately enclose parts of the Earth. As such, the exclusive possession of property becomes quite literally a matter of "obedience" to God and thus a practice in accordance with the natural order of things.[108] This dual notion of obedience and nature rests on the fact that, in Locke's conception, property held in common is "wasted" property, whereas property that has been made private and productive through subjection to human labor and industriousness fulfills the divine and natural purposes for which it was made, thereby authorizing exclusive possession of it.[109] Understood in such a way, the eurochristian colonial capitalist pursuit of absolutely exclusive private ownership of the Earth becomes what political theorist Onur Ulas Ince calls a "divinely sanctioned" moral endeavor.[110]

As a political theology of the relationship between persons and things and of the purpose of creation, Locke's thinking on private property possession also entails an implicit anthropology, a theory of personhood. Locke, as well as Hobbes and others, understands the fullness of personhood in terms of what political theorist C. B. Macpherson calls the "possessive individual." The possessive individual is marked by freedom *from* dependence on others, on the one hand, and freedom *for* self-interested disposal of one's capacities and possessions, on the other, owing nothing to anyone or to society as a whole.[111] For Locke, this essential freedom or capacity to possess oneself and the world not only makes a person a person but is itself a kind of property that normative persons—European men of wealth—possess.[112] Property, then, under the Lockean conception, consists not only in things themselves but in the allegedly inherent right or capacity of self-possessing individuals to possess them.[113]

Elaborating on and extending Macpherson's theory of possessive individualism, political philosopher Étienne Balibar argues that in Locke's work as a whole—including both his philosophy of property and his philosophy of human consciousness—we see a theory in which possession is foundational to normative human personhood.[114] By "binding together" "identity" and "appropriation," Locke transforms the idea of personhood so that "*having*" and "*being*" are not two fundamentally distinct phenomena but rather two ways of talking about the same thing: to be a (normative) person is to possess oneself and to use one's labor, or the labor of others under one's control, to possess the world.¹¹⁵ Appropriation, then, in Locke's view, is not a secondary but primary expression of what it means to be a human person—or at least a certain kind of human person. Indeed, Locke understands the capacity for the unlimited acquisition and exclusive possession of property to be natural or inherent only to those who are gifted with superior degrees of rationality and industriousness, which, for Locke, would have meant wealthy men of European origin, as opposed to poor European laborers, Africans, or Indigenous peoples in the Americas or other European colonies.¹¹⁶

Arising from the gendered and racial foundations of capitalism, absolutely exclusive private property possession in its formative stages was also a thoroughly gendered and racialized regime. European men, in Locke's framework—and indeed in most philosophical and theological systems of the time—were the only persons seen as natural bearers of the capacity to possess property privately. As Silvia Federici's work demonstrates, capitalism depends on the reproductive labor of women who give birth and so supply more bodies for a labor force that builds wealth that those laborers—reproductive or otherwise—will scarcely enjoy. Women, according to predominant thought in the modern era, lack the natural capacity to possess and manage the Earth privately. Indeed, women—whether of European, African, Indigenous, or other descent—not only could not, whether by nature or by custom, possess property but themselves *were* the property of men, though not all in the same ways.¹¹⁷ Women of European descent functioned as "extensions" of their husband's property and existed at the disposal of men in general.¹¹⁸ And yet, married European women still enjoyed beneficial access to private property through their husbands in a way that African and Indigenous women did not.¹¹⁹ In any case, even if only certain people get to be private possessors, in the Lockean view of property, the private possession of a few is understood to benefit not only those few but all of human civilization.¹²⁰ Because Locke's vision of society entails an understanding of the normative—European, male—human person as private possessor, he subsequently understands the primary purpose of civil government to be protecting and preserving property against those who would do harm to property both in persons and possessions and to punish those guilty of such trespasses.[121]

Locke's theological-political conception of private property ultimately reflects not just an elaboration of the work of political philosophers before him but a philosophy and theology worked out in tandem with his own personal colonial commercial investments, his role in the political and economic institution of the Carolina colonies, and his stake in the wider enclosure movement that was well under way in his home country of England.[122] Though the process of the enclosure of commonly tenured lands began as early as the thirteenth century in England, it reached its peak during the late sixteenth and early seventeenth centuries and served as the basis of the formation of unlimited and absolutely exclusive private property as a central institution in the ever-expanding eurochristian capitalist world.[123] Building off a tradition that sees private property as a safeguard against the chaos that ensues from human finitude and sin and building off the popular theological-political rationales of wealthy landowners in the early modern era, pro-enclosure elites, Locke, religious leaders, and others who follow them elaborate a political theology of private property that establishes the right to relatively unlimited, absolutely exclusive private property—property possessed without regard for the rights or well-being of others—as a right of both transcendent theological and political grounding. Property possessed privately, it would become widely accepted, corresponds with and concretely materializes God's intentions for the created world.

Patriarchal Whiteness and/as Private Property

Absolutely exclusive and relatively unlimited private property— from its early modern origins in the English enclosure movement to its worldwide proliferation via European colonialism, racial and plantation capitalism, and global imperialism and up through the neoliberal present—creates, because it relies on, economic dispossession: privatizing land and resources otherwise held in common requires *dis*possessing those who had utilized them for their livelihood up to that point, a reality made evident by more than a thousand years of theological and political tradition that decries private property as a form of theft in which the few steal from the many.

Thus far, I have outlined the historical formations of whiteness and of absolutely exclusive private property regimes, only implicitly pointing to the actual relationship between the two. So what, specifically, is the nature of the relationship between patriarchal whiteness and private property? To begin with, as noted earlier, in addition to land and commodities produced by slave labor, slaveholding racial capitalism transformed people of African descent into property "that could be transferred, assigned, inherited, or posted as collateral" by owners primarily of European descent.[124] As such, the "value" of African life for white plantation owners was a matter not of any inherent dignity, mutual relation, or any other measure but primarily of its labor and reproductive capacities.[125] In addition to transforming enslaved Africans into a kind of property, though, whiteness is intimately tied to the institution of private property in another important sense that is crucial for understanding the racial, classed, and gendered criminalization that defines the modern eurochristian world. In addition to the possession of other people, whiteness itself, as critical race theorist Cheryl Harris shows, constitutes a kind of "property" in the sense that its earliest eurochristian colonial articulations ascribed to it an allegedly inherent and superior capacity to possess the world absolutely.[126]

The history of English enclosure is typically narrated as a matter of purely economic class relations, but as detailed earlier, even within Europe, the exploitation and dispossession that generated capitalism already took on racial or proto-racial forms.[127] Before, and eventually simultaneous with, England's conquests of Africa and the Americas, it colonized Ireland and Scotland, whose inhabitants English colonizers characterized in terms that anticipate and approximate the "racial" in the sense that Cedric Robinson conceives it.[128] Powers like England carried out the dispossessing work of enclosure in tandem with global colonial conquest and war making, deploying enclosure as a tool of colonial conquest in itself, including in the Indigenous territories of the Americas. In the end, the racial capitalism of eurochristian colonial expansion and African enslavement was the same racial capitalism that undergirded the mass displacement of economically dispossessed Europeans, including in the Scottish Highlands, where enslavers and former enslavers used profits accrued through enslavement to forcibly evict at least five thousand people from their land during the late eighteenth and early nineteenth centuries.[129] Pro-enclosure elites across the British Empire regularly characterized poor commoners in subtly racial or proto-racial terms not only in Ireland and in the Highlands of Scotland but in England, and they did so by deploying the same terms of derision that were simultaneously used in service of the profit-generating enslavement of African peoples and the settler colonization of Indigenous lands in the Americas and beyond. "Critics of commons loathed commoners with a xenophobic intensity," historian J. M. Neeson argues. "They were a 'sordid race,' as foreign and uncultivated as the land that fed them. Like commons they were wild and unproductive. They were lazy and dangerous. If wastes must be subdued, so must they."[130] Far from a matter of a narrowly conceived notion of class alone, the political theology of private property and enclosure fused differentiations based on race and class (and gender) by deploying "racialist" terms to disparage and thus justify the displacement of commoners within the boundaries of Europe.

As private enclosure spread, by way of colonialism, across the globe, the implicit racial character of private enclosure became more explicit in such a way that naturalized conceptions of absolutely private property possession and absolutized conceptions of race became inseparable. According to Harris, the histories of European colonialism, chattel slavery, and the formation of law in the United States show that "rights in property are contingent on, intertwined with, and conflated with race" in ways that produce and reproduce racial subordination. Just as Malcolm X said of racism and capitalism—that you cannot have one without the other—so Harris says of the modern formation of race and private property: "The origins of property rights in the United States are rooted in racial domination. Even in the early years of the country, it was not the concept of race alone that operated to oppress Blacks and Indians; rather, it was the *interaction* between conceptions of race and property that played a critical role in establishing and maintaining racial and economic subordination."[131] Conceptions of race and property first "interacted" in the sense that "possession—the act necessary to lay the basis for rights in property—was defined to include only the cultural practices of whites," in contrast to the lack of capacity to properly possess that Europeans projected onto Indigenous peoples in North America. As Harris writes, "The possession maintained by the Indians was not 'true' possession and could safely be ignored. This interpretation of the rule of first possession effectively rendered the rights of first possessors contingent on the race of the possessor," thereby legitimating the violent *dis*possession of Native Americans from their land.[132] Together with the "seizure and appropriation" of Native American land, the "seizure and appropriation" of African labor undergirding the system of chattel slavery "facilitated the merger of white identity and property."[133] Indeed, according to legal theorist Brenna Bhandar, the histories of European colonialism and racial capitalism show that "racial subjectivity and private property ownership" do not merely "interact" with each other but, more fundamentally, come into existence in and through each other.[134]

In the process of coding and implementing private property possession racially, white identity itself came to be understood as a kind of natural property right, namely, the property of the right to inherited power, security, and the assumed capacity to privately possess and govern the world in a way that excludes and yet is ultimately understood to benefit others.[135] As outlined earlier, modern notions of property deriving from Locke understand property to consist not only in things themselves but in the right or capacity to possess them.[136] As such, the "property of being white" guaranteed not only greater access to physical properties in land but also freedom from the status of slavery. The "color line" that eurochristian settler colonialism, racial capitalism, and chattel slavery helped produce and reproduce was more than an abstraction; it was "a line of protection and demarcation from the potential threat of commodification," of *being* someone else's property as opposed to possessing someone else as property. The property of being white, ultimately, was freedom *from* bondage and freedom *for* self-determination through securities, rights, and powers that African and Indigenous peoples—and women of all races—allegedly did not have the rational capacity to enjoy.[137]

While a coherent notion of "whiteness" had not yet fully emerged when Locke was investing in the African slave trade and theorizing a natural right to absolutely exclusive private property, by defining the capacity for private property possession in direct relation to European notions of personhood, Locke's work, Roediger argues, "made the idea of race both possible and necessary."[138] As Tinker puts it, "Although [Locke] would not yet have called himself White, his philosophical argumentation and socioeconomic practice clearly place him in the context of burgeoning White european supremacist thinking."[139] In short, Locke's work catalyzes an anthropology not just of "possessive individualism" but of what George Lipsitz calls the "possessive investment in whiteness."[140] As noted earlier, this fusion of whiteness and private property is, like the larger systems within which they emerge, an inherently gendered phenomenon. While predominant views in the early modern West held that women were not capable of property possession but were, rather, property themselves, women of European descent also enjoyed access to property and were seen as belonging to the private domestic sphere that private property made possible. Whiteness as property is also gendered in the sense that it was understood as a means of hedging European women in against the projected threats of African and Indigenous peoples, often defined as inherently sexual threats, despite the fact that propertied European men could and did enact sexual violence against their wives—and practically anyone else—without repercussion. The gendered nature of whiteness as property can further be seen by the fact that, in a context in which whiteness and private property obtain conceptual and material cohesion by way of each other, men of European descent who did not possess property were for that reason viewed as men who failed to adequately perform both masculinity and their "superior racial status."[141] And yet, even when poor, propertyless white men are perceived as having failed to live up to their whiteness and their manhood by virtue of their possessing no property, their whiteness and masculinity still afford them a semblance of security, no matter how small or ultimately illusory that security may be.[142]

On the most basic level, Harris argues, what whiteness and property share is "a common premise—a conceptual nucleus—of a right to exclude."[143] Whiteness and property mutually reinforce and extend each other: whiteness, a "species of property," extends the conceptual and material structure of private property possession racially, just as private property extends whiteness into the world in a concretely material, spatial, and relational way.[144] Crystallized through eurochristian colonialism and racial capitalism, whiteness, always patriarchal, came into existence not as a neutral descriptor of human difference but as a means of possession and dispossession, inclusion and exclusion, empowerment and disempowerment. The function of enclosures—hedges, fences, gates, and walls—is to keep in and to keep out. Like the hedges and fences that early modern elites raised across England and colonial America, the basic function of whiteness from its beginning was—and is—to keep out and keep in and to police those boundaries vigilantly. Grounded in the necessity of exclusionary boundary policing, patriarchal whiteness and private property are deeply intertwined with, and indeed emerge alongside, the police power to dispose threats to social order, as I explore in the chapters that follow. As a manifestation of exclusive possession, whiteness as property, what Bhandar calls a "racial regime of ownership," dispossesses whatever and whoever falls outside or trespasses against its lines of demarcation.[145] The line of protection formed by patriarchal whiteness and private property—by patriarchal whiteness *as* private property—is one of the most significant lines of demarcation in modernity because it marks out spaces and identities not only of trespass and belonging but of death and life. As centuries of mass resistance indicate, patriarchal whiteness and private property possession are far from merely neutral markers of personhood and materiality. On the contrary, as I show in what follows, patriarchal whiteness and private property are ways of arranging the world that deploy carceral capture and captivity as means of determining access to life and proximity to death for populations conceived and arranged according to functionally sacred hierarchies of race, class, and gender.

Willie Jennings writes that "whiteness comes into being as a form of landscape"—a landscape arranged according to the sacred supremacy of private property and its possessors.[146] In a world where whiteness is supreme, to be Black—or to be anything other than white, for that matter—is to be fundamentally "out of place."[147] In a world ordered according to the oppositional supremacy of whiteness *as* property, to be Black, to be anything other than white, and even to possess no property at all is to engage in material and moral trespass, which, for the managers of such a world, necessitates the police power to eliminate the dispossessed as a means of restoring, and indeed *saving*, the social order. As will become clearer in what follows, threat and salvation, ever fused in opposition, are integral to the function of racial capitalist settler colonial order and the police power that helps to create and sustain it: colonial racial capitalism generates crises that threaten its existence and so generates new measures, including criminalization, to *save* itself from itself, over and over again—or, more precisely, "forever and ever, Amen."[148]

2

"Ownership of the Earth Forever and Ever, Amen!"

Understanding mass criminalization as a manifestation of religion requires understanding how the violent forces of patriarchal whiteness and absolutely exclusive private property that police exist to serve and protect are themselves manifestations of religion. Whiteness and property are religious, on the one hand, in the sense that European and European-American Christian theological reasoning, biblical appeals, and religious practices played indispensable roles in their formation during the modern era. But the role of religion in the formation and maintenance of whiteness and property is more than that of a mere legitimating instrument in service of seemingly nonreligious dimensions of reality thought to be more fundamental, like the social, political, or economic. Beyond being simply influenced or shaped by religion, patriarchal whiteness and private property are, in themselves, religious phenomena, functionally sacred centers of the social order that revolves around them. How is it that forces typically understood to be essentially social, political, economic, or cultural in nature are also inherently religious in nature?

Religion, broadly speaking, consists of the practices and orientations by which peoples seek to transcend, transform, and make ultimate meaning of the conditions of mortal finitude. As such, religion is an inherently human practice, embodied by both individuals and collectives, which means there is no such thing as religion apart from the social creatures who build and practice it. As an inherently earthbound practice, a way of being directed within the limitations of space and time—even if directed toward that which lies beyond space and time—religion is very much concerned with and helps establish the arrangement of material life here and now. And the ordering of material life is a matter of sociality, of politics, economics, culture, and other dimensions of shared existence. As a fundamentally social phenomenon, religion plays a central role in the creation and cohesion of many kinds of communities, not only in the sense that communities carry out religious practices together but in the sense that the deities or aspects of the deities that religions revere often function as implicitly projected manifestations of the collective identity of those who are doing the worshiping.[1] As a result, the reverence that communities direct toward a society's god or gods often functions doubly as a kind of reverence for the social order itself. As such, religion might be understood, at least in part, as an exercise in collective self-deification. For some religious traditions, broadly conceived, deification is primarily a matter of greater proximity to the divine, of integration into the ultimate order of things, while for others, deification is an inherently competitive process in which becoming divine requires that others be understood as falling outside the bounds of divine favor and moral belonging. Making gods of some, such traditions work only if they also render others not merely human but less than human, even demonic. The colonial and racial capitalist manifestations of eurochristianity that forge patriarchal whiteness and absolutely exclusive private property regimes constitute one such tradition.

One of the primary means by which many religious traditions establish a sense of ultimate meaning and order is by clearly delineating sacred from profane, orderly from disorderly, pure from polluted. In so doing, religions provide structures of meaning and orientation that make it possible to live in a world that might otherwise seem chaotic and dangerous. Whatever disrupts that sense of order is thus experienced as a disruption of the sacred and thus of life itself. According to anthropologist Mary Douglas, the religious pursuit of purity—an inherently boundary-making desire that separates, demarcates, and punishes prohibited crossings—is, at its root, a manifestation of the desire to establish metaphysical and social order in the face of the threat of disorder that "impurity" seems to pose. The symbolic locus of impurity, Douglas suggests, following Freud, is "dirt": "matter out of place" that, simply by being out of place, poses danger to a social order that depends on clear social, spatial, and cosmic delineations.[2] Elaborating on Durkheim's work, Douglas argues that eliminating the threat that "dirt" and "pollution" pose to the moral and social order by punishing transgressors is not merely an act of negation but a "creative" act that unifies experience and creates social structure for a society as a whole.[3] Punishing boundary transgressions that pose a threat to the integrity of moral and social order, in other words, is as much, if not more so, about reproducing and maintaining the order itself as it is about the person accused of trespassing against it.

The order-establishing pursuit of purity integral to many forms of religiosity—eurochristian colonial and capitalist traditions in particular—thus entails an inherently oppositional dynamic: one can only be defined as pure if others are marked as impure, one can only become God if others are understood to be opposed to God. This is why, according to Douglas, moral and social pollution is articulated as a threat most prominently in contexts "where the lines of structure, cosmic or social, are clearly defined."[4] The more solid the system of order and classification, and thus the more accentuated and absolute the lines of demarcation between differentiated peoples and practices, the more likely it is that certain peoples and practices will register as transgressions of the lines that maintain a sense of cosmic and social order. And demarcations—cosmic or social, immaterial or material—continue to exist and serve their social, order-establishing function only if they are policed, secured, and reinforced. To fail to protect those borders is to risk a chaos and disorder that threatens the foundations of the social order itself. Indeed, it is here, at the production and defense of the boundaries of social order, that police power emerges and becomes discernible as inherently religious, a dynamic I explore more thoroughly in chapters 3–5.

In the end, the lines, boundaries, and borders that manifest the religious aspiration to maintain self-preserving purity against the dangers of pollution are more than theoretical or abstract; they are material, and they structure the physical spaces we inhabit in the world, shaping people's lives in concrete ways, even when we do not perceive it. Demarcating the sacred from the profane in our midst, religion constructs heaven and hell and the boundaries between them not merely as immaterial states of life after death but as material manifestations of life and death in space and time, here and now.[5] As a fundamentally social phenomenon that makes meaning of the limitations of finitude and then makes that meaning material, religion establishes material and conceptual structures through which people experience and arrange the world and the relationships between people living in it. Whatever enables people to transcend, transform, or make ultimate meaning of the conditions of finite reality, therefore, performs a function that not only resembles but constitutes the "religious."

Patriarchal whiteness and absolutely exclusive private property regimes come into being via religious rationale, as outlined in chapter 1. But more crucially, whiteness and regimes of private ownership reorganize life, landscapes, and ways of thinking, perceiving, and being embodied in so all-encompassing a way that they are best understood as religious phenomena in themselves, as opposed to simply social, political, or economic realities that just happen to be influenced by religious ideas at various points of their historical formation. Patriarchal whiteness and private ownership transform and reframe reality, imposing implicit and explicit demarcations of sacred and profane, pure and polluted, moral and immoral on real peoples and places. They make and impose those meanings, materializing them through systems of power, value, culture, and law. They build walled, gated, fenced, and psychic boundaries to keep their demarcations—simultaneously religious, political, social, economic, and cultural—and the larger social orders that they uphold in place. They provide a means for a few to obtain godlike power over the Earth and its peoples. They soothe the anxieties of mortal finitude by building mechanisms of exclusive transcendence and invulnerability that work only by exposing others to vulnerability and harm. They create access to life for some and "vulnerability to premature death" for many others.[6] They provide a path to heaven for a few by creating hell for many. They deify some by destroying others. Such determinations are not without breaks and disruptions forged by acts of refusal and reconstitution. And yet, because whiteness and property have contributed so profoundly to making the world as we know it, critical analysis of their functionally religious power, reach, and resilience is an indispensable step in breaking mass devotion to them and their power over our lives.

The mass criminalization of Black and economically dispossessed peoples is a function of the production and vigilant defense of a eurochristian racial capitalist settler colonial social order that, for its managers and beneficiaries, functions as sacred, ultimate, heavenly. The social order that revolves around patriarchal whiteness and private ownership is functionally sacred not in the sense that it manifests actual divine presence and power but, rather, in the sense that it is a manifestation of a human aspiration to the godlike power to both transcend and possess the world at the expense of those who are cast outside the bounds of cosmic and social belonging. The religiosity of patriarchal whiteness and private property is therefore neither neutral nor innocent. As an inherently world- and person-transforming power, religion, broadly speaking, has the capacity to be either life-affirming or death-dealing. The religiosity of whiteness and property is a tragically illusory, exclusive, paranoid, hierarchical, scarcity-fabricating, and therefore deadly religiosity that is powerful only when it makes others powerless, that possesses the world only when others are dispossessed of it, that obtains transcendence only when others are caged, that secures life only when others die. A functionally sacred subject-making, meaning-making, and world-ordering orientation and set of practices, patriarchal whiteness and private property determine access to life and proximity to death for populations conceived according to differentiations of race, class, and gender, as well as sexuality, ability, and other eurochristian markers of personhood and normativity. Because they seek their godlike power at the expense of others, patriarchal whiteness and private property are ultimately not divine but deadly. And yet, the fact that they function in ways that mimic and aspire to a kind of divine power requires that we understand the scope of their world-transforming pretensions in terms of religion.

White Apotheosis

One of the best guides we have in understanding the religiosity of whiteness in its connection to regimes of private ownership is the twentieth-century Black radical scholar and activist W. E. B. Du Bois. In addition to being one of the first to thoroughly uncover and analyze the systemic connections between white supremacy, European colonialism, and the political economy of global and plantation capitalism, Du Bois was also a keen interpreter of the ways religion functioned as both a foundation of death-dealing oppression and a means of freedom for oppressed peoples.[7] In his 1920 essay "The Souls of White Folk," Du Bois subtly traces the subject-making and world-rearranging religiosity of whiteness as a force that produces and depends on Black subjugation and dispossession. If his classic 1903 text *The Souls of Black Folk* is a meditation on the spirit of Black survival in a world where to be Black is to be a "problem" from the moment one is born, then "The Souls of White Folk" is a meditation on the religious spirit of white supremacy that depends for its survival on Blackness being at once a "problem" and an exploitable resource.[8] The art and depth of the meditation that opens his text invites quoting at length:

> High in the tower, where I sit above the loud complaining of the human sea, I know many souls that toss and whirl and pass, but none there are that intrigue me more than the Souls of White Folk. Of them I am singularly clairvoyant. I see in and through them. I view them from unusual points of vantage. Not as a foreigner do I come, for I am native, not foreign, bone of their thought and flesh of their language. Mine is not the knowledge of the traveler or the colonial composite of dear memories, words and wonder. Nor yet is my knowledge that which servants have of masters, or mass of class, or capitalist of artisan. Rather I see these souls undressed and from the back and side. I see the working of their entrails. I know their thoughts and they know that I know. This knowledge makes them now embarrassed, now furious. They deny my right to live and be and call me misbirth! My word is to them mere bitterness and my soul, pessimism. And yet as they preach and strut and shout and threaten, crouching as they clutch at rags of facts and fancies to hide their nakedness, they go twisting, flying by my tired eyes and I see them ever stripped,—ugly, human. The discovery of personal whiteness among the world's peoples is a very modern thing. . . . The world in a sudden, emotional conversion has discovered that it is white and by that token, wonderful! This assumption that of all the hues of God whiteness alone is inherently and obviously better than brownness or tan leads to curious acts; even the sweeter souls of the dominant world as they discourse with me on weather, weal, and woe are continually playing above their actual words an obligato of tune and tone, saying: "My poor, un-white thing! Weep not nor rage. I know, too well, that the curse of God lies heavy on you. Why? That is not for me to say, but be brave! Do your work in your lowly sphere, praying the good Lord that into heaven above, where all is love, you may, one day, be born—white!" I do not laugh. I am quite straight-faced as I ask soberly: "But what on earth is whiteness that one should so desire it?" Then always, somehow, some way, silently but

clearly, I am given to understand that whiteness is the ownership of the earth forever and ever, Amen![9]

Du Bois's depiction of whiteness begins with the precision of Black knowledge and perception. "High in the tower," Du Bois the Black philosopher claims clairvoyance, the special ability to perceive what cannot otherwise be perceived, namely, the spirit of that power that orders the modern world of colonialism, capitalism, and imperialism: whiteness. What for others is a mystery—the substance of the souls of white folk—is, from his vantage point, no mystery. This ability to discern the heart of whiteness is a consequence not of the kind of distance that permits an aerial view, Du Bois suggests, but of an intimacy derived from the original contingency of the "races" on one another. Whiteness depends for its existence on the devalued Blackness that it had to invent for its own supremacy.[10] Du Bois can see in and through whiteness because whiteness created—pseudo-divinely spoke into existence—a world in which Blackness exists only as "problem."[11] This Black ability to perceive the hidden secret of whiteness embarrasses and infuriates white people, Du Bois writes. Like the Jewish and Christian God whose fullness transcends conceptual grasp, so whiteness is godlike only if it transcends Black knowledge's threatening circumscription of it: as the thought and language that creates devalued Blackness, whiteness is supposed to be the power to circumscribe Blackness conceptually and materially, not the other way around. Black knowledge of the whiteness that is supposed to transcend it is precisely the threat that Black agency and freedom pose to white supremacy, which is why Black knowledge of the true nature of whiteness makes white people "embarrassed" and "furious."[12] In response to the expression of Black knowledge of the "entrails" or inner workings of whiteness, and the agency of which that knowledge is an expression, whiteness unmasked of its illusory power lashes out, denying the right of Black people "to live," to "be," redefining Black existence as "misbirth," an abnormality in the natural order of things. Calling to mind the fervent fire-and-brimstone religiosity of white evangelical Christians, Du Bois describes the angry desperation of white people to hide the shame of being as finitely human as their allegedly inferior others, calling to mind biblical narratives of first awareness of sin in Genesis: "And yet as they preach and strut and shout and threaten, crouching as they clutch at rags of facts and fancies to hide their nakedness, they go twisting, flying by my tired eyes and I see them ever stripped,—ugly, human." Du Bois's vision of whiteness is a vision of a base, sinful humanity stripped of its idolatrous, illusory aspirations to wield a godlike power that it pursues in an effort to cover the anxiety and insecurity of its own finitude. Like Adam and Eve, who sinned by aspiring to divine knowledge and power, white people are naked and ashamed before a Black vision that sees through their pseudo-divine mimicry.

"The discovery of personal whiteness among the world's peoples is a very modern thing," Du Bois writes. But the word "personal" should not lead us to understand whiteness as an exclusively "personal" matter. Whiteness is not just skin deep but worldwide: "the world in a sudden, emotional conversion has discovered that it is white and by that token, wonderful!" When Du Bois writes that "the world . . . discovered that it is white," he does not mean that all the people of the world realized they were white. Du Bois is suggesting, rather, that the discovery of personal whiteness implied the whitening of the Earth itself, the global extension—through capitalism, colonialism, imperialism—of the white power to possess the world, which is a power to remake the world in its own image: with the religious zeal of "conversion," the world itself is transformed into the exclusive possession and extension of whiteness. Even relatively well-meaning white people, Du Bois suggests, presume without question the God-ordained naturalness of racial hierarchy: "My poor, un-white thing! Weep not nor rage. I know, too well, that the curse of God lies heavy on you. Why? That is not for me to say, but be brave!" All the same, Du Bois perceives behind their pity an urging to accept Black subjugation as a means of racial and religious salvation: work hard—"do your work in your lowly sphere"—and pray "that into heaven above, where all is love, you may, one day, be born—white!" Blackness, according to white mythology, is a state beyond the reach of heaven. The only way to reach heaven is to become white, and the only way to become white, or at least to live relatively untroubled in the midst of whiteness, is to accept one's place beneath it.

If one asks what is whiteness that it should be so desired—which is to say, so inherently valued above all else—the answer is that whiteness is the means by which humans come into possession of the world, like

God, without limitations of time or space. The value of whiteness is therefore expressed in terms of a social, political, economic, and ultimately divine capacity: "ownership of the earth forever and ever, Amen!" Whiteness is the pretension to infinite possession. The "Amen!" in Du Bois's description of whiteness is far from a mere rhetorical flourish. On the contrary, punctuating "the ownership of the earth forever and ever" with "Amen!" clarifies that time-and-space-transcending possession of the Earth constitutes a capacity of godlike proportions and presumptions. The central prayer of the Christian tradition, the Lord's Prayer, which has its source in the gospel of Luke (11:2–4), is a confession of dependence on the power of a universe-creating God whose loving provision makes human flourishing possible. It ends by proclaiming the infinite, merciful power of the God who provides for and empowers reconciled, trespass-forgiving human community: "For thine is the kingdom, the power, and the glory, forever and ever, amen." The "forever and ever, Amen!" of Du Bois's definition implies that whiteness takes the place of the God to whom, in the Lord's prayer, belongs "the kingdom, the power, and the glory," which is to say, "ownership of the earth forever and ever, Amen!"

Whiteness, Du Bois helps us see, is not just an identity position. Nor is it merely a form of political power. Whiteness is not even simply a god that people worship. Whiteness is the means by which those who inhabit and possess it get to be as powerful as gods—gods to whom belong "the kingdom, the power, and the glory." Born of European colonialism, capitalism, and Christianity, whiteness is pseudo-divine, world-encompassing possession. It is the aspiration to a power that transcends—in order to exercise authority over—human finitude, that owns and governs the world from a security beyond the world's vulnerabilities and the anxieties they produce. Indeed, the transcendent power of whiteness does not merely avoid worldly precarity; it aspires to transcend the precarity of finitude by trapping others within it. Whiteness escapes the world by climbing on the bent backs of Black people, Indigenous people, other people of color, and even white people who have failed to live up to their raced, classed, and gendered calling as private possessors that have mastered self and others. The aspiration to world-encompassing ownership is not merely a by-product of whiteness; it is, Du Bois suggests, its "soul." Whiteness comes into being via theological reasoning expressed through social, political, and economic machinations, conceptualizing itself as the apex of moral and anthropological superiority and indeed as a mode of pseudo-divine transcendence in relation to the rest of humanity. As such, whiteness not only emerges but continues to subsist as a functionally divine presence and power in the world, even when it is not explicitly articulated as such.

Written during the early twentieth-century rise of US imperialism—and mass resistance to it—across the globe, Du Bois's essay keenly discerns that the death-dealing, world-possessing pretensions of whiteness are "more than a matter of dislike" but are, rather, "a great religion, a world war-cry: Up white, down black; to your tents O white folks, and world war with black and parti-colored mongrel beasts!"[13] Whiteness is religious in a way that is inherently oppositional, competitive, and thus violent. Whiteness is religious violence. Claiming a "title to the universe," Du Bois writes, white folks act like "world-mastering demi-gods" guided by "the doctrine of the divine right of white people to steal," an allusion to European-American colonial and imperialist doctrines of discovery and manifest destiny, both of which imagine an Earth empty and waiting to be possessed according to God's will.[14] Such a divine right is, of course, utterly illusory, Du Bois argues. And yet, it is precisely such a "phantasy"—and the material accumulations of wealth and power deriving from it—that spirals the world, especially Africa and other non-European places, into "Hell."[15] The godlike claim to "ownership of the earth forever and ever, Amen!" may be a false one, but the power of such a pretension, such an aspiration, has altered and continues to alter the shape of the world in deep and abiding ways.

Du Bois is not the first or only figure who discerns and resolutely criticizes the world-upending, pseudo-divine aspirations of whiteness. Writing nearly a century before Du Bois, Black revolutionary abolitionist David Walker, an early member of the African Methodist Episcopal (AME) tradition, a member of "Mother Emanuel" AME Church in Charleston, South Carolina, and an early forerunner of the Black liberation theology tradition, wrote that white Christians were far more evil than the white "heathens" who preceded them.[16] Like Du Bois, Walker berates the hypocrisy of white Christians, preachers, and slave owners who claim a faith that requires treating others as one wants to be treated and yet claim ownership of African peoples as "their natural inheritance," holding them in wretched, degrading, and deadly conditions. White Christians, Walker suggests, enslaved Africans with a zeal that can only be described as religious—as indeed it was.[17] Having "always been an unjust, jealous, unmerciful, avaricious and blood-thirsty set of beings, always seeking after power and authority," white people, and especially white Christians, Walker argues, aspired to take the place of God in the world. Even if "God were to give them more sense," Walker writes, "if it were possible, would they not *dethrone* Jehovah and seat themselves upon his throne?"[18] Whiteness, Walker critically discerns, is the aspiration to become and even to displace God, deifying oneself by dehumanizing others. If white humanity believes the lie that to be white is to be more than human—divine—then all forms of nonwhiteness, and Blackness in particular, must, by necessity, be only human and, indeed, *less* human than the finite humanity that whiteness actually embodies but pretends to transcend. In this way, the "lie" that is whiteness is, as James Baldwin argues, "genocidal": it exists only insofar as others are made inferior in relation to it, and it thrives only when the rest of humanity is brought "to the edge of oblivion."[19]

Building on the early Black political theologies of Walker, Denmark Vesey, Henry McNeal Turner, and others that emerged out of generations of enslavement and struggles for abolition and catalyzed by the Black freedom movements of the 1950s, '60s, and '70s, James Cone and other theologians of Black liberation also critically discern in whiteness the death-dealing aspiration to become God at the expense of all others. Whiteness, Cone writes, is the sinful "desire of whites to play God in the realm of human affairs," a desire that is sinful not simply because it offends God but because it is "the source of human misery in the world."[20] Indeed, a world in which white people get to be God, Cone writes, is a world in which Black people "live under sentence of death."[21] As such, Cone argues, whiteness is not godly but "satanic," "the symbol of the Antichrist."[22] The godlike power of whiteness is a result not simply of white people constructing God as a white man but of the lived presumption that whiteness is a kind of divine or divine-proximate inhabitation in itself. As womanist theologian Kelly Brown Douglas writes, "Not only did the early American Anglo-Saxons believe their mission to be one of erecting God's 'city on a hill' but they also came to believe that they essentially had divinity running through their veins. The Protestant evangelicals in particular believed themselves to be as close a human manifestation of God on earth as one could get."²³ As the pretension to godlike power over the world and its peoples, whiteness becomes the "gateway to divinity, the key to salvation." If all who inhabit whiteness are "essentially human incarnations of a divine reality," then all who fall outside the bounds of whiteness, Douglas writes, inevitably register as "an offense against God," "an expression of sin."²⁴

Whiteness is not simply a god that people worship but a means of becoming as powerful as gods. The eurochristian vision of creation was quite literally one in which European Christians were presumed to possess powers akin to God. Through their colonial transformation of the relationship between peoples and places, Willie Jennings writes, European Christians "performed a deeply theological act that mirrored the identity and action of God in creating."²⁵ Just as, for predominant Christian theology, God is revealed through the divine action of creation, so European Christians' action in the world reveals Europeanness to be a pseudo-divine "creative authority" that *re*-creates the world according to its own "boundary-less" supremacy.²⁶ Inhabiting a "God-position" characterized by the presumed power to determine the eternal—and temporal—fates of racialized populations, the powers of whiteness are a manifestation of the European aspiration to infinite control over the Earth and its peoples.²⁷ As such, J. Kameron Carter writes, whiteness should be discerned not merely as a matter of "pigmentation" but as "a regime of political and economic power for arranging . . . the world."²⁸ Whiteness is a manifestation of the desire not merely to become *like* but to *become* God in relation to the Earth and its peoples, a desire fulfilled only when others are sacrificed in pursuit of it.

The kind of power that "ownership of the earth forever and ever, Amen!" implies is unmistakably political, economic, and territorial in scope: "ownership" designates a relationship between humans and the world characterized by absolute possession and control. Whiteness *is* the power to possess the world because whiteness first came into being through violent acts of land theft and displacement. As such, whiteness is more than a neutral descriptor of human difference, a category in a list of races; whiteness is a strategy for exclusively owning and ordering the world infinitely and thus divinely—"forever and ever, Amen!"

Sacred Partitions

The story of patriarchal whiteness is a story of private ownership, and the story of private ownership is only fully understood in relation to histories of modern racialization. As Jennings puts it, "whiteness comes into being as a form of landscape," a force that reconfigures the Earth through colonial acts that separate people from places—places transformed into "raw, untamed land" in service of Christian European and European-American wealth, power, and control.[29] Whiteness is and always has been a possessive force, an aspiration to "ownership of the earth forever and ever, Amen!"[30] Fused with acts of possession, whiteness is an inherently spatial phenomenon. More than simply an isolated identity position abstracted from the geographies in which we live, whiteness is the pseudo-godlike power to transform actual landscapes according to its own presumed supremacy, the capacity to forge and implement anthropological delineations geographically through social, political, economic, and cultural means and to do so under the presumption—implicit or explicit—of divine legitimacy and power.

From the point of view of what political philosopher Charles Mills calls the "Racial Contract"—the white supremacist political contract that establishes modern Western social orders and nations—the peoples and spaces out beyond whiteness are inherently savage and in need of taming. As such, the Racial Contract that constitutes modern social order entails "an active *spatial* struggle" against "savage and barbaric" peoples and spaces waged in pursuit of the "Europeanization of the world," the imperial and colonial process that Du Bois referred to when he wrote that "the world in a sudden, emotional conversion has discovered that it is white and by that token, wonderful!"[31] From colonialist and imperialist European mapping projects that delegitimized and eliminated nonwhite spaces to the violent and religiously legitimated acts of possession and dispossession that correspond to them, the Racial Contract demonizes the "unholy land" of the world beyond its ever-expanding borders in a way that frames "Europeanization" as the only possible means of "moral redemption."[32] Racial order is eurochristian order.[33] In a racially partitioned world "divided between persons and racial subpersons," a world in which white peoples and spaces are constructed as orderly and holy and in which nonwhite peoples and spaces constitute chaotic threats, clear and rigid boundaries are necessary to keep nonwhite peoples in their place.[34] From the perspective of the Racial Contract, "the nonwhite body is a moving bubble of wilderness" that must be vigilantly policed in order to securely maintain the social order.[35] Eurochristian racial order can exist, in other words, only if it eliminates those who stand in the path of its infinite possession.

The act of marking out, claiming, and enclosing space—an act fundamental to racial capitalist settler colonial order—is an act with both political and religious lineages. As political philosopher Wendy Brown notes, enclosure both "lies at the origin of the sacred" and "marks out the beginning of the secular" by founding civil society and forging a sovereign power that is at once theological and political.[36] Acts of enclosure are functions of the sacred in the sense that enclosures produce space deemed sacred by "marking it off from the common or the ordinary," as in the case of shrines, temples, and other traditionally conceived sacred spaces set apart from the space and time of mundane life.[37] Thus conceived, there can be no sacred space without some material mechanism or symbol of enclosure that enacts its material distinction from other space. In addition to bearing a religious lineage, Brown argues, the material mechanisms of enclosure also help bring modern conceptions of the political into existence by concretizing claims of mine and thine, as in the case of acts of private possession that theorists such as Hobbes, Locke, and Rousseau associate with the founding of modern social orders. Walls and fences help establish the sacred as a spatial reality, and they also help establish and spatially manifest social and political orders and the laws that maintain them. These two functions of enclosure, Brown suggests, are ultimately inseparable: even seemingly secular political partitions contain within them a religious pretension and aspiration that confers a power and reverence that is best understood as religious.

This dynamic can be seen most clearly in John Locke, whose work, outlined in chapter 1, shows that asserting rights of possession over against the nonexclusive, non-European modes of inhabitation practiced by Indigenous peoples in the Americas may constitute a political act, but one that is nevertheless rationalized theologically. In Locke's interpretation of sacred scripture, God mandates humans to "subdue" and make industrious use of the Earth, making private property possession a matter of "obedience" to God and the failure to possess privately and exclusively a manifestation of disobedience to God. For Locke, enclosures are both sacred and politically necessary—and they are both of these things at one and the same time. As Eugene McCarraher argues, Locke's political philosophy of private property was simultaneously a political "theology of improvement" that "vindicated the divine right of capital."[38] Locke himself was invested in acts of enclosure beyond the merely theoretical: in addition to his colonial commercial investments, his role in the political and economic institution of the Carolina colonies, and his stake in the wider enclosure movement that was well under way in his home country of England, enclosures functioned as a meaningful conceptual cornerstone of his work in the *Second Treatise* and thereby represent a crucial point of convergence between his scholarly work and personal life.[39]

On the most practical level, the function of enclosures—hedges, fences, gates, walls—is to keep in and keep out. As such, enclosures are sites of inherent political contestation. In early modern England, enclosure appeared as a dramatic disruption that separated people from the common lands on which they worked and gleaned for their livelihoods. Enclosures during that era were the result of wealthy landholders, motivated by new market opportunities, illegally—and often by way of violence and terror—reclaiming commonly tenured farmland and woodland as their own exclusive possession, literally closing it in with hedges or fencing in order to transform it into sheep pasture to serve more profitable forms of production.[40] Over the course of the fifteenth through seventeenth centuries, the enclosure of commonly tenured land displaced many thousands of rural tenants whose livelihood depended on access to the commons. As historians Peter Linebaugh and Marcus Rediker write, "By the end of the sixteenth century there were twelve times as many propertyless people as there had been a hundred years earlier. In the seventeenth century almost a quarter of the land in England was enclosed."[41] By the eighteenth and early nineteenth centuries, enclosures obtained the authority of the law, with approximately four thousand enclosure acts passed during those centuries legalizing the appropriation of upward of six million acres of land, transferring land that was once held in common into the hands of a small number of "politically dominant landowners."[42]

The process of the enclosure of commonly tenured lands paved the way for the establishment of unlimited and absolutely exclusive private property as a central institution in the modern European colonial and capitalist world.[43] Beginning as an illegal process of theft and evolving into a legal process of theft, the enclosure movement's mass expropriation, Linebaugh and Rediker, echoing Marx, write, "was the source of the original accumulation of capital, and the force that transformed land and labor into commodities."[44] The original expropriation or "primitive accumulation" catalyzed by the enclosure movement virtually eliminated the commons that sustained the livelihood of a majority of the population, replacing it with private, exclusively possessed property. In so doing, the enclosure movement reconfigured legal, political, and economic orders in a way that deepened the distance and distinction between a propertied owning class and a dispossessed working class and underclass displaced to industrializing cities where the only option was to work as a "free" but "rightless" wage laborer in a system that was, according to historian Christopher Hill, "little better than slavery."[45] In tandem with the related processes of European war making and colonial and enslaving ventures, the enclosure movement helped forge the political economy and concomitant legal buttresses of racial capitalism in its earliest manifestations.[46]

Enclosures are sites of inherent political and economic contestation. But they are also sites of theological contestation. Much like Locke, whose political philosophy of private property relies in significant part on biblical interpretation and theological reasoning carried out from his elite social position, the early modern proponents of enclosure rationalized their dispossession-by-enclosure through engagement with Christian scripture and popular conceptions of Christian morality. Much as for Locke, for landowning enclosers in early modern England, hedges, fences, and gates functioned not only as practical mechanisms for privatizing land but as sacred mechanisms for fulfilling God's mandate to exercise private dominion over the Earth and to promote the industriousness to which God calls all humans. Under both the manorial arrangements of feudalism and the transition to early agrarian capitalism, enclosers viewed the work of "improving" the Earth—a term widely deployed by centuries of enclosers—as an inherent moral good. Echoing the legal treatises and commentaries popular at the time, a widely read

English husbandry manual from 1578 cites Genesis 3:19: "In the sweat of thy face shalt thou eat thy bread." The author cites this passage not to establish, as Genesis does, the sinful state of all human existence before God after the fall but to suggest that God ordains obtaining wealth through the industrious labor of agriculture.[47] The political theology of primitive accumulation can be seen, moreover, by the way in which a number of other husbandry manuals from early modern England argue in no uncertain terms that commonly tenured land promotes immorality that contradicts God's will and weakens the strength of the nation. In the words of a manual published two decades prior to Locke's *Two Treatises*, common lands are "the producers, shelterers, and maintainers of vast number of vagrants, and idle persons, that are spread throughout the great part of England; and are encouragements to theft, pilfering, lechery, idleness, and many other lewd actions, not so usual in places where every man hath his proper lands inclosed, where every tenant knows where to find his cattle, and every labourer knows where to have his days work."[48] Likewise does the anonymous author of a pro-enclosure pamphlet published in England in the 1650s argue that "God is the God of order, and order is the soul of things, the life of the Commonwealth; but common fields are the seat of disorder, the seed plot of contention, the nursery of beggary." The same author also falsely claims that there is "no example of common fields in all the divine word" of Christian scripture, which he takes as evidence of the fact that private enclosure accords with God's intentions and that common property contradicts God's will and produces immoralities that threaten the order of things as God intends it.[49]

Viewed in light of such threats, historian Nicholas Blomley points out that seventeenth-century husbandry manuals "characterized improvement as a divine imperative. Passive ownership was an affront to God's will; innovation and enterprise were to be encouraged."[50] By materializing God's vision for creation, the hedges, fences, and gates of agrarian enclosure served the purpose of guarding against and disciplining the alleged moral depravities of poor vagrants and "disorderly" villagers who regularly damaged enclosures in retaliation against the dispossession that enclosure generated. Indeed, Blomley posits, the figure of the hedge in early modern England functioned, for both theologians and other social commentators, as "a common metaphor for impenetrability, and the prevention of misrule."[51] As a kind of organic barbed wire, the thorns of certain species of hedges served as instruments for physically "disciplining" the bodies of poor commoners who tried to break or climb them.[52] As such, they constituted what one husbandry manual called "Defence" against "rude persons," protection against "the lusts of vile persons," thereby playing an important material function in enclosers' understandings of God's intentions for creation.[53]

In addition to transporting landless, criminalized Europeans and enslaved Africans to the American colonies, English colonialism brought the property-owning political theology of enclosure to the "New World," as well. John Locke is best known for his *Two Treatises of Government* (1689), but he also authored the *Fundamental Constitutions of Carolina* (1669), which, according to Nancy Isenberg, functioned as "a declaration of war against poor settlers" from Virginia and other colonies, whom Locke and other elites viewed as an inherent moral and economic threat to the success of the Carolina colony.[54] Despite their attempts at exclusion, North Carolina gained the reputation as a place where the illegitimate, landless refuse of the Earth settled. In the early eighteenth century, the governor of the Virginia colony bemoaned one particularly notorious North Carolina county as "a common Sanctuary for all our runaway servants," attacking the place and its vagrant peoples for their "total Absence of Religion" and deriding them as "renegadoes," a term that denoted both lawlessness and irreligiosity.[55] On both sides of the Atlantic, to be poor and landless was to trespass against the sacred order built around private accumulation and enclosure.

We can understand the inherently religious function of modern Western criminalization if we understand the oppositional relationship between the constructed morality of private property possessors and the constructed immorality of those who do not possess—and are in fact dispossessed *by*—private property. If hedges, fences, and gates were understood as sacred mechanisms, then those who threatened them merely by having no property at all were inevitably perceived as embodiments of immorality and evil. As historian E. P. Thompson wrote of the early modern era in which private property was becoming legally dominant, "the greatest offence against property was to have none."[56] The history of enclosure, however, does not consist only in powerful agents exercising limitless power over poor passive victims. Indeed, people dispossessed of common land in early modern England, for example, regularly deployed an array of tactics in opposition to enclosure, including calculated foot-dragging to slow the process of their dispossession, refusal to mark out property lines for surveyors, theft and destruction of surveyor maps, "grumbling" to neighbors as a form of base building and organizing, distributing "complaints" to neighbors and landowners, and submitting petitions to Parliament. When these measures failed to stop the tide of enclosure that threatened their livelihoods, villagers regularly resorted to gathering by the tens, hundreds, and even thousands to physically level hedges, break and burn fences, and demolish the gates that enacted their displacement.[57] As private property owners did in regard to the bothersome "vagrants" who roamed the countryside, they likewise disparaged more militant anti-enclosure commoners in the same terms as embodiments of the worst kind of immorality. According to Sir John Cheke, the rebels of a series of rural anti-enclosure uprisings in England in 1549 were nothing more than "nastye vagabundes," "idell loyterers," "robbers," "ungodly rablementes," and "loitering beggers."[58]

Or take the case of a late eighteenth-century anti-enclosure uprising in the small village of Raunds in the East Midlands of England. There, in 1797, a group of landless sheep and cattle grazers, artisans, and small proprietors presented a petition to Parliament as that governing body prepared to pass an act of enclosure that would cut off villagers' access to the town's common lands. Having seen how the enclosure of commonly tenured lands ravaged neighboring communities, the villagers expressed their concern at the inevitable "injuries" to themselves and the broader community that would follow their displacement from the land. However, given that Parliament in the late eighteenth century had become highly sympathetic to the desires and wishes of wealthy enclosers—as Linebaugh points out, Parliament was at that time "composed exclusively of landlords"—the villagers' petition was, like most such petitions at that time, ignored.[59] The enclosure proceeded as planned. About two years later, J. M. Neeson writes, the "petitioners" of Raunds became the "rioters" of Raunds: "led by the village women and some shoemakers they pulled down [enclosure] fences, dismantled gates, lit huge bonfires and celebrated long into the night."[60] A young boy by the name of James Tyley, the nephew of an area vicar, was a witness to the events. Tyley, too, would later become a clergyman. As rector of a neighboring village,

Reverend Tyley wrote a poem celebrating the sacred glory of enclosure and recollecting the evil of those who attacked it when he was a child. "Meanwhile the greedy crowd," he wrote,

> as if maddened by Bacchus, the thyrsus-bearer, rage horribly when they recall their pleasant little thefts, their sheaves of corn snatched from the scattered harvest and their hidden guile.... To such [mobs], brawls and din and mad riot are dear, and all hatred of kings, and contempt of sacred law. Like a swarm of locusts the dark tribe burst from their noisome hovels, abandoning their unfinished soles and wooden benches. Seditious, filled with Paynim poison, they spread contagion among the gaping mob. Trusting overmuch to such leaders and void of reason, the people remove the fences and wildly riot over the length and breadth of the fields.[61]

Like so many other pro-enclosure texts of the time, Tyley depicts the commoners of Raunds as fundamentally godless, depraved, and immoral, almost demonic, and characterizes the larger threat they pose in terms of a social, moral, and implicitly racial "contagion." Tyley accuses the commoners of greed and theft for claiming entitlement to gleanings from the edge of the field—an irony given the imperatives in Deuteronomy and Leviticus to leave gleanings for the poor of Israel (Leviticus 19:9–10; Deuteronomy 24:21–22).[62] Likening the crowd, at once, to a bloodthirsty, spear-wielding Roman god of agriculture and wine and then to the biblical threat of "a swarm of locusts," Tyley disparages the ramshackle dwellings of the shoemakers and woodworkers who lazily abandon their work in order to incite a riot. "Seditious," seemingly against both God and country, Tyley poeticizes that the rioters are "filled with Paynim poison." "Paynim" is a European Christian term for heathen, especially Muslims, indicating a demonization that is inherently religio-racial in nature. As Charles Mills explains, the early modern distinction between Europeans and non-Europeans "is essentially a theological one, developed in large part through the wars in the East and South against Islam," a context in which "paynim" came to denote heathen Blackness: "both anti-Christ and anti-Europe."[63] The threat that such racially and religiously constructed commoners posed, from Tyley's perspective, was the threat of "contagion," a poisonous pollutant that threatens the moral purity on which the social order rests. So possessed, according to Tyley's recollection, the leaders of the riot gain the mindless trust of other allegedly irrational commoners, who subsequently tear out the town's enclosing fences en masse. Thus does Tyley encapsulate and dramatize the political theology that builds enclosures: enclosure is a mechanism that manifests God's vision for the world; those who build and protect themselves through enclosures are proximate to and even act on behalf of God; and those who would so disrespect enclosures counter God's will and are therefore embodiments of sin and evil.

Building off a tradition that sees private property as a safeguard against the chaos that ensues from human finitude and sin and building off the popular theological-political rationales of wealthy landowners in the early modern era, pro-enclosure elites, John Locke, religious leaders, and others who follow them elaborate a political theology of private property that establishes the right to relatively unlimited, absolutely exclusive private property—property possessed without regard for the rights or well-being of others—as a right with both theological and political grounding. Property possessed privately, it would become widely accepted, corresponds with and concretely materializes God's original intentions for the created world. Acts of enclosure, of marking off, separating, and excluding people defined as godless and immoral from particular places, manifest the intertwining of political and religious rationales that permeate modern colonial and racial capitalist order.

Emerging in tandem in the early modern period, patriarchal whiteness and absolutely exclusive private property regimes are best understood as manifestations of the pursuit of infinite, pseudo-godlike possession—"ownership of the earth forever and ever, Amen!" By materializing a vision of a world arranged according to the white European fantasy of infinite possession, the early modern and present-day mechanisms of enclosure—hedges, fences, gates, walls—help establish and secure the functionally sacred spaces of patriarchal whiteness and private property by eliminating the chaotic threats of moral and political trespass that nonwhite and propertyless peoples embody in the eurochristian imagination.

Pseudo-Divine Attributes

Identifying patriarchal whiteness and private ownership with "godlike" or "pseudo-godlike" power is more than a merely hyperbolic characterization. Indeed, analyzing the characteristics of patriarchal whiteness and private property through the lens of the Western metaphysical and Christian theological and religious traditions from which they emerge, as I do in this section, helps to clarify the actual extent to which their characteristics resemble the so-called attributes or traits of God as articulated by theologians across millennia. Doing so helps clarify the religious pretensions of whiteness and property in a way that deepens our understanding of their shape, scope, and impact in the world. It also ultimately enables us to perceive the inherent religiosity of the police power with which they are so intimately connected, as I show in the remaining chapters.

The tradition of the divine names or attributes first developed as a way of conveying the nature of the Christian God as discerned through sacred scripture, tradition, and human experience, the premise being that the divine attributes apply, by definition, only to God, which is why it is so significant that they also seem to apply in significant part to the human inhabitations of patriarchal whiteness and private property ownership.[64] The purpose of identifying the pseudo-divine attributes of patriarchal whiteness and absolutely exclusive private ownership is thus not to suggest that they are manifestations of real divine power or goodness. On the contrary, patriarchal whiteness and absolutely exclusive private property are threats to the Earth and to all living beings—a threat, that is, to nonwhite peoples, propertyless peoples, *and* to those white and propertied peoples who have inherited and continue to stake their existence, knowingly or unknowingly, on a deadly illusion, a genocidal lie.[65] In short, the purpose of identifying the pseudo-divine attributes of patriarchal whiteness and private property is to more clearly demonstrate that they are manifestations of the desire to become God by exposing others to living hell and thus that they are death-dealing illusions—what Jewish and Christian theological traditions call "idols"—that must be more clearly understood in order to be disempowered and ultimately dismantled.

Transcendence and Infinitude

Most Western metaphysical and Christian theologies hold that God is absolutely "transcendent," which is to say that God in God's fullness cannot be fully grasped or encountered from within finite human conceptuality or materiality.[66] Transcending all delimitations of finite existence, God, in contrast to God's creation, is *infinite*, without limitation of any kind.[67] For many ancient and medieval Christian theologians, God is transcendent and infinite in the sense that God is ultimately incomprehensible and unknowable.[68] The notion of God's incomprehensibility is the notion that God exceeds—meaning God cannot be conceptually circumscribed by—human faculties of reason and imagination. As Augustine writes, "If you think you have grasped him, it is not God you have grasped."[69] In addition to conceptual transcendence, God's transcendence is also transcendence of all spatial and temporal boundaries, which is to say that God can be both everywhere and nowhere, dwelling in past, present, and future at one and the same time. God can be both everywhere and nowhere because God in God's self, according to Christian traditions, is distinct from the order that God created. God is in no way bound by the laws of materiality: "God . . . does not live in shrines made by human hands" (Acts 17:24). God, in short, possesses the attribute of omnipresence: "God cannot be localized or circumscribed" within the dimensions of space and time because God is the author of the dimensions of space and time.[70] For thinkers like Augustine, God's omnipresence is not a matter of being partly here and partly there.[71] Exceeding the laws of space and time, God is at once intimately present and yet absolutely uncircumscribable within the finite world that God created. God is nonlocalizable, omnipresent, because God transcends the finite world absolutely.

Patriarchal whiteness is a manifestation of the human aspiration to transcend—and thereby to exercise absolute power and control over—the finite world. In the modern West, particularly in the US, the power of whiteness is all-pervasive, approximating omnipresence, and yet, both its presence and the extent of its power remain largely hidden from popular view. As George Lipsitz argues, whiteness is at once "everywhere" and yet "very hard to see."[72] Having helped order social, political, and economic life in modernity, whiteness structures Western society in such a way that being "white" means the likelihood of access to greater wealth, health, employment, education, security, and power.[73] And yet, because it is "the unmarked category against which difference is constructed, whiteness never has to speak its name, never has to acknowledge its role as an organizing principle in social and cultural relations."[74] Jennings likewise argues that whiteness in the context of theologically legitimated European colonial ventures came to signify not just European identity but "the rarely spoken but always understood organizing conceptual frame" of the modern world altogether, thereby leaving Blackness to signify "the ever-visible counterweight of a usually *invisible* white identity."[75] The pseudo-godlike invisibility and unspokenness of whiteness is a consequence of its self-construction as absolutely distinct from—transcendent in relation to—nonwhiteness to the point that whiteness tends, in most casual discussions of race today, to transcend the category of race altogether. To talk about "race" in most contexts, in other words, is to talk about being anything other than white. Whiteness operates as the nonracial position—or position that seems to transcend positionality altogether—against which "race," in any form of nonwhiteness, comes into existence and into view.[76] As such, philosopher George Yancy writes, "whiteness as a racial marker [is] the 'great unsaid'" that, under a Western dualist frame that opposes spirit and matter, occupies the transcendent universality of immaterial, disembodied mind, in contrast to the particularity of irrational, material bodiliness occupied by all forms of nonwhiteness.[77] Patriarchal whiteness articulates manhood and womanhood in much the same dyadic and oppositional terms: men generally and white men in particular manifest transcendent, disembodied rational intelligence, while women in general and Black women, Indigenous women, and other women of color in particular manifest irrational fleshliness.[78]

Patriarchal whiteness tends not to name itself as a racial category because to do so would mean that "whiteness becomes simply one more element in a system of differences as opposed to the transcendental norm or that site from which racial differences are established and identified," which would threaten the basis of its supremacy.[79] Indeed, from its European colonial beginnings, Jennings writes, "whiteness transcended all peoples because it was a means of seeing all peoples at the very moment it realized itself."⁸⁰ Whiteness, in short, comes into being as a way of viewing, ordering, and exercising power over the world "from the commanding heights."⁸¹ This transcendent nonpositionality of patriarchal whiteness describes the seemingly innocent but actually violent power of white men in particular to stand "above and apart from history," gazing on, categorizing, and colonially managing the white and nonwhite worlds from a "godlike, dissymmetrical" vantage point.⁸² As Dana Nelson points out, it is precisely this transcendence-aspiring nonpositional gaze on and control of the world that helped to solidify not just whiteness in general but patriarchal whiteness in particular—what Nelson calls "white manhood"—as the unifying normative personhood on which the United States took shape as a nation in the first place.⁸³

Patriarchal whiteness is a manifestation of the aspiration to infinitude. In philosopher Jacques Derrida's essay "White Mythology," he interrogates the world-transcending pretensions of the language of Western philosophy, which works by erasing evidence of its own finite invention, casting itself as natural and original and thereby of universal, infinite value.⁸⁴ Such universalist aspirations are evident, Derrida suggests, in the fact that Western metaphysics makes meaning and articulates reality by way of concepts that negate, transcend, and strive for mastery over worldliness: "*ab-solute, in-finite, in-tangible, non-Being.*"⁸⁵ The world-transcending aspirations of metaphysics, Derrida ultimately argues, make it a "white mythology" for the reason that it "reassembles and reflects the culture of the West" and in so doing serves as the means by which "the white man" defines himself and his reason as the manifestation of "universal" "Reason" writ large.⁸⁶ Like the traditions of modern Western philosophy and metaphysics, whiteness, too, is characterized by the desire to negate, transcend, and master the world.⁸⁷ Derrida also explores the value-producing effacement of origins and transcendence of finitude through the concept of "phantasm." For Derrida, "phantasm" is that which aspires to transcend finitude in pursuit of an "unscathed" "life beyond life," an existence beyond the limits of vulnerable facticity.⁸⁸ Phantasm names a theological-political power because it consists in the "omnipotent fantasy" that it is possible to pseudo-divinely transcend and master time, space, and life itself.⁸⁹ The illusory aspiration to infinitude, Derrida argues, is an aspiration at the heart of "religion" and one that leads to the pseudo-godlike calculating pretensions to mastery that produce death penalties of all kinds.[90]

For Derrida, white supremacist, anti-Black racism is a prime manifestation of the finitude-transcending pursuit of purity, particularly in the context of state racism, as in the case of South African apartheid.[91] "Deconstruction"—the philosophical project with which Derrida is most popularly associated—is, according to philosopher Michael Naas, "first and foremost, a deconstruction of the phantasm, a deconstruction of any putatively pure origin, indeed, of any phantasm of purity."[92] Because deconstruction is the deconstruction of illusory aspirations to purity, deconstruction is also, Derrida suggests, "the deconstruction of racism," of "the conditions of the possibility of racism," of "the roots of racism."[93] Phantasm names the religious aspiration to exercise godlike powers and capacities that transcend the limits of finitude and its manifold vulnerabilities, securing it against the threats posed by allegedly impure, out-of-place forms of life. Elaborating on Derrida's theorization, more than just "racism" in general, whiteness in particular constitutes a phantasm, an instantiation of the religious pursuit of a purity beyond the limits of finitude and its vulnerabilities.[94] Freed from the limits of racial particularity, and indeed of time and space, whiteness takes on an "inestimable value"—or at least so it seems.[95] As a phantasm, whiteness's aspiration to divine power is ultimately only that: an aspiration. For Derrida, phantasm only "*seems*" to do what it sets out to do, without actually doing so, because phantasms are ultimately unreal.[96] And yet, making the unreal seem real is precisely what makes phantasms like whiteness so powerful and thus so dangerous.

The Christian idea of God's transcendence is, according to theologian Kathryn Tanner, the idea that "God is not a kind of thing among other kinds of things," "a kind of being over against other kinds of beings," but is instead "beyond any such contrasts."[97] The point of positing such a radical divine distinction or transcendence, Tanner argues, is not to posit a God who exists at a radical distance from humans but to clarify that God, as loving creator, redeemer, and giver of gifts to God's creation, can only be the God who gives God's own self to humans if God is radically distinct from humans. For these reasons, creatures and God exist in what Tanner calls a "non-competitive relation," which simply means that God's increase does not require that creatures decrease: "The glorification of God does not come at the expense of creatures."[98]

Despite whiteness imbuing itself with infinite moral value and thereby imitating aspects of divine power, the "transcendence" of patriarchal whiteness, in contrast to classical Christian understandings of God's transcendence, does not enable life-giving, humanity-embracing relation but is rather what Robert Birt calls "exclusive transcendence."[99] Theorizing an existentialist philosophical anthropology in which humans are understood to exist authentically only when they accept both their transcendence *and* their finitude, Birt argues that whiteness exemplifies "bad faith" self-deception that seeks to escape the facticity of existence precisely by denying transcendence to its nonwhite others. Whiteness, as a form of exclusive transcendence, Birt writes, "can live as such only through the denial of the transcendence of an Other, the reduction of that Other to an object, to pure facticity. At least in America, that Other has been primarily the black. Whiteness could not exist without that Other."[100] Whiteness is an inherently oppositional religious force produced by the aspiration to transcend and master the material world by holding its nonwhite others in the captivity of finite facticity, a captivity that takes many forms, including carceral ones.[101] Just as there is no such thing as whiteness without the Blackness against which whiteness defines itself as superior in every way, so there is no such thing as white transcendence apart from Black and nonwhite captivity. As David Roediger puts it, whiteness is "the empty and therefore terrifying attempt to build an identity based on what one isn't and on whom one can hold back."[102] A mode of "self-definition by negation," whiteness depends for its existence and survival on the devaluation and destruction of all forms of nonwhiteness and of Blackness in particular.[103]

Omnipotence and Invulnerability

As transcendent, infinite, omnipresent, and omniscient, God is also known within Jewish, Christian, and Western metaphysical traditions to be "omnipotent," all-powerful. Jewish and Christian scripture convey an "almighty" God whose power knows no bounds, made manifest in the creation of the world and all that is in it, the preservation or holding together of the universe, and the (promised) power to restore and redeem the world from the power of death and sin. Christian scripture and many Christian theologies also understand God as a beneficent sovereign Lord whose providential power embraces and maintains the cosmos and all who live in it. A power without limitation, God's omnipotence is literally the power to do anything—so long as it is in continuity with God's nature as loving and good.[104] More than a mere intention, God's will—the enactment of God's limitless power—is absolutely effective, meaning that the good that God wills to create or bring about, God creates or brings about. Because God is all-powerful, God's beneficent will is, for such theological traditions, what orders reality itself: what God wills is what is, and what is—with the exception of the creation negations of sin and evil—is what God wills. From justifications of state violence based on the idea that God ordains all authority (Romans 13) to casual acceptance that whatever happens in one's life must be "God's will," the idea that the way things are is the way God wants them to be is a powerful political theology that has justified many a status quo. An important implication of God's omnipotent will, according to Christian traditions, is that sin and evil are privations of the good, which is to say, the absence of the good that God can only create. God, according to this tradition of thought, does not—strictly speaking, *can*not, as a good God—create sin or evil, only a world in which humans have the agency to choose to create sin and evil and the death that Christian scripture understands to derive from them (Romans 6:23). Whatever evil or sin that exists, then, comes not from God but from the sin that free humans enact through seeking to become God themselves.

Because God, in most Christian theologies, is understood to radically transcend the limitations of finitude, God is also said to possess the attribute of "aseity," which means originating and existing "in oneself" and therefore utterly independent in the most absolute sense: God originates from God's self and therefore depends in no way on anything outside God's self.[105] As the creator, origin, or cause of all things, the force that puts all created things into motion, God, according to Aristotelian and Thomist theologies, is the "unmoved mover."[106] Deriving from God's own self, Aquinas argues, "God is his own being."[107] The notion of God's aseity is a way of apprehending how it is that God creates the world without having first been created by someone or something outside God. Additionally, God's aseity is a way of understanding how God exists in relation to humanity without that relation implying that God *needs* humanity in any sense. The notion of aseity, therefore, is related to the notions of divine "impassibility" and "immutability." Impassibility describes the state of being invulnerable to or unaffected by anything outside oneself, a notion that derives in part from the ancient Greek philosophical concept of *apatheia*, which means "nonsuffering, freedom from suffering, a creature's inability to suffer."[108] Stoic and other Greek philosophies encouraged pursuit of a life that rose above or avoided pain and conceptualized God as one who, transcending finitude, logically speaking, cannot be affected in any way by the forces of finitude and thus can be said to "feel" no "pain." In Stoic and Platonic philosophy, the so-called passions are understood as marks of bodily creaturehood that, opposed to transcendent, universal "reason," sharply distinguish humans from God. Though Jewish and Christian scripture depict a God who "feels" various emotions regarding the state of creation—love, anger, and so on—the idea of a passionless God who does not, properly speaking, "need" and likewise is not impacted by creation ultimately took hold in many strands of Christian theology as the more logically consistent way of conceptualizing the God who transcends finitude absolutely.[109] As impassible—invulnerable to feeling and therefore invulnerable to suffering—God is also understood to be characterized by the divine attribute of immutability, the inability to change. To be human is to be finite and vulnerable, which means being affected by what is outside oneself, whether for better or for worse. In contrast to humans, God, being "perfect," is invulnerable to finitude and thus impassible; for that reason, God is also immutable, free from the possibility of being changed by anything finite or infinite.[110]

Patriarchal whiteness is "ownership of the earth forever and ever, Amen!" because it is a manifestation of the human aspiration to world-encompassing power that enables world-transcending invulnerability. As noted earlier, the "Amen!" in Du Bois's definition clarifies that the aspiration to infinite possession that constitutes whiteness is an aspiration of religious proportions in that it claims the godlike power to rearrange the world in powerfully concrete—material and spatial—ways. The aspiration to infinite possession inherent to whiteness ultimately gives shape to what Lipsitz calls the "white spatial imaginary." Characterized by a "hostile privatism" and "defensive localism" that pursue "pure" and "homogeneous spaces, controlled environments, and predictable patterns of design and behavior," the white spatial imaginary, Lipsitz writes, "promotes individual escape" instead of collective and democratic engagement in the problems of society.[111] Whiteness shows up in the world as an expression of the desire to escape the vulnerabilities of the world in order to safely possess it to the exclusion of others. Viewing the material "space" of the created world "primarily as a locus for the generation of exchange value," Lipsitz writes, the white spatial imaginary is a settler colonial imaginary that functions by purging space of those whose presence registers as threat or impediment to the progress that whiteness is understood to inherently bring about. In a world where whiteness and property rule, Blackness in particular inevitably constitutes trespass. As imprisoned Black radical George Jackson wrote of the white racist who creates and yet does not take responsibility for the deadly conditions that Black people are forced to live in, "We were never intended to be part of his world."[112] In a world made by and for whiteness, Blackness is "matter out of place."[113]

Whiteness as property is a right not only to possession but to protection from the vulnerabilities that others experience in the world.[114] Functioning like the material guarantor of a kind of human aseity and impassibility, independent from and unmoved by the world beyond its boundaries, whiteness as a mode of property both transforms and aspires to transcend the threatening complexities of finitude. Absolutely exclusive private property itself, reinforced as it so often is with hedges, fences, and gates, helps realize this transcendent aspiration of whiteness and/as property in quite material ways. If the peoples and places beyond the bounds of whiteness and property are dangerous, "wild," and potentially criminal or moral threats, then the function of fences, gates, and walls is to secure and maintain what is moral and godlike, enabling life "unscathed" by the contaminating threats of nonwhite, nonpropertied peoples.[115] The security that the boundary markers of whiteness and private property establishes gives to whiteness and property a kind of pseudo-impassibility—a material, even architectural invulnerability to the suffering of others, including the suffering that whiteness and property create, suffering that they keep at a comfortable distance through mechanisms of security, enclosure, and, as we will see, police power.

As explored earlier, private property in its more absolutely exclusive forms—starting with the private enclosures of early modern England—was viewed as sacred insofar as it helped align creation with what ruling-class elites understood to be God's intentions for a world subdued, accumulated, and made industrious by human labor. As historian Douglas Hay puts it, private property in early modern England was functionally "deified" through the proliferation of laws focused on managing the behavior and mobility of dispossessed people whose condition of forced poverty led to acts of survival that propertied people experienced as threatening and disorderly.[116] In the words of political theorist Mark Neocleous, this was an era marked no longer simply by the "Divine Right of Kings" but the "Divine Right of Property."[117] Much like—and eventually continuous with—what Du Bois called the "color line," the private property line has long been conceived as a sacred means of defense against the chaos of a dangerous and immoral world filled with people perceived and defined in terms that emphasized their creaturely finitude in contrast to the almost divine transcendence of those who dwell safely behind the walls of private property.[118]

Patriarchal and possessive whiteness, from its origins in European colonialism and racial capitalism up through today, is a fundamentally spatial, geographical phenomenon, a force that transforms an Earth inhabited in common into privately possessed property on which people without property, and people without the property of whiteness, register as trespassers who, for the sake of the social order, must be captured and exiled. More than just a secular political vision of the world, the white spatial imaginary is, in Lipsitz's words, a "moral geography," a simultaneously religious and political frame that views racial capitalism's accumulative, value-generating practices as a faithful response to God's mandate to subdue, privately enclose, and make industrious use of the Earth, such that those who are perceived to be either unable or unwilling to fulfill this mandate are viewed as inherent threats to the social order.[119] The limitless accumulation that John Locke understands to create value and capital through exclusive possession of the Earth does not just respond to the divine will but imitates it: from colonialism to imperialism to present-day gentrification and displacement, possessive whiteness functions as a divine-omnipotence-mimicking "creative authority" that re-creates the world by rearranging peoples and places in life-altering ways.[120] Akin to the power of God to create goodness and life out of the chaos of nothingness, whiteness as property forges economic value out of the constructed valuelessness and nothingness of the "wasted" commons or "blighted," not-yet-exploited geographies abandoned by the state. For all these reasons, the "landscape" through which whiteness comes into being functions as sacred space—space in which the mere presence of Black life, Indigenous life, all other nonwhite life, and even poor white life registers as a threat to a moral and social order that creates exclusive heaven for a few by exposing many to hell.

God's omnipotence means that whatever God wills becomes reality. White, propertied will approximates the creative and re-creative authority of divine omnipotence in the sense that it is effective: what it wills it creates, what it desires to possess it finds a way to possess, what it needs for its power it makes material, and whatever stands in its way it either moves or destroys with the help of the police power of the state. The omnipotent will of possessive and patriarchal whiteness is especially discernible in what Cornel West calls the "normative gaze."[121] The normative gaze is the powerful vision of whiteness that both surveys and surveils and thereby transforms its nonwhite others, optically capturing Black and other nonwhite lives within conceptual and spatial boundaries as a means of determining, controlling, and protecting itself against the "dark world" outside its boundaries.[122] While it might seem that a mere "gaze" would be rather innocuous, the opposite is true of the gaze of a whiteness that pretends to godlike authority: what the normative gaze of whiteness sees or needs to see becomes materially and conceptually—and even legally—"real" through its seeing, regardless of whether it is actually reflective of reality or not. The normative gaze sees Blackness and other forms of nonwhite and nonpropertied existence as inherently inferior and potentially criminal threats to the security of whiteness and property. Just by surveying and surveilling the dark world from a perspective that can only see its others as antagonistic threats or exploitable resources, patriarchal and possessive whiteness transform nonwhite and nonpropertied life into the dual resource and threat that it needs it to be for its own fragile cohesion and power.

God's all-powerful will is the power to do anything, with the exception of create sin or evil, which is why sin and evil are understood in orthodox Christianity to be manifestations of the absence of God's goodness, as opposed to divinely created realities in themselves. Within this framework, it is fallen, inherently sinful humans who generate the sin and evil under which they suffer and by which they are bound. The notion of divine innocence and human culpability for human suffering finds a racialized parallel in a pseudo-godlike whiteness that maintains absolute moral innocence in the face of the harm that it creates, while simultaneously placing blame for that harm on those who are trying to survive it. This dynamic of transferring responsibility for the suffering that whiteness generates to those who are enduring it can be seen in the widespread idea that Black and Indigenous people experience disproportionately higher rates of poverty and lack of wealth not as a result of centuries of white racial capitalist accumulation made possible by the systematic exploitation and dispossession of Black, Indigenous, and other people of color but because of deficiencies inherent to Blackness and Indigeneity. In making such a claim to moral innocence and inherent goodness despite the harm it generates, patriarchal whiteness is a deceiving and self-deceiving moral confusion that maintains its power and pursues its legitimacy by hiding the harm it creates from both others and itself. As Yancy puts it, whiteness is "a master of concealment," a deliberate misinterpretation of the world.[123] Blaming its victims for the violence that it enacts—what we might understand as a kind of racial gaslighting—whiteness is inherently manipulative, not only of others but also of those who possess or inhabit it, to the point that whiteness is best understood as a condition of delusion under which white people are incapable of seeing the violence and suffering around them as violence and suffering that their own functionally religious devotion to whiteness has helped create.

Gazing on, capturing, and exercising power over the world from its pseudo-transcendent nonposition, patriarchal whiteness is, in the words of Biko Mandela Gray, Stephen Finley, and Lori Latrice Martin, "the existential disposition of seeing without having to be seen, of looking at and therefore constituting the world without having to take responsibility for the implications of such constitution." Faced with contestations of its innocence, accusations of culpability, and challenges to its presumed power and authority, patriarchal whiteness lashes out in raging resentment, often resorting to acts of violence to reassert its innocence, its moral goodness, and its authoritative power in governing the world.[124]

Fused with notions of racial and sexual purity, the claim to moral innocence that undergirds patriarchal whiteness has long enacted anti-Black violence in the name of alleged self-preservation against fabricated threats of Black violence in general and Black sexual violence in particular. This can be seen especially clearly in the history of lynching in the US, in which, after the period of Reconstruction, as whiteness strove to exert its supremacy anew, white mobs accused—most often falsely—Black men of sexual predation against the moral innocence and purity of white women, whom white men also conceived of as extensions of their property, thus making alleged acts of Black violence against white women matters of literal trespass against private property. With lynching, the threat of Blackness was constructed as a voracious, animalistic sexual threat to white womanhood, which itself posed the larger threat of racial contamination of white bloodlines enacted through alleged sexual violence carried out by Black men. From the point of view of the proponents and beneficiaries of a social order based on maintaining the purity and thus power of whiteness, such alleged acts of Blackness, even when completely fabricated, warrant the most brutal violence, and even death, in response. Permitted and sometimes implicitly authorized and sanctioned by agents of the state, the brutal act of murdering Black people by hanging them from trees as part of religiously oriented rituals in front of large crowds of white men, women, and children is a violent manifestation of the idea that whiteness possesses inherent godlike qualities of absolute goodness and innocence that requires defending, even with the blood of others on its hands.[125] This is why the violence inherent to whiteness—a violence that seeks to maintain purity and power to the exclusion and at the expense of others—is best understood as a form of religious violence. Like predominant conceptions of God in many Western traditions, whiteness is authorized to carry out or allow violence insofar as doing so is understood as an act necessary to preserving the sacredness and moral integrity of social and cosmic order.

This double presumption of moral innocence and right to absolute authority is part of what makes whiteness, and white rage in particular, a thoroughly "religious disposition."[126] White rage is religious, in other words, not only in the sense that it is a guiding "orientation in the ultimate sense," in the words of Charles Long, but because it is a means by which human beings act from the pretension to godlike authority over others and over the world as a whole.[127] The "religious disposition" of whiteness operates from the pretension that "whiteness has a primary relation with and to the Divine," thereby granting it a presumed authority that legitimates violence in the name of preserving moral, social, and cosmic order.[128] As Gray, Finley, and Martin write, "Whiteness may not be a 'G-d,' but it sure acts like one."[129]

Independence and Mastery

The finitude-transcending aspiration of patriarchal whiteness expresses the desire not just to escape facticity but to maintain godlike invulnerability to worldly precarity altogether, to manage and govern the world from beyond the vulnerabilities of the world. As noted earlier, the Christian doctrine of aseity holds that God does not derive causally from and is not sustained by anything outside of God, meaning God is utterly independent and self-existent.[130] Related to it, the doctrine of divine impassibility holds that God is not affected by and thus does not suffer as a result of anything outside God. Like such conceptions of God in relation to God's creation, patriarchal whiteness and absolutely exclusive private ownership share a common pretension to absolute independence from the rest of the world. In colonial and postrevolutionary America, the prerequisite for "full patriarchal authority" was absolute independence in all spheres of life, private and public.[131] During that period, ideas of "manhood" were measured by the degree to which one was able to obtain economic and other forms of independence, culminating especially in the possession of private property. Because capacities for private property possession were first defined according to modern European and patriarchal ways of "knowing, doing, and being," private property possession emerged as a right belonging inherently only to men of European descent.[132] In addition to claims to property, the title and rights of "citizen" belonged first to white, propertied men, before only later being granted to white men without property, women, and nonwhite peoples, if at all. As the condition for full citizenship, rights, and access to resources in the United States, patriarchal and possessive whiteness are manifestations of white "national manhood," a resolutely antidemocratic and individualistic mode of absolute independence from and power over anyone who is not a white, propertied man.[133]

In these ways, patriarchal and possessive whiteness can be understood as manifestations of the aspiration to the independence and invulnerability of a kind of divine aseity and impassibility in the sense that it consists of the desire to secure itself—socially, politically, economically, psychically, and so on—against that which it perceives as a threat against it and even against basic creaturely finitude or facticity itself, enabling it to survive on itself, by itself, and for itself. Patriarchal whiteness imagines itself to have come into existence and acquired its power by its own resources. It is a state of (imagined) absolute independence, an allegedly natural capacity to manage and possess the finite world without being subject to the vulnerabilities that come with being a creature in it. The reality, however, is that the seeming self-existent independence of patriarchal whiteness comes not from some sort of self-generating pseudo-divine power but by extracting resources from nonwhite and even dispossessed white labor and suffering and from the Earth itself, which is why its aseity and impassibility, like all its other godlike attributes, can only be said to be approximate or aspirational. As a phantasm, patriarchal whiteness operates on the illusion that it possesses the power to transcend and master the vulnerabilities of finitude, sustaining itself by its own inherent resources, when the reality is that whiteness is powerful only by accumulating others' resources through violent acts of accumulation by dispossession and displacement, the evidence of which it subsequently erases from its history. In so doing, patriarchal whiteness makes the power it does possess seem natural and original, as though it always has been and therefore always should be.[134]

The pursuit of absolute independence from and mastery over the world is a religious pursuit because it manifests an aspiration to exercise godlike power and authority in relation to the rest of the world. Aspiring to and reflecting attributes of a God conceived in terms of absolute independence from, invulnerability to, and mastery over the world, patriarchal and possessive whiteness hinge on casting women—especially Black, Indigenous, and other women of color—as well as nonmasculine men and gender-nonconforming people, as thoroughly consumed by fallen finitude and thus as a threat to the moral sanctity of the social order.[135] As theologian Ellen Armour argues, modern conceptions of "Man" are grounded in the patriarchal desire to master self, world, and others through institutions and practices that secure "his" preeminence through the dehumanization of others. A project and product of the modern Eurocolonial era, the figure of "Man," Armour writes, came into being as the subject who replaces God as the ultimate "one-who-knows-things," who "stands above and outside of things."[136] The paradox of the normative Man of modernity is that his aspiration to a kind of god-like independence from and power over others ultimately depends on the presence and labor of those whom he defines as inferior to him.[137] The patriarchal illusion of pseudo-divine separability and independence necessitates the presence of people defined as inherently inferior and exploitable. In Armour's words, with the advent of modernity, "Man occupies the center, while his others surround him like a network of mirrors that reflect him back to himself, thus securing his sense of identity and of mastery—over self, over nature, and over his others."[138] In the end, though "he periodically tries to deny it," the self-, world-, and others-mastering Man of modernity is ultimately as finite as those "others" he seeks to control.[139]

Whether to establish itself or to reassert itself after it has been challenged or weakened, patriarchal and possessive whiteness requires violence—racial violence, sexual violence, gender violence, police violence—to sustain its delusional pretension to godlike power over peoples and places. According to critical race theorist Angela Harris, gender violence is the masculine enactment of violence against women—as well as against other men and gender-nonconforming people—that uses sexualized violence to harm and reduce others as a way of attempting to liberate men from their anxiety about an inability to fulfill their masculinity and thus to reempower them as superior in a patriarchal social system premised on the promise of a material and psychic sense of mastery. As Harris notes, "violent acts committed by men, whether these break the law or are designed to uphold it, are often a way of demonstrating the perpetrator's manhood," a manhood that has been questioned or compromised in one way or another, often through real dispossessions catalyzed by racial capitalism. In order to remedy the compromising of that notion of manhood, the compromising of the right to operate as master in every social environment, men—and white men in particular—resort to acts of violence that reestablish that sense of mastery.[140] Because patriarchy in general, and white patriarchy in particular, consists in the aspiration to and promise of godlike transcendence and mastery, challenges to that pretension to mastery produce insecurities that catalyze violence against others—a desperate grasping after some sense of power and control that men, and white men in particular, are habituated to identify as a natural birthright. Manifesting in both interpersonal and systemic ways, the illusory quest to both transcend and master—to stand absolutely independent from and over—finitude at the heart of patriarchal and possessive whiteness is a quest that ultimately wreaks havoc on the world, including even on those who cling desperately to the power it affords.

Despite projecting godlike power and might, patriarchal and possessive whiteness derives from a profound sense of anxiety over the vulnerabilities of finitude, powerlessness, and existential limitation. Put another way, whiteness in all its patriarchal and possessive manifestations is a deadly expression of a fear of death and, by extension, a fear of life as a finite, mortal creature among other finite, mortal creatures.[141] Patriarchal and possessive whiteness seeks to outrun vulnerability by exposing others—and even the Earth itself—to increased vulnerability and harm. Guided by the illusion that it is possible to dwell, godlike, above and outside finite, mortal existence, patriarchal and possessive whiteness is a truly deadly force that bears itself out in ways large and small—from settler colonial violence to the white mob violence at the US Capitol on January 6, 2021—throughout history and up to the present. Such realities help explain why movements for liberation led by Black, Indigenous, and other people of color have traditionally deployed rhetoric of the "white man" as the source of all that is wrong in the world.

The Christian and Western metaphysical tradition of enumerating the divine attributes is a means of making sense of God's nature, including the various ways in which God is understood to transcend finitude, and the implications of God's transcendence for the life of faith. The divine attributes are premised on the fact that each attribute can only apply, by definition, to God. The fact that the dynamics of patriarchal whiteness and absolutely exclusive private property so closely resemble traits of God according to these traditions—the same traditions out of which, in their European contexts, patriarchal whiteness and private property emerge in the first place—clarifies that patriarchal whiteness and private property are not simply the result of the interplay of raw social, political, or economic forces but are, in a much deeper sense, religious phenomena, manifestations of the desire to become God by transcending and transforming the world into heaven for a few and hell for many.

Deification and Destruction

In Mircea Eliade's classic text *The Sacred and the Profane*, the historian of religion theorizes the "sacred" as a concretely spatial reality that is "qualitatively different"—ontologically distinct—from profane space divested of divine presence or power. The difference between the space of the sacred and the space of the profane is, on Eliade's analysis, so absolute that sacred space constitutes "absolute reality," whereas profane space is absolute "nonreality," "absolute nonbeing," with the "threshold" between the two functioning as a firmly fixed "limit" or "boundary" that "distinguishes and opposes two worlds." Indeed, so distinct is the space of the sacred from the space of the profane that simply dwelling in sacred space enables one to "transcend" the surrounding profane world altogether.[142] For Eliade, while the construction of sacred space may take place in part through human labor, it is ultimately a reality constituted by divine power: marking out space as sacred in an otherwise profane world quite literally "reproduces the work of the gods."[143] Religious scholars have rightly criticized the rigid, absolute nature of the distinction between sacred and profane in Eliade's theory, as well as his failure to adequately attend to the preeminent role that human labor and contestation actually play in the formation of sacred spaces.[144] And yet, the divine intransigency of the boundary between the two realms as Eliade imagines it offers important insight into the deifying and destructive border-making religiosity of patriarchal whiteness and absolutely exclusive private property, and the settler colonial, racial capitalist order of which they are a part.

In Eliade's analysis, the work of demarcating a given space as sacred is not limited to the construction of traditionally conceived sacred sites or places of worship. Indeed, Eliade argues that simply occupying and settling in a new, so-called unoccupied territory establishes sacred value because it imposes cosmic order and meaning where once there was only the "unknown" and "foreign," the profane, which, for Eliade, is a form of "nonreality." To settle in a territory, Eliade argues, is thus to establish that space as cosmically meaningful and thus is "equivalent to consecrating it."[145] Indeed, more than simply making it meaningful, settling in a territory is, according to Eliade, an inherently creative, godlike act: "settling in a territory is equivalent to founding a world."[146] Likewise, Eliade argues, religiously or ritually consecrating a space is an act that authorizes claims to possession of that space. In short, to claim space as one's own is to make it sacred, and to make it sacred is to make it one's own. It is precisely this religious orientation to space that undergirds patriarchal and possessive whiteness as a set of forces forged in the fires of eurochristian settler colonialism and racial capitalism. Patriarchal whiteness is properly understood as religious, from Eliade's framing, because whiteness regards the acts of possession inherent to it as divinely ordained—"ownership of the earth forever and ever, Amen!" Whiteness is the godlike power to transcend the profane world and to transform it by claiming it as one's own and thus as sacred. As Eliade writes, consecrating and thereby claiming space as "mine" or "ours" transforms that space into "holy ground, . . . *the place nearest to heaven*," thereby imitating the world-creating "work of the gods."[147] European settler colonizers stole land and violently displaced people from it over and over on the basis of exactly these religious rationales.

Just as space that has been transformed into a private, enclosed possession—"our world"—is space made holy, so whatever lies beyond "our world" represents danger: settled and occupied space is space in which cosmic and social order has been imposed, whereas "unoccupied territory" is inherently disorderly, chaotic, and thus threatening. In Eliade's words, "Since 'our world' is a cosmos, any attack from without threatens to turn it into chaos. And as 'our world' was founded by imitating the paradigmatic work of the gods, . . . so the enemies who attack it are assimilated to the enemies of the gods, the demons. . . . 'Our' enemies belong to the powers of chaos."[148] If the territory one claims as one's own is, by such claiming, holy, then whatever dwells beyond it represents the threat of annihilation, a threat that must be neutralized to secure the social and cosmic order. Under such a framing, the possessive dynamics of settler colonial expansion are ascribed an inherently sacred character, as they so often have been throughout history and up to the present. Much as Wendy Brown argues that enclosures are inherently religious because they cordon off the holy from the mundane, Eliade likewise suggests that walled fortifications in cities find their origin in the double desire to protect one's society from the Devil, on the one hand, and to protect it from foreign enemies, on the other—a multivalence that is easy to comprehend if, as Eliade writes, one's "enemies" are functionally "the enemies of the gods."[149] Within such a framework, any "victory" over those who are deemed a threat or attack against the sacred space of the social order "*reiterates the paradigmatic victory of the gods over . . . chaos.*"[150]

Intertwined from their early modern origins to the present, patriarchal whiteness and private property are fundamentally exclusive phenomena that survive only by drawing strong boundaries that delineate, insulate, and protect themselves against the perceived threat that lies outside their enclosures: whiteness *is* only by defining and defending itself against what it is not, just as private property can be said to exist only by making an absolute, exclusive claim of possession over against the claims of others. As such, whiteness and property are, by definition, fundamentally *threatened* and thus paranoid phenomena: by defining their existence oppositionally and defensively over against what they are not, they exist and subsist by constructing nonwhite and unpropertied peoples as hindrances to their supremacy or threats to their survival. As Mark Neocleous writes, the self-interested bourgeois liberal principle of a right to absolutely exclusive private property "makes us see others as a barrier to our own freedom" and thus "as a threat or source of harm," thereby "turn[ing] each of us into a source of the other's insecurity."[151] A world ordered according to the pseudo-godlike power of whiteness as property is a world ordered by fear of danger—by insecurity—and thus, as we will see, a world that needs police power to survive.[152]

More than a purely secular political or social dynamic, the absolute boundary making inherent to patriarchal whiteness and private property is a function of their self-deifying, others-demonizing religiosity. Guided by a doctrine of divine scarcity, the pursuit of godlike power that undergirds patriarchal and possessive whiteness is a zero-sum game that requires the destruction or displacement—immediate or eventual—of all who dwell outside their gate. As religious scholar Eric Weed writes, "The elevation of space beyond the limits of finitude necessarily means no other space can stand beside it. . . . To make a space sacred, as in the spatiality of white supremacist Christianity, necessitates the elimination of all other space."[153] Anything that stands in the way of infinite white possession and power must be destroyed. Despite claims to moral innocence, the long history of organized and systemic white violence against Black people, Cone writes, makes it clear that "whites have only one purpose: the destruction of everything which is not white."[154] As a zero-sum religiosity, a religiosity that brings life to some only if it also brings death to others, patriarchal and possessive whiteness perceives that which is not white and not propertied as a potential combatant, an inherent danger that must be eradicated for the sake of the survival of the social order that revolves around them. In the spatial terms of the white settler racial imaginary, if all the world is or will eventually be white property—"ownership of the earth forever and ever, Amen!"—then to be anything other than white and propertied is to trespass against the social order. Blackness in particular is viewed with suspicion in a white world because Blackness is the foundational enemy against which whiteness articulates itself in the first place, which means that Blackness, by definition, does not belong in a white world and indeed constitutes a threat to it—a threat, as I explore in chapters 3 and 4, that necessitates the carceral interventions of police power.

Coming into existence as an expression of the aspiration to functionally godlike power and control over the world and all who live in it, patriarchal whiteness and private property are not neutral, naturally occurring, or value-free identity positions or possessions. Forging heaven for a few by exiling many to hell on Earth, patriarchal whiteness and private, exclusive ownership are, to repeat the words of Du Bois, "more than a matter of dislike" but, rather, "a great religion, a world war-cry."[155] As religious calls to war, whiteness and property are manifestations of religious violence against those who whiteness and property explicitly or implicitly cast as the enemies of God, which is to say, their own enemies. As aspirations to a godlike power that depends on the dispossession, containment, or outright elimination of others, patriarchal whiteness and absolutely exclusive private property exist and subsist as such only if others are dehumanized and destroyed in pursuit of them.

It is important to understand whiteness, property, and the criminalization with which they intertwine as religious phenomena because doing so helps us discern the *why* behind the insistent durability of these systems in the face of challenge, which in turn better enables us to dismantle them. Put otherwise, whiteness and property—and the criminalization that they engender—are so rigorously defended and maintained because their grounding is transcendent, because they play not just a mundane, logistical, or order-maintaining function but an ultimate, sacred function in the larger social order that revolves around them, such that challenges to them constitute existential threats that cannot be tolerated. More than the raw interplay of social, political, and economic forces, whiteness, property, and criminalization persist because they are widely presumed, both implicitly and explicitly, to be mechanisms through which divine will or ultimate reality manifests itself in the world.

In the end, there is no question that the first people exploited, dispossessed, criminalized, and discarded by European colonialism, racial capitalism, and the whiteness and private property they create are Black people, Indigenous people, and other people of color. And yet, while poor and working-class white people certainly enjoy what Du Bois called the "public and psychological wage" of being white, the fact that possessing whiteness does not always mean possessing the wealth and security that are supposed to be inherent to whiteness clarifies that whiteness, based as it is on accumulation by dispossession, is so narrowly self-obsessed that it does not even consistently care for all its own, and indeed never intended to. Whiteness is the willingness to sacrifice anyone—including other white people—in pursuit of transcendent power and control.[156] "White people don't *give* nothin' to each other," Baldwin writes, "so I know they ain't gon' *give* to me. They had children dragging carts through mines before they got to me."[157]

Patriarchal whiteness and private property possession are historical manifestations of the anxiety that emerges from the inability to fully transcend the vulnerabilities that come with being a finite creature and not God. The desire to transcend human vulnerability and become like God in relation to the Earth and its peoples is a desire often generated by fear of finitude, fear of scarcity, and thus a fear of others. Treating the vulnerabilities of finite, creaturely existence as threats to be avoided rather than means of communion with others or with the divine, the pursuits that animate patriarchal whiteness and property constitute what Baldwin calls the futile pursuit of "safety instead of life."[158] Such a pursuit of an all-encompassing, absolute safety, Baldwin argues, is integral to the function of religion, especially American Christianity.[159]

Fearful and paranoid, the religiosity of patriarchal and possessive whiteness seeks "refuge" by terminating everything in its way, which eventually includes even itself: "as long as white Americans take refuge in their whiteness—for so long as they are unable to walk out of this most monstrous of traps—they will allow millions to be slaughtered in their name," Baldwin writes. "They will perish (as we once put it in our black church) in their sins—that is, in their delusions."[160] The pursuit of a safety born of fear—safety that treats life itself as a danger to be escaped, safety secured only by exposing others to harm—is ultimately a danger not only to others but to oneself and thus is no safety at all.

Patriarchal whiteness and absolutely exclusive private property destroy others at the same time that they destroy their possessors through alienation from the interrelations that give life. Lashing out against their limitations, the possessors of patriarchal whiteness and private property maim others; flailing wildly to cover the shame of being human among other humans in a finite world, patriarchal whiteness and private property eventually harm even those who possess them, even if in less immediate or obvious ways. Seeking to outrun the finitude they share with those whom they imagine to be inherently inferior or threatening, whiteness and property are means of transforming those whom they render other and inferior into a ladder on which they try to escape the world into some imagined paradise purified of those whom they perceive as threats. Seeking to reach heaven alone, they create hell for others, only to eventually find themselves there as well.[161]

3

The Mortal God of Police Power

On Christmas morning 2015, a fifty-nine-year-old Black man named Vernon sat in a cold Nashville jail cell, awaiting his court hearing for aggravated criminal trespass. Vernon couldn't read very well, took care of his diabetes as best he could, worked whatever odd jobs he could find, and stayed with his partner, Miss Dorothy, in a boarding house in the North Nashville zip code with the highest incarceration rate in the nation.[1] A historically Black community and thriving Black commercial and cultural hub before federal, state, and local governments drove an interstate highway through it in the late 1960s, demolishing one hundred square blocks—including 650 homes, twenty-seven apartment buildings, and dozens of Black-owned businesses—North Nashville has long endured decimating economic divestment of public goods and equally decimating hyperinvestment in policing and jails: carceral control posed as the solution to the instabilities that massive economic disruption and divestment helped create.[2] As a direct result of these dynamics, by 2015, North Nashville was becoming one of the last frontiers in the city for real estate speculators and developers to reap profit off foreclosed and still-affordable land and housing. Displaced by gentrification from another part of the city, my wife and I became Vernon's neighbors in late 2014.[3] The highway that tore the neighborhood in two half a century earlier hummed day and night at the end of the block. Vernon was the first neighbor to introduce himself to us. He prided himself on his lawn-care services and made sure we knew he was looking out for us, always telling us he would keep an eye on our house when we were out of town. Vernon prided himself, of his own initiative, on being a good neighbor.

On December 12, 2015, I was taking out the trash when I saw police surrounding Vernon in front of his house across the street. I hurried over, and Miss Dorothy's adult niece told me that a white man flipping a house two doors down—a house that would soon list for nearly three times as much as other houses of the same size on the street—called the police on Vernon for allegedly breaking into a vacant, boarded-up apartment across the street. The white house flipper was working on the roof when he saw who he was certain was Vernon breaking into the vacant property before walking back across the street to the boardinghouse. As it turns out, the gentrifier saw not Vernon but another man whom Vernon and Miss Dorothy knew. After allegedly breaking the plywood covering the front doorway, the man walked to Vernon's house and left out the back door when the police came. Vernon, who had been visiting with Miss Dorothy's family when it all happened, fit the description: a thin Black man, about five foot six. When the police showed up at his door, they asked him questions to which they already presumed answers, confirmed with the house flipper that Vernon was the suspect, and placed him under arrest.

While Miss Dorothy wept on the sidewalk, the white gentrifier stood on the porch, arms crossed, chest out, watching it all unfold. When he spotted me—another white man—on the sidewalk talking with my neighbors and questioning the police, he called me up to where he stood so he could speak privately, presumably beyond earshot of my Black neighbors. "Do you live around here?" he stood close and asked quietly. When I pointed to our house a few doors down across the street, he responded, "A word of advice: watch your back around here." His white construction coworker, a wiry man with stubble on his face, warned me about the "riff-raff" in the neighborhood who were out to get people like me. Both men named their anticipation for the changes—clearly both racial and classed—that would soon come as more houses were flipped in the neighborhood. I was shocked but not surprised. I told them that they had been misled, that they did not in fact understand this neighborhood, and that Vernon would not and could not have broken into the abandoned home, because he prides himself on keeping watch over the neighborhood. The house flipper who called me up to offer his racist word of warning expressed a patronizing regret: "I know it must be hard," he said. "I know you thought you knew your neighbor, but I know what I saw." What the white male property defender perceived the police believed, and they placed Vernon in handcuffs while Miss Dorothy wailed on the sidewalk and her niece filmed the police while she excoriated them for taking an innocent man.

"They're tryin' to take me downtown—for *no reason*!" Vernon called out while the officer wrapped steel around his wrists. "Why?" he kept asking the white officer arresting him. "I'm not the one!" He already knew what his arrest meant for him and Miss Dorothy, hardly able to afford rent as it was, especially during the winter months when he didn't have any lawns to cut. "I gotta get on and make my money, man," he said to the officer. "I ain't the one!" he repeated, incredulous, while the officer turned him around, moved him against the car, asked him to spread his feet apart, took Vernon's wallet out of his back pocket, and tossed it on the trunk of the cruiser. A moment later, as the officer guided him into the back seat of the squad car, Vernon glanced up toward the porch where the house flipper stood, then drew his eyes back down. "They lyin'," he said matter-of-factly. From the rolled-down window of the cruiser, Vernon tried to explain once again that it was not him. "He was in the house talking to our daughter!" Miss Dorothy implored him. The officer, in a patronizing *I'm-only-doing-my-job* tone, responded, addressing Miss Dorothy, now shaking with tears. "The people who called us ID'd him to a T," he said. "Now, that being said, that doesn't make him guilty." Mispronouncing his presumption of guilt as a presumption of innocence, the officer turned to me: "I'm sorry, I never did catch your name, sir." "Andrew," I responded. He turned to Vernon and Miss Dorothy: "So, like Mr. Andrew and everyone else, we're gonna try and figure out what's going on, okay?" Much like the house flipper who called me to his porch as an expression of our shared white possessive manhood in a predominantly Black neighborhood, the cop subtly but clearly adopted me, a white male property owner, into a position of authority in a way that the situation clearly did not warrant, especially given that I was inside my house when it all happened. Meanwhile, unlike the word of white men on roofs and inside houses across the street, the word of every Black person present was treated as inherently nonauthoritative, lacking any legal claim to truth, and was thus ignored. What the godlike gaze of whiteness sees becomes real through its seeing, regardless of whether it is actually reflective of reality or not.

My wife and I went to the night court judge to speak to Vernon's character and to implore him not to move forward with any charge. We ran into the house flipper outside the night court chambers, where he told us and the arresting officer that he would be carrying his gun onto the property for the remainder of the renovation. Vernon spent weeks behind bars without ever being formally convicted of any crime, keeping him from being able to earn any money to support himself and his partner during the holidays. In the year that followed, both Vernon's and Miss Dorothy's health deteriorated, and Vernon eventually had no choice but to move in with his daughter. He died less than five years later at the age of sixty-three. Shortly after the armed white house flipper finished his work on the house, it was converted into a short-term rental property for tourists. Nearly ten years later, it is occupied with guests, at most, five days out of every month. If the owner decided to sell, they could easily get more than half a million dollars for it. The abandoned property across the street remains unfilled, plywood covering the windows and doors, grass grown up high around the porch in spring. Meanwhile, thousands of people struggle to survive in shelters and camps, under overpasses, and on the streets of Nashville every night.

Vernon's arrest and his premature death are manifestations of racial capitalism and settler colonialism—the same forces that ran a highway through the neighborhood at the end of the block, divested resources and sent in cops for decades, threw a generation of Black people from the neighborhood in cages by criminalizing forced acts of survival, created conditions of foreclosure and displacement, vacated an apartment across the street, functionally deputized a white man flipping a house two doors down, and predisposed the cops to treat the house flipper's perception as reality against Black people accused of trespassing in an ever-whitening landscape. Indeed, the words, actions, and presuppositions guiding both the house flipper and the police he called illuminate the long history and deep intertwining of the pseudo-sacred powers of patriarchal whiteness, private property, and police. By defending even vacant property from Black presence and by making clear his intention to contribute to the whitening of predominantly Black space through territorial reclamation and displacement, the house flipper invoked a white settler colonial and carceral imaginary.[4] Historically speaking, the white settler colonial imaginary encounters all nonwhite space as dangerous space that requires taming, profane space that requires purifying, in order for it to come under sacred white possession. It is the logic that guided manifold acts of white terror and violence against Black and Indigenous communities throughout US history and that guides the dynamics of gentrification and displacement enforced by police in the "new urban frontier" today.[5] Much as in the histories of eurochristian colonialism, imperialism, and manifest destiny that destroyed Indigenous and Black communities, for the white house flipper, taming and purifying a nonwhite landscape requires vigorously held claims to absolutely exclusive private possession that generate white wealth and contribute to the displacement of nonwhite, working-class, and underclass residents. Though it was not even his own property that was threatened, the house flipper defended it because threat to any private property is potentially a threat to all private property and thus to the white settler vision that guided him.

Patriarchal and possessive whiteness is a manifestation of the human aspiration to godlike transcendence and power. What the story of Vernon's arrest shows, among other things, is that merely asserting "ownership of the earth for ever and ever, Amen!" is not always enough to make patriarchal and possessive whiteness materially omnipotent. The order that revolves around whiteness and property depends for its existence—and its sacredness—on the vigilant management and elimination of all that threatens to desecrate it. Managing or eliminating threats to sacred order requires ordained violence. And in a white racial capitalist settler colonial social order, the "violence work" of identifying, managing, and eliminating threats to whiteness and property, and of thereby actualizing their inhabitants' godlike power to possess and control the world, belongs to police.[6]

For centuries, the most predominant term for the state power to use violence to eliminate threats to the social order and those whom it serves has been "police power."[7] Before it referred to organized, uniformed, armed agents of the state, the notion of police power referred to the broad, patriarchally defined, God-ordained, and discretionary power to govern the social order in the way that a divine or human father exercises authority over his household. Under such a view, the police power of the state not only protects civil society but brings it into being.[8] Without the discretionary state power to eliminate threats, the modern liberal story goes, civil society, given over to the disorder and chaos of the state of nature, would cease to exist. With the proliferation of racial capitalism and settler colonialism over the course of the seventeenth, eighteenth, and nineteenth centuries, this broad state power to exercise godlike authority over people and planet became institutionalized and eventually professionalized in the form of armed agents of the state—"police"—tasked with using violence to produce and maintain the hierarchies and boundaries of colonial racial capitalist order.

Whiteness, property, and police entered the world in and through one another; they are coconstitutive, inextricably intertwined. There is no sacred whiteness or property without police, and apart from whiteness and property, there would be no such thing as police as we know them today. As concrete manifestations of the "right to exclude," patriarchal whiteness and private property already contain within them the seeds of criminalization and indeed come into being in and through the police power to criminalize and eliminate those who, by status or by act, trespass against and thereby desecrate them.[9] As such, we should understand whiteness, property, and police as conceptually and materially contiguous: the sacred fences, gates, and walls that hedge in whiteness and private property and hedge out their trespassers extend into and serve the same function as the fences, gates, and walls of the carceral institutions that partition and order our world.

Most commentaries on modern policing fail to apprehend the foundational role that police power plays in the creation of modern society itself: police power helps bring racial capitalist and colonial order into being, defends and protects it from all that threatens to undermine it, and thereby ensures the order's continued existence.[10] In these ways, the very structure and function of police power resembles a kind of divine power in relation to society: police power *creates*, *saves* from threat, and *sustains* a social order that grants near-transcendent power to a few by criminalizing and dispossessing many.[11] Fulfilling the role of a kind of God who acts on behalf of the white propertied few, the police power to criminalize threats to moral and social order helps to realize the transcendent aspirations of the possessors of whiteness and property by eliminating all that stands in the way of their social, political, economic, and cultural omnipotence. There can be no heaven for a few without forcibly capturing and exiling the many alleged enemies of God and society to hell.

One of the greatest seeming contradictions of the modern capitalist and colonial state is that while it cannot exist without purging itself of its internal and external enemies, it also cannot exist without them. The state's dependence on its internal and external enemies often takes the form of economic reliance on their exploited, wealth-generating labor. But it also takes the shape of a more fundamental dynamic wherein the state must posit and construct an enemy in order to prove itself powerful and superior at all. Just as whiteness and property define themselves hierarchically in relation to what they are not, so the racial capitalist and settler colonial state is only able to articulate and actualize itself through hostility to those whom it dispossesses. Indeed, there is no such thing as the modern state apart from its enemy, defined as the "Enemy of All Mankind."[12] Far from hyperbolic, the concept of the "Enemy of All Mankind" shows up throughout modern history as a central political frame that gives shape and coherency to state power. From at least the late medieval and early modern era on, the figure of the "criminal," embodied predominantly by forcibly dispossessed, colonized, Black, and Indigenous peoples, has been foremost among the named enemies of state and order. As early as the sixteenth century, and for many centuries thereafter, English legislators cast the criminalized "idle" vagrant as an "enemy of the commonwealth."[13] Throughout the modern era, state actors, political philosophers, and colonial-capitalist commentators deployed the same carceral language of inherently "criminal" "common enemies" to refer to a wide array of working-class and underclass peoples whose rebellious activity and "abnormal" personhood seemed to threaten the very foundations of order across the globe.[14] After touring some of the United States' most brutal penitentiaries in the 1830s, the French diplomat Alexis de Tocqueville observed that the criminal in the United States is "an enemy of the human race and every human being is against him."[15] More recently, during the late twentieth-century rise of mass incarceration, politicians and public theologians regularly declared carceral war on Black and economically dispossessed Americans, whom they decried as a monolithic "godless," "criminal," "enemy of the human race."[16]

There can be no white racial capitalist state without its Black, dispossessed, criminalized enemy. Or, as Baldwin put it, "the State creates the Criminal . . . because the State cannot operate without the criminal," which is to say, the police power to construct, capture, and eliminate those who threaten sacred social order—criminalization—is the foundation on which the racial capitalist settler colonial state depends for its very existence.[17] As a tool deployed to maintain the supremacy and security of some by managing, caging, and disappearing others, criminalization is not an anomaly within but a manifestation of the social order from which it arises: capturing and containing threats to sacred order makes the order possible and, with every police intervention, ensures its continued existence.

The police power to criminalize and thereby eliminate the enemies of order does not merely defend whiteness and property; it deifies them and thereby sacralizes the order that revolves around them. In this way, eliminating threats to sacred social order is not merely an act of negation but, for those who manage and benefit from that order, a fundamentally creative, life-giving, and thus godlike act. As Durkheim and others argue, the punishment of those who are defined as "criminal" gives society a foundational sense of cohesion, bringing people together in a shared response to the "blasphemy and sacrilege" that the criminal desecration of sacred order enacts.[18] By capturing and containing predominantly Black and Indigenous people, other people of color, and propertyless peoples of all races, police power and carceral captivity make white propertied life possible—and pseudo-divinely powerful. The elimination of some makes life for others. Deification for a few means destruction for many.

Sacred Law and Order

What at first seems a contradiction—that the modern state can live neither with nor without those whom it constructs and captures as "criminal"—is in fact a foundational and implicitly religious rationale that structures the racial capitalist settler colonial state. As outlined in the introduction and chapter 2, aspects of the oppositionality that shapes capitalism and colonialism also characterize the dynamics of many forms of religion and of sacred space in particular. The partitions forged by the geographies of the sacred and profane, of belonging and trespass, take shape not just in some heavenly beyond but here and now, in the social, political, economic, and cultural orders in which we live. Indeed, social order itself often registers as sacred because it manifests the living, collective embodiment of a group of people's shared values and orientations toward what they take to be ultimate.[19] This is true both for societies in which institutionalized religion plays a clear and predominant role and in societies in which it does not: even modern secular social orders, Durkheim argues, are characterized by a "sacred," "transcendent" sense of morality that, when violated, "keeps violators at arm's length, just as the religious domain is protected from the reach of the profane."[20] Whatever disrupts social order is thus experienced as a desecration of life itself. For the social body, such disruptions register quite literally as threats to existence that cannot be tolerated and that must be eliminated to maintain the order at all.

The eliminatory response to the disruption of sacred sociality is an expression of the deep religiosity at the heart of police power and carceral punishment. As Durkheim suggests, the original and overarching purpose of identifying, capturing, and punishing those who threaten social and moral order is not to deter crime or to create safety or to facilitate processes of accountability; the purpose of carceral capture and punishment is to defend and restore the sacred social order desecrated through actions deemed "criminal."[21] Thus, despite the seemingly individualized application of police, judicial, and carceral procedures, the idea of criminality is a matter of offense not primarily against individuals or even against the law but against the functionally sacred social order itself, which the law exists to maintain. This is why, according to carceral logic, caged people "pay their debts" not to impacted individuals or to the law but to "society" and, by extension, to those who manage and benefit from its hierarchies. The eliminatory response to disruptions of order is inherently religious because it embodies the same dynamic of oppositionality—between sacred and profane, orderly and disorderly, pure and polluted—that undergirds religious thought and practice, particularly in its eurochristian iterations. In the end, sacred order is only sacred insofar as it maintains its purity, which requires eliminating the profane and polluting disorder of "matter out of place." And the work of eliminating the social and moral threat of matter and people out of place is, by modern historical definition, the work of police.

By eliminating impurities, police perform the godlike function of creating, redeeming, and maintaining sacred order, a function that secures near-transcendent power for its managers and beneficiaries. Likening the police power of the state to divine power is far from hyperbolic. Indeed, the association of political authority with divine authority has a long history beginning in the ancient world and continuing, in evolved form, to this day. In the ancient world, ways of thinking about the divine and ways of thinking about the law and the political sphere were often mutually formative. Predominant among the many ways that monotheistic Jewish and Christian scripture image God, for instance, are as sovereign king or lord and as just judge or lawmaker.[22] Following the conceptual frameworks and metaphors of the Christian tradition's sacred texts, many ancient, medieval, and early modern theologians also conceptualized God as a kind of sovereign or judicial authority whose divine action—including condemnation and justification, damnation and salvation—reflects the "justice" that is understood to be essential to God's very nature. From scripture to theological tradition, Jewish and Christian ways of thinking about who God is and what God does borrow from the political realm in order to help humans understand something of God's nature: we know what kings, lords, and judges are like, and we can understand God analogously, even if God's power ultimately exceeds such earthly powers. In an effort to convey the fundamentals of God, sin, and salvation for the life of Christians, many of the most influential theologians throughout the tradition posit who God is and what God does through political frames of slavery, captivity, punishment, debt, law, and freedom, among many other phenomena. While conceptions of God often borrow from the political realm, God concepts shape the political realm, as well, such that it is sometimes difficult to discern if a concept originates in theology or politics. Despite late modern presumptions about their inherent distinction, the theological and the political have long been—and to continue to be—mutually formative.

The intertwining of Christian theological and political rationales throughout history also reflects the fact that Christian traditions have positioned themselves in proximity to political power in multiple ways. After a few centuries of relative unalignment with political authorities, starting in the fourth century, when the Roman emperor Constantine made Christianity the official religion of the empire, Christianity has fused with political authority in both thought and practice in a multitude of ways. "Satisfaction" theory, which emerged in eleventh-century Europe at the nexus of Christian theology and legal practice, elaborated on the ancient political theologies and philosophies that preceded it, fusing theological and legal concepts in ways that would significantly shape the religious and legal landscape from that point forward.[23] By the sixteenth-century Protestant Reformation, theology and politics continued to intertwine at a fundamental level: Martin Luther viewed the punishing apparatuses of civil government as "God's hangmen," and John Calvin figured God as a kind of Absolute Monarch. Built on analogous conceptualizations of God and state, Protestant doctrines of moral law also directly informed key features of Anglo-American criminal law and punishment. As legal scholar John Witte Jr. writes, early modern Protestant jurists and theologians "regularly collaborated in formulating criminal doctrines and inflicting criminal punishments" and were unified in the belief that God "imposes divine punishments" and that civil magistrates are "God's vice-regents" who carry out God's will in the world.[24] Much as in earlier eras, in the modern Protestant European context out of which racial capitalist settler colonial powers emerged, most moral and political authorities understood the work of salvation and the work of government to be not only analogous but functionally intertwined, serving the same ends.[25]

The theological-political rationales developed by ancient, medieval, and early modern moral and political authorities contributed to a long-standing social imaginary—one that has taken different forms throughout history up to the present—in which political authority is understood to be an extension or approximation of divine authority. Under such a frame, the social order that political authority governs and the law by which it governs are treated as inherently sacred, which is to say, grounded in something inherently moral, transcendent, ultimate, and thus worthy of protection at any cost. Even when the state and its order no longer articulate themselves in explicitly theocratic or religious terms, this implicitly religious frame endures. In Thomas Hobbes's seventeenth-century political philosophy of the origins and function of the state and civil society, he narrates a process by which people willfully give up their right to absolute self-governance in exchange for security from the state. As noted earlier, in a pre-state world marked by the sin of pride—excessive self-concern that leads to a "war of all against all"—Hobbes characterizes the state that forms through the collective renunciation of individual self-governance as a "mortal God" that governs under and with the authority of the "immortal God."[26] The state maintains its godlike authority and power only when all its subjects submit entirely to its pseudo-divine authority. If the state that the people's will allegedly generates is a mortal God, then the social order that the mortal God maintains through its governing inevitably registers as sacred.

Such a conception of modern political order, one that still informs the social imaginary of the present, even if not always in explicitly theocratic ways, bears an inherently religious structure: conceptualizing the state as a mortal God empowers the state to treat the internal and external enemies that threaten its sacred social order as immoral enemies of God. Indeed, the "criminal," order-disrupting "enemies of all mankind" have long been understood as manifestations of "the original Enemy of All Mankind," the Devil. The state power to eliminate threats to sacred social order—the power of Hobbes's "mortal God"—is, by definition, the power of police.[27] As such, the police power to eliminate criminal threats to social order amounts to a divinely derived power to exorcise the demonic from our midst. As Mark Neocleous writes, "God's Adversary is the embodiment of all (social) disorder on earth. Defeat the Devil and one defeats disorder. Conversely: maintain order and one defeats the Devil."[28] Indeed, the earliest architects and defenders of private property, settler colonialism, and African enslavement made abundantly clear time and time again that the commoners they dispossessed, the Indigenous peoples they eradicated, and the Africans they enslaved were immoral enemies of God who, without the violence of forced subjection, would unleash intolerable disorder on society. In the words of Justice Isaac F. Redfield's majority opinion in the 1848 Vermont Supreme Court case *Spalding v. Preston*, a case that helped solidify the expansive nature of police power, the overarching task of the mortal God of the police is "stifling the fountains of evil."[29]

In the Christian tradition, divine power is, among other things, the power to "save." Modern police power, which entered the world through European Christianity, capitalism, and colonialism, is also the power to save. By eliminating that which threatens sacred social order, police power "saves" both sacred order and, by returning them to their proper place, those who trespass against it. Bearing more than an accidental resemblance to salvation, police and carceral power both emerged from and draw from a largely European Christian tradition of thinking on sin and salvation based in the idea of subjection to authority.[30] Most Christian theologies conceptualize human personhood as a combination of two fundamental facts: God created all humans *imago Dei*—in the image of God—and all humans are, at the same time, fundamentally corrupted by the condition of sin, alienating humans from God and thereby placing them in a state of condemnation, indebtedness, and ruination before their creator.[31] The tension of these two concurrent realities finds its resolution for most Christian theologies not in human effort but in the saving power of God. While understandings of what precisely sin and salvation entail vary across Christian thought, a predominant trajectory within Christian theology interprets sin and salvation in terms of human obedience and subjection to divine authority that properly reflects the radical difference in power and ontology between humans and God. Within this framework, which I term a *carceral soteriology of subjection*, sin is understood as a disobedient refusal to be subject to a benevolent, life-giving authority, while salvation is understood to entail an obedient return to subjection to that authority.

The stream of Christian thought that sacralizes subjection cannot be traced to one single figure. However, brief engagement with the work of three theologians in particular, whose interpretations and elaborations of scriptural themes help shape dominant Western theological and political thought broadly, will help illuminate some of its central features. Augustine (354–430), Anselm (1033–1109), and Calvin (1509–1564) lived and wrote centuries apart from one another. Though it might otherwise be methodologically suspect to attempt to synthesize thought from figures who each lived approximately five hundred years before or after the next, tracing connections across the work of three of the most influential theologians in the Christian tradition will demonstrate important continuities in theological thought that persist not only from the fifth to the sixteenth century but to the present moment, as well. The carceral soteriologies of these figures interpret and elaborate on scripture, using images and metaphors for God-human relations used in both the Hebrew Bible and New Testament, and the Pauline corpus in particular. Each makes sense of the theological problem of sin and the resolution of salvation by way of penal and economic frameworks that both borrow from and contribute to political conceptualities based in subjection and captivity. Understanding the dynamics of their political theologies will enable us to better understand the dynamics of the police and carceral power that draw implicitly and explicitly from them. Far from a purely ecclesial matter of theological debate, Augustine's theory of atonement paved the way for Anselm's satisfaction theory, which influenced the retributivism of broader legal and social imaginaries of Europe for five hundred years, eventually informing Calvin's political theology of penal substitution and criminal punishment, which in turn gave shape to the modern European and American criminal punishment systems from which our present systems derive.

Corruption, Subjection, and Self-Willed Punishment

For most Christian theologies, "sin" describes, among other things, the corruption of human will and nature that results in a breach between humans and God. And for most Christian theologies, crystallized first in the work of Augustine, the essence of that corruption and the source of that separation is "pride." At its root, pride is a turning in toward oneself and away from God, a disordered desire in which one worships created things, including oneself, rather than the creator.[32] In Augustine's interpretation, the Garden of Eden represents creation as God intended it: God gives us everything we need, which means we need not look to ourselves for our own sustenance or survival. When Adam and Eve ate from the tree of the knowledge of good and evil, thereby becoming "like God," they disrupted God's intentions for creation by disrupting the benevolently hierarchical dynamics of the God-human relationship, mistaking themselves for God and thus failing to acknowledge God as God.

Implicit in Augustine's theology of the origins and essence of sin is that humans are made for life-giving subjection to their benevolent maker and master. When humans reject the subjection to God for which they were made, Augustine argues, they render themselves captive to the Devil instead. For Augustine, then, and for many after him, the sin of pride is the disobedient refusal to be properly subject to the divine source of all life. On this basis, and assuming an implicit connection between divine and political authority, Augustine characterizes the rebellious nature of sinful humanity by analogy to unpunished prisoners and runaway slaves seeking a freedom that belongs only to God.[33] More than just isolated acts, sin, for Augustine, is a condition, a disorder in human nature that results in a state of guilt, indebtedness, and "condemnation" before God.[34] And to be condemned before God, Augustine suggests, following the writings of the Apostle Paul, is to be bound, in the sense of captivity. "Your wrath was heavy upon me and I was unaware of it," he writes. "I had become deafened by the clanking chain of my mortal condition, the penalty of my pride."[35] Importantly, because God does not and cannot create sin, he argues, it is humans who create the chains that bind them and under which they groan.[36] Enslavement to sin, in other words, is its own self-willed punishment.[37] Augustine also posits that punishment is a form of mercy, just as fire purges impure elements, and brings us back to God.[38] Indeed, he argues, the self-willed punishment that results from sin against a just God is not only deserved but a merciful good—sacred.

For Anselm, much as for Augustine, the condition of humanity is a state of ruination and captivity resulting from sin.[39] To sin, Anselm argues, is to refrain from giving God the honor that God is owed. Because honor is rightfully God's to begin with, refusing to give it constitutes an egregious act of theft: "everyone who sins is under an obligation to repay to God the honor which he has violently taken from him."[40] And yet, because, theologically speaking, it "is impossible for God to lose his honor," the refusal to honor God is ultimately the refusal to be properly subject before God, to orient oneself as though God is not sovereign, as though God is not God.[41] The consequence of the refusal to recognize and be properly subject to the divine sovereign is cosmic disorder: when one sins, Anselm writes, one "dishonors God . . . since he is not willingly subordinating himself to God's governance, and is disturbing, as far as he is able, the order and beauty of the universe."[42] Emphasizing and elaborating on the implicit economic dynamic of Augustine's soteriology, Anselm posits that the disorder-inducing failure to honor God establishes a relation of guilt and obligation—an indebtedness—that demands satisfaction.[43] For Anselm, as for Augustine, one of God's most basic traits is that God is just, which, for Anselm, has to do with a sense of order and proportionality rooted in God's absolute power and supremacy over God's creatures: creatures must be in their place and God in God's place in order to maintain the just order that God creates. Conceived in terms of a sovereign whose sovereignty depends on his being honored, Anselm's God ultimately requires the satisfaction of God's justice—and the restoration of God's honor—through either recompense or punishment: "either the honor which has been taken away should be repaid, or punishment should follow."[44] Anselm, again following Augustine, argues that the human condition of indebtedness and condemnation, and thus the need for recompense or punishment, is a fundamentally self-willed state.

In connection with the notion of economic and legal obligation, Anselm also follows Jewish and Christian scripture, Augustine, and others in characterizing the human condition before God in terms of purity and impurity. Humanity, Anselm writes, is God's "most precious piece of workmanship" that has been "completely ruined" by sin.[45] Expanding this metaphor of ruination, Anselm also likens God to a "rich man" and humans to a pearl: if God drops the perfect pearl in mud, it becomes "stained with the filth of sin," and he will not pick it up and put it back in his treasury without first washing it off because leaving it dirty would contaminate the otherwise pure space of God's sacred order.[46] By imaging God as a wealthy possessor of human pearls at the same time that he figures God as a sovereign to whom guilty humans owe a debt, Anselm carries forward a long-standing equivalency between impurity and debt and thus between the remedies of "washing" and "recompense" to a God conceived in terms of political and economic power. Human pearls can only be washed through payment that satisfies—"absolves"—humanity's debt of sin.[47] In these ways, Anselm's work enacts an important shift in emphasis in Christian soteriological thought, namely, from seeing sin as hurting primarily humans to sin as a "violent" offense against a sovereign, property-possessing God.[48] In the end, the disobedient refusal to honor—to be properly subordinate to—God is an offense against God and God's cosmic order, which corresponds directly to the long-standing notion that political disobedience, the refusal to be subject to a political authority, is an offense against both the sovereign and the sacred social order over which they rule.

Finally, building off the work of Augustine, Anselm, and others, Calvin argues that the root of sin is disobedience, which leads to pride, which leads to selfish ambition, which leads to rebellion against divine law and order, which Calvin understands as an attempt to destroy the glory of God.[49] Like those before him, Calvin argues that humanity is a "seed-bed of sin," which they inherit from their first progenitors and cannot escape on their own. Likewise, building off the writings of Paul, Augustine, Anselm, and others, Calvin deploys frames of slavery and captivity to convey the dynamics of sin. God gives humans free will, but instead of acting freely, Calvin writes, each human becomes a "voluntary slave" "enchained" to sin.[50] Under "bondage" to sin, the corrupted human will is utterly incapable of pursuing God's will.[51] Also like theologians before him, starting with the acts of the first human, Adam, it is the "depravity" of humans, not God, that is to blame for the ruination and corruption of their created nature.[52] This state of ruin is a "polluted" state of "degeneracy" and guilt, a state of condemnation. Much like Anselm before him, who viewed sin and salvation in terms of a synthesis of ontological purification, economic payment, and penal retribution, Calvin theologizes about sin and salvation on the basis of a fundamental fusion of notions of purity and punishment. However, whereas Anselm's theology posits either recompense or punishment as a means of satisfying debt, Calvin emphasizes punishment as the primary means of addressing humans' pollution and guilt.[53]

Salvific Subjection

If sin is the refusal to be properly subject to—to disobey, to dishonor, to rebel against—a life-giving God, then central to salvation is a restoration to proper subjection to God. To obey, to honor, to be subordinate: salvation restores the proper hierarchical relation between God and humans, ensuring that God is God and humans are not. There are certainly important distinctions between the God-human dynamics of these soteriologies and the state-subject dynamics of the carceral orders that draw from them. There is no question, for instance, that the subjection implicit in these soteriologies is, unlike the reality of carceral systems, ultimately about redeeming dependence on the loving and self-giving source of all life. Nevertheless, the hierarchical power dynamics embedded in these soteriological frames are central to the meaning they make and thus the worlds they help create. Understanding what exactly salvation entails for theologians in this tradition of thought will enable us to better discern the connections between carceral soteriology and carceral practice, which I explore in the final section of this chapter.

For practically all Christian theologies, there is no salvation apart from Jesus Christ. While his life before his crucifixion and his resurrection after are also central to most Christian theologies, for carceral

Christian accounts of salvation, Jesus's death—and what is understood to take place therein—plays the most crucial part. Augustine's ransom theory of salvation channels the biblical notion of propitiatory blood sacrifice that releases one from debt. In Augustine's narration, God, hearing the groans of humans under captivity to the Devil, interposes Christ's blood, which is so costly that the Devil has no choice but to release humans from his grasp. This act pays the debt that held humanity captive to the Devil, releasing them from the debt bondage of sin. In the ancient world in which Augustine wrote, debt was not an abstract relation of obligation but a relation by which multitudes were bound, including physically, by imperial power. Debt was also widely understood as a cognate of sin. "Redemption" in its literal sense refers to a "buying back," a release or "ransom" or "deliverance" from bondage, which is why Christ's death that brings release from debt captivity is understood as inherently "redemptive."[54] While this way of narrating salvation certainly bears potential for liberatory theologies of God's work among humans, it also remains tethered to a frame of obedience and subjection that has served various forms of human subjection. For Augustine, just as it was human pride and disobedience that, under God's justice, delivered humans *to* the Devil, so it was the opposite—God's humility and Christ's obedience to his Father on the cross—that delivered humans *from* captivity to the Devil, modeling for humankind the way of redeeming subjection to God. Indeed, the liberation that God initiates in Christ is not freedom to do whatever one wants but freedom that consists in a journey from rebellion and pride to proper obedience and submission to a God who gives us all we need. Since self-centered pride is the root of sin, self-relinquishing submission is the key to its correction.

Anselm takes up Augustine's notion of sin as the refusal to be subject and of salvation as a return to proper subjection, deepening emphasis on the impact of sin and salvation on God and on the God-human relationship in particular. Anselm also deepens and shifts the economic dimension of Augustine's account of what Christ's death accomplishes in the passage from sin to salvation. Having dishonored and thereby accrued a debt to God, finite, sinful humanity faces the conundrum of the fact that (1) it owes a debt it is incapable of paying and that (2) its debt to God can be satisfied only when humanity pays it. What are humans to do if they owe a debt they cannot pay? The answer to this conundrum, for Anselm, is the God-Man, Jesus Christ, who, as human, pays the debt that humans owe and, as God, is capable of satisfying it. Six hundred years before Anselm, Augustine had written that Jesus, as God, became human "in order that He might pay for us, the debtors, that which He Himself did not owe."[55] Both conceive of sin in terms of guilt and indebtedness, and both understand salvation as a kind of payment to "satisfy" an obligation and atone for guilt. The difference, however, is that for Augustine, the payment of Christ's blood is made to the Devil, who holds humanity captive to sin. For Anselm, it was unthinkable to suggest that God would owe the Devil anything. Anselm therefore shifts the terms of satisfaction so that it is the God-Man who pays to God, rather than the Devil, the debt that humans owe. Much as for Augustine, for Anselm, if it is disobedience that "dirties" and renders humans indebted, it is the God-Man's obedience that restores and cleanses human life by reestablishing proper proportional and hierarchical order.[56] Because Christ the God-Man was in need of nothing, the surplus that the Father gave him in return for his obedient, satisfactory righteousness to the point of death on the cross could be transferred to someone else instead, and so he gave it to humankind, securing their release from the bondage of their debt—their sin.[57]

Once again, since sin cannot actually—ontologically—take anything away from God, restoring God's honor that humans have "violently taken from him" is ultimately about the restoration of right hierarchical relation between a divine sovereign and his finite subjects. As such, Anselm argues, to strive to live in accordance with God's will is simply to return God's property: "the things you are giving are not your property but the property of him whose bondslave you are, and to whom you are making the gift."[58] Beyond what human striving can accomplish, recompense or punishment "satisfies" God because God is a just sovereign whose power depends on being honored as sovereign, which requires a relation of subjection. Salvation saves humans by returning them to proper subjection to their benevolent, life-giving sovereign and saves God from the threat of not being honored as God, of not being God. Recompense and punishment, voluntary or involuntary, restore the divine-human hierarchy on which cosmic and social order depend.[59]

Following and elaborating on the soteriologies of Augustine and Anselm, Calvin understands the corrupted human will through the prism of "the antithesis between the rebellious movement of the heart, and the correction by which it is subdued to obedience."[60] Held captive by a corrupted, rebellious will, humans are, by themselves, utterly incapable of the obedience that God requires and that humans' own well-being necessitates. The answer to the problem of a rebellious and condemned humanity, for Calvin, is not Christ paying a ransom to the Devil, as for Augustine, or the God-Man paying humans' debt to God, as for Anselm, but Christ interposing himself as our substitute, taking on the punishment due to us, thereby saving us by rendering us just before a God conceived as a kind of judge. Calvin's penal substitutionary atonement theory, as it is often called, hinges on the idea of God's justice. In this way, Calvin operates on the same basis that Anselm did: the divine and natural order of things dictates that wrongdoing demands retribution in some form, which includes punishment. For both thinkers, punishment is a mechanism that fundamentally rights wrongs and restores a sense of cosmic order and justice. Condemned humanity deserves punishment in a cosmic framework in which that "deserving" is simply part of the grain of God's created order and the foundation of God's just and benevolent character. While Anselm's soteriology does not entail a God-Man who must take on humanity's punishment, it does build off the presumption that punishment is a legitimate and even sacred means of restoring order in the wake of dishonor, debt, impurity, and condemnation. Such a presumption makes it possible for Calvin to center divine punishment as *the* mechanism through which salvation takes place.[61]

Like Augustine and Anselm, Calvin argues that since it is human disobedience that warrants our condemnation and punishment, it is Christ's human obedience to the Father's will, even to the point of punishment and death, that secures our pardon and restores the possibility of life-giving subjection to God.[62] Utilizing the language of "satisfaction" that Anselm used, Calvin holds that the punishment and condemnation due to humans that Christ took on through his voluntary and obedient death is the "price" by which "the justice of God was satisfied."[63] On the cross, Christ became "our substitute-ransom and propitiation" such that his blood "acted as a laver [wash basin] to purge our defilement," once again highlighting the inseparability of economic, judicial, and cleanliness metaphors in predominant conceptions of salvation.[64] Christ on the cross undertook our "expiation" "in order to remove our condemnation."[65] Indeed, Calvin argues, Christ's punishment—which he took on as our substitute on our behalf—is our acquittal: it justifies humans before God, bringing us to "the final goal of safety."[66] Thus can we discern the predominant modern political philosophy that punishment makes safety as a manifestation of carceral theology.

From Carceral Soteriology to Carceral Practice

Christian carceral soteriologies both draw from and help reinforce the idea that sovereign political authority is a natural feature of social order, either as an unfortunate but necessary means of preserving order or as a divinely ordained attribute of creation.[67] From these presumptions derive political theologies that reinforce the intertwining of hierarchical forms of divine and political authority. For Augustine, civil government exists because sin does: human sinfulness unrestrained inevitably leads to chaos and evil. Government exists to restrain and punish sin and evil and thus to preserve order and a semblance of peace. Building off the groundwork laid by Augustine, Anselm, and others, Calvin posits a theocratic conception of government, in which political authority exists to protect piety, Christian worship, and property and to keep the peace against "evil-doers and criminals" of various kinds.[68] The righteousness of government, Calvin argues, is in defending the innocent and oppressed. Governmental magistrates "have a commission from God," are "invested with divine authority," "represent the person of God," and so may be considered a kind of "substitute" for God on Earth.[69] As such, Calvin argues, when the "magistrate" inflicts punishment, "he acts not of himself, but executes the very judgments of God."[70] Civil authority is sacred and lawful—indeed, the most sacred and honorable station among mortals, a "sacred office" whose heads are "ambassadors of God." Whatever the form of government, God intended it and authorizes it, and so it is our duty to "obey and submit."[71] Obedience is an inherent good because it submits to power that is utterly benevolent in the case of God and divinely ordained in the case of political sovereignty. Thus are sovereignty and subjection understood to be basic features of God's will for the material world.

Following a line of thinking nourished by Augustine and Calvin, among others, modern liberal European political philosophers including Hobbes, Locke, and Jean-Jacques Rousseau developed a theory of social contract in which civil government exists to guard against chaos and protect the property and personhood of its citizen-subjects, all in exchange for their law-abiding obedience and submission. Elaborating on Hobbes's mythology of the state as a mortal God that saves humans from the chaos of the state of nature and Locke's theory of government as a means of the protection of life, liberty, and property, Rousseau posits the sovereignty of state power as the right over life and death: a sovereign gives security and liberty, and therefore the possibility of life itself, to humans who would otherwise struggle to obtain and maintain it, in exchange for obedience to the law and renunciation of limitless freedom.[72] And historically speaking, the power to determine life and death by eliminating threats to order is the power of "police." Thus is the police power to create, redeem, and sustain sacred social order the power of a mortal God.

A central outcome of these political theologies and philosophies is that they naturalize the exclusion and death of those who are accused of refusing to be subject to divine and political order and the law that upholds it. As early as Augustine, to refuse subjection to the source of all life was to expose oneself to death, establishing a kind of self-inflicted death penalty at the heart of God's law: God commands "obedience" under "pain" and "penalty of death."[73] Mirroring the carceral soteriology of subjection that narrates punishment for sin as a self-willed condition and death as a reasonable outcome, the mythology of the modern liberal social contract posits that those who refuse to submit to sovereign power and sacredly derived law effectively will their own punishment, exclusion, or death. Because the sovereign is the living embodiment of the people's collective will for the good, obedience to the sovereign is effectively obedience to one's own will. As such, Rousseau writes, one who violates the state's laws literally "ceases to be a member of [his country]; he even makes war upon it," which is, in turn, to consent to social—or, when necessary, biological—death.[74] From this viewpoint, to be a member of society is to consent to the loss of certain freedoms by obeying the law in exchange for protection. Those who pridefully seek to exercise their own freedom without limit disobey the law and thereby antagonize the social order itself. By antagonizing sacred social order, the story goes, criminal enemies will their own captivity and death. As Augustine argued well before the modern era, the chains in which humans exist are chains of their own making: those who refuse proper subjection to divine and political will opt for the subjection of a spiritual and material captivity that, by nature and necessity, follows as a consequence of such disobedience.

The idea that punishment, by both nature and divine necessity, consequentially follows wrongdoing makes it possible to presume, as many people do today, that anyone captured, convicted, or caged as a "criminal" is held captive because a transcendent principle of "justice" demands it. It is not even that actions defined as criminal or disorderly require punishment but that, by a seemingly natural and sacred arithmetic, crime essentially *causes*—in the sense of leading inevitably to—the punishment of those who commit it. In this way, carceral logic characterizes punishment as a natural consequence when in fact it is a fabricated response that seeks to restore subjection to social hierarchy. To escape what the state characterizes as the natural and sacred consequence that is punishment is, according to the state, to disrupt the natural and divine order of things. Moreover, if all punishment is effectively self-willed, then it is not authorities who punish but criminals who punish themselves. Punishment, in this way, becomes its own evidence of the criminality of the punished. This widely held presumption makes it difficult to discern carceral capture and captivity as anything other than a manifestation of the way things are just supposed to be, foreclosing any possibility of understanding human caging as unjust or evil in its own right. Additionally, if punishment is natural, a self-willed consequence of disrupting sacred social order, then the technologies of the state—handcuffs, squad cars, razor wire, concrete walls, surveillance technology, and weaponry—are naturally occurring and divinely willed phenomena. If sinners and criminals will their own captivity, then the mortal gods who hold the keys fulfill a crucial task in the natural and divine order of things. Thus, when it comes to the elimination and death of those who trespass against sacred order, the mortal God of police power can only, by definition, be innocent. He is, like the officer who arrested Vernon, only doing his job.

In an order that deifies whiteness and property by capturing and confining nonwhite and propertyless peoples at rates that far exceed those of all others, carceral captivity comes to be viewed in the popular imaginary not only as a natural consequence of disorderly or "criminal" actions abstractly conceived but as the natural destination of ontologically criminal Black, Indigenous, and propertyless life itself. If there happen to be more Black and dispossessed people in carceral captivity, this line of reasoning concludes, then it must be because they are more inherently criminal—inclined to refuse proper subjection—than the rest of us. In reality, it is racial capitalist settler colonial authority, including police power, that defines what constitutes criminality and projects it onto people who, according to ruling classes, embody an existential threat to order. As Ruth Wilson Gilmore writes, "Laws change, depending on what, in a social order, counts as stability, and who, in a social order, needs to be controlled."[75] Under a police power that hinges entirely on discretion, policing is the selective enforcement of laws for the maintenance of social and cosmic order.

While "law" and "order" have long been paired both conceptually and rhetorically, the early modern history of criminalization shows that the racial capitalist state is concerned first with order—hierarchical order in which a few exercise social, political, and economic power over many—which it subsequently forges and preserves through the sacredly authorized force of the law. The capitalist state and the law it enforces exist to preserve economic inequality, because, under capitalism, economic inequality is the basis of wealth, wealth is the basis of order, and the law exists to serve that order. As Adam Smith, author of the 1776 text *The Wealth of Nations*, a key text in the canon of capitalist theory, states plainly, "Civil government, so far as it is instituted for the security of property, is in reality instituted for the defence of the rich against the poor, or of those who have property against those who have none at all."[76] In a society in which wealth sits at the center of popular conceptions of morality and order, a society in which police power helps forge and maintain the hierarchies inherent to wealth, dispossessed peoples inevitably register as social and moral enemies who must be eliminated or controlled for the sake of us all.

The crux of constructions of criminality is disorder, and the crux of disorder is matter—and people—out of place.[77] In a fundamentally hierarchical order like that of the United States, being out of place means disrupting the divinely ordained hierarchies of power and security that constitute racial capitalist settler colonial order. In both a literal and symbolic sense, to be out of place is to "trespass." "Trespass" carries multiple meanings that are helpful for apprehending the dynamics of the religion of criminalization. Etymologically, since at least the fourteenth century, "trespass" has signified both an offense or a sin, on the one hand, and, on the other, an act of crossing over or passing across—both spatially and morally—that violates or infringes on law or norm.[78] We can also observe the historical and material formation of "trespass" as it relates to notions of debt, particularly through the Lord's Prayer of the Christian tradition. In speaking of what is forgiven in that prayer, Luke 11:2–4 and Matthew 6:12 use the Greek *aphiemi*, which signifies release from debt in both an economic and spiritual sense. Matthew 6:14, however, uses *paraptoma*, which signifies a trespass or sin. While most translations have retained both "debt" and "trespass," in the early modern era, at the same time as the birth of capitalism and the enclosure of common lands, English translations opted to use only "trespass." According to biblical scholar Dale Irvin, different early modern European translations, associated with different Christian movements, probably reflect subtle differences in social and economic contexts: those translations more closely tied to merchant classes emphasized debts, while those more closely tied to landed aristocracy emphasized trespass.[79] In any case, the distinction between "trespass" and "debt" is ultimately a distinction in emphasis, as opposed to a radical distinction in kind: moral trespass against God establishes a relation of indebted obligation to God.

Just as to trespass against God is to place oneself in a relation of guilt and obligation to God, so trespassing against the social order is to enter a relation of guilt and obligation to the social order and its managers. Likewise, just as salvific order is restored in carceral soteriology through a satisfaction of debt or punishment, so the punishment of carceral captivity has long been posed as a means by which people who have trespassed against law and order "pay their debt to society," as noted earlier. In ancient, medieval, and modern societies, a relation of debt was and is a relation of bondage, both in the sense of a relation of interpersonal obligation and in the material sense of the caging of people unable to pay off debts or, in the present day, unable to pay money bail or afford their own attorney. "Paying one's debt to society" is therefore not just a rhetorical flourish but a precise way of describing the theological-political dynamic between the mortal God of racial capitalist settler colonial order and its criminalized subjects. The modern carceral "payment" of debt "satisfies" not in the sense of freeing and restoring relation, as in some renderings of the Christian narrative, but in the sense of restoring hierarchical power relations in perpetuity. Unlike the God of the Christian tradition, the mortal gods of patriarchal and possessive whiteness do not desire restored relation with their inferiors but the maintenance of a deliberately subordinating, exploitative, and violent relation.[80] This is why people who have "paid their debt to society" by completing their sentence in prison are not freed from a relation of obligation and condemnation but remain in it through ongoing disenfranchisement and dispossession from housing and employment and through other forms of discrimination postrelease.

It is important to note that obligation itself is not an inherently dehumanizing dynamic; indeed, it is often a consensual feature of noncarceral modes of accountability and justice. The difference with the carceral obligation under which criminalized people live is that it is a set of deliberately dehumanizing modes of forced subjection that the state defines as a natural consequence of wrongdoing, when in fact it is a fabricated response to the order-disrupting offense of failing to be properly subject within existing social hierarchies. Moreover, whereas obligation in a noncarceral key is concerned with repairing harm by meeting the needs of those who have been harmed, the indebtedness of carceral obligation, oriented as it is around the idea that dispossessed "offenders" victimize the state, has nothing to do with meeting the complex needs of people who may have actually been harmed by an interpersonal violation made all but inevitable by the mass inequality on which capitalist order depends. Carceral obligation is obligation to a state that maintains hierarchies and is satisfied only when hierarchy is restored. As such, the debt that criminalized peoples owe cannot in fact be satisfied in a way that releases one from obligation: its satisfaction is secured only in its permanence.

In both carceral soteriology and carceral practice, the refusal to be properly subject to divine and political authority is understood to be a manifestation of a corrupted moral state: in theological terms, an inherent sinfulness, and in political terms, an inherent criminality. Carceral soteriology and modern liberal theory both rest on the presumption that the existence of sin necessitates the sword of the state: the state exists to prevent the descent into chaos that sin generates without subjection, as well as to maintain security and protect property. While a general sense of human finitude and sinfulness undergird theologies and philosophies of political authority throughout history and into the modern era, with the formation of the racial capitalist state, the order-maintaining violence of the state is justified on the basis not of the sinful criminality inherent to humanity generally but of the criminality inherent to nonwhite and propertyless peoples in particular. As a projected manifestation of something essential rather than happenstantial, the criminality of criminals is, for the racial capitalist settler colonial state, an expression of a nature disposed to an evil that threatens sacred social order and that must therefore be eliminated or brought under control.[81] In the end, the refusal to be properly subject that whiteness and property project onto their enemies is an invention of their own making, an invention that they need in order to exist at all. Thus, despite the seemingly individualized orientation of police and judicial processes in the United States, police power is only concerned with the individual "criminal" offender insofar as their punishment or elimination saves the social order that they disrupt by failing to be properly subject within it.

In an order built to materialize the divine aspirations of patriarchal and possessive whiteness, the personhood and self-determining agency of Black, Indigenous, other people of color, and propertyless peoples of all races register as acts of disorderly trespass—matter out of place. Much as in the divine scheme narrated by Christian carceral soteriology, police power restores order through punishment or elimination that returns people to their proper place in social and cosmic hierarchies, ensuring that the possessors of whiteness, property, and police power are God and that nonwhite and propertyless peoples are not. Indeed, as I explore more in chapter 4, the police power to eliminate the criminal enemies of the state reinforces the pseudo-divinity of both police power and the whiteness and property that it serves and protects and in so doing forges heaven for a white propertied few by disappearing many to carceral hell.

Taken up and elaborated by both religious and ruling-class architects of criminal punishment in the modern West, the carceral soteriologies developed by Augustine, Anselm, and Calvin, and many others along with them, have contributed to a conception of "justice" and a broader social imaginary in which disruptions of hierarchical social order are designated as "crime" and in which punishment or death are defined as the natural consequences of such disruptions—consequences that restore order, both social and cosmic alike. The European-American Christian, capitalist, and colonial societies that birthed police and carceral institutions produce order by proliferating the theological idea that sin against God—mortal or immortal—disrupts order and demands order-restoring satisfaction, which requires sacrifice. "That the answer to violence in the community is the violence of sacrificial death is taught Christian society by its faith," theologian Timothy Gorringe writes. "Criminals die to make satisfaction for their sins as Christ died for the sins of all."[82] More than just influencing systems of police power and carceral punishment, soteriologies of subjection provide conceptual infrastructure that sacralizes and becomes material infrastructure for police and carceral practice.[83] The mortal gods of police and carceral power mimic and strive to facilitate the world-rearranging power of salvific subjection that otherwise belongs only to the immortal God. As such, if we only see in prisons, jails, and police politically neutral mechanisms for facilitating "justice" in response to individual instances of lawbreaking, then we miss how they fulfill a much larger, mythological, and indeed religious function by helping to create and vigilantly defend the hierarchies of a functionally sacred racial capitalist settler colonial order.

4

Criminalization and Deification

Dispossession and criminalization are the sacred cornerstones of colonial racial capitalist order, without which it would cease to exist. Those whom racial capitalism dispossesses with one hand it criminalizes with the other: criminalization—and institutionalized police power more broadly—first emerged in the early modern era as a means of enforcing the allegedly God-ordained mass theft of land and wealth via the enclosure of the commons and of preserving the functionally sacred order of inequality that enclosure produced.[1] Through centuries of "bloody legislation," western European legislators and landowners treated those whom they dispossessed as trespassing, thieving, monstrous embodiments of evil engaged in war against moral and social order, while portraying their own, far greater acts of theft as natural, necessary, and even sacred.[2] An anonymous English poem captures the contradictions of privatization and criminalization well:

> The law locks up the man or woman
> Who steals the goose from off the common,
> But lets the greater villain loose
> Who steals the common from the goose.[3]

Through the enclosure of commonly tenured lands, capitalism took the ground under people's feet and called it someone else's sacred property, rendering those who were still standing on and obtaining their livelihood from it trespassers—literally matter out of place, which is to say, a disorderly desecration. In the wake of such evictions, western European states like England forced people displaced by capital to submit to the precarity of life as a wage laborer at the disposal of capital. While the life of a wage laborer was technically "free" from the feudal bonds that preceded it, in the absence of either customary rights to the commons or formal rights assuring adequate wages and fair treatment under increasingly expansive compulsory labor laws, the life of a wage laborer was—and still is—highly precarious and exploited, leading many people throughout the early modern era to regard it as "little better than slavery."[4]

Unsurprisingly, many of those who were already dispossessed by privatization in early modernity refused to be exploited through wage labor, a refusal that they enacted either through impromptu or organized acts of resistance or through simply opting to wander and beg for means of subsistence instead. Those who did not properly submit to the allegedly God-ordained task of laboring to produce other people's wealth, the state criminalized, captured, punished, and treated as a criminal threat to the social order itself, all for trying to survive a condition into which the theologically legitimated greed of landowners and legislators forced them. In these ways, those who were dispossessed by early agrarian capitalism were stuck between a rock and a hard place, forced to choose between an unprotected existence at the disposal of exploitative bosses or a life of vagrancy criminalized through punishment, forced labor, torture, imprisonment, or death. The dispossession that the state, in coordination with wealthy landowners, created through mass theft and displacement with one hand it exploited and criminalized with the other. The birth of racial capitalism and the birth of modern police and prisons constitute not two histories but one: the dual task of enforcing capitalist dispossession and managing its outcomes gave us police and carceral power as we know them today.

The Refusal to Be Subject to Capital

For the early modern pro-enclosure ruling class, "God is the God of order" who secures wealth and power for those who are ordained to possess them. As such, those who disrupt the accumulation of capital were "disorderly" enemies of God who must, for the sake of sacred order, be brought under control or eliminated altogether.[5] One of the main means by which the early modern state controlled and eliminated dispossessed peoples was through vagrancy laws. Emerging in tandem with compulsory labor laws that ensured a steady labor supply and counteracted organized resistance to enclosure and exploitation, vagrancy laws naturalized mass accumulation that generated dispossession by locating the origins of poverty in the alleged moral failing of the dispossessed rather than in the capitalist acts of theft that actually caused it.[6] Vagrancy laws prohibited a wide range of activities that were seen as potential or actual disruptions of public order and political economy and as a sign of a person's propensity for immoral and criminal activity.[7] Among the terms by which modern authorities coded the allegedly immoral and disruptive character of the masses of unemployed commoners, few were more prominent than "idleness." Viewed by legislators and property owners as "the primary cause of social disorder," idleness was a term that helped delineate what Matthew Beaumont calls "the Devil's poor," those who were allegedly able-bodied but unwilling to labor for a wage, from "God's poor," those who were physically disabled and thus unable to labor.[8] The idle vagrant who, "although able to work, refuses to do so," was, both de facto and de jure, guilty of what the English jurist William Blackstone called in 1769 a "high offence against the public economy," both because their idleness was understood as the first step down a slippery slope toward further criminality and because it constituted a willful refusal of the religious, patriarchal, and capitalist virtue of industriousness on which the "public economy" depended.[9] In every case, idleness was widely perceived not as a mere annoyance but as the refusal to be properly subject to capital and thus as an intolerable threat to the state and economy that should be punished accordingly.[10]

Like the God of carceral soteriology, the God of capital can be omnipotent only when many are made subject beneath him. To be idle in a capitalist order is to refuse proper subjection to the laws of capital and, by extension, to the laws of God and nature. Idleness, then, for the ruling class, constituted a manifestation of order-disrupting immorality, and for both liberal political mythology and carceral soteriology, to disrupt order is to render oneself an enemy and thus to will one's own punishment or even outright elimination, both of which restore order by restoring the hierarchy on which order depends. Under a 1536 act against vagrants prohibiting and punishing public begging, upon their third infraction, vagabonds "should suffer execution as a felon and an enemy of the commonwealth."[11] A 1547 act prescribing punishment for vagabonds proclaimed that anyone who "refuses to work . . . shall be condemned as a slave to the person who has denounced him as an idler. The master has the right to force him to do any work, no matter how vile, with whip and chains. If the slave is absent for a fortnight, he is condemned to slavery for life and is to be branded on forehead or back with the letter S; if he runs away three times, he is to be executed as a felon."[12] Under a 1572 act, rogues, vagabonds, and "sturdy beggars" who were caught "wandering, and mis-ordering themselves" were deemed "outrageous enemies to the common weal" who, upon conviction, should be "whipped and burnt through the gristle of the right ear with a hot iron, manifesting his or her roguish kind of life."[13] In the words of a sixteenth-century English financial administrator, idleness, "the very mother of all vice," is "the deadlie enemy to this tree of common wealth."[14] To refuse subjection to capital is to declare oneself an enemy of all humankind. And to be an enemy of all humankind is to be an enemy of God. From the enclosure of the commons to vagrancy acts and compulsory labor laws, wealthy property owners and state authorities created the conditions of mass disenfranchisement and then defined and treated those who were forced into such conditions as dangerous enemies of the state who, for the sake of sacred order, must either be brought under state control or disposed of altogether.

Modern police and prisons first came into existence to enforce racial capitalist dispossession and manage its outcomes. In the early modern era, much as today, to exist outside the spatial and temporal partitions of the owner-laborer relation was—and is—to embody the disorder of matter out of place. By the seventeenth century, English vagrants and able-bodied beggars were often targeted by proto-police night watch and constable forces who apprehended and forced them to give a good reason as to their idleness or wandering. If they were unable to offer a satisfactory explanation, they were often sent to the jail attached to the court and from there to newly created houses of correction, including the famous "Bridewell." Founded in the mid-sixteenth century in London and replicated in England and beyond in the centuries that followed, the central purpose of these early "houses of correction" was to correct the allegedly immoral dispositions of dispossessed vagrants and beggars who, by refusing to labor to generate other people's wealth, disrupted capitalist order.[15] If the problem of idleness was the problem of the refusal to be subject to capital, the refusal to work, then the primary means of such correction was forced labor under conditions of confinement.[16] According to historian Adam Hirsch, idleness in England and colonial

America was often "likened to a degenerative disease" that could only be treated with the "therapy" of hard labor in houses of correction, as well as in workhouses, an institutional offshoot of the Bridewell.[17] First emerging as a state response to resistance among working-class weaver communities in London who agitated against mechanization that benefited owners but further dispossessed workers, workhouses became what Peter Linebaugh calls "locations of struggle" for freedom that shaped both capitalism and the state's defense of it in the era that followed.[18]

Born of the aspiration to subdue and eliminate dispossessed populations whose alleged refusal to be subject to social and economic hierarchy was viewed as inherently "injurious to the state," police power—and, by extension, the carceral caging power of the Bridewell, workhouse, and later the penitentiary—first emerged, in the words of Mark Neocleous, "to *make the working class work*."[19] More than simply enforced by police, vagrancy laws served as a premise for the full, institutionalized emergence of police power more broadly. As political theorists David Correia and Tyler Wall write, "The hunting and capturing of vagrants across Europe . . . was the 'founding act' of police power, and vagrancy would continue to be a central object of police pursuit in essentially every historical stage of the police."[20]

For the police-power-wielding state and the ruling-class architects of the Bridewell and workhouse, the primary purpose of capture and forced labor under confinement was to counteract the disruptions of both idleness and working-class resistance by teaching the "discipline of production" and thereby instilling a moral ethos of "submission" and "obedience" to authority outside the walls.[21] Bearing the imprint of a carceral soteriology that locates salvation in subjection to sovereign authority, the discipline of labor that early carceral institutions sought to instill was at the same time a thoroughly religious discipline as well. Indeed, according to Georg Rusche and Otto Kirchheimer, "the use of religion as a means of inculcating discipline and hard labor was an essential feature" of houses of correction across Europe.[22] One seventeenth-century Jesuit priest advocating the establishment of houses of correction for vagrants and beggars in Paris captured the fusion of religious and capitalist rationales when he argued that the institutions would be "at once a religious institution, a seminary, and manufactories."[23] The power of police is the power to forge and defend sacred social order by coercing into submission—or outright eliminating—the enemies of God and order. The power of police is the power of the mortal God.

Wealthy modern enclosers, clergy, legislators, and philosophers propagated the idea that privatization corresponded to God's will, that God institutes state power to preserve property, and that people dispossessed of property disobeyed God. In the same way, vagrancy laws enacted by the police power of the state further solidified the idea that poverty was a direct result of dispossessed people's "moral disorder" and disobedience to God.[24] By the end of the seventeenth century and the full arrival of capitalism, Christopher Hill writes, "Labour, the curse of fallen man, had become a religious duty, a means of glorifying God in our calling. Poverty had ceased to be a holy state and had become presumptive evidence of wickedness."[25] By naturalizing and sacralizing the capitalist causes of poverty, blaming the dispossessed for their own hardships, and punishing those struggling to survive it, vagrancy laws and houses of correction facilitated the conceptual merger of poverty and criminality in the popular imaginary, a conflation that persists to this day. Poor people are poor, the story goes, because of an immorality exemplified by the refusal to be subject to God's law and the laws of capital and property that derive from it. And by refusing to be properly subject, one becomes a danger to the social order: a "criminal." As one nineteenth-century British commentator argued, crime arises most predominantly from those who "will not work."[26] It was on this premise that early modern proto-police forces captured those who refused to be subject to an order based on capital and then caged them as a means of restoring them to proper subjection to "the discipline of wages," a discipline framed at nearly every stage in terms of morality.[27]

The connection between the refusal to be subject and the notion of criminality is also evident in the language that propertied and lawmaking classes used to refer to working-class and underclass peoples in early modern England and colonial America. A common designation used for people dispossessed of access to land in those times and places was "masterless" people. Masterless people were masterless, first of all, in the sense of illegally existing outside of master-serf or owner-laborer relations. Masterless people were also so defined because they were characterized as inherently disposed to rebellious, disobedient, and criminal behavior. In short, one is masterless—literally without a master—because one has refused subjection to any authority. Much as for carceral soteriology, for the ruling class, the central threat posed by the refusal to be subject to capital is that it upsets the social hierarchies and power dynamics on which the social order depends. Likewise, just as subjection to God in carceral soteriology is a dependent form of subjection to the source of life that meets all human needs, so subjection to capital and the discipline of labor is falsely framed as a form of dependence on a system that provides for one's needs. As hundreds of millions of people across the globe can attest, capitalism does not meet people's most basic needs and indeed deliberately prevents it. As with those who refuse submission to the sovereign God, those who refuse submission to capital are understood to will their own poverty and thus their exile, punishment, and premature death. As such, those who suffer or are captured or caged at the hands of an order that does not in fact meet everyone's needs are said to be responsible for their own conditions of precarity: capital is circulating as nature intends, and the mortal God of the state is just doing its job of controlling and eliminating those whose disorderly refusal to be subject poses a threat to the continued functioning of sacred order.

Puritans and Penitentiaries

In the wake of the proliferation of vagrancy laws, two of the most foundational examples of the religious making of the pseudo-divine state power to capture and confine the enemies of God and order are the covenantal criminalization facilitated by the Puritans and the mortifying salvation facilitated by the penitentiary. The Calvinist Puritans of the sixteenth and seventeenth centuries in England and colonial America built their order-maintaining criminal punishment institutions as expressions of their understandings of their social covenant with God. From the point of view of early American Puritans, civil society is bound by a covenant with God such that social life must align with God's precepts or else be exposed to God's wrath. In Puritan theology and law, the state exists in large part to bind disobedient sinners and criminals to proper subjection to God and state.[28] As such, the Puritans believed that criminal sanction or punishment was a means by which to uphold their covenant with God. For the Puritans and many after them, crime was, in the words of Hirsch, "an outgrowth of the offender's estrangement from God" that threatened the whole community by compromising the community's covenant with God. "Puritans conceived that they had bound themselves to obey the Lord's commands; sins accordingly represented an affront to God, and their punishment constituted an expiatory obligation to His authority."²⁹ Channeling an explicitly carceral soteriology, the Puritans arranged their society on the basis of the idea that the refusal to be subject to divine and political authority offends God and threatens sacred social order and that only punishment can restore that order. Puritan ministers often formally accompanied colonial processions to the gallows and regularly proclaimed, in the words of historian Jennifer Graber, "that civil government served as God's institution for keeping social order" and that "lawbreakers under judgment represented the entire community's sins."³⁰

Predominant Protestant political theologies in colonial America, including that of the Puritans, articulated a carceral soteriology by defining criminality as a refusal to be subject to divine and political authority. As theological ethicist Christophe Ringer outlines, in Puritan politics and theology, Blackness and Black criminality in particular were understood as manifestations of a disobedient desire for a freedom that, according to eurochristian political theology, was not natural to Black life.³¹ The popular Puritan minister Cotton Mather characterized this sinful Black desire as a "fondness for freedom" that leads only to ruin and death.³² Benjamin Wadsworth, a minister and contemporary of Mather, equated the alleged disobedience of unruly enslaved Africans with "disobedience to God" and the rebellion of freedom-seeking enslaved peoples as "rebellion against [God]." By living out their fondness for freedom, Wadsworth proclaimed, enslaved Africans "trample God's law, his Authority, under their feet."³³ Thus did Mather and Wadsworth articulate a racialized carceral soteriology of subjection: criminality—and Black criminality in particular—is a matter of the disobedient refusal to be properly subject to divine and political authority, an intolerable disobedience that, by jeopardizing society's covenant with God, threatens the very existence of social order itself.

The dynamics of this racial-carceral soteriology come into even sharper focus in the sermon that Mather preached as part of the 1721 execution of a formerly enslaved African man named Joseph Hanno, who was charged with killing his wife. Employing the theo-carceral logics of punishment and purity alongside the covenantal theology of Puritan governance that renders sin a threat to the entire community, Mather proclaimed that "*Sin* must be punished," that "the Infinite *Justice* of GOD must be satisfied," and that, were Hanno's life to be spared, the land in which they lived would be "polluted."[34] For Mather and the Puritans, criminal punishment that excises moral pollution maintains the purity of sacred social order by maintaining Puritan society's good standing with God the just judge. As such, Hanno's execution constituted what Ringer calls "an act of expiation."[35] For the Puritans, and for American society more broadly, Ringer suggests, to contain, punish, and even execute disobedient Black life is to defend and purify social order.[36]

Up until the late eighteenth century, in addition to forced labor under conditions of confinement, punishment for vagrancy, petty theft, and other crimes against the order of property was often public and gruesome and included public torture, whippings, and executions. Starting in the late eighteenth and early nineteenth centuries, in response to the growing ineffectiveness of more public and corporal punishments, and with a desire for an approach that married effectiveness and more humane treatment, Protestant religious reformers and officials in the postrevolutionary United States developed a new carceral form, the penitentiary, which combined the forced manual labor under confinement that characterized European bridewells and workhouses with an added emphasis on morally redemptive isolation.[37] Despite popular framings of the penitentiary's seemingly humane focus on rehabilitation, the rehabilitation that the penitentiary sought to facilitate was, with only minor differences, the same rehabilitation that animated the English houses of correction: rehabilitation to the moral and social discipline of sacred subjection to capital and all other forms of authority, which is to say, the discipline of returning to one's proper place within sacred social hierarchies. Thus, contrary to many historical accounts, the penitentiary—an institution established and managed by a racial capitalist settler colonial state—represented not so much a break from but an elaboration of early capitalist carceral power and as such was an institution populated predominantly with people forced into precarity by racial capitalist settler colonial order.

With brick and stone, the early nineteenth-century penitentiary gave material form to the idea that sinners and criminals are guilty of the failure to be subject to divine and political authority and that salvation demands a return to supposedly life-giving subjection. Through the penitentiary, reformers cast solitary confinement and forced labor as a just, effective, and allegedly humane punishment designed to draw feelings of remorse out of criminals and, in the case of dispossessed people guilty of idleness or crimes against order and property, to "spark a craving for employment."[38] If criminality, as reformers believed, was "an outgrowth of the offender's estrangement from God," then prison, they argued in explicit terms, should be a kind of church.[39]

Despite the veneer of humanitarian concern, however, the penitentiary was in fact a site of immense state violence, violence that administrators and chaplains framed as an extension of divine violence necessary for the restoration of order. As literary theorist Caleb Smith shows, literature produced by reformers, theorists, and writers from the late eighteenth and early nineteenth centuries typically figures the prisoner in one of two ways: "a reflecting, self-governing soul," on the one hand, and a mortified and "dehumanized body," on the other. While these two seem to be utterly distinct and irreconcilable—one emphasizing a redeemed soul and the other a kind of living corpse—they are both in fact "fundamental to the carceral imagination of the last two centuries." Contrary to common presumption, dehumanization and redemption represent two dimensions of a single process that the penitentiary sought to facilitate. In Smith's analysis, the logic or "poetics" of the penitentiary was "organized around a narrative of rebirth," which "required, as a precondition, the convict's virtual death." For the administrators and chaplains of the penitentiary, redemption is only possible through the mortification and death of the old self that makes way for the resurrection of the new self. As Smith summarizes,

> The prison adapted ancient myths of resurrection to the demands of a post-Revolutionary social contract. It was a "living tomb" of servitude and degradation as well as the space of the citizen-subject's dramatic reanimation. Its legal codes divested the convict of rights; its ritualized disciplinary practices stripped away his identity; it exposed him to arbitrary and discretionary violence at the hands of his keepers; it buried him alive

in a solitary cell. But it also promised him a glorious return to citizenship and humanity. It mortified the body, but it also claimed to renovate the soul. Its ideal subject was one who, in the words of one great Philadelphia reformer, "was dead and is alive."[40]

The language of dehumanization did not come exclusively from those who were protesting the conditions of penitentiaries. Indeed, Smith writes, "The very reformers who built the prison system understood it as a place of deliberate mortification."[41] Deploying the concept and practice of civil death, which is central to the mythological origins of the social contract that sacrifices liberty in exchange for security, the penitentiary shared with the plantation the power to strip all power and identity from those who were confined therein to such an extent that social commentators at the time argued that the convicts who endured the "living death" of the penitentiary approached "the condition of a Slave."[42]

The death-like passage from the free world to the penitentiary cell in nineteenth-century America took the form of what Smith calls a "political ritual, a drama of power and subjection" that enacted the story of the modern social contract whereby those who transgress the social contract lose their right to life and liberty and in essence will their own virtual death.[43] Upon the entrance of a newly convicted person into the prison, penitentiary staff removed all semblances of their selfhood—their clothing, hair, and name—and placed them in a hooded garment resembling a burial shroud while escorting them to their cell.[44] As the warden of New York's Auburn Prison told his inmates in 1826, "While confined here . . . you are to be literally buried from the world."[45] Auburn and other prisons across the Northeast, Smith writes, regularly "depicted the convict's initiation to penitence as a ritualized burial."[46] When Charles Dickens visited Eastern State Penitentiary in the early nineteenth century, he observed that the prisoner is "a man buried alive."[47] The seeming paradox between reformers' vision of a humane institution for moral rehabilitation and the reality of carceral dehumanization was hardly a paradox for those who envisioned and operated such institutions: in order to be reborn, one has to die, and the penitentiary helped realize that civil and social death. As imprisoned Black Panther George Jackson wrote in 1970, a century and a half after the birth of the penitentiary, "Capture is the closest thing to being dead that one is likely to experience in this life."⁴⁸ One early nineteenth-century prison chaplain, the Reverend John Stanford, preached his very first prison sermon from Isaiah 48:10: "Behold, I have refined thee, but not with silver; I have chosen thee in the furnace of affliction."⁴⁹ According to Graber, Stanford argued that "the prison hosted the fullness of divine action, including the suffering necessary for redemption. He believed that criminals necessarily experienced state-imposed physical and psychological pain. While humiliating and awful, such torments were necessary."⁵⁰ While redemption was available to convicted criminals, those who "obey not," Stanford would say, "shall perish by the sword."⁵¹ Carceral violence was and often still is understood as a medium of divine violence and thus wholly legitimate, even sacred.⁵²

For a carceral soteriology of subjection, the problem of the sin of the refusal to be subject is that, by claiming more power for oneself than God or nature allow and thereby failing to acknowledge God as God and oneself as not God, humans disrupt the hierarchy of the God-human relationship. The problem of sin, in short, is the problem of people out of place vis-à-vis divine authority. Similarly, for carceral, racial capitalist settler colonial society, the problem of criminality is the disruption of hierarchical order: people out of place, which is to say, people claiming more freedom, power, and self-determination for themselves than the mortal God of the state allows. To be idle in a capitalist order, to trespass in a propertied order, to inhabit space communally in a privatized order, to be Black in a white order, to claim for oneself what racial capitalist order reserves for only a few—these are what it means to be out of place, disorderly, in a colonial racial capitalist world. As I have shown, the world of inherently oppositional boundaries, borders, fences, and gates is a world conceptualized in terms of the sacred, such that physically or symbolically transgressing such partitions is an act of desecration, a rebellious rejection of God's will for the world. Just as sin disrupts distinctions in kind between God and humans, criminality disrupts distinctions in class—and race and gender—in a capitalist society. In response to such disruptions, the police power to capture and the carceral power to contain the enemies of God and order reestablish order by reestablishing the hierarchical distinctions that criminality disrupts and on which order depends. As Massimo Pavarini writes, the criminalization and confinement of dispossessed peoples reasserts "the clear distinction between the world of property owners and the world of the propertyless."⁵³ In the face of the disorder unleashed by the disruption of hierarchy, police and carceral power reestablish the "*vertical relations*" on which sacred social order depends.⁵⁴ The telos of carceral soteriology and practice is to secure the Godness of God, mortal and immortal alike.

Despite the attempts of some reformers to develop penitentiaries as a formally religious institution, the form that stuck packaged prison's religiously conceived functions in more secular terms.⁵⁵ And yet, regardless of how it was articulated, the overall vision of an institution that forcibly restored people to proper subjection to divine and political authority, and thus to their proper place within social and cosmic hierarchies, remained the same. Syncretizing religious and political rationales, penitentiaries articulated a spiritual-secular morality based in obedient citizenship, respect for property, and the discipline of wage labor, a morality they sought to instill through processes of subjection that would, in Foucault's words, "restore to the state the subject it had lost."⁵⁶ Producing good citizenship and instilling the principle of obedience to authority were core purposes of penitentiaries because those who were caged inside their walls were understood to have refused proper subjection and obedience to authority, thereby misplacing themselves within social hierarchies and in turn generating disorder. As such, for the sake of both the sacred social order and those who were accused of disrupting it, the penitentiary used mortifying violence in an attempt to transform dispossessed peoples from disorderly to disciplined, from savage to civilized, from rebellious to obedient.⁵⁷

Before, during, and on the other side of the penitentiary's predominance, carceral institutions have been places for disciplining, punishing, and managing primarily dispossessed and propertyless peoples whose actions under conditions of forced precarity form the basis of state definitions of immorality and criminality. Even the charitable spirit of some nineteenth-century Protestant prison reformers was nevertheless a paternalistic one that still viewed dispossessed peoples as particularly depraved people whose agency and inclinations necessitated carceral intervention to restore subjection and order. While reformers, legislators, and state authorities determined people previously proximate to patriarchal whiteness and property to be more inherently capable of rehabilitating to their previous state prior to their crime, almost everyone else was deemed inherently incapable of staying in their proper place apart from state coercion. As such, a primary purpose of the state power to capture and confine was—and is—to incapacitate and warehouse the most disorderly and rebellious members of society's "dangerous classes."[58] While many early reformers and legislators believed that at least some caged people were capable of restoration, others believed that anyone whom police brought to the jail, the courthouse, or the prison gate was already inherently irredeemable.[59] As one chaplain put it, prisoners are, by definition, a "great moral waste."[60] The police power of the mortal God is the power to serve and protect—and thus to save—sacred social order by redeeming the redeemable and eliminating the irredeemable, ontologically corrupted enemies of all humankind.

Controlling the "Dangerous Classes"

The desecrating "disorder" that racial capitalism fears most is a manifestation of the inequalities it produces and on which it depends. Disorder, for capitalism, is anything that threatens to disrupt the pseudo-sacred hierarchies and differentiations that produce and reproduce wealth and power, which includes people who fail or refuse to labor to produce other people's wealth, people who transgress pseudo-sacred racialized, classed, and gendered boundaries of property and containment, and people who organize themselves to undermine the arrangements that produce their conditions of dispossession. In every case, the threat of disorder is the threat of the immoral refusal to be properly subject, the threat of matter and people out of place, all of which amounts to a threat to the sacred as defined by the architects of order. Controlling the movement and activity of those whose actions and personhood register as a threat to sacred social order—the so-called dangerous classes—was thus a foundational impetus behind the state power to formally "police" populations and specifically in the creation of formalized, professionalized police departments across the United States and Europe in the nineteenth and early twentieth centuries.

While police power did not formally institutionalize as municipal or state police forces until the nineteenth century, the state and private power to monitor and control populations had existed in a variety of forms for centuries. Derived from the broad patriarchal power of the state to exercise discretionary force for the sake of preserving order, the English precursors of the formal police forces instituted in England—and in parts of the United States—in the early nineteenth century originated in the eleventh-century Norman frankpledge system that deployed "shire-reeves" or "sheriffs" to collect fees and represent the king in shires (districts) across England.[61] So-called justices of the peace and constables later came to replace sheriffs and fulfilled duties on behalf of the state, such as collecting taxes, inspecting highways, and serving as magistrates in towns and cities.[62] In the thirteenth century, well-populated English towns instituted a system of night watch that surveilled the allegedly criminal behavior of dispossessed peoples who walked the streets at night.[63] In an early modern era in which wage labor was "gendered as male" and women's work was largely unrecognized and uncompensated, dispossessed women who, lacking any other means of subsistence, turned to sex work for survival were widely criminalized not only for engaging in morally impure acts but for disrupting the daily rhythms of capitalism by posing "nocturnal temptations" to men whose wealth-building productivity during the day depended on a restful night.[64] Beginning as a compulsory, unpaid duty fulfilled by adult men, in the eighteenth century, London's night watch became a semiprofessionalized policing body that paid and equipped its officers and, as such, Kristian Williams argues, "came very nearly to resemble the modern police department that replaced it."[65]

As the highly exploitative wage-labor system—and the wealth it produced—grew from the late seventeenth to the nineteenth century, so did the need for means of security to maintain and reinforce it, which led to a drastic expansion of acts constituting capital offense before the law, a significant portion of which focused on crimes against property.[66] Building on the night watch, and in response to a series of working-class uprisings, legislators and elites of the late eighteenth century created numerous proto-police forces, including Henry Fielding's Bow Street Runners in 1749, a force tasked with hunting and capturing people suspected of theft and subduing popular working-class revolts in an increasingly stratified society. In 1800, the West India Company, together with Patrick Colquhoun, formed what would come to be known as the Thames

River Police for the specific purpose of criminalizing London dock workers' long-permissible custom of taking gleanings from the products of their labor, an act that authorities redefined during the late eighteenth century as a criminal act of theft that undermined both profit and the wage system as a whole.[67]

Through writings and legislative advocacy, Fielding, Colquhoun, and other leading figures in commerce and police power built on the tradition of criminalizing dispossessed peoples by arguing for the expansion of police on the basis of the idea that the corrupted morality of dispossessed peoples posed a threat to society as a whole. In Fielding's words, the criminal conduct of the lower classes "tears both the moral fiber and the social fabric of the community," and "criminal punishment serves to mend that tear."[68] Likewise, for Colquhoun, the "evil," morally corrupted nature of the "lower classes" was the primary source of the criminal disorder that "injured and endangered" "public and private property and security."[69] The conditions of precarity and desperation that racial capitalism generates both produce wealth and threaten to undermine it. To counteract the disorderly threat of the dangerous classes, both Fielding and Colquhoun proposed and developed forms of state subjection and violence as means of maintaining capitalist order. Mirroring the acts of enclosure that criminalized the acts of survival of those who were displaced from the commons, Fielding, Colquhoun, and industrial capitalists of the late eighteenth and early nineteenth centuries expanded the reach of capital by expanding the reach of the police power to criminalize the allegedly immoral, irreligious masses of people that capital forcibly dispossessed.[70]

During the late eighteenth and early nineteenth centuries, an informal "patchwork of public and private police forces" kept watch over the "dangerous classes" of dispossessed Londoners until, in response to an alleged rise in property crime and ongoing working-class uprisings across England and its colonies, Parliament passed the Metropolitan Police Act in 1829, developed by Sir Robert Peel, creating the Metropolitan Police of London, one of the first formal state-run police departments in the modern era.[71] As the manager of Britain's colonial occupation of Ireland, Peel developed highly organized "police" strategies to impose colonial rule and manage the threats posed by dispossessed peoples who organized themselves to challenge the sources of their exploitation and suffering. Britain's colonial expansion and warfare around the globe meant traditional military forces were not as readily available to respond to social unrest in Ireland, and even when they were, they proved themselves incapable of the kinds of agile social control Peel desired. As a result, Peel formed proto-police "peace" forces that surveilled local communities from which anticolonial resistance emerged, which eventually led to the formation of the Royal Irish Constabulary that policed rural Ireland and helped preserve British colonial control of the region for a century. What Peel learned and developed in the occupation of Ireland he proposed as a solution to English authorities' inability to adequately subdue strikes, uprisings, and property crime across England, all of which threatened to undermine a social order based on wealth-generating exploitation in the form of wage labor. After a state cavalry murdered working-class demonstrators protesting the effects of industrialization in Manchester in 1819—an event remembered as the "Peterloo Massacre"—the British state passed new vagrancy laws designed to funnel people into productive wage labor. But without a well-organized professional police force, it was impossible to adequately enforce such laws or neutralize the threats to order posed by dispossessed peoples.[72] Building on the work of John Fielding, Henry Fielding, Patrick Colquhoun, and others before him, Peel posed professional police forces as the answer to the challenge of how to maintain the social hierarchies necessary for capitalism to function. Indeed, despite claims to "political neutrality," Alex Vitale argues, the history of the genesis of the London Metropolitan Police clearly demonstrates that its "main functions" were to "protect property, quell riots, put down strikes and other industrial actions, and produce a disciplined industrial work force."[73]

By the middle of the nineteenth century, northern US cities including Boston, New York, and Chicago began implementing the London model approach to policing to disrupt and quell working-class organization and resistance similar to that which emerged in response to industrialization in England.[74] Most major US cities had incorporated a professional police force before the end of the nineteenth century. Newly formed northern police departments during this era overwhelmingly articulated their reason for existence in relation to the presence of a morally "dangerous" underclass and working class composed in large part of new European immigrants. As the general superintendent of police in Chicago wrote in 1876, "There is in every large city, a dangerous class of idle, vicious persons, eager to band themselves together, for purposes subversive to the public peace and good government."[75] Much like the English authorities of the seventeenth through nineteenth centuries, police chiefs in the US perceived the threat posed by dispossessed peoples, on the one hand, in terms of a criminality rooted in idleness that creates disorder and, on the other, in terms of the potential for organized resistance, as when poor and working-class people "band themselves together." Subtle and not-so-subtle racialized white Protestant resentment against working-class European immigrants—before many of those immigrants became racialized as "white"—also helped expand the reach of urban police forces in the Northeast and Midwest, where so-called vice or morality laws gave officers a legal basis to surveil and capture working-class immigrants, disrupting both their daily lives and their ability to organize effectively against exploitative industry.[76]

In response to industry owners unwilling to relinquish their wealth and control over the working-class populations that helped produce their wealth, a widespread organized labor movement emerged in the late nineteenth century that deployed a diversity of tactics in pursuit of achieving more equitable compensation, benefits, treatment, and control of their workplaces. Created as state means of social control in an increasingly industrialized and stratified society, northern police forces responded to the labor movement with duties ranging from targeting the behaviors of poor and immigrant workers using retooled vagrancy laws to surveilling labor organizing and violently disrupting workers' strikes in factories and mills. Before municipal police forces took on this duty, many industry owners contracted with private parties to commit violence against workers in the interest of preserving their property and the inequities inherent to their workplaces. When this proved too costly and difficult for company owners to fund and coordinate over time, the duty of keeping a lid on working-class resistance passed to state and local police forces that used violence and terror against workers as a means of preserving the interests of wealthy business owners. During the Great Railroad Strike of 1877, for instance, in which railroad workers from the Midwest, Appalachia, and the Northeast ceased work in opposition to the mass exploitation of their labor, police and militias defended the interests and properties of owners through mass violence. In Chicago, police killed as many as thirty-five people. Whereas previously, many northern elites had become skeptical that police were adequately effective in defending their interests, police silenced their ruling-class doubters through their violence in 1877 and further ensured their place as defenders of capitalist order.[77] Antilabor strikebreaking, carried out on behalf of wealthy industrialists, was central to late nineteenth- and early twentieth-century policing, helped legitimate police in the eyes of elites, and thereby solidified their role as defenders of the hierarchies required by a functionally sacred racial capitalist order.

In order for patriarchal and possessive whiteness to attain to godlike "ownership of the earth forever and ever, Amen!" the criminal threat of disorder posed by the people whom racial capitalism and settler colonialism dispossess must be managed and ultimately eliminated. As I posited in chapter 3, eliminating threats to sacred order requires divinely ordained violence, and the divinely ordained use of violence belongs to police. Police are best understood as a mortal God in the sense that police power creates the conditions for whiteness to be divine and for property to be sacred, defends whiteness and property from the enemies of God and order, and sustains them by reproducing their pseudo-divine status through the order-maintenance interventions they carry out. As forces that come into being and reproduce themselves through antagonism and violence toward those whom they construct as other, whiteness and property can only exist at all, and can only approximate godlike power, through the dispossession, suffering, and death of those whom they exploit and against whom they define themselves as superior. It is therefore not simply that whiteness is first divine and that property is first sacred and that police subsequently defend that divinity and sacrality; rather, the very act of criminalization, by eliminating living disruptions to racial accumulation by dispossession, reinforces the functional omnipotence of whiteness and property within the social order that revolves around them. In short, police power fulfills—actualizes—the aspiration of patriarchal and possessive whiteness to possess and control the world; apart from the creative, world-making violence of police, it is only an aspiration. Criminalization deifies some by destroying others.

Criminalizing Blackness, Deifying Whiteness

In addition to and in connection with acts of enclosure and exploitative wage labor, racial capitalism's most significant form of mass dispossession was the system of chattel slavery through which European and European-American colonizers kidnapped, confined, abused, and exploited more than ten million people of African descent, forcing them to build wealth and infrastructure for people who came to be known as "white" on the colonized lands of Indigenous peoples. As outlined in chapter 1, for many European slave owners, slavery was not just an economic and social good but a moral, divinely sanctioned good. Jewish and Christian scripture seemingly refrain from ever outright condemning enslavement, they reasoned, and natural law dictates that different peoples have different natures, making them fit for different places within social hierarchy.[78] Constructed as an approximation of divinity, whiteness, and white propertied manhood in particular, was constructed as an eminently moral ontological position characterized by superior capacities for reason, management, and governance. European colonizers constructed nonwhiteness, on the other hand, and Blackness in particular, as a manifestation of alienation from God, constructing people of African descent as more inherently depraved than others. Blackness, from the eurochristian perspective, meant inferior reasoning capacities, animality, sexual insatiability, uncivilized savagery, and a "natural" disposition for manual labor. Indeed, slave owners went so far as to suggest that because liberal freedom does not suit Black nature, it would in fact destroy Black people and, by extension, the white people endangered by their free presence. Simply put, from the perspective of those who forged racial capitalism and the system of chattel slavery at its heart, whiteness entails freedom, authority, and ownership, while Blackness entails—and indeed is made for—subjection. Just as the Apostle Paul enjoined Christians to a kind of "slavery to God," many eurochristian colonizers and missionaries enjoined enslaved Africans, through conversion, to enter a state of subjection not only to God but to the godlike power of whiteness.[79]

Much as with racial capitalism's other modes of wealth-generating dispossession, chattel slavery both depended on and reproduced police power as a means of functionally deifying a few by controlling a demonized and racialized many. Indeed, at the exact same time that seventeenth-century English landowners and legislators were forging early manifestations of police power by forcibly displacing people from common lands and then criminalizing them as a means of forcing them into exploitative wage-labor relations, English colonists in Barbados and other Caribbean colonies were forging police power by instituting slave patrols to exercise near total control over the Africans whom they enslaved and whose forced labor generated their wealth. Taking shape in and through one another, Europeanness became so enmeshed with the work of surveilling and controlling dispossessed and African peoples that the two became functionally inextricable: the mortal God of police meets and becomes the mortal God of whiteness.

European colonizers' aspiration to exercise godlike control over their human property was rooted in a combination of racialized fear and capitalist necessity. From the perspective of the colonizers in Barbados, articulated in the 1661 law they instituted, the "heathenish," "brutish," and "dangerous" African peoples they enslaved were naturally inclined to refuse subjection, commit acts of theft, and organize rebellion, all of which manifested their allegedly inherent immorality.[80] By rejecting subordination and by trespassing against the laws of property, colonizers suggested, enslaved Africans posed the order-desecrating threat of matter out of place. To counteract that threat, Barbadian plantation owners in the early seventeenth century enlisted overseers and privately hired slave catchers to enforce slave codes that regulated the movement and activity of those whom they enslaved and to capture and return to proper subjection those who escaped their captivity. When private overseers struggled to adequately surveil and control the growing number of enslaved Africans imported to the colonies, Barbadian legislators implemented new slave codes in the late seventeenth century that deputized all men of European descent to act as patrollers and even required them to stop, question, whip, and detain any enslaved person they found off the plantation without a proper pass. According to the text of the law, requiring enslaved Africans to carry a pass and requiring people of European descent to exact violence on those who failed to do so was "absolutely necessary to the Safety" of the colony.[81] If the Black refusal to be subject threatens divinely ordained order, then the distinctly white power to restore Black subjection secures it.

Following the model of Barbados, the English colonies of South Carolina, North Carolina, and Virginia instituted slave codes in the late seventeenth century that instituted pass systems, curfews, prohibitions against secret gatherings, and more measures to control the movement of—to keep in their proper place—enslaved Africans in those colonies. South Carolina's law mandated that all people of European descent were required to stop, capture, whip, and return any enslaved person without a proper pass. Those who complied with this legal requirement received a reward, while those who failed to do so were subject to a fine. Through such measures, historian Sally Hadden writes, South Carolina lawmakers "effectively turned the entire white population into a community police force."[82] During the early eighteenth century, fearing rebellion among the increasingly large numbers of enslaved African peoples, South Carolina, followed by North Carolina and Virginia, consolidated its various slave code enforcement practices into formalized patrols that closely monitored and controlled nearly every movement and activity of the people enslaved within their borders. By the late eighteenth century, authorities in Charleston combined the city watch, constable, militia, and slave patrols into what was arguably the world's first professional police force, called the Charleston Guard and Watch, composed of a chain of command and a large paid, armed, uniformed force. By 1831, Charleston's police force already consisted of more than one hundred foot and mounted patrol officers who worked in shifts twenty-four hours a day keeping order by keeping close watch—with the threat of violence—over the city's subjugated populations, which, in addition to enslaved Africans, also included propertyless Europeans and Native Americans.[83]

Recorded testimonies from slave patrolmen during this era resound with the theo-carceral logic according to which the refusal to be properly subject legitimates violence. Armed with "guns, whips, and binding ropes," slave patrollers were ordered to "apprehend every negro whom [they] found [away] from his home; & if he made any resistance, or ran from [them], to fire on him immediately, unless he could be stopped by other means," and to search "the negro cabins, & take every thing [they] found in them, which bore a hostile aspect, such as powder, shot &c."[84] Other patrollers reported rounding up free and enslaved Black people gathered in groups at night—a prohibited activity—bringing them before the authorities, and physically beating them with a whip. One Charleston Guard and Watch officer summarized his job, simply, as "keeping down the niggers."[85] By controlling the movement and activity of enslaved Africans, including by disrupting any kind of social gathering of enslaved Africans outside of white supervision, slave patrols strove to prevent and punish enslaved people's refusal to be properly subject to functionally godlike whiteness and capital. In so doing, the police forces that evolved out of slave patrols produced and reproduced the functionally sacred partitions of the color line that marked where one could be and where one could not.[86] As a man formerly enslaved in North Carolina named W. L. Bost recalled in a 1937 interview, "If you wasn't in your proper place when the paddyrollers come they lash you 'til you was black and blue. The women got 15 lashes and the men 30. That was jes bein' out without a pass."[87]

Though the system of chattel slavery through which modern racial hierarchy and police power took shape formally ended with the passage of the Thirteenth Amendment to the US Constitution in 1865, the distinctly white capitalist powers of policing and caging that it produced remained. Indeed, the legal basis for the carceral reenslavement of Black Americans after emancipation was the same constitutional amendment that brought about slavery's end. The Thirteenth Amendment, which, in political theorist Joy James's words, "ensnares as it emancipates," formally outlawed slavery in one sense while legalizing it in another: "Neither slavery nor involuntary servitude, *except as a punishment for crime whereof the party shall have been duly convicted*, shall exist within the United States, or any place subject to their jurisdiction."[88] With this exception, the United States opened the door to the continuation of a kind of legal servitude in perpetuity and cleared a path for police and carceral power to provide white propertied Americans with the cheap labor and social control that the outlawed institution of chattel slavery no longer could. As a result, for many Black Americans, life after enslavement was hardly any better, if not in fact worse. As Du Bois wrote in his account of Reconstruction, after emancipation, "the slave went free; stood a brief moment in the sun; then moved back again toward slavery."[89]

One of the first ways that former planters and lawmakers reexerted their control over Black life and ensured the endurance of their godlike power after slavery's end was through legal mechanisms including so-called Black Codes, which repurposed prior slave codes that placed severe limits on the movement of enslaved people, antebellum laws that applied to free Black people, and the English tradition of vagrancy laws that criminalized dispossessed peoples in order to funnel them into exploitative labor.[90] To enforce these codes, municipalities throughout the South developed formalized police departments out of their slave-patrol precursors that, while seemingly race-neutral on the surface, were fully oriented in practice toward the task of maintaining Black subordination in practically every realm of life, particularly employment.[91] Cities and towns also deployed vagrancy laws toward this end, giving police officers a new and widely manipulable legal basis for surveilling and criminalizing the activity of newly freed Black people, including by stopping and detaining them if they did not have proper proof of employment. Georgia's vagrancy statute, like most, did not explicitly specify Black people as its target, though it certainly implied it as it articulated an equivalency between idleness, immorality, and the propertylessness that characterized the vast majority of Black people at that time: "All persons wandering or strolling about in idleness, who are able to work, and who have no property to support them; all persons leading an idle, immoral, or profligate life, who have no property to support them and are able to work and do not work; all persons able to work having no visible and known means of a fair, honest, and respectable livelihood . . . shall be deemed and considered vagrants, and shall be indicted as such."[92] Mississippi's vagrancy law, passed in 1866, was more explicit about its targets: "all freedmen, free Negroes, and mulattoes in this state over the age of eighteen years, found . . . with no lawful employment or business, or found unlawfully assembling themselves together, either in the day or night time . . . shall be deemed vagrants."[93] Alabama's vagrancy law went so far as to define the offense to include "stubborn servant[s]." While most laws were formally race-neutral on the surface, a planter, former slave owner, and Ku Klux Klan member clarified popular white understandings of the intended purpose of postbellum vagrancy laws when he stated that the "vagrant contemplated" by such laws "was the plantation negro."[94]

Channeling centuries of eurochristian ideology that regarded subjugation as the natural and God-ordained condition of people of African descent, one Alabama planter after the Civil War made clear, in the absence of a legal basis to outright enslave people of African descent, that carceral control could help maintain Black subjugation and, by extension, white civilization: "We have the power to pass stringent police laws to govern the Negroes—this is a blessing—for they must be controlled in some way or white people cannot live among them."[95] For former planters and other members of the white capitalist class, laws that required Black people to labor were necessary not only to maintain an order in which whiteness was still functionally divine and Blackness was still subservient but to forge a class of Black laborers large enough to maintain white wealth in an increasingly industrialized economy after the Civil War.[96] To these ends, police, sheriffs, judges, and other legal authorities captured, convicted, and sentenced recently freed Black people charged with petty or altogether fabricated crimes into forced labor inside prisons and on prison farms, including some built on the site of former plantations, as well as on railroads, in mines, on farms, and in other dangerous working conditions that often resulted in death.[97] Convict leasing, a system that enabled authorities to lease out Black people convicted of a crime to commercial bidders on a contractual basis, was another predominant postemancipation means by which authorities forced Black people to generate white wealth. Systematizing the exploitation and control of Black people "duly convicted" by the courts, convict leasing authorized white southern elites to hold Black people captive to labor for white wealth, thereby also keeping the alleged threat of unsubjected Black people under control.[98]

Even as convict leasing declined in the late nineteenth century, states continued to sentence an increasingly disproportionate number of Black Americans to longer and longer prison sentences, creating what Michelle Alexander calls "the nation's first prison boom."[99] Late nineteenth- and early twentieth-century census numbers revealed that Black prison populations indeed skyrocketed in the decades following emancipation, which a majority of sociologists and white Americans at the time interpreted as confirmation of the inherent criminality of Black people, when in fact it was a direct result of racist legal measures including Black Codes and vagrancy laws that rapidly funneled recently freed Black people into state captivity.[100] In contrast to the predominant view among white America, Du Bois argued that "it was blackness that was condemned and not crime."[101] As such, Du Bois writes, Black Americans in the decades following emancipation "came to look upon courts as instruments of injustice and oppression, and upon those convicted in them as martyrs and victims."[102] By the late nineteenth century, only a few decades after emancipation, crime and Blackness had become so conflated in the eurochristian imaginary that, for white Americans, the fundamental identity of Black Americans was no longer "slave" but "criminal," a reconstituted conception of Blackness as inherently savage, dangerous, and hostile to the order of whiteness and property.[103]

Whiteness, from its beginnings, has been fundamentally patriarchal and possessive. Indeed, white lawmakers and men of property during the postemancipation era deliberately produced anxiety around "Negro crime," Andrea Ritchie outlines, by constructing Black women as "prostitutes," "savage beast[s]," and "true monster[s]" who committed "barbaric acts of cruelty." They also did so by proliferating fabricated stories of "crazy negresses" inclined to attack white men, women, and children, to act in "immoral, deranged, and atrocious ways," to lure white children into the sex trade, and even to kill their own children. In Ritchie's words, "These images fueled the arrest, incarceration, and lynching of Black women, and the constitution of Black women 'as subjects outside of the protected category "woman.""'[104] Patriarchal whiteness and police power remained closely tethered well into the twentieth century as Black women who exercised agency beyond the submissive and maternal "mammy" stereotype were—and still are—subject to physical and sexual violence at the hands of police.[105] With Black women cast as either hypersexualized "Jezebels" or "domineering, emasculating" "Sapphires," their refusal to be subject to white patriarchal circumscriptions renders them vulnerable to the violence of a police power that exists to maintain long-standing hierarchies of race, class, and gender.[106] Indeed, Black women—as well as Indigenous women and other women of color—who have sought to survive white supremacist capitalist patriarchy by any means necessary have long been defined and punished as criminals throughout the history of the United States. The same remains true today.[107]

Despite the promises and hopes for repair entailed in the multiracial "abolition democracy" of Reconstruction, it was ultimately southern "Redemption"—a white supremacist movement for the reentrenchment of white political and economic power via Black subjugation—that triumphed in the decades following emancipation.[108] The term itself—"Redemption"—signals quite clearly that, for white southerners, saving the violent order that they held as sacred from the threat of its dismantling resembled and was perhaps even intertwined with the redemption at the heart of their eurochristian tradition. Indeed, despite the fact that "redemption" literally refers to release from subjugation, the kind of saving that southern Redemption entailed was a deeply carceral one, as the mass return of Black people to subjection to patriarchal whiteness by way of capture and caging was central to it. From the *Plessy* decision that enshrined racial segregation to the Jim Crow policies and practices that enforced it, Redemption restored whiteness as a functionally godlike power, and it did so, at every stage, through the power of police to coerce Black people to their proper subjected place within racial capitalist order. Even the technically extralegal, anti-Black terror of lynching, which a Georgia newspaper in 1901 called "part of the religion of our people," along with the terror of white supremacist organizations like the Ku Klux Klan, relied on coordination with police forces, many of which employed Klan members as officers.[109]

Police helped reconstitute racial order not only in the South, where chattel slavery prevailed the longest, but also in the Northeast, Midwest, and West, where millions of Black Americans, many fleeing Jim Crow and racial terror, were forced to migrate as refugees from the South during the first part of the twentieth century, only to find variations of the same violence, including from police, in their new places of residence.[110] By the second half of the twentieth century, as racial capitalism forged new ways to dispossess and contain Black Americans for the sake of white wealth and power, and as a new wave of the long Black freedom movement emerged to contest systemic racial discrimination and disenfranchisement, the still clear anti-Black violence endemic to policing in major US cities beyond the South was an unmistakable fact widely understood among people living there.[111] James Baldwin gave voice to this common understanding when, in 1966, he described the hypercriminalized Black neighborhoods of New York, Chicago, Detroit, and "every Northern city with a large Negro population" as "occupied territory." "The police are simply the hired enemies of this population," Baldwin wrote. "They are present to keep the Negro in his place and to protect white business interests, and they have no other function."[112]

For Baldwin, the police power to keep Black people in their place is a power built on deeply religious pretensions. The "white fundamentalist minister" and the "sheriff," he writes, "entered my life in the same breath." Both claim Christianity, and both "believe that they are responsible, the one for divine law and the other for natural order. Both believe that they are able to define and privileged to impose law and order; and both, historically and actually, know that law and order are meant to keep me in my place." In a republic built on the idea that Blackness itself is a manifestation of sin, Baldwin concludes, the minister and the sheriff exist "to keep the Republic white—to keep it free from sin."[113] In 1965, the rising evangelical preacher Billy Graham condemned the Watts Rebellion carried out by dispossessed Black underclass and working-class residents in southern Los Angeles. According to Graham, leftists and civil rights demonstrations were the cause of the rebellion, as they represented "an organized attempt to down-grade the policeman," which in turn led to "a breakdown of law" that transformed city streets into "jungles of terror," a clearly racist dismissal of the real life-and-death concerns that catalyzed the uprisings in the first place. "We need salvation from lawlessness," he preached to a gathering of evangelicals in North Carolina. Condemning the mass disrespect for law and order on display in Watts and declaring that police must be central in restoring it, Graham envisioned "tough new laws" as an integral component of the "great spiritual awakening" that a nation rife with Black rebellion so desperately needed.[114] Less than six months later, the predominantly white National Association of Evangelicals followed Graham in decrying the "godless," "un-American," "revolutionary" actions of the disorderly masses. Warning of the implicitly racialized dangers posed by disobedient disrespect toward "all authority of God and country," the association proclaimed that "law and order are essential principles in the divine economy" and thereby declared its unwavering support of "law enforcement agencies who seek to fulfill their divinely endowed function of maintaining peace and safety."[115] The mortal God of police saves—and becomes—the mortal God of whiteness.

And yet, the fundamental intertwining of the pseudo-divine powers of whiteness and police does not mean that all white people benefit fully from whiteness or are fully immune from the police violence it deploys. Indeed, patriarchal whiteness is a deadly lie not only in the sense that it deals death to nonwhite peoples but also in the sense that it deliberately deceives and even dispossesses those who inherit it. As outlined in chapters 1 and 2, this has been the case from the very emergence of whiteness in the eighteenth and nineteenth centuries, when ruling-class European colonizers gave poor European laborers and servants the impression of solidarity by granting them privileges and powers that were in fact severely limited. The partial empowerment and partial dispossession and criminalization of its own is a fundamental feature of patriarchal whiteness, a feature that takes shape not only through hierarchies of race and class but also, at the same time, through raced and classed hierarchies of gender. From the policing of alternative reproductive health practices and sex work to the criminalization of women's attempts at surviving gender and sexual violence, police and carceral systems have long policed the lines of gender by policing the behaviors of women, gender-nonconforming people, and transgender people, most predominantly women, gender-nonconforming, and transgender people of color.[116] The state also perceives white women who fail to live up to their race, class, and gender inheritances as disruptors of race, class, and gender hierarchies that must be punished accordingly. Indeed, for centuries, white women who have failed to live up to the social norms of white womanhood by failing to be properly subservient and reproductive have, in the words of Angela Davis, been "more closely associated with blackness than their 'normal' counterparts," resulting in their being denied the protections otherwise promised to them as white women.[117] As a result, the same police and carceral systems that have long entrapped Black women, Indigenous women, and other women of color have also entrapped economically dispossessed white women, even if to a lesser degree.

A similar dynamic has long played out through the racial capitalist state's criminalization of working-class and underclass men of European descent deemed to have failed to live up to their divinely ordained raced, classed, and gendered standards, namely, to master and possess oneself and one's world. The thoroughly patriarchal power of police to manage the social household by eliminating threats to its hierarchies reveals itself in the rhetoric of American penal reformers of the late eighteenth and early nineteenth centuries who regularly sold their carceral proposals to legislators and the public in terms of "caring civic fathers" who would do the seemingly harsh but allegedly benevolent and godlike work of capturing and caging in order to transform "childish criminals into mature men and trustworthy citizens."[118] The primary targets of such carceral interventions were men widely viewed as having failed to meet the masculine standards of economic independence, self-control, mastery, authority over one's family and others, and respect for masculine governing powers.[119] Carceral and legislative authorities perceived men who deviated from such norms as essentially effeminate and thus inherently criminal, deserving of the godlike, patriarchal power of police intervention.[120]

Additionally, as historian Kelly Lytle Hernández documents, late nineteenth-century white settlers seeking to transform a conquered Los Angeles into an "Eden for the Saxon Homeseeker" "disparaged, criminalized, and caged poor white itinerant men who, by migrating constantly, living in homosocial communities, and loving in homosexual ways, either could not or would not abide by Anglo-American settler norms such as heading nuclear families, acquiring Native land, and permanently settling down."[121] For some social commentators, poor white men were "human parasites" that embodied "contagious" "evils" that should be "quarantined and prevented from spreading." If Los Angeles was to be a kind of sacred settler space built around patriarchal whiteness and private property, as settlers envisioned it, and if poor white men presented a menacing threat to that dream, then police and cages were necessary to contain and ultimately eliminate the problem they embodied. Casting white "tramps," "hobos," and "vagrants" as "degenerate," "incorrigible," "irreclaimable," and "utterly depraved," white settlers and elites in California literally built prisons specifically to deal with the seasonal influx of largely white itinerants into the city. As a lieutenant with the Los Angeles Police Department announced at a press event for the unveiling of a new stockade in 1908 said, "Now let the hoboes come; we're ready for them."[122] The caging of white propertyless men in a world built for white propertied men is always justifiable insofar as such caging defends the social order from those who have failed to live up to society's patriarchal and possessive standards and thus cannot handle liberty unrestrained.[123]

More than just interrelated, patriarchal whiteness and the patriarchal power of modern police—mortal gods over the world—cannot exist apart. The early American police power of slave patrols deputized—functionally deified—men of European descent to serve racial capital by surveilling and controlling Black people, understood to be inherently uncivilized and thereby made for subjection. In so doing, slave patrols contributed to the emerging coherence of patriarchal whiteness as a godlike capacity for exacting legitimate forms of violence in pursuit of economic and political power.[124] At the same time that they tethered emerging conceptions of possessive whiteness to emerging conceptions of police power, slave patrols defined and treated Blackness not only as "heathen," "savage," and uncivilized but as inherently outlaw, criminal—literally outside and against the law, thereby necessitating organized forms of social control to secure the racial and social order. Evolving from slave patrols, as well as anti-immigrant, strikebreaking, and settler colonial forms of police power, the "divinely endowed" mortal God of police power in the US has helped create, "Redeem," and sustain a functionally sacred racial order, rendering whiteness a power of functionally godlike proportions in the process. More than simply simultaneous, whiteness and police are, at their points of germination and throughout their evolution, mutually dependent, cogenerative phenomena that depend on each other for their existence. As Frank Wilderson III puts it, "White people are not simply 'protected' by the police. They are—in their very corporeality—the police."[125]

Criminalizing Trespass, Sacralizing Property

Whiteness came into existence, via police power, not merely as an abstract identity marker but as a status imbued with material value, power, and godlike authority. As outlined in chapters 1 and 2, one of the foremost ways that the all-encompassing, pseudo-godlike power of patriarchal whiteness manifests itself in the world is as a kind of property, a pretension to the natural right to possess the world absolutely—"ownership of the earth forever and ever, Amen!" Like the whiteness with which it is intimately fused, the story of property is also a story about the police power to criminalize, capture, and dispose of trespassers as a means of producing and securing private possession. In a world ordered according to the boundaries of the color line and the property line, police perform the pseudo-divine function of eliminating the order-desecrating threat of matter and people out of place. In the end, property is made sacred not only by the partitions that demarcate and constitute it but by the power to eliminate those who desecrate it. Criminalizing trespass does not merely *protect* property; it makes property sacred.

To better understood the connection between property and police, and the religiosity that constitutes that connection, it is helpful to return once again to John Locke. For Locke, as well as for Adam Smith and other theorists of liberal capitalist order after him, the primary purpose of civil society, and the reason for its existence at all, is "the preservation of property."[126] Premised on the idea that the private possession of enclosed land is a natural and God-mandated foundation of social order that extends from one's own self-possession and that ultimately benefits all of humankind, Locke's myth of the origins of a society built for the preservation of property hinges on the elimination of property's enemies, which is to say, the enemies of God. In the state of nature, Locke argues, it is reasonable to "kill a thief" because a thief takes away the most sacred right of preserving one's own life, liberty, and property, a right on which Locke understands the entire social order to depend. "Criminals" in general, and those who transgress against real property—thieves—in particular, for Locke, constitute a threat not just to individuals but to the social order as a whole. As such, Locke likens criminal thieves to "wild Savage Beasts, with whom men can have no Society nor Security," and thus as beings deserving of destruction.[127] Violating the social contract, thieves declare themselves enemy aggressors against an order in which individual private possession is held as ultimate, sacred.[128] For the sake of social order itself, then, those who offend against property and its preservation—those who, in Locke's words, "trespass against the whole Species, and the Peace and Safety of it"—must be eliminated.[129] The preservation of property, in Locke's highly influential mythology of civil society, requires force, whether from the rational, civilized, individual European possessor or from the police power of the state that, according to Locke, quite literally exists for exactly such a purpose.

More than just a matter of individual proprietors, the state's police power to preserve property establishes the right to private possession as a principle that orders all of social life and the forms of relation that constitute it. Indeed, rather than simply protect an already existing order of property, police power—the power to coerce and eliminate people who dwell out of place—is the condition of order's possibility. The mortal God of police creates a partitioned world of property and calls it good, rendering evil those who, in their state of forced precarity, seem to threaten it. The owners who benefit from that order, who are themselves defined by proximity to divine power, share with other propertied people a common interest to defend not only their own property but the property of others and, by extension, the order that makes private possession possible at all, as I showed in chapter 3. Colquhoun, writing a century after Locke, argued that any act of trespass against one private property owner is an act of trespass against the entire society and that all members of such a society should be functionally deputized to neutralize any such threats.[130] The boundaries arranging a social order that exists to preserve property are thus the boundaries of property, making any act of trespass against property "a trespass against the whole Species," a criminal act of war against the sacred and natural that warrants social exclusion or even death.[131]

Working in tandem with acts of enclosure that generated dispossession by privatizing property in the hands of fewer and fewer people, the majority of criminal statutes developed in England, colonial America, and the early American republic over the course of the seventeenth through nineteenth centuries were concerned with offenses "against property."[132] As E. P. Thompson writes, in eighteenth-century England, "property and the privileged status of the propertied were assuming, every year, a greater weight in the scales of justice, until justice itself was seen as no more than the outworks and defences of property."[133] Having been essentially "deified" through the legal and economic orders that revolved around it, private property in early modern England, Douglas Hay argues, functioned as "the measure of all things."[134] So sacred was private property that, for a period of time in eighteenth-century England, crimes against property—including seemingly minor acts of theft against wealthier property owners—were, following Locke's influence, punishable by death. In practically all cases, those who determined penalties for crimes against property were themselves land and property owners, often of the same upper-middle or ruling class as those who were allegedly "victimized" by minor thefts.[135] Detailing the history of the widespread execution of working-class and underclass "criminals" during that time, Linebaugh writes, "Most of those hanged had offended against the laws of property, and at the heart of the 'social contract' was respect for private property. It could therefore be argued that, just as each hanging renewed the power of sovereignty, so each hanging repeated the lesson: 'Respect Private Property.'"[136] While a penalty of execution for property offenses was replaced in the late eighteenth and early nineteenth centuries with less explicitly violent means of carceral "correction"—including workhouses and penitentiaries—the criminal punishment systems in both England and the colonies that England established in the Americas continued to treat people dispossessed by the divinely ordained accumulation of capital as a desecrating threat that required the divine violence of the mortal God to correct and control.[137]

In the same places where police power emerged as a means of placemaking, of producing and protecting geographies of private possession, it also emerged as a means of race-making.[138] In other words, whiteness emerged not only from private ownership but from private ownership's vigilant protection against Black, Indigenous, and propertyless peoples constructed as rebellious, thieving threats to colonial racial capitalist order.[139]

In the immediate aftermath of slavery's abolition, the antagonistic relationship between white property and Black agency at the heart of chattel slavery deepened and took on new form as white planters and lawmakers developed new ways to reinforce boundaries against newly freed Black Americans. By the late 1860s, private ownership had long been designated a capacity natural only to Europeans of wealth, in sharp contrast to the incapacity to possess that Europeans projected onto allegedly "uncivilized" Indigenous and African peoples in the Americas. In light of the possibility that freed Black Americans might have access to land after abolition, many white southerners and "Redeemers" made it clear that Black property possession was an intolerable "evil."[140] While the state could no longer explicitly discriminate against Black ownership, anti-Black white solidarity and implicitly anti-Black laws succeeded in keeping most Black people from owning land for generations, thereby ensuring the enduring permanence of Black dispossession.[141] Additionally, in the years following emancipation, even previously held customs that allowed all people to hunt, fish, and forage on other people's land before the Civil War were eliminated in states across the South, predominantly in counties with large Black populations, through criminal trespass laws that lawmakers and landowners strengthened in order to exclude and criminalize Black people, thereby funneling them into exploitative labor relations and securing—sacralizing—white property and wealth in the process.[142] Showing the implicit connection between property, whiteness, and carceral logics, one planter in South Carolina argued that allowing people to hunt and fish on someone else's land "led to crime," while another argued that trespass laws "would keep the negroes more confined."[143] Beyond merely exacting punishment for the sake of punishment, these trespass laws, deliberately created and enforced in racially disparate ways, reinforced the original intertwining of whiteness and property by criminalizing one of the few means that dispossessed and formerly enslaved Black people had to support and feed themselves.[144] In so doing, white lawmakers and elites reproduced white property as functionally sacred space that must be defended no matter the cost.

In a world of private possession forged through acts of mass dispossession, "crimes" against property committed by people dispossessed of it are all but inevitable.[145] Even the proponents of such an order have long understood that property is inherently vulnerable and so can go on existing only if it is rigorously defended, which, according to Locke, is the reason for the formation of civil societies in the first place. Understanding the inherent vulnerability of property and the need to protect it, Colquhoun writes, "where Property is exposed, a preventative Police must be resorted to, in order to be secure."[146] Written into the legal rationales undergirding European colonial and imperial powers like the United States, the vigilant defense of sacred property is fundamental to the work of the state, which necessitates agents of the mortal God ordained to defend property, by force if necessary, against those who, by status or by act, pose a threat to it.

In the end, the police power that eliminated dispossessed commoners in England by punishing and shipping them to labor in the "prison without walls" of the American colonies was the same police power that surveilled and controlled the movement of enslaved Africans, which was the same police power that carried out the settler colonial task of the "elimination of the Native" from the lands that colonizers, following Lockean logic, claimed as their own.[147] Channeling the tradition of English agricultural capitalism and husbandry, Locke defined common property—and, by extension, the Indigenous peoples and commoners who dwelled there—as "waste" land.[148] Inspired by Locke's work, and operating from within the same set of rationales, European settlers defined colonial expansion into Indigenous "waste" lands and the requisite eviction of Indigenous peoples from those lands as a kind of purification, one typically accomplished through force at the hands of individual settlers, settler militias, and/or police.[149] Over the course of centuries, settlers characterized Native peoples using many of the same terms that European property owners and elites used to characterize the Africans they enslaved and the English commoners they dispossessed—as savage, godless, immoral, depraved, and violent—all in order to justify their violent displacement. European colonizers also deployed a rigid gender binary to criminalize Indigenous and African peoples who seemed to deviate from the gender and sexual norms of European femininity and masculinity.[150] With European colonizers convinced of the sacredness of their settlement and the deviant savagery of those who stood in their way, the resort to a divinely conceived violence—both vigilante and police—has been integral to settler colonialism from its origins. "The colonial project," Sherene Razack writes, is "a lethal project."[151]

By literally eliminating Native peoples through physical violence and death, cultural genocide, and the violence of forging and maintaining racialized boundaries of exclusion and containment, police power *makes space*—pseudo-divinely *creates a world*—for the expansion of seemingly infinite white possession.[152] As Mircea Eliade helps us understand, for the eurochristian imaginary, the settler colonial work of marking out, displacing people from, taking, and thereby making new worlds for whiteness constitutes a sacred work in that it "reproduces the work of the gods."[153] Much as with other forms of European boundary making, transforming the lands of Indigenous peoples into exclusive white space requires "the production of Indigenous bodies as out of place in the settler city," a process that takes place through many social, political, economic, and cultural means but that ultimately depends on the state's use of force through police.[154] The police power that forges racialized property lines and that eliminates Native peoples as trespassers on their own lands is the same police power that used—and still uses—violence to impose and secure the borders of settler states. The US-Mexico border, for instance, still today a site of immense settler police violence, took shape over the course of generations, not merely as a tool for antirefugee exclusion but as a manifestation of what theorist and activist Harsha Walia summarizes as "imperialist expansion, Indigenous elimination, and anti-Black enslavement."[155] Through the "frontier fascism" of Andrew Jackson's Indian Removal Act of 1830, which displaced and killed thousands of Indigenous peoples, and the 1848 Treaty of Guadalupe Hidalgo, which moved the US border south, annexing more than 525,000 square miles of Mexican territory, the US state deployed its police power to eliminate those who impeded or challenged the divinely ordained "manifest destiny" of its colonial acquisitions.

In the context of these brutal acts of border making, one of the most well-known American police and militia forces, the Texas Rangers, formed in 1835 through acts of mass violence against Indigenous peoples that they deployed as a means of establishing and maintaining functionally sacred space for white settlement.[156] After the passage of the Fugitive Slave Act in 1850, which allowed slave owners to retrieve enslaved Africans who had fled their plantation, including those who had escaped to nonslaveholding territories, border militias including the Texas Rangers added former slave patrollers to their ranks and conducted raids across the southern border to recapture Black people seeking freedom in Mexico.[157] In the late nineteenth century, the federal government passed laws that authorized police forces including the Texas Rangers to criminalize Chinese migrants seeking entry at the nation's borders, which paved the way for the formation of the formal US Border Patrol in 1924, with its earliest agents "recruited from the ranks of the Texas Rangers and Klansmen."[158] The Border Patrol remains active a century later in the work of racial exclusion and control as part of the long project of white settler possession.[159] The godlike power of white settler possession—"ownership of the earth forever and ever, Amen!"—and the mortal God of police power go hand in hand.

From Sir Robert Peel's police management of England's colonial occupation of Ireland to the colonial development of slave patrols in Barbados to the border-making settler colonial elimination of Indigenous peoples in pursuit of infinite white ownership, American policing has been a colonial and imperial—and thus international—project from its beginnings. The US-Philippine War of the late nineteenth and early twentieth centuries, for instance, played a major role in developing twentieth-century US policing as an inherently race-making and place-making power. From the perspective of the US government, the Philippines was, in the words of Nikhil Pal Singh, "a blackened and disordered space" that required occupation in order to come under US control.[160] After a series of imperial contestations, the US formally acquired and imposed colonial rule in the Philippines in December 1898. President William McKinley, who facilitated the imperial acquisition, showed the religious rationale that animated that occupation when he later characterized his violent capture of the Philippines as an unexpected "gift from the gods." Faced with the possibility of acquisition, McKinley described his deep consternation over the right course of action to take. "I walked the floor of the White House night after night until midnight," McKinley said. "I went down on my knees and prayed Almighty God for light and guidance." After prayerful deliberation, McKinley reported, he received clarity that the only option was to "take," "educate," "uplift," "civilize," and "Christianize" the Filipino people. The next morning, he made his orders to "put the Philippines on the map of the United States" where it remained for nearly half a century.[161]

After securing occupational rule, the US established the Philippine Constabulary to maintain order in the colony, especially over its anti-colonial revolutionary forces. More than a mere military venture, the US occupation of the Philippines became what one historian describes as a "laboratory" for US officials to experiment with new police practices rooted in counterinsurgency, methods that it would soon import back to the US.[162] The Pennsylvania State Police, for instance, founded in 1905, was directly modeled after the Philippine Constabulary and, much like the Constabulary, was concerned primarily with serving state and corporate interests by brutally suppressing working-class uprisings and strikes.[163] August Vollmer, who is widely credited with pioneering twentieth-century US policing and who authored one of the most influential textbooks on the subject, got his start in the Philippines before later becoming police chief in Berkeley, California. Beyond the Philippines, Marine General Smedley Butler, who developed colonial policing in Haiti and Nicaragua, became Philadelphia's police chief in 1924.[164] Other examples abound.[165] Beyond actual police counterinsurgency in the imperial context, the deep connection between US imperialism abroad and domestic policing at home is also evident in the rhetorical and conceptual connection between war power and police power that developed during the twentieth century. As Singh points out, after World War II, state authorities often described imperialist wars as "police" endeavors, while domestic police forces in the US regularly described their work in terms of "war."[166] It is little surprise, then, that James Baldwin would describe the great urban centers of the US in 1966 as "territories" "occupied" by police, who performed what he described as the inherently religious task of exercising total control over Black people.[167]

As President McKinley's racial-religious rhetoric and imperial prayers attest, white possession via colonial occupation, made possible by the police power that maintains it, is best understood as a matter of functionally sacred proportion, which is to say, for the managers of imperial power, a manifestation of nothing less than the power of God, mortal and immortal alike. Indeed, the Philippines was not merely "a gift from the gods," as McKinley quipped; it was a gift secured by the organized violence of the mortal God of police. Following patterns first established as early as the seventeenth century, police power in the twentieth century was—and remains today—a means by which the colonial racial capitalist state engages in race war, class war, frontier war, and global imperial war to secure exclusive "ownership of the earth forever and ever, Amen!" Without police there is no white possession, and apart from white possession, there is hardly any need for police.[168] White possession necessitates mass elimination.[169]

Writing about the precarious conditions and organized movement of the working classes in early 1840s England, Friedrich Engels remarked that, for the ruling classes, "law" and "order" are "sacred." The "sanctity of the law" and "the sacredness of order," he wrote, do not derive from divine influence; law and order are "sacred" because the ruling classes create them for their own "benefit and protection." Law and order are sacred, in other words, because they absolutize the will of those who forge them. To render one's own will the law of the land is to presume a position of godlike power over people and planet, and indeed, Engels noted this dynamic when he wrote that the English bourgeois "finds himself reproduced" not only in "his law" but in "his God." Indeed, in the context of 1840s industrial England, and well beyond, white propertied men did not merely serve the gods of racial capital; they *were* the mortal gods of racial capital. Ruling-class power is a mode of self-deification, and importantly, as Engels implies, the condition of its possibility is the "wonderfully soothing power" of the "policeman's truncheon," which is to say God's truncheon.[170] If police power is the power of the mortal God, then police violence is divine violence that makes, saves, and sustains heaven for a few at the expense of many. Criminalization makes white propertied men divine.

5

Measuring Salvation in "Chains and Corpses"

In James Baldwin's November 1970 letter to imprisoned Black radical feminist freedom fighter and intellectual Angela Davis, he reflected on the meaning of the ongoing reality of "chains on black flesh." "Dear Sister," he writes, "One might have hoped that, by this hour, the very sight of chains on black flesh, or the very sight of chains, would be so intolerable a sight for the American people . . . that they would themselves spontaneously rise up and strike off the manacles. But no, they appear to glory in their chains; now, more than ever, they appear to measure their safety in chains and corpses."[1] Aren't chains a relic of history? Why do they persist? As Baldwin indicates, measuring safety by chains and corpses was not a phenomenon unique to the 1970s.[2] Indeed, three hundred years before Baldwin ever put pen to paper, the European aspiration to a transcendence obtained through chains on Black flesh helped give birth to the racial whiteness by which some come into "ownership of the earth forever and ever, Amen!" at the expense of others. For the inherently oppositional force of whiteness to be something like divine—socially and politically omnipotent, infinite, transcendent, invulnerable—Blackness must be damned to chains, rendered powerless, captive, exploitable. The modern history of chains and corpses—from chattel enslavement to carceral confinement and beyond—is not arbitrary, without reason, but purposed, a manifestation of a world-possessing desire at the heart of the eurochristian project. Chains continue to capture Black flesh, Baldwin writes, because the idolatrous, pseudo-religious aspirations to absolute safety, power, and control inherent to racial capitalism demand it: "We know that we, the blacks, and not only we, the blacks, have been, and are, the victims of a system whose only fuel is greed, whose only god is profit. And we know that, for the perpetuation of this system, we have all been mercilessly brutalized, and have been told nothing but lies, lies about ourselves and our kinsmen and our past, and about love, life, and death, so that both soul and body have been bound in hell."[3]

White America obtains its wealth and power, and thus its "safety," only when Black people, along with Indigenous people, other people of color, and propertyless people of all races, are "brutalized" for white profit and eventually "bound in hell." The image of hell in Baldwin's letter is not incidental but intentional and one he deployed throughout his work. To be Black in America, to be Black in any white supremacist society, Baldwin later wrote in a letter to Desmond Tutu, is to have visited hell and to know an inherent kinship and solidarity with others so dispossessed and held captive.[4] White people, on the other hand, he writes, live by the illusion that "hell is a place for others," a place and system that "they control."[5] For white propertied folks to live in their own exclusive heaven, Black folks, and many others besides, must be damned to living—and dying—hell. The aspiration to render oneself infinitely secure by controlling the destiny of people and planet may be based in an illusion, but its effects are all too real.

Safety, Security, and Salvation

To be human is to be finite, mortal, to live facing the reality of one's own end—and, increasingly, in our time, the end of the world as we know it. To be alive, in other words, is to be vulnerable. Indeed, religions, cultures, philosophies, and politics can be understood as means by which humans have interpreted, navigated, and determined how to arrange their lives in the face of mortality. At the most fundamental level, then, the desire for safety is inherent to human existence: the world can be a mortally dangerous place, and we are right to want to survive those dangers, to be safe in the midst of them. And yet, what begins as a natural desire often transforms into an illusory desire for a safety that is absolute, invulnerable, even transcendent—what Baldwin calls "safety instead of life."[6] The pursuit of absolute safety requires total control of one's environment, especially of those who are perceived as threats to individual or collective well-being: if I can control the movement and agency of others, the illusion posits, then I can obtain a semblance of control over my own existence, my own destiny. In the end, controlling others necessitates force, coercion, even elimination, which is why, on a mass scale, the pursuit of "safety instead of life" is an inherently "genocidal" pursuit: it requires the destruction of anything that interrupts the mirage of its heavenly destination.[7] Absolute safety requires absolute control, and absolute control requires violence.

The desire to transcend human vulnerability and become like God in relation to the Earth and its peoples is a desire generated by fear of finitude, fear of scarcity, and thus a fear of others. This anxious aspiration to pseudo-divine transcendence and power, I have argued, is the story of patriarchal and possessive whiteness and the mass violence and dispossession it has wrought over the past three to four centuries. For whiteness and property to transcend finite vulnerability—to be like God—others must be posited as inferior to their own sacred power and dehumanized and exploited as such. Indeed, whiteness and property manifest the self-aggrandizing paranoia and fear that are central to the liberal mythology of the origins of the state, a mythology that, in the words of Mark Neocleous, "makes human beings see in others not the realization of their sociality and freedom but rather the barrier to them." Under such a rationale, "we come to see other members of civil society as a threat or source of harm," thereby turning "each of us into a source of the other's insecurity."[8] Treating the vulnerabilities of finite, creaturely existence as threats to be avoided rather than means of life-giving communion with others or with the divine, the religiosity of patriarchal and possessive whiteness at the heart of US society seeks "refuge" by terminating everything in its way, which eventually includes even itself: "as long as white Americans take refuge in their whiteness—for so long as they are unable to walk out of this most monstrous of traps—they will allow millions to be slaughtered in their name," Baldwin writes to Angela Davis. "They will perish (as we once put it in our black church) in their sins—that is, in their delusions."[9] Such a hyper-individualist, wholly self-interested orientation to human existence helps give rise to modern "necropolitical" order, characterized by what political philosopher Achille Mbembe calls the "relation of enmity" whereby humans perceive "the existence of the Other as an attempt on my life, as a mortal threat or absolute danger whose biophysical elimination would strengthen my life potential and security."[10] To pursue safety *instead* of life is to pursue death—death for others and eventually for oneself as well.

What Baldwin calls safety, Neocleous and other scholars of police power call "security," the illusory aspiration at the heart of racial capitalist order.[11] The mass wealth-generating dispossession on which racial capitalism depends produces populations deprived of the means of subsistence, which in turn threatens the system's security, either by way of dispossessed people organizing to challenge the systems that dispossess them or by the mere unproductive and thus, according to capitalist logic, *worth*less presence of dispossessed people at all. Capital, in other words, is inherently insecure and proliferates further insecurity, which in turn gives rise to a politics centered around maintaining the order's security, no matter the cost. Central to the task of securing order is the power of police.[12] When racial capitalist orders speak of police and prisons as institutions of "public safety" or "security," then, they are actually talking primarily about the safety and security of racial capitalist order itself and its managers and beneficiaries, as opposed to all people living under, exploited by, or made vulnerable by it. Police power is the power to eliminate threats to sacred social order. And yet, the insecurity that racial capitalist settler colonial order creates through mass dispossession can never be fully eliminated so long as the order keeps on dispossessing and destroying nearly everyone and everything in its path, which it must do in order to survive. At best, the outcomes of racial capitalist inequality can be managed but never eliminated. Thus, the pursuit of absolute safety and security, Baldwin and Neocleous suggest, is ultimately futile, unattainable, an illusion. Nevertheless, the state continues to pursue its own fragile security, at immense human and public financial cost. Just as racial capitalist order is a human fabrication that pretends to be natural, so the police and carceral power that strive to secure it are rooted in "an illusion that has forgotten that it is an illusion," or at least an illusion that pretends it is real.[13]

In pursuit of its own security, racial capitalist settler colonial order transforms the organic human desire for safety into a weapon with which to force others into either subjection or manufactured consent to its own pseudo-godlike power.[14] At nearly every stage of racial capitalism and settler colonialism—from the first slave patrols in Barbados to present-day ruling-class rhetoric about the urgent need for more cops and cages to combat "rising crime"—the police and carceral power to control the enemies of God and order have been framed as means of producing a general "safety" for all. The reality, as I have shown, is that police and carceral power have, from their beginnings to the present, been concerned above all with pursuing the ultimately unattainable security of hierarchical order and the safety of its white propertied managers and beneficiaries, all at the expense of the many lives cast outside the bounds of racial capitalist belonging. The colonial racial capitalist pursuit of absolute security endangers us all.

At the end of the day, the deeply revered idea that cops and cages keep us safe amounts to a kind of religious devotion, what Charles Long calls "orientation in the ultimate sense."[15] For many people, especially most white people, the idea that cops and cages are natural, that they have always been with us, and that they make us safe is so seemingly self-evident that it rarely warrants any further investigation. Thus, to suggest otherwise registers, for many, as a kind of sacrilege that elicits scorn that is at once religious, racial, and classed in nature. The religiosity of mass consent to state violence is an expression of the structured opposition inherent to phenomena—like whiteness, property, and the racial capitalist state—that need a demonized "criminal" enemy in order to exist at all. To put it another way, the functionally religious quest for transcendent safety is a quest animated by fear—the kind of fear that ultimately devolves into vigilance and then violence against its own shadows that it unwittingly casts on the wall. In Baldwin's 1962 essay "Down at the Cross," he writes of the fear that animated the religiosity he first experienced as a young Black teenager in Harlem. "I became, during my fourteenth year, for the first time in my life, afraid—afraid of the evil within me and afraid of the evil without." Afraid of himself, the world, others, everything, Baldwin inherited and embraced the idea that "God and safety were synonymous." Indeed, he writes, "The word 'safety' brings us to the real meaning of the word 'religious' as we use it."[16] Demarcating sacred from profane, orderly from disorderly, pure from polluted, religion, broadly construed, provides structures of meaning and orientation that make it possible to live in a world that might otherwise seem chaotic. In many cases, such demarcations draw distinct boundaries between "us" and "them," which is to say, between the safe and the dangerous. In the white propertied imaginary, whatever or whoever disrupts such a deeply revered sense of order destroys the sacred boundary that protects us from danger, thereby jeopardizing not only the sacred but life itself.

As such, on the other hand, whatever preserves moral and cosmic order by defending and maintaining the boundaries that protect it fulfills what amounts to an inherently religious function. In the popular imaginary, cops and cages not only make us safe but save us. To make safe is to *save*: the English terms "save" and "salvation" derive from the Latin *salvus*, meaning "safe," and the Late Latin *salvare*, meaning to "make safe, secure."[17] The original Latin term for "save" later evolved through French and into English to convey acts that "protect," "redeem," "rescue," "preserve," or "deliver" from danger, death, or eternal damnation. Bearing both general nonreligious and explicitly religious meanings throughout its usage, the multiple dynamics signified by safety and salvation are, both etymologically and conceptually, deeply intertwined, perhaps even inextricable. Christian salvation, from its earliest to its most contemporary articulations, involves deliverance from danger. Likewise, human acts of protection or deliverance from danger, real or imagined, are often articulated in ways that draw on religious connotations of rescue from evil. As I outlined in chapter 3, predominant theocarceral conceptions of sin and salvation in the Christian tradition hold that (1) sin consists in a disorder-generating refusal to be subject to a benevolent and sovereign God, a refusal that establishes a state of condemnation and debt, and that (2) salvation consists in a debt-satisfying sacrifice or punishment that restores cosmic order by restoring humans to proper life-giving subjection to God. In Calvin's scheme, Christ's obedient, self-sacrificial subjection to penal death, which he took on as humanity's substitute, restores humanity's hierarchical relation to the sovereign God, saving humans from permanent damnation and thereby delivering us to "the final goal of safety."[18]

From Augustine to Anselm to Calvin and beyond, the sacrifices of debt payment, punishment, and death not only "satisfy" divine justice but *save*, which is to say, "make safe." For carceral soteriology, the salvation that sacrificial death generates is the restoration of the necessarily hierarchical divine-human relation, a relation understood to benefit and thus save humanity. By restoring proper divine-human relation, sacrificial punishment and death restore divine—and, by extension, social—order, restoring humans to their proper subjected place within cosmic and social hierarchy. For the irredeemable, the surplus, and the expendable, restoration to proper place within cosmic and social hierarchy effectively means outright elimination: for such people, one's proper place is no place at all. The philosopher René Girard argues that the function of systems of sacrifice is to redirect the Hobbesian violence of "all against all" by transforming it into the violence of "all against one," in which a scapegoat absorbs and thereby breaks the cycle of social violence.[19] Formerly incarcerated political theorist Timothy Malone, engaging Girard's work, argues that prisons constitute a "sacrificial stone" at the root of social order. By casting responsibility for social disorder on criminalized peoples, the sacrificial violence of carceral institutions against and between its subjects founds and stabilizes order. As such, Malone argues, the prison is not simply a site of judicial consequence for unlawful actions but a "sacrificial chamber" that, by eliminating the criminalized, founds and secures society itself.[20] Just as the sacrificial punishment and death of the God-Man Jesus restores divine order in the wake of its sinful disruption, so the sacrificial punishment and death of "criminals" restores the sacred social order disrupted by its disorderly desecration, either by restoring dispossessed peoples to their proper subjected place within social hierarchy or by channeling social and racial antagonisms to eliminate "sacrificable" peoples altogether.[21] The eliminatory violence of penal and mortal sacrifice is not merely an act of negation, therefore, but an act of creation and an act of sacralization. Indeed, the etymological origin of the term "sacrifice" is the Latin *sacrificium*, from *sacer*, "sacred" or "holy," and *facere*, "to make": to "sacrifice" is, quite literally, "to make sacred."[22] Sacrifice establishes social order as sacred order. Sacrifice "gives rise to the sacred."[23] Sacrifice saves. The punishment and death of some secures—*saves*—life for others.

Salvation in a carceral key requires subjection, acts of sacrifice that, through debt payment, punishment, or death, restore allegedly life-giving hierarchical relation. In short, carceral salvation is a paradoxically redeeming return to subjection, to one's proper place within hierarchical order.[24] As such, for the managers and beneficiaries of functionally sacred colonial racial capitalist order, the violence of police and carceral power is a manifestation of divine violence and thus of salvation. The police and carceral power of the state is the power of a mortal God. What and in what sense, then, do police and prisons save? Police and prisons save sacred social order by securing it against threats, and they secure it by restoring the inherently threatening, out of place, disobedient, and rebellious enemies of God and order to their proper subjected place within social hierarchy, or by eliminating them from social order altogether.

Police and carceral power, at their root, are manifestations of the patriarchal power to manage the social household, to keep it in order, by whatever means necessary. From the point of view of the lawmaking managers of order, refusing one's place in the social household disrespects and damages not only the household but oneself as well. As such, the managers and beneficiaries of order, along with those who consent to their rule, often characterize forced return to subjection as a kind of salvation both for the larger society and for those whom they make subject, in the sense that it habituates disobedient people to the redemptive discipline of obedience in a context of control made necessary by their allegedly corrupted nature. As legal scholar Markus Dubber, writing on the rationale of vagrancy laws, puts it, "Any correction inflicted for such an offense . . . occurs for the benefit of its object *as a member of the household*, and therefore ultimately for the benefit of both the micro and macro household and its respective heads."[25] Indeed, Dubber writes, the regulations of police power, according to its patriarchal logic, "are said to benefit their objects" as a kind of paternal discipline.[26] A vagrancy statute passed in Maine in 1821 gave local "Overseers of the Poor" the police power to capture vagrants who failed to productively contribute to the social household and to take them to a workhouse where they would be habituated to their proper place and practices within the social order. An 1834 Maine Supreme Judicial Court decision in the case of a woman taken to a Portland, Maine, workhouse for vagrancy upheld the statute on the basis of the patriarchal idea that subjection under state confinement was a sacred benefit not only to the community, which, through her social elimination, was "preserve[d] . . . from contamination," but also to the woman herself. As the court wrote, "When enlightened conscience shall do its office, and sober reason has its proper influence, she will regard the imposition as parental; as calculated to *save* instead of punishing."[27]

The first European and American prisons were likewise structured around the idea that subjection—even mortifying, near-deadly subjection—was salvific in that it restored sacred social order by restoring those who disrupt it to life-giving subjection to divine and political authority. In the context of chattel slavery and its police afterlives, the police power to control the movement and activity of enslaved and formerly enslaved Africans was said to be necessary both for African peoples, who, according to white people, were made for subjection, and for the white social order that sought to contain the dangerous threat of disobedience that African peoples posed if left unrestrained. Similarly, in the context of early European-American settler colonialism that claimed the divinely ordained and godlike right to "ownership of the earth forever and ever, Amen!" the violence of police power that made it possible was said to be a means of saving not only a settler society regularly cast as a kind of heaven on Earth but also, perversely, the Native peoples victimized by that violence. As the authors of *Red Nation Rising*, quoting Sherene Razack, write, "The violence of the settler colonial state against the Native is depicted as a purifying violence, a violence that releases the Native from her subjugation, in which 'killing becomes saving, and murder brings redemption.'"[28] Present-day police similarly often characterize broken windows policing as a benefit to those whom it targets, including unhoused people who obtain temporary "shelter" through confinement in jail.[29]

Another example of the racial capitalist patriarchal police logic that holds that criminalization and salvation can take place at the same time is the case of the Hamilton County, Tennessee, sheriff deputy Daniel Wilkey, who, around 10:00 p.m. on February 6, 2019, followed Shandele Marie Riley as she left in her car from a gas station before eventually stopping her outside her former mother-in-law's home. During the encounter, Wilkey, who is the subject of multiple other lawsuits for excessive force and sexual assault during traffic stops, assaulted Riley by groping her during a body search and ordering her to remove and shake out her bra. After searching her car and allegedly finding a single marijuana roach in a box of cigarettes, Wilkey used the discretion fundamental to his police power to tell Riley that she could avoid being arrested by being baptized and receiving only a citation instead. Riley reports that Wilkey both called her a "piece of shit" and asked if she was "saved," telling her that he felt God's spirit while he searched her car. After agreeing, under coercion, to being baptized, Wilkey took Riley to a nearby lake, where Wilkey stripped out of his deputy uniform down to just a T-shirt and underwear and waded with Riley, who refused Wilkey's request to remove her clothes, into the frigid lake waters, where he assaulted and baptized her while another deputy filmed it all with his phone. A few months later, Riley filed a lawsuit against the deputies.[30] In 2022, Riley was found dead, allegedly from a drug overdose.[31] It is important to note that the state both rejected and defended the legitimacy of Wilkey's actions: though he was indicted on multiple charges in the case, as of November 2022, Hamilton County had spent more than $1 million providing him with legal defense.[32] Moreover, while his actions may seem exceptional, the reality is that they simply express in unusually explicit form the mythological synthesis of violence and salvation that lies at the heart of police power more broadly. In other words, calling Riley a "piece of shit" and sexually assaulting her and at the same time "saving" her by baptism are, for the police and carceral imaginary, not mutually exclusive. Like the penitentiary, vagrancy laws, slave patrols, and colonial police power deployed against dispossessed peoples from the early modern period to the present, Wilkey's actions sought to save the social order precisely by "saving" Riley via violence, returning her to proper subjection to the state and to God, in so doing returning both to the state and to God "the subject [they] had lost."[33]

Or at least that is what police mythology tells us. Despite the perennial ruling-class claim that police and carceral power benefit both those who are targeted by it and the social order that is rid of their presence, the reality is that, for subjugated peoples, forced subjection feels a lot less like salvation and a lot more like damnation to hell on Earth.[34] Thus, in the end, the forced restoration to proper subjection of people marked as criminal constitutes salvation—in the sense of both transcendent safety and deification, becoming God—not primarily for those who are held captive but for the managers and beneficiaries of racial capitalist settler colonial order who are able to enjoy their illusory heaven precisely because others are confined to hell. The functionally sacred order that revolves around patriarchal and possessive whiteness measures its safety—its *save*-ty, its salvation, and ultimately its godlike power—in chains and corpses.

The Lord's Work

The religious drama of criminalization has been playing out, with dehumanizing and death-making effects, for centuries. Institutionalized police power has from its beginnings been widely understood as a function of divine power that exists to impose moral order on the immoral disorder of the "dangerous classes." The rhetoric and function of the earliest iterations of police make it easy to identify its origins as religious, but what about the past half century, during which criminal punishment institutions seem to have secularized in their rhetoric and function? As many scholars have shown, the story of late modern secularization, which narrates the seeming disappearance of religion as a force that structures social life, is inadequate for helping us understand the ongoing influence of eurochristian religion in the West, and the religiosity of policing, which has only deepened over the past half century, is no exception.

To begin with, in the late nineteenth century, many Protestants in both Britain and the United States viewed police as agents fulfilling not merely a political duty to establish order by enforcing the law but a divine duty to protect the good and fend off evil. In the late nineteenth and early twentieth centuries, popular organizations like the Christian Police Association characterized police as embodiments of God's will in the world, and popular Christian authors like Charles Sheldon defined police as "missionaries" sent to bring about a kind of salvation from the nation's moral ills. By the 1920s and '30s, a range of social commentators and religious leaders in the US began to articulate the problem of "crime" as one of the most critical moral and social crises facing the nation. Having already been widely established as moral agents who maintain sacred social order, police were once again called on to hold the front line in the war against social immorality. Indeed, as historian of American religion Aaron Griffith writes, the "first 'war on crime' was a religious war."[35] Built on a foundational synthesis of religious and secular political rhetoric, the characterization of police as inherently moral agents expanded into the second half of the twentieth century, channeled by figures like Billy Graham and groups like the American Association of Evangelicals in the mid-1960s, both of whom demonized Black rebellion and sacralized "law and order"—which is to say, police—as the moral answer to it.

As Griffith outlines, by the early 1970s, the burgeoning point of neoliberal abandonment and violence, the sacralization of policing began to spread more thoroughly into Protestant and evangelical cultural realms in the form of multiple books and films that figured police as God's foot soldiers in a sinful world. In addition to cultural productions, in 1971, a new translation of the Bible called *The Living Bible* was published. Exceedingly popular among evangelicals and many others—it was the best-selling book in the US in 1972 and 1973—the translators further sacralized policing by rendering the God-ordained "rulers," to whom the Apostle Paul in Romans 13:3–4 says Christians owe their obedience, as "police": "For the policeman does not frighten people who are doing right; but those doing evil will always fear him. . . . The policeman is sent by God to help you. But if you are doing something wrong, of course you should be afraid, for he will have you punished."[36] Romans 13 had long been deployed as a slave-owning and ruling-class means of sacralizing political power that dispossesses and controls masses of people, and *The Living Bible*'s translation further cemented its role toward such ends. One California cop reported that he had a religious epiphany while reading Romans 13 from this translation, which he said resolved the dissonance between his faith and his police work. As he put it, "God put the government in power, the laws on the books and officers on their jobs. Enforcing the laws of the land are [sic] enforcing God's law."[37] The cultural, theological, and exegetical seeds planted in the early 1970s produced in the decades that followed a significant number of ministers, politicians, cultural commentators, and police officers who further naturalized the idea that police do God's work. For instance, Los Angeles Police Department officer Robert Vernon wrote in his 1977 memoir that police work is "the Lord's work," and in 1985, he made clear at a gathering of evangelicals that the religious crime war that began more than half a century earlier was still very much playing out when he said, quite plainly, "We are at war."[38]

A few years later, in the early 1990s, popular evangelical ministers like John MacArthur were proclaiming that the masses rising up in the wake of the police beating of Rodney King "are not just opposing the police; they're opposing God, almighty holy God."[39] In more recent years, multiple new editions of the Christian Bible marketed specifically for police officers and their families have grown in popularity and in correspondence with broader pro-police "thin blue line" culture that idealizes the work of police as the moral work of defending civilization by eliminating threats posed by the enemies of God and order. As a police officer speaking at a 2015 Christian law enforcement retreat put it, "we're not cops, we're servants of God."[40] Built on centuries of religious conceptions of police power, the idea that police are divinely ordained actors who protect us from evil remains firmly set today not only in hearts and minds but in stone. On a wall near the entrance of the Metropolitan Nashville Police Department headquarters stands a memorial plaque honoring the "devotion," "courageous service," and "honorable sacrifice" of fallen officers.[41] Below it appears a passage of Jewish and Christian sacred text often deployed by police culture to characterize police as soldiers in God's army: "I heard a voice of the Lord, saying, whom shall I send, and who will go for us? Then said I, here I am, send me" (Isaiah 6:8).

Protestants and evangelicals have played a significant role in maintaining the idea that police power is a manifestation of divine power. And yet, evangelicalism only makes explicit in new terms what has been present all along, namely, the presumption that God ordains the state and its frontline agents to impose the sacred hierarchies of colonial racial capitalist order wherever they seem to be disrupted. Thus, whether police officers are self-proclaimed Christians who consciously carry out their duty as "servants of God" or not, policing fulfills what amounts to the religious task of protecting the good and defeating evil. As sociologist Peter Manning writes, "The police view their position as marking the boundaries of the social order, standing between the higher and the lower, the sacred and the profane, the clean and the dirty."[42] In Manning's analysis, the work of police is fundamentally "dramaturgical," meaning it publicly dramatizes myths about the foundations of and threats to social order, myths in which police perform a central role. The myth of police is a myth in the tradition of "the downfall of evil and the eventual triumph of the gods." In narrating and performing a story about good and evil, police forge the boundaries of social order as the boundaries of sacred order, providing an existential "reassurance" of a safe, "bounded" existence.[43] As such, Manning writes, police power transcends the mere professional performance of a task and instead "becomes a sort of 'creed.'"[44] In the face of the threat of the "criminal" that "represents the apotheosis of evil," police embody the mortal God that serves and protects sacred order by overcoming chaos and evil wherever they manifest themselves.[45] In short, police are mythologically integral to the popular imaginary that undergirds contemporary social order: they make, defend, and sustain sacred order by using ordained violence to fight off evil and maintain the boundary between heaven and hell. Because police occupy a central place in the popular political and religious imaginary, to question or organize to diminish or abolish police power registers as an intolerable desecration of the sacred partitions that seem to keep chaos and evil at bay. Returning the favor of their protection, the racial capitalist state and social order defend and sustain police by any and every means necessary.

Neoliberal Racial Capitalism

The history of pseudo-salvific police and carceral power in their intertwining with racial capitalism and settler colonialism is a history not just of the distant past but of the present. From the beginning of the twentieth century through to the 1950s, '60s, and '70s, mass social movements emerged around the globe, including in the US, to challenge the industrial capitalist, white supremacist, and imperialist forces that created conditions of precarity and premature death across the globe. From labor to Black freedom to feminist, socialist, decolonial, and other mass movements demanding a world where oppressed peoples could thrive, social movements of the first seventy years of the twentieth century created significant crises of legitimacy and power for the systems that thrive by way of people's dehumanization and exploitation.[46] Faced with new challenges, especially by organized people directly impacted by the systemic violence of the social order, the state power to accumulate wealth through dispossession and eliminate threats through criminalization pivots and shape-shifts into new forms that, despite seeming to soften its inherent brutality, ultimately reproduce and often expand the same violence under new guises. Following a well-worn cycle, ruling-class and state powers beginning as early as the 1940s and emerging more fully in the 1970s and '80s shifted toward what David Harvey and Ruth Wilson Gilmore call "organized abandonment," a multifaceted process whereby the capitalist state divests public funds previously used for social welfare and funnels it to private corporate entities, as well as to the carceral and police forces of "organized violence" that manage those who are victimized by organized abandonment and repress those who rise up to challenge it.[47]

The term for these social, political, and economic arrangements that privilege economic privatization and market deregulation, eviscerate social welfare programs, prize a culture of individualism and self-interest no matter the cost, and do so according to an underlying racial logic is "neoliberalism." More than some kind of natural evolution in capitalist political economy, neoliberalism in the era of deindustrialization should be understood as a deliberate "revanchist" retaliation meant to recover and expand the economic and political power that ruling classes lost through the victories of decades of radical social movements. While some commentators focus exclusively on the strictly economic dimensions of neoliberalism, neoliberalism cannot be adequately understood apart from the racial foundations of the capitalist order out of which it emerges. Though the architects of neoliberal order tend to avoid the language of race except for token calls for diversity, a eurochristian logic remains in the neoliberal language of "culture" and "civilization," terms that, for the key architects of neoliberal order, stand over and against the profane finitude of nonwhite, uncivilized peoples who fail to submit to and align with sacred market order.[48] As an act of revenge against the wins of movements for liberation, the organized abandonment and organized violence of neoliberal racial capitalism are best understood as modes of race and class war.[49]

Much as in previous eras of capitalist restructuring, raced, gendered, and class-based moral panics about the threat of crime and disorder emerging from the margins of society have dominated the turn to neoliberal racial capitalism. Building on the "law and order" and "war on crime" politics of the 1950s, '60s, and '70s, neoliberalism resorted to police, jails, prisons, and surveillance as central solutions to the problem of "surplus" peoples—the masses of people who, having been dispossessed by neoliberal capital accumulation, cannot be absorbed into wealth-generating markets, making them economically worthless and thus disposable in an order devoted to capital.[50] By situating capture and confinement as the answer to the problem of surplus peoples, neoliberal revanchism helped create the most massive and rapid growth in criminalization and incarceration that the world has ever seen.[51] Indeed, the late twentieth-century rise of the carceral state is itself a manifestation of the rise of neoliberalism: the mass elimination of social goods and the mass expansion of state means of social control and elimination are two sides of the same coin.[52] As sociologist Loïc Wacquant puts it, under neoliberal capitalism, "the prison operates as a judicial garbage disposal into which the human refuse of the market society are thrown."[53] Under such an order, the insecure wage-labor class that the neoliberal state creates with one hand, it punishes and disappears through police, jails, and prisons with the other.[54] The mass criminalization of the late twentieth century, therefore, did not emerge as a response to a real rise in crime but as a counterinsurgent means of managing surplus populations forged by neoliberal racial capitalism and organized resistance to it.[55] As the frontline soldiers in the race and class war that is the ongoing anti-Black, antipoor "war on crime," police since the end of Jim Crow have played a role in continuity with their original purpose of managing the outcomes of the mass dispossession they help create. In short, the police power of criminalization is a prime instantiation of what Gilmore calls "capitalism saving capitalism from capitalism."[56]

"Now, more than ever," Baldwin wrote at the precipice of the era of neoliberal abandonment and mass criminalization, "they appear to measure their safety in chains and corpses." For those who seem to benefit from it, the idea of safety built on capturing and caging the enemies of God and order is so existentially and mythologically significant that it is best understood as *save*-ty: the "safety" produced by chains and corpses of which Baldwin spoke was, in the words of Billy Graham in 1965, "salvation from lawlessness," a salvation made possible by the revanchist power of the mortal God of police—salvation not primarily for those who are captured but for the sacred social order and its managers. Framing the function of police in the era of neoliberalism in terms of salvation is hardly an exaggeration. Indeed, despite emerging in the midst of what by many accounts was an era of secularization, neoliberalism has, from its beginnings, borne the "signature" or imprint of a deeply religious and political-theological rationale.[57] The leading mid-twentieth-century neoliberal economist Friedrich Hayek conceptualized the neoliberal market as a transcendent and inscrutable force that demands faithful subjection to its mysterious workings in exchange for net positive outcomes that strengthen eurochristian civilization. Though committed to secular rationality, Hayek nevertheless figured the forces of neoliberal capitalism in universalizing, pseudo-godlike terms, thereby imbuing the inner workings of neoliberal order with an infinitude that functions benevolently only when obeyed, thereby resembling the God of the soteriology of subjection.[58] More than simply religious, neoliberalism is best understood as salvific, salvific in the same way that the white supremacist "Redemption" movement of a century earlier was salvific: it deified—gave godlike power to—a few by sacrificing many. Restoring the white propertied ruling class to godlike power by subjugating or eliminating its enemies, the dispossessive revanchism at the heart of both Redemption and neoliberalism require the order-saving organized violence of police. Without police, there could be no neoliberal racial capitalism, and without neoliberal racial capitalism, there would be no need for police.

In short, the pretensions to godlike power that have characterized patriarchal and possessive whiteness for centuries persist in neoliberal order. Likewise, as a manifestation of racial capitalism, neoliberalism needs enemies of God and order in order to function at all, and just as in the stages of racial capitalism that preceded the rise of neoliberalism, the counterinsurgent soldiers responsible for securing sacred racial and class order are the police.[59] Now, more than ever—so much more than ever that we use the word "mass" to describe its enormous scope—the managers of racial capitalist order measure their safety, their *save*-ty, their salvation through the organized and often deadly violence of cops and cages.

Broken Windows Policing

Police power, from its earliest manifestations, much like the patriarchal and possessive whiteness with which it is intimately intertwined, has resembled the patriarchal power of a transcendent God.[60] According to the early nineteenth-century congressman, Supreme Court justice, and enslaver Philip Barbour, police power is a power innate to sovereignty and as such should enjoy an "indefinite supremacy," an "undeniable and unlimited jurisdiction over all persons and things."[61] A few decades later, Supreme Court justice Samuel Miller declared that police power "is, and must be from its very nature, incapable of any exact definition or limitation." Founded on an infinitely indefinable principle of discretion, police power transcends the law for the sake of sacred order.[62] Indeed, the legal and political authorities who helped enshrine police power understood it as an inherently creative power in the cosmological sense. As literary theorist Bryan Wagner, summarizing an 1851 majority opinion written by Justice Lemuel Shaw, writes, "Without the police power, there would be no society to protect in the first place." Transcending limits both conceptual and material, the state's police power, under such a rationale, becomes "a precondition for social existence."[63] The practically divine nature of popular and ruling-class legal conceptions of police power from its germination and over the course of centuries has meant that superficial or reformist challenges to its institutionalized manifestations rarely, if ever, effect any significant reduction in its functionally infinite power or scope. If police cannot be a godlike power, if they cannot force into moral subjection those who otherwise refuse it, they cannot *be* at all.

For centuries up until the early 1970s, vagrancy laws were central to the inherently vague and indeterminate discretionary power of police and were used to punish a wide range of statuses and actions that the state and ruling classes deemed threatening to the smooth functioning of social order.[64] As a result of social movements challenging the social injustices that police power helped create and defend, in the early 1970s, the Supreme Court ruled that most vagrancy laws were unconstitutional. The Court's ruling did not, however, signal the end of police power's status as a mortal God, as indeed the decision came around the same time that the Court also reaffirmed other aspects of the broad-ranging police power to intervene in the lives of people or actions deemed, by the discretion of police, out of place.[65] In one of those cases, *Terry v. Ohio* (1968), the Court decided that police officers are permitted to stop, search, and question people without concretely informed "probable cause," so long as officers have "reasonable articulable suspicion" that the person may be committing a crime and posing a danger to others. The Court's ruling, which sacralized the "suspicion" of state agents that exist to defend racial capitalist order, opened the door to stop-and-frisk policing, which enabled the mass criminalization of youth and adults of color as well as economically dispossessed people of all races whom individual officers—or their superiors—find suspicious and who they determine pose some threat to public "order," as defined by propertied classes, no matter how vague or abstract that threat may be.[66]

Thus, in the absence of the straightforward social control enabled by vagrancy laws, municipalities during the early neoliberal era resorted to alternate and legally viable means of controlling and eliminating the threats posed by masses of people dispossessed by neoliberalism's mass elimination of social goods. In 1982, in the middle of these social, political, and economic rearrangements, George Kelling and James Q. Wilson, two officials with the Police Foundation—a neoliberal organization that pushed law-and-order politics under the umbrella of "police reform"—published an article in the *Atlantic Monthly* that laid out a theory of urban crime and disorder that would soon reconstitute antivagrancy policing under a new name. Elaborating on the French aphorism that "he who steals an egg, steals an ox," Kelling and Wilson's "broken windows" theory of urban crime and disorder rests on the sociologically dubious assertion that small signs of disorder—like a broken window—have the effect of inviting further, more serious crime. Premised on the idea that "disorder and crime are usually inextricably linked," broken windows theory reasons that the way to combat serious crime is to combat the small signs of disorder that supposedly make serious crime possible: by fixing broken windows, you repair a neighborhood's vulnerability to the crime that "broken windows" inevitably draw. According to the theory, behaviors associated with chronically unhoused and other underclass populations—like panhandling, loitering, or public drunkenness—are the signs of disorder, the broken windows, that invite more serious crime to proliferate. By "fixing broken windows" in the form of low-level disorderly behavior and crime, police unite their traditional "order-maintenance" and "crime-prevention" functions into one. Kelling and Wilson write,

> The citizen who fears the ill-smelling drunk, the rowdy teenager, or the importuning beggar is not merely expressing his distaste for unseemly behavior; he is also giving voice to a bit of folk wisdom that happens to be a correct generalization—namely, that serious street crime flourishes in areas in which disorderly behavior goes unchecked. The unchecked panhandler is, in effect, the first broken window. Muggers and robbers, whether opportunistic or professional, believe they reduce their chances of being caught or even identified if they operate on streets where potential victims are already intimidated by prevailing conditions. If the neighborhood cannot keep a bothersome panhandler from annoying passersby, the thief may reason, it is even less likely to call the police to identify a potential mugger or to interfere if the mugging actually takes place.[67]

Much like early modern views that perceived idleness and propertylessness as the root of all crime and disorder and that defined crime in opposition to the traits and possessions of propertied people, broken windows theory defines the behaviors—and indeed the mere presence—of working-class and underclass populations as problems to be fixed through criminal statutes that disappear the problem from public view, allegedly preventing more serious crime and disorder in the process. Also like the measures implemented by early modern legal and political authorities and wealthy elites, neoliberal broken windows policing abstracts poverty from the broader social forces that create it, reducing it to a manifestation of individual immorality rather than the social forces that actually create it and, in so doing, rendering it a status inherently threatening to social order. As two-time New York Police Department (NYPD) and one-time Los Angeles Police Department (LAPD) police chief William Bratton, who helped develop and implement broken windows policing across the globe, put it, "The cause of crime is the bad behavior of individuals, . . . not the consequence of social conditions."[68]

Working around the unconstitutionality of explicitly criminalizing the status of poverty and other supposedly order-disrupting modes of existence, broken windows policing criminalizes alleged behaviors associated with people deliberately abandoned by the state and, in so doing, functionally criminalizes their very existence. As "a technique for the invisibilization of the social 'problems' that the state . . . no longer can or cares to treat at its roots," the criminalization of people forced into conditions of poverty is essentially a means of eliminating such people from social existence.[69] In the decade-plus following Kelling and Wilson's 1982 article, right-wing think tanks like the Manhattan Institute and the Heritage Foundation popularized broken windows by posing it as a solution to social and economic problems facing cities, while public officials including New York City's Mayor Rudolph Giuliani and Bratton implemented broken windows through city policy and policing strategies starting in 1994. Under Giuliani and Bratton, "squeegee men," drug dealers, sex workers, panhandlers, unhoused persons, "street people" with mental illness, graffiti artists, and people who play music too loudly became reviled threats to public order and security and were targeted as such. Much as lawmakers understood dispossessed peoples four centuries earlier, for Bratton, such people were quite literally "the enemy" of the city, its authorities, and its residents.[70] In sharp contrast to the progressive notion that the so-called disorderly behavior and low-level misdemeanor crimes of dispossessed peoples are relatively harmless, Bratton claimed that quality-of-life crimes do not so much "victimize" individuals as the entire social order itself: "The victim was the neighborhood. The victim was the borough. The victim was the city."[71] The low-level crimes of dispossessed people, Bratton proclaimed, are "crimes committed against the community."[72] Under the banner of two phrases that would soon become and remain central to policing in municipalities across the country, New York City implemented a "zero tolerance" approach to such criminal activity in order to restore the "quality of life" of the public, which is to say, those who are not poor or unhoused. Following New York and later Los Angeles, broken windows was exported to and implemented in police departments and courts across the country and even abroad.[73]

Wealth-accumulating organized abandonment cannot be sustained in the long term without organized violence, and in the neoliberal era, that violence has taken the form of broken windows policing. Indeed, there can be no neoliberal racial capitalism without it. The state violence of broken windows policing is often spectacular and high-profile, including the police murders of Eric Garner, George Floyd, and literally tens of thousands of others over the past thirty to forty years. Broken windows policing is also extremely mundane, and when mundane, no less violent. Broken windows policing has radically expanded the rate at which Black, brown, and Indigenous people and poor people of all races are stopped, questioned, searched, cited, or arrested and detained by the police. As a result, broken windows policing has radically expanded the machinery of the multifaceted carceral system required to keep up with so many state interventions into people's lives. The rate of police encounters—both those ending in arrest and those that do not—in large cities like New York as well as smaller municipalities have skyrocketed between the mid-1990s and today, impacting millions of people every year. As legal scholar Babe Howell argues, order-maintenance and quality-of-life policing have become the "most common point of contact between the public and the criminal justice system."[74] The full scope of the impacts of broken windows policing on people's lives is so enormous that it is difficult to quantify. In addition to the thousands of lives lost to the immediate violence of broken windows policing, the life-disrupting fines and fees that often result from encounters with order-maintenance policing, and that fall most heavily on already dispossessed communities, turn into city revenue often adding up to millions of dollars every year. For those who are arrested, even a brief stint in jail, before one has ever been found guilty, can destabilize a person's life in irreparable ways.

Even when encounters with the police do not result in death, arrest, or imprisonment in jail or prison, the impacts of contact with the punishment system regularly jeopardize people's housing, employment, schooling, parenting, and family statuses, in turn deepening the social, racial, and economic inequalities on which the social order is already built.[75] Legal scholar Issa Kohler-Hausmann argues that focusing critical attention exclusively on imprisonment in prison or jail "understates" and "misrepresents" the vast majority of interventions that police make in people's lives.[76] According to Kohler-Hausmann, taken as a whole, the work that the criminal punishment system does under broken windows is ultimately more "managerial" than "adjudicative."[77] In other words, through broken-windows-style mass criminalization, the state intervenes in people's lives in ways that are less concerned with innocence and guilt and more concerned with managing, testing, and controlling populations through administrative procedures that, together, forge neoliberal "order" by keeping people in their proper "place" within that order. Structured according to wealth-generating and thus deeply dispossessive racial, class, and gender hierarchies, the neoliberal order that mass criminalization creates and sustains is an order of wealth and power for a few and vulnerability to premature death for many. Thus, while technically the result of formal shifts in police strategy, the dramatic increase in police encounters over the past three to four decades is, at a deeper level, a manifestation of neoliberal racial capitalism saving itself from itself. The mortal God of police saves the social order by eliminating the living manifestations of dispossession that it produces. As such, the abolition of police is also the abolition of the order they uphold, which helps explain why the racial capitalist state responded to the global call to defund and abolish police by pouring more cash into police than ever before.

In continuity with the social imaginary undergirding white settler colonialism, Kelling and Wilson's broken windows theory likens the neighborhood where the "disorderly" behaviors of "undesirable" lower-class people go "unchecked" to a "frightening jungle," a "threatening place" vulnerable to "criminal invasion."[78] Such language articulates the warmaking and threat-elimination function central to police power. More broadly, broken windows theory borrows from and contributes to the long-standing mythologies about the central role of police power in the creation and protection of civilization itself.[79] In a world depicted as utterly chaotic and disorderly, police power brings order and thereby makes it possible for communities to go on existing in the face of monstrous, existential threats from within and without. Indeed, the mythology of broken windows is a mythology based in what legal historian Bernard Harcourt calls "a continual struggle of good versus evil."[80] That broken windows envisions the world in such a way is not surprising given the intellectual and political lineage from which Kelling and Wilson emerge. One figure in particular, Edward Banfield, who taught Wilson at the University of Chicago, helped shape neoliberal social thought and policy, including that of Kelling and Wilson, with the publication of his landmark 1970 text *The Unheavenly City*. In it, Banfield blamed the problems facing cities not on systemic forces but on the moral pathologies of poor people. Much like the white settlers of California who hoped to create a patriarchal Anglo-Saxon "Eden" by eliminating vagrants only a few decades earlier, Banfield envisioned a society made "heavenly" by the carceral correction or police elimination of people allegedly disposed to criminal immorality. Through their antisocial, order-disrupting behavior, Banfield argued, poor people "generate social problems," including "violent crime," and thereby threaten "the 'quality-of-life' or, as it used to be called *civilization*."[81] By eliminating disorderly threats to social order, the mythology goes, police make it possible for human society not only to thrive but to exist at all.[82]

While the state's formal, public-facing rhetoric regarding broken windows policing seldom deploys explicitly religious or moralistic language to describe either the work of the police or the behaviors of the lower-class populations it targets—perhaps with the exception of sex workers—some of its advocates have nevertheless discerned in broken windows philosophy an implicit Christian logic of order, purity, and obedience.

In addition to a number of online devotional reflections and sermons that utilize broken windows as a conceptual frame through which to enjoin Christians to repair the moral and spiritual broken windows in their lives, one of the clearest interpretations of the religious character of broken windows theory comes from the evangelical prison ministry leader Charles Colson. In a 1997 article published in *Christianity Today*, titled "Cleanliness Is Next to Crimelessness," Colson wrote that advocates of the new broken windows and community policing philosophy "may not know it, but they are reviving a classic Christian understanding that crime is not only an individual act but also a violation of the social order." Like Durkheim and others before him, Colson characterizes criminality—particularly that of lower and racialized classes—as an offense against order, which amounts to an offense against God's order and thus a desecration. Decrying the Supreme Court's dismantling of police powers against the disorder of vagrancy and loitering that, in the seeming absence of adequate social control, promised to destroy American cities, Colson praises the advent of broken windows as a means of reempowering cities to purify themselves of "antisocial behavior" like the "scribbling of graffiti and panhandling."[83]

Parroting the playbook of Kelling, Wilson, Banfield, Giuliani, and Bratton, Colson locates the source of crime in disorder and thus the elimination of crime in the imposition of an order that is at once secular and religious. "To reverse the destruction of our cities," he wrote, "we need to revive the classic Christian understanding of order." Referencing Augustine, Colson argues that societal justice and peace are impossible without the "tranquility of order."[84] All things considered, the title of Colson's article, more than anything, clarifies the fundamental religiosity of the broken windows logic: like the sacred partitions that separate pure and impure, good and evil, orderly and disorderly, broken windows equates crime with "dirt"—which, as Mary Douglas notes, signifies moral disorder—which is why Colson equates the elimination of crime with the elimination of dirt. Channeling the phrase attributed to John Wesley, founder of Methodism, that "cleanliness is next to godliness," Colson implies that the elimination of the social dirt of criminality is a manifestation of the cleansing—saving—power of God. Whether articulated, as with Colson, in an explicitly religious idiom or not, the widespread presumption remains that the eliminatory violence work of policing, and broken windows policing in particular, is a manifestation of inherently moral, even divine authority in the form of political authority and is thus inherently sacred—necessary for life.

Salvation from Unhoused People

In early modern Europe, political, economic, and religious authorities forged a popular imaginary according to which poverty was a result not of forced dispossession but of one's own moral failing. To be poor was to be distant from God. While the dynamics of this fabricated illusion have shifted over time, they have not disappeared: the state and ruling classes today continue to blame poor folks as the cause of their own precarity, when in fact it is the direct result of systems that create increasingly massive wealth for a few through the disenfranchisement of many. As a result, most people take widespread forms of extreme poverty like mass homelessness to be a more or less natural or inevitable reality in US society. The actual reality, however, is that it was only a few decades ago that massive federal cuts in affordable housing, mental health care, and other social goods displaced people from housing on an unprecedented scale.[85] As a product of neoliberal abandonment, the explosion in numbers of people without housing took place at the same time as the expansion of the organized violence of the prison industrial complex and the birth of broken windows policing in particular. The same neoliberal order that creates "surplus" peoples—people who are no longer useful for the production of other people's wealth—regards and treats the visible presence of people enduring poverty as an offense against it.

Enter, once again, police, whose work today often includes the deliberate harassment, perpetual displacement, citation, and arrest of unhoused people in cities and municipalities across the US. Why do police continue to spend so many resources on eliminating dispossessed and unhoused people, as they have for as long as they have existed? Today, they do so because just by existing within view, unhoused people threaten to disrupt the flow of capital, potentially diminishing the wealth of the managers and beneficiaries of neoliberal order. Police also continue to hunt unhoused people because, under broken windows logic, people visibly enduring poverty—which has always been associated with criminality—constitute a "broken window" that, left unfixed, threatens to invite further criminality and thus disorder. Like conceptions and realities of "vagrancy" and its criminalization in earlier eras, the deliberate *creation* of mass houselessness and its *criminalization* cannot be separated: the same forces that create mass houselessness define and punish it as an offense against law and order. Police exist to make and purify sacred order by eliminating what threatens to pollute it. By eliminating unhoused people, people who are widely presumed to be inherently immoral and thus potentially criminal, from public and private space, police secure—save—sacred order from those whose mere presence seems to threaten its very existence.

The rhetoric of movements against the criminalization of homelessness, derived from the testimonies of unhoused people themselves, often proclaims that "it's not a crime to be homeless." Technically, there is no law explicitly prohibiting homelessness as such. Practically speaking, however, the combination of police discretion, municipal and state "quality of life" ordinances prohibiting life-sustaining functions in public, laws banning camping on public property, and the demands of the racial capitalist social order that police serve and protect have all rendered homelessness a punishable offense against the social order, resulting in millions of stops, searches, citations, arrests, and convictions every year.[86] Despite the unconstitutionality of the criminalization of an individual's status, broken windows and quality-of-life policing continue to effectively criminalize the status of unhoused people by using discretion to apply the law selectively against people performing basic human functions—sleeping, sitting, standing, walking, eating, using the bathroom, and so on—without housing and thus in public.

There are many ordinances that police, in coordination with state and municipal government officials, business owners, and developers, use to criminalize unhoused people today, including prohibitions on criminal trespass, obstructing a passageway or sidewalk, loitering, sitting or lying down, panhandling, sharing or serving food, living in vehicles, defecating or urinating, scavenging or dumpster diving, disorderly conduct, public intoxication, being out past curfew, truancy, and more.[87] Much like during the Reconstruction era, criminal trespass remains one of the foremost tools at the disposal of police to remove specific people from private and public properties. In most major North American cities, where populations of unhoused people are concentrated and where numbers of unhoused people are on the rise, there are seldom nearly enough shelter beds to hold the number of people without housing, and even if there were, shelter systems are only a temporary solution. Moreover, most shelters operate with barriers that make it impossible for a significant number of people—including especially couples, pet owners, and queer and gender-nonconforming people—to utilize their services.[88] As a result, public camping has also been on the rise for some time. While a few municipalities formally allow designated homeless encampments and some look the other way, most cities send the police in to "sweep" encampments, often slashing tents and demolishing what few belongings people have before citing, arresting, or evicting their residents, who, once displaced, often just set up a new camp at a site the police have not found yet. Many camp evictions are the result of a private property owner issuing a complaint or developers conferring with municipalities to clear all visual signs of homelessness in advance of a commercial or luxury housing construction project. In other cases, special interests converge to advocate for the passage of laws such as one passed in 2022 in Tennessee that makes unapproved camping on any public property in the state a felony offense.

In other cases, unhoused people are arrested for trespassing not while camping but for simply trying to survive the elements without reliable means of shelter. A twenty-eight-year-old unhoused woman named Charlotte, for instance, was digging through a trash can outside a Rite Aid at the corner of Rosa Parks Boulevard and Jefferson Street in Nashville, Tennessee, before the sun rose on the morning of April 7, 2013, when a police car approached. Moments later, Charlotte was in the back of the police car en route to the city jail. As Charlotte's arresting officer wrote in the affidavit, "Defendant was observed at arrest location going through trash can. Right next to where defendant was standing in plain view there was a sign posted no trespassing, loitering, or standing." After spending four days in a jail cell for digging her arm through a trash can in the middle of the night, Charlotte was released back to the streets.[89] Much like Charlotte, Charles, a Black queer man experiencing homelessness, was given a citation for trespassing while trying to stay out of the rain on the property of a closed business directly next to the Nashville Rescue Mission, just south of downtown Nashville. "I felt harassed in a way, you know, being homeless—and they know who I am," he said.

"I think that it is kinda like a way of taking away my freedoms, because I wasn't breaking or entering, I was just trying to get in out of the rain."[90]

In addition to criminal trespass, ordinances prohibiting obstructing a passageway or roadway, which have legal roots in the criminalization of labor strikes and were routinely used against protesters during the Black freedom movement of the 1960s, are another means by which police disappear unhoused people from public spaces, usually for sitting, sleeping, or even just standing in place, which is to say, out of place.[91] As I also recount in the preface, a few months before the police got to Charlotte and Charles, in the middle of a frigid February night, a Metro Nashville police officer gave a criminal citation for "obstructing a passageway" to Anthony, a disabled, unhoused Black man who had parked his motorized wheelchair alongside two other people on a large heating grate to keep warm as temperatures dropped. As the arresting officer wrote in his affidavit, he initiated a *Terry* stop on Anthony because he was "blocking the sidewalk" and "observed an individual try to pass the group that was blocking the sidewalk, and the individual had to walk off the sidewalk in the gardening area to get past them." Anthony reports that the officer talked to him "very disrespectfully" and that he had to bite his tongue to avoid going to jail. "Four o'clock in the morning," Anthony quipped in disbelief at the idea that he was obstructing pedestrians: "Who's on the sidewalk?" Anthony spent the rest of the night, without heat, shivering outside the bus station. After pleading guilty, Anthony's court costs totaled $259.33.[92]

Tina, a white, unhoused woman in her twenties, was cited for obstructing a passageway in October 2009, while standing next to a park bench on Church Street where her friends were sitting. The bench was located outside Morton's, an upscale steakhouse, and directly across from the Downtown Public Library. The officer told Tina that he wrote the citation because the restaurant had called in a complaint about her allegedly blocking the sidewalk outside the business. "I thought it was a little strange because I wasn't in the way," she said. After she blew off the ticket, not realizing its seriousness, a warrant for her arrest was put out. More than two years later, in January 2012, police tracked her down. She was arrested and spent ten days in jail. "I just hope it doesn't happen to anybody else," she said, "'cause, I mean, it's pointless, you know. Find somebody else that is doing something worse than standing in a sidewalk." After her jail stay, Tina owed the city $344.10.[93] Like Tina, a disabled, middle-aged, unhoused Black man who went by the name "Dr. John" received a criminal citation for obstructing a passageway while propping up his ankle—swollen from lack of housing and subsequently untreated medical conditions—on a crate under a bridge in the middle of a rainy night in July 2013. Because he could not afford the fines, he was, until his death in 2021, technically still indebted to the city and liable to be arrested at any time. In his words, "Ain't no way I'm gonna build up no daggone $120. Ain't no way. So they want to eventually put me in jail. It's nothing you can do. You're never right. You're always wrong."[94]

Among the many physically, psychologically, financially, and socially harmful impacts of such forms of broken windows criminalization is that, by placing legally enforceable prohibitions on basic life-sustaining functions when performed outdoors, they leave unhoused people feeling as if their very existence is illegal. A middle-aged white man who goes by Doc and lives on the streets of Nashville was arrested for criminal trespass in 2013 for sleeping among trees behind a brick ledge at the top of a hill that descended down toward the Cumberland River. Doc says there wasn't a "No Trespassing" sign anywhere within view. He petitioned the officer to use his discretion to let him off with a warning instead, but the officer cited him anyway. "I felt like I was charged for being homeless and for breathing air," he said.[95] An unhoused Indigenous person living in Seattle named Tom was arrested for being in a park after being served with a park exclusion notice. "I can't go anywhere," he said, echoing Doc's words. "Just bein' anywhere I'm committing a crime."[96] As housed and unhoused anticriminalization activists often put it, the fight against the criminalization of homelessness is a fight for "the right to exist." In a racial capitalist society, however, the right to exist is, by definition, not guaranteed. Forged through enclosures that displaced and rendered people perpetually "out of place," and ultimately disposable, racial capitalism in its neoliberal iteration continues to enclose and displace people from the spaces where they struggle to survive. For the managers of order, the proper place for unhoused people in a neoliberal society is no place at all.

To some readers, the police criminalization of people already struggling to survive without a safe, affordable place to call home will seem senseless, irrational. The reality, however, is that the criminalization of people simply trying to survive is neither an outlier in the scheme of police work nor unreasonable within racial capitalist settler colonial social order as a whole. Michel Foucault argues that the power that structures a carceral society organized according to hierarchies of race is not reducible to repressive power *against* but is better understood as power *for*—power that produces things, that brings about life, order, and even pleasure.[97] The same goes for policing. The negations imposed on criminalized people is an act of creation for the order, its managers, and its beneficiaries. As key terms in the lexicon of broken windows imply, policing strives to "improve" the "quality of life" itself—just as enclosure has been said to "improve" the "waste" land of the commons from the beginning of capitalism to the present.[98] The question, as social movements have asked for decades, is *whose* quality of life broken windows policing serves and protects and who must suffer—which is to say, who must be sacrificed—for that life to be possible? The answer, by now, should be clear. The state and police power structure spaces of belonging and trespass that disappear people like Charlotte, Anthony, Tina, Dr. John, and Doc so that the managers and beneficiaries of the deliberately inequitable social order disrupted by their presence might have life to the fullest, which is to say, so that they might be secured, saved, again and again, "forever and ever, Amen!"

Salvation from Blackness

Arising from the same racial capitalist settler colonial social order that deployed slave patrol and antivagrancy policing to keep Black people in their subservient "place" beginning more than three hundred years ago, broken windows policing that targets unhoused people also targets Black people as potential or actual trespassers in a world ordered around the sacred properties of whiteness. The broken windows police power to stop and search people on the street without probable cause that took the place of the police power to enforce vagrancy laws beginning in the 1970s paved the way for the mass criminalization of Black people at the hands of police in municipalities across the US, thereby forging the era of mass incarceration in which we still live today. It is difficult to capture the impact that broken windows policing has on the lives of those who are caught in its web. Every year, broken-windows-style policing unnecessarily burdens hundreds of thousands, if not millions, of Black people, Indigenous people, other people of color, and economically dispossessed people of all races and ethnicities with criminal records, jail or prison time, and traumas that impact employment, housing, education, wealth, family, physical and mental health, and general well-being for years after the fact, often in ways that lead to premature death.[99]

Exactly one hundred years before the birth of broken windows policing, Frederick Douglass identified that, in the wake of the Civil War and the abolition of slavery, the Black Codes and vagrancy laws that legislators and former planters proliferated and police enforced served to "impute crime to color."[100] The conflation of Blackness and criminality continues to permeate the popular white, propertied social imaginary today, and broken windows policing is a primary means by which it does so. Just as Black Codes and Jim Crow fulfilled the function of Black subjugation that chattel slavery no longer could, so broken windows manages or eliminates people dispossessed by the organized state abandonment of neoliberal racial capitalism through policing and incarceration that captures a disproportionate number of Black people and other people of color on the basis of legal infractions for which white people are either not arrested or receive lesser punishments. Despite the claims of its founding theorists and practitioners, broken windows policing does not prevent crime so much as construct the criminality of nonwhite and economically dispossessed peoples in order to justify state interventions that incapacitate, disappear, and in effect purify the social order of those who are constructed as inherent threats to it.[101] Multiple studies show that, despite being seemingly race-neutral or colorblind on the surface, broken windows policing that engages in frequent stops and searches of people without probable cause has an impact that is severely racially disparate, creating individual and collective traumas that linger and multiply.[102] While few police today would say that they understand their role as present-day slave catchers, the impact of broken windows policing is functionally the same in that, by capturing and so dispossessing Black and economically dispossessed people far more than others, it quite concretely reproduces the same centuries-old racial, class, and gender hierarchies on which the United States was founded.

Broken windows policing dispossesses and traumatizes Black and other dispossessed peoples. It also kills.

As a means of managing the outcomes of neoliberal racial capitalist abandonment, broken windows policing led to the death of twenty-two-year-old Kalief Browder in 2015. Police arrested Browder at age sixteen for allegedly stealing a backpack, which he insisted he did not do. Browder spent three years in jail at Rikers Island without ever being convicted of a crime. Two of those years he spent in solitary confinement. After enduring physical and mental abuse at Rikers, Browder attempted suicide in 2012, and he did so again after he was released in 2013. After multiple hospitalizations for physical and mental health difficulties, Browder committed suicide on June 6, 2015, at his family's home in the Bronx.[103] Browder may have died by suicide, but in the larger scheme, it was broken windows policing and the abuses he endured in jail that created the conditions for his death. While not every police stop for a petty or fabricated low-level crime ends the same way it did for Browder, the ripple effects of harm that begin with a *Terry* stop often lead to premature death.

Sometimes the path toward death that broken windows policing initiates takes place over years. In other cases, the fists, arms, knees, batons, and bullets of broken windows policing kill in an instant. One of the most widely known instances of a fatal broken-windows-style *Terry* stop is the case of Eric Garner, a forty-three-year-old Black man choked to death on the sidewalk by white NYPD officer Daniel Pantaleo on July 17, 2014. Officers confronted Garner in Staten Island under suspicion that he was selling untaxed loose cigarettes on the street, an action that is consequential only under a philosophy of broken windows policing that views such a petty crime as an offense against racial capitalist order and a gateway to more serious crime. Garner had been targeted for petty offenses by Staten Island police for at least seven years before the day of his murder, and a civil rights lawsuit he filed in 2007 alleged public sexual violation at the hands of officers. As officers approached him on July 17, Garner protested, "Every time you see me you arrest me. I'm tired of it. It stops today." After begging for the officers to leave him alone, Pantaleo put Garner in an illegal chokehold. After repeating the words "I can't breathe" eleven consecutive times, Garner fell unconscious and died one hour later. Garner was a large Black man whose very figure, read through the prism of white supremacist projections of Black animality and violence, already registered as a potential threat to white security and thus as a kind of transgression of public space coded according to approved forms of racial capitalist commerce. The father of six children and grandfather to three grandchildren, Garner was no longer able to work more traditional jobs due to health problems. By selling untaxed cigarettes as a means of survival outside an economy from which he was effectively barred, Garner trespassed against an order that is based on and even encourages theft on an enormous scale yet polices every move of those who try to survive via unapproved forms of capital exchange, even to the point of death.

The police murder of Eric Garner was the result of a decade-long attempt to "fix" a "broken window" by disappearing it altogether. And yet, thanks to the uprisings and organizing that emerged in response, the effort to disappear Garner instead illuminated for the world the deadly injustice of the racial capitalist and carceral systems that killed him and keep on disappearing and killing others like him. Garner's dying words—"I can't breathe" and "this ends here"—became rallying cries of a new era of Black-led racial justice and abolitionist movements to dismantle the racial capitalism and carcerality embedded in the foundations of US society.[104] The uprisings of 2015 paved the way five years later, in the summer of 2020, for the largest protest movement in US history, which emerged in response to multiple police and vigilante murders of Black people. Among the victims was George Floyd of Minneapolis, whom officer Derek Chauvin killed by pressing his knee into Floyd's neck for more than nine minutes during an arrest after a corner-store clerk called the cops on him for allegedly using a counterfeit $20 bill to buy a pack of cigarettes. After Floyd called out for his mother and repeated the words "I can't breathe" over and over, he died. Under neoliberal racial capitalism, those who are deemed out of place often die quite literally out of breath at the hands, arms, and knees of the mortal God of police, the embodied "muscle" of racial capitalism.[105] In a world made for whiteness and its properties, from the streets of Minneapolis to New York to Nashville, Black people, as well as Indigenous people, other people of color, and propertyless people of all races who step out of place by simply trying to survive in a world that thrives by way of their suffering are made vulnerable, again and again, to premature death at the hands of the state. The mortal God of broken windows police power saves the sacred order of whiteness and property by subjecting disorderly peoples to chains and, when necessary, by reducing them to corpses.

Geographies of Salvation

The racial capitalist settler colonial aspiration to maintain orderly purity by eliminating the disorderly pollution embodied by the enemies of God and order gives rise to functionally sacred partitions that must be protected at all costs. Without clear boundaries that demarcate the safe from the dangerous, the innocent from the monstrous, the good from the demonic, the sacred from the profane, there can be no safety, which is to say, no salvation from the existential threat of disorder posed by the "dangerous classes." As I have argued, the work of creating, defending, and sustaining sacred order and the partitions that make it possible is the work of the mortal God—police. At the end of the day, the boundary-forging, order-protecting power of police does not operate by sheer force alone but by mythologies that make ultimate meaning and that make that meaning material, even spatial. As Correia and Wall write, police are central not only to race-making but to "place-making."[106] And central to the police work of place-making is the mythology that police embody the fragile boundary between chaos and civilization.

The Sacred Thin Blue Line

Patriarchal whiteness and private property—the beating heart of racial capitalist settler colonial order—are manifestations of the anxious human aspiration to transcend mortal finitude and exercise godlike power over the world and its peoples. As phenomena that define and obtain their power in and through the dispossession or outright destruction of others, whiteness and property can exist and keep on existing only when they are empowered to hold those whom they dispossess and disempower in subjection, keep them in their proper "place," or eliminate them altogether. If those who, by ruling-class definition, belong on the other side of sacred partitions encroach on those borders, the ruling-class mythology goes, disorder ensues. According to capitalist, colonial, and carceral logic, police exist to hold that line using whatever force necessary, because the entire social order depends on it.[107] In contemporary police mythology, the name of the border that police hold and embody is the thin blue line.

Well before the advent of uniformed, badged, armed, salaried police officers, the earliest articulations of the police power of the state established itself as the ordained capacity to eliminate threats to order and so to make order and thus civilization possible in the first place. Western political philosophy in the lineage of Thomas Hobbes amounts to a philosophy of police power, the power to create order from out of the chaos of the state of nature by drawing masterless people into subjection to a sovereign who in turn maintains peace through the use of legitimate violence against the enemies of God and order.[108] Hobbes's mythology of the state thus constitutes what Correia and Wall call a "police conception of history," according to which "the police powers secure the conditions for civil society . . . based on racial capitalist, colonial, social relations of private property, the wage relation, and accumulation."[109] Hierarchical social relations generate and indeed run on the basis of relations of enmity, which is to say, enemies, enemies against which the managers of order must in turn protect themselves. Without the power to eliminate or manage the enemies that capitalist and colonial order itself generates, capitalist and colonial order could not survive. In these ways, police power, according to this mythology, is an inherently creative power, in the cosmological sense: it is, like God, the omnipotent power apart from which the world as we know it could not exist.[110]

The cultural symbol that has come to embody this police mythology in the present era, the thin blue line, derives from the mid-nineteenth-century characterization of a British battalion in the Crimean War as a "thin red line." Starting in the 1920s, New York City police commissioner Richard Enright began to refer to the role of police in terms of a "thin blue line," and by the 1950s, the image took hold among a growing number of police officials and politicians. The phrase reached new cultural significance through the cultural influence of LAPD chief William H. Parker, who, in addition to working with Hollywood producers to incorporate police as heroes into popular television shows, racially disparaged Indigenous immigrants from "the wild tribes of Mexico" and described Black participants in the Watts Rebellion as "monkeys in a zoo."[111] Imagining the work of police well beyond that of mere law enforcement, Correia and Wall write that the thin blue line casts police in "sacred, mystical" terms as "the very line—the border or boundary—dividing wickedness from the good life, morality from depravity, and the sacred from the profane."[112] Deriving from a war metaphor, and considering that police have long articulated themselves as agents of ordained violence against the criminal enemies of all humankind, the thin blue line should be understood as "a battle line" and thus as a manifestation of a "mythology of war" against "evil incarnate."[113]

Members of the ruling class have also articulated the violence work of the thin blue line in implicitly colonial and racialized terms as an antidote to the immoral savagery of nonwhite peoples who remain in the state of nature. Speaking at the 1981 meeting of the International Association of Chiefs of Police in New Orleans, Louisiana, President Ronald Reagan identified the source of the problem of crime in the United States as the systematic weakening of our individual and collective morals. If the problem of crime is a problem of morality, then it demands a "moral" and "spiritual solution," and central to that solution, he asserted, is strengthening the "criminal justice system," which "acts as the collective moral voice of society." With clear racial and colonial overtones, Reagan warned that the moral threat of crime is the threat of a "jungle" where "the darker impulses of human nature thrive," a "jungle [that] is always there waiting to take us over." Reagan concluded his speech with a word of ruling-class gratitude to the defenders of racial capitalist settler colonial order: "I commend you for manning the thin blue line that holds back a jungle which threatens to reclaim this clearing we call civilization."[114] Less than a year after Reagan's speech, Kelling and Wilson wrote in their article outlining their broken windows theory that a neighborhood in which police do not maintain order will inevitably devolve into "an inhospitable and frightening jungle."[115] In the eurochristian settler colonial imaginary, jungles are sites of racial hostility, zones from which Black and Indigenous peoples launch attacks against Western colonial and imperial power. As such, the thin blue line between the "clearing" of civilization and the "jungle" of savagery is not just a boundary marker but a battle line that extends into and becomes the fences, gates, and walls of the property line, the color line, the border, the jail, and the prison.[116] The thin blue line is the front line in the state's sacred racial class war.

As with most mythologies of good versus evil, police mythology both produces and is produced by anxiety and fear. In *Police Strategy No. 5: Reclaiming the Public Spaces of New York*, a memo published in 1994, NYPD Police Chief Bratton and Mayor Rudy Giuliani announced the advent of the era of broken windows policing beginning with the NYPD, the world's largest police department. In the memo, Bratton and Giuliani argue that New York was "a city out of control" and thus a city of mass disorder that generated fear among its residents.[117] According to *Police Strategy No. 5*, as for all racial capitalist settler colonial and police strategies, the disorder and fear it produced are fundamentally geographical, embodied, and spatial phenomena. As the memo's subtitle—*Reclaiming the Public Spaces of New York*—strives to indicate, the physical spaces of the city were so overrun with people dispossessed by neoliberal racial capitalism that it was as if it had been seized by enemies. Just as Reagan, Kelling, Wilson, and other managers and architects of racial capitalist order identified their enemy as a creature of the jungle of disorder, so Bratton and Giuliani decried people trying to survive dispossession in public space as savage enemies of sacred order who must be vanquished. By eliminating the underclass enemies of order, Bratton and Giuliani reasoned, "civility," which is to say, civilization, would be restored. At the end of the day, the spatial and geographical reclamations that broken windows policing makes possible are indispensable to neoliberal order. Indeed, territorial reclamation by force—the ordained force of both racial capital and police power—is central to the organized abandonment and violence through which the ruling classes displace and eliminate those surplus peoples who impede the smooth functioning of order.

The inherently fear-based mythology of police power, especially in its broken windows iterations, deifies those who inhabit and possess patriarchal whiteness and property by demonizing and destroying those who do not. The dynamic of deification and destruction that structures racial capitalist settler colonial society and the mortal God of police that helps forge and maintain that society is not abstract but quite concrete, geographical, spatial—"ownership of the earth forever and ever, Amen!" Claims to absolute possession generate borders and boundaries marking off the functionally sacred from the functionally profane and dividing humanity into owners and trespassers. Indeed, "trespass," a term that has long designated both moral transgression and physical invasion of property, is especially salient for understanding the foundational dynamics of a social order built on antivagrancy and broken windows policing. In a social order in which property—private property, public property, whiteness as property—is functionally sacred, those who trespass against (physically invade) whiteness as property, by extension, trespass against (morally transgress) the social order in which whiteness and property are held as sacred, thus rendering trespassers both moral and criminal enemies of the social order itself, as the earliest vagrancy laws explicitly indicated. If, for the managers of racial capitalist order, property lines and color lines are sacred, then so is the living thin blue line that reinforces them: by eliminating threats to a social order based on the sacred right of whiteness as property, police do the sacred work of both constituting and saving the social order from all that seems to desecrate it.

An illuminating example of the border-making spatiality and materiality of the sacred thin blue line of police power is the advent of what neoliberal theorists beginning in the early 1970s called "defensible space."[118] Much like the early modern notion that hedges were a kind of natural barbed wire that would "discipline" the bodies of those who trespassed against the sacred order of property and the boundaries that constitute it, defensible space and the related concept of crime prevention through environmental design (CPTED) are built on the idea that architectural design and urban planning can incorporate a kind of police or self-policing power into the very structure of private and public space in order to neutralize criminal threats to it.[119] As extensions of the color line, the property line, and the thin blue line of police, defensible space is premised on the implicitly religious and political idea of "territoriality," the idea that one's home is "sacred" and that it should be defended as such.[120] Defensible space and CPTED emerge from the same rationale that produced broken windows theory and eventually paved the way for the practice of installing literal gates, spikes, and other physical obstacles in public and private urban spaces such as ledges, windowsills, and doorways as a means of dissuading and/or physically harming anyone who dares to stop and rest on them, thereby forcing underclass and unhoused people to move along, producing private and public space purified of the disturbances posed by the mere presence of such people.[121] In cities including Nashville, where I live, police power and property also intertwine in the form of trespass waivers, a legal mechanism whereby police actively petition faith communities and businesses to register with the police department to empower police to forcibly evict any unhoused person found on their property after hours without having to call the property owner before doing so.[122] Incorporating police power into the very brick, mortar, sidewalk, and pavement of the racial capitalist built environment, the state in effect conflates property possession and police power, establishing invisible thin blue razor wire lines that stretch through space and secure sacred order from the threats that its own acts of dispossession generate. Through the work of what legal scholar Aya Gruber calls "bluelining," police serve as a kind of border patrol securing heaven for a few by displacing many to the living hell of handcuffs, the back of a squad car, a jail cell, or even just another hidden campsite or overpass in the shadows of another multimillion-dollar development project.[123] The thin blue line of police power maintains the functionally sacred racial capitalist line between possessor and dispossessed, keeping people in "their spatial and social place."[124]

A neoliberal racial capitalist order that prioritizes and sacralizes the right to private property also includes property that is technically "public" in nature, dwindling as those spaces inevitably are. In such an order, public property, while it is allowed to exist, is nevertheless contingent on the ethos and boundaries of private possession. For more than three hundred years, private property rights have largely trumped rights to the commons, and owners have viewed the commons as an existential threat to the security of their wealth and power, which is why claims to private possession determine the boundaries and existence of public or common property and not the other way around. As such, even commonly enjoyed spaces in a racial capitalist social order—including parks, libraries, sidewalks, and other state-owned properties and resources—often operate according to implicit standards of exclusion defined by the hierarchies of racial capitalism, making them subject to the same kinds of surveillance and carceral defense on which private property depends. In most modern US cities, the "public" for whose enjoyment public spaces like parks exist is a public often defined by middle- and upper-class norms and behaviors and, most fundamentally, by the priority of capital and its uninhibited flow. As such, whatever or whoever disrupts the "sanctity of public space" inevitably registers as a hostile and invasive disruption and thus a cause for police intervention to cite, arrest, or even just force to move along.[125] In an order that prioritizes privatization, political theorist Randall Amster notes, the exclusivity at the heart of private property expands outward into public space, "literally and legally converting supposedly prized havens of public space into exclusionary domains of private property."[126] Despite the fact that property owners and elites often accuse unhoused and other underclass people of stealing, invading, or colonizing public spaces where they dwell—hence the ruling-class call to "reclaim" public spaces—unhoused people, Amster writes, are in fact "the immediate victims" of the colonization of public space by neoliberal racial capital, which transforms the ground on which they struggle to survive into privatized space in which they can only trespass.[127]

Police power is the pseudo-divine power to make, redeem, and sustain a world partitioned according to social differentiations and hierarchies of every kind. More than simply abstract, police power, like the whiteness and property alongside which it came into the world, "takes place" in the most literal sense. In addition to the ways already established, another of the ways that police power forges and defends thin blue lines in space and time is by clearing the way for the present-day settler colonialism of gentrification. Driven by the potential for immense profit, gentrification is the multifaceted process whereby racial and finance capital, aided and abetted by the state, empowers possessors to accumulate properties in the "frontier" of the predominantly nonwhite and working-class communities decimated by neoliberal abandonment and state violence. At its core, gentrification, like settler colonialism, is a mode of generating wealth and geographically expanding omnipotence by displacing people from the spaces, neighborhoods, and communities they inhabit and call home. As geographer Neil Smith identified in the 1990s, gentrification manifests the racial capitalist and revanchist aspiration to reclaim urban property, violently reversing the supposed "theft" and disordering of the city by propertyless, nonwhite, and otherwise nonnormative peoples.[128]

Police regularly use their discretionary powers of stops, searches, and arrests to put in motion the displacements on which gentrification depends.[129] One of the incidents that helped catalyze the uprisings of the spring and summer of 2020 was the police killing of twenty-six-year-old

Black woman Breonna Taylor, whom police shot and killed after barging into her Louisville, Kentucky, apartment. As her lawyers later pointed out, Taylor's apartment complex was the site of a city campaign to evict residents in order to clear the way for profit-generating redevelopment. Despite the city's denial of any coordination between elected officials, police, and the real estate industry, the same pattern has unfolded many times over in municipalities across the US since at least the 1980s. For a racial capitalist settler colonial state that must grow or else die, Breonna Taylor and her working-class neighbors—as well as people living in dilapidated apartment complexes and trailer parks on valuable property, groups of unhoused people camping in the path of a new high-rise luxury apartment complex, and Indigenous communities inhabiting sacred lands in the proposed path of corporate energy projects—constitute not mere inconveniences but savage instantiations of trespass that block the path to pseudo-divine "ownership of the earth forever and ever, Amen!"[130] For the managers of an order that runs on increased profit, such people constitute the inherently profane disorder of matter out of place, which is to say, people impeding the steady and increasing flow of sacred capital. And the answer to the disorder of matter and people out of place is returning people to their proper place as defined by racial capital and as geographically established by the functionally sacred thin blue line. The work of using ordained violence to return people to their proper place has belonged to police for as long as they have existed.

Purity and Pollution

If the essence of disorder is matter out of place and the essence of matter out of place is dirt, then the desire for order is a desire for purity, a desire that is, as Mary Douglas suggests, fundamentally religious. Likewise, if pure order is sacred, then so is the work of eliminating whatever threatens to pollute it. The police power to maintain the thin blue line between order and disorder, civilization and savagery, is, according to the police imaginary, the power to hold the boundary between "the clean and the dirty."[131] Since at least the early modern period, dirt has been associated with poverty and propertylessness, while the "proper" of property possession has been associated with cleanliness. Fused with property, whiteness, too, has long been associated with moral purity, and Blackness with moral impurity. During the seventeenth, eighteenth, and nineteenth centuries, when policing was emerging as a distinct expression of the state power to eliminate threats to a social order based on racialized property, metaphors of pollution and moral contagion pervaded social commentary. The preeminent architect of police and capitalist order Patrick Colquhoun characterized dispossessed and working-class peoples of late eighteenth-, early nineteenth-century England as "contaminated," "polluted," and "depraved" peoples whose immoral nature in turn contaminated and polluted others.[132] In the 1837 US Supreme Court case *Miln v. New York*, which decided on the right of the state to exercise police power to protect against threats both internal or external, the Court affirmed the legitimacy of the need "for a state to provide precautionary measures against the moral pestilence of paupers, vagabonds, and possibly convicts," likening that state protection to the state imperative to guard against "physical pestilence," such as from "an infectious disease."[133] Much as with the rhetoric underlying the displacing territoriality of settler colonialism, including Locke's commentary on the "wastes" of Indigenous and common lands, from the seventeenth century to the present, metaphors of "street cleaning and refuse collection" have been essential to descriptions of police work, from Adam Smith's eighteenth-century incorporation of "cleanliness" in his definition of police work to twentieth- and twenty-first-century police rhetoric in which police liken themselves to "uniformed garbagemen" who "clean" the streets of "social dirt," "polluted" people, "waste," and "scum."[134] Political philosopher Pasquale Pasquino argues that in the nineteenth century, the object of carceral and police power shifted from one who commits a crime to one understood to be inherently criminal, evil, malformed, a kind of "waste" within the social order. Under such a view, Pasquino writes, the criminal is regarded "as an excrement of the social body, at once a residue of archaic stages in the evolution of the species and a waste-product of social organization."[135] The same logic continues into the neoliberal era of broken windows policing. As Giuliani, along with Bratton, was fond of repeating throughout the mid-1990s, the greatest enemies to the city of New York were "squeegee pests"—people dispossessed by neoliberal organized abandonment who attempted to earn a meager income by washing windshields at stoplights.[136]

As noted earlier, the logic of purity, pollution, and punishment also finds expression in the long history of anti-Black criminalization in the United States. In a world where whiteness—and property and manhood—are understood to be something like divine, Blackness, and particularly Blackness unrestrained, poses a moral threat. Religious ethicist Rima Vesely-Flad argues that Blackness has been constructed in Western society as a kind of "social pollution" that has been framed in fundamentally "moral terms" from the start, the result of which is that "Black people are constructed as internal enemies that threaten the moral foundations of white, Christian, democratic, capitalist nations."[137] If Black people constitute a form of "moral pollution" that threatens the purity of a social order that revolves around whiteness, then carceral institutions that criminalize and confine disproportionately high numbers of Black people should be understood as pseudo-salvific mechanisms for cleansing that order.[138] The widespread idea during the nineteenth century that Black people were "intellectually and morally degraded" provoked anxiety in white elites in both the North and South concerned about the inevitable threat such people pose when left free and uncontrolled. Carceral institutions including the penitentiary, Vesely-Flad argues, were posed as moral solutions to the threat of moral pollution that free Black people posed in a world made for whiteness.[139] While the explicit articulation of Black moral pollution has receded from the formal language of most—though certainly not all—present-day state and ruling-class reasoning about the need for cops and cages, the fact that police still utilize rhetoric of purity and pollution and still disproportionately criminalize Black people shows that the logic remains.

Neoliberal racial capitalism is a regime of mass dispossession and criminalization. The hard right turn toward mass divestment from social welfare and mental health care in the 1980s generated mass houselessness on a scale never before seen and then deployed the organized violence of police to eliminate unhoused people from public and private space, all so that racial capital might multiply unimpeded. In continuity with popular conceptions of people forced into conditions of poverty during the eighteenth and nineteenth centuries, the stigmatization of houselessness since at least the early 1980s has hinged on metaphors of moral and physical pestilence that pollutes and thereby threatens the social body through disorder and disease.[140] Whether the dirt of projected immorality or of physical decay, in the popular imagination, homelessness represents the "dirt" of "matter out of place."[141] "A polluting person is always in the wrong," Mary Douglas writes, echoing Dr. John, quoted earlier.[142] "He has developed some wrong condition or simply crossed some line which should not have been crossed and this displacement unleashes danger for someone."[143] For the racial capitalist settler colonial state, the most tried and true answer to the "danger" of matter out of place is elimination, banishment—social and spatial sanitation.[144] By harassing, citing, arresting, or simply ordering to "move along" people trying to survive the social order that dispossesses them, police fulfill their function as purification workers who undertake the work of "spatial cleansing" on behalf of a social order that depends on it.[145]

The idea that criminality pollutes and that "cleanliness is next to godliness" does not emerge from nowhere. As I outlined in chapter 3, the language of moral impurity or pollution is a feature of predominant Christian soteriological rhetoric on the nature of sin and what takes place in salvation-by-subjection. Anselm describes the ruined state of humanity in terms of a pearl dropped in mud: God, figured as a wealthy man, would not put the pearl back in his purse until it is cleansed of its "filth," the implication being that it would contaminate those clean pearls with which it comes into contact. Similarly, Calvin argues that the condition of humanity is a corrupted or "polluted" state, which subsequently condemns us and warrants punishment. In a social order that defines all of reality in relation to pure, godlike whiteness and property, Black, Indigenous, and other people of color, as well as unpropertied, gender-nonconforming, transgender, and disabled people of all races, inevitably pose the polluting threat of matter out of place. As a power approximating the power of a mortal God, the police power to criminalize and thereby eliminate the enemies of sacred order is, for the managers and beneficiaries of that order, a power of salvific proportions.[146] Criminalization purifies—saves—the sacred order of whiteness and property by chains and corpses.

Beasts, Monsters, and Demons

In addition to metaphors of purity and pollution, police have long defined their work as a mythological and courageous fight against beasts, monsters, demons, and other subhuman threats to the human species. According to popular police rhetoric, police patrol the "wild" "waste" of unsettled lands in which "savage" Indigenous or "uncivilized" Black people dwell, in which the criminal "wolf" or "lion" preys on property and thereby threatens civilized society. In an order in which to be properly human is to be subject to God—mortal and immortal, political and divine—to refuse subjection is, in Tyler Wall's words, "to lethally mark oneself as bestial."[147] In Hobbesian terms, the "Leviathan" of state and police power exists to contain the "Behemoth," a term that in Hebrew signifies both "beast" and an "aggregation of monsters."[148] As Foucault writes, the advent of disciplinary modes of punishment casts the criminal, "the enemy of all," as one who has removed himself from citizenship and entered the "wild" state of nature and, in so doing, appears as "a monster."[149] Without the state power of Leviathan, Behemoth reigns; without the mortal God of police, criminal beasts and monsters unleash chaos on the Earth. The British political theorist and Parliamentarian Antony Ascham wrote in 1649 that "Governours of men are like keepers of beasts." When irrational or revolutionary animality takes hold of humans, Ascham argued, they break loose from their cages and threaten all of society. Thus did Ascham, warning of the threat of revolution, call for a carceral power "to tame Monsters or usurpers."[150] Under such a mythology, the violence of police is not an aberration but a necessity insofar as we understand the criminal recipients of that violence to be civilization-threatening antagonists.

Another common narrative within contemporary police mythology depicts citizens as innocent and naïve sheep and police as sheepdogs that herd and protect the sheep in ways the sheep could never imagine. Author and police trainer Dave Grossman has helped proliferate this narrative, including through children's literature in which police and other military personnel hunt vicious wolves. As Wall notes, casting criminal enemies as wolves and police as sheepdogs builds on colonial frontier mythology that imagines "police as the settler state moving through untamed wilderness, hunting dark predators in civilization's shadows."[151] Channeling the idea that police are the thin blue line holding order together in the face of chaos, Grossman and Stephanie Rogish write that without heroic sheepdogs—police—"our civilization could not exist."[152] In Grossman and Rogish's portrayal, police are kindly but tough animals committed to the domestic sphere but called into the shadows to capture far more beastly and terrifying creatures. In one illustration from their children's book *Sheepdogs*, a bipedal sheepdog dressed in a police uniform pats his dog-child's head as he prepares to leave the house on duty. Next to the door hangs a key holder on the wall with words from John 15:3: "Greater love has no one than this: That they give their life for their friends."[153] Cast as heroic, self-sacrificial shepherd-Christ-figures, police mythology holds that police make safety—*save*-ty—in ways both mundane and cosmological. Even beyond the figure of the sheepdog, the rhetoric of hunting beasts is common within present-day police work.[154] Some police rhetoric even casts police as what Wall calls "noble beasts," dangerous but benevolent creatures that hunt and eliminate beasts that threaten humanity, thereby allowing society as we know it to continue to exist. As an anonymous author wrote in *Law Enforcement Today*, the only reason citizens can take their kids to school and "sleep in peace at night" is because the police hunt and capture their prey—the beastly enemies of all humankind. "As they prepare to come for you ... I pounce. I am not kind. I am not merciful. I take the fight out of them. Then I take them out of the fight. Their throat is my prize. Their end is my glory.... I do it for my children. I do it for my God. I do it for my country. I do it for you. I am the wolf. And tonight, like every night, I will hunt."[155] Police mythology does not deny but actively justifies the inherent violence of policing as humanity's last defense against chaos and evil, a violence that destroys some in order to purify—to glorify—others.

Police fight beasts and monsters, and embodying the power of a mortal God, they also fight demons. On August 9, 2014, twenty-eight-year-old white St. Louis County police officer Darren Wilson shot and killed eighteen-year-old Black teenager Michael Brown in the middle of the street outside the Canfield Green apartment complex in Ferguson, Missouri, a predominantly Black and working-class community near St. Louis. Wilson's pursuit of Brown was not a random act of cruelty but the outcome of what a US Department of Justice investigation identified as an intentionally discriminatory program of targeting and extorting Black and economically dispossessed residents through criminal citations and fines.[156] More than a month after Wilson killed Brown, he testified before a grand jury about some of the alleged details of the events and circumstances that led to Brown's death. At one point during the testimony, Wilson claimed that Brown gave his friend Dorian Johnson a handful of cigarillos so that Brown could free his hands up to reach into Wilson's police car window, allegedly in order to attack him. St. Louis County police would later claim Brown stole the cigarillos from a convenience store, with alleged video evidence, thereby presumably justifying Wilson's pursuit and substantiating the supposed criminality that would, in turn, legitimize Brown's death. "I tried to hold his right arm and use my left hand to get out to have some type of control and not be trapped in my car any more," Wilson told the grand jury. "And when I grabbed him, the only way I can describe it is I felt like a five-year-old holding onto Hulk Hogan." The interviewer asked for clarification: "Holding onto what?" Wilson replied, "Hulk Hogan, that's just how big he felt and how small I felt just from grasping his arm."[157] A few minutes later, after further describing his portrayal of a struggle that Wilson claimed ensued through the window of his squad car, Wilson said his gun fired, breaking the window. After Brown, shocked from the gunfire, stepped back from the window of the car, Wilson reported, "[He] looked up at me and had the most intense aggressive face. The only way I can describe it, *it looks like a demon*, that's how angry he looked."[158] Moments later, Wilson fired on Brown at least six times, killing him. His lifeless body remained face down in the street for four and a half hours. On Monday, November 24, 2014, St. Louis prosecutor Bob McCulloch announced during a televised press conference that the grand jury had decided not to indict Wilson for Brown's death.

Police exist to use ordained violence to defeat and eliminate the enemies of all humankind. If the enemies that police fight are, by definition, beasts, monsters, and demons, then it follows that anyone whose life the police end must have been a beast, a monster, or a demon, which is to say, worthy of elimination. When it comes to acts of violence, including lethal violence, against allegedly aggressive enemies, the police can only be innocent: they are in fact just doing their job—holding the line that protects what the state discerns as the good from what the state discerns as evil. If Michael Brown was a demon, then his death was not only justified but an act of God, mortal and immortal alike. Indeed, putting to death those who constitute a demonic threat against sacred order, against the innocent who dwell within that order, is, for the religion of mass criminalization, a death that brings life, the sacrificial production of a corpse that makes safe.

Among the inherent traits that beasts, monsters, and demons share in common is a spirit of rebellion, a natural disposition toward disobedience, an inclination to refuse to be properly subject within the hierarchies of natural, social, and sacred order. Throughout the colonial modern era, ruling-class actors on both sides of the Atlantic characterized dispossessed and enslaved peoples from every nation in terms of beastly monstrosity and evil.[159] As I have already shown at length, Blackness in particular has long been associated with savage animality, monstrosity, and immorality and, as such, has been characterized as instantiating a natural disposition toward disobedience and rebellion. The beastly, monstrous, and demonic enemies that the mortal God of police strives to eliminate are enemies precisely because they refuse subjection to divine and divinely derived political authority. The refusal to be subject poses a threat because it jeopardizes the sacred hierarchies on which the order of things is built, the collapse of which would lead to a dangerous chaos in which finite, sinful people's latent capacity for rebellion would be unleashed without any force to restrain it. The thin blue line registers as sacred for the ruling class, then, because it maintains sacred social order against the constant moral threat of masses of people refusing to be subject in all manner of ways.

By being Black—literally, by *being* Black—while also allegedly stealing from a corner store, walking in the street, and refusing to show deference to whiteness, Michael Brown registered to Wilson, a white officer of the colonial racial capitalist state, as a monstrous, demonic, and thus inherently dangerous embodiment of the refusal to be subject to political and thus divine authority. For both the soteriology of subjection and modern social contract theory, one who fails to abide by divine covenant or social contract by refusing to be properly subject disrupts order and thereby renders themselves an enemy aggressor willing their own expulsion or death. As Augustine argued, the chains under which sinful humans groan are chains of their own making, and as Rousseau put it, one who violates the state's laws quite literally "makes war upon it," thereby inviting their own death. Thus, according to the state, the grand jury, the district attorney, and the popular white carceral imaginary, by refusing proper subjection to an officer of the racial capitalist state, Michael Brown in effect willed his own death, which means the state could not be held responsible. As a violence worker, a purification worker, an eliminator of threats to sacred order, Darren Wilson was only doing his job.

The disorderly refusal to be properly subject is the refusal to remain in one's proper place, and the refusal to remain in one's proper place—to trespass—is, within the popular imagination, a feature of the demonic. As scholar of demonology S. Jonathon O'Donnell shows, religious and political rhetoric has long articulated demons in opposition to the borders and walls meant to secure geographically partitioned sacred order: "dark [demonic] forces are usually framed as coming from outside, or—when internal—as owing allegiance to that outside. This projection of threatening alterity enables the creation of a phantasmatic image of a walled enclosure—a *paradise* in its etymological sense."[160] As O'Donnell notes, the etymological root of "paradise" is "enclosure," conveying "a sense of both sovereignty and sacredness," which further clarifies the innate connection between private property and the transcendence of a heavenly beyond.[161] The demon is, like the "criminal," an existential enemy that sacred order cannot tolerate and yet also cannot exist without. As O'Donnell puts it, "the demon . . . gives to Paradise its self-consolidating other, providing it with a narrative of self-legitimation that justifies the arguments that frame Paradise's walls as necessary for existence itself, enabling rigid demarcations of order from chaos, life from death, self from other—even and perhaps especially when such borders blur or are breached."[162] As one who "*passes through space*, traversing borders that should remain stable," the demon disrupts the partitioned geographies that constitute a sense of sacred order: the demonic is that which trespasses, and that which trespasses is subject to being discerned as demonic, which is to say, monstrous, beastly, an enemy in concert with the "original Enemy of All Mankind," the Devil.[163]

When Darren Wilson described Michael Brown with the words "it looked like a demon," he was not merely trying to avoid a criminal indictment by characterizing his victim hyperbolically; on the contrary, in demonizing Brown, Wilson was speaking fluently the language of police mythology, an imaginary that is, as Neocleous puts it, "riddled with demons." It is, indeed, the threat of disorder posed by the monstrous and demonic enemies of God and order that generates police power in the first place.[164] Without the sacred thin blue line of police power, the mythology goes, paradise would quite literally succumb to the powers of hell: as a 1967 FBI memo put it, police "alone stand guard at the upstairs door of Hell."[165] When a white police officer characterizes the Black teenager he killed as demonic, we should believe him, not in the sense that we should believe that Brown was in fact demonic but in the sense that we should believe what that characterization tells us about the imaginary within which Wilson operated, namely, that cops keep us safe from evil—save us—by eliminating the enemies of God and order. Had Wilson not killed Brown, Wilson's testimony implies, all hell would have broken loose. Paradise is only paradise thanks to the thin blue line. Salvation is only salvation thanks to chains and corpses.

The Religion of Mass Criminalization

Religion, broadly construed, consists of the practices and orientations by which peoples seek to transcend, transform, and make meaning of the conditions of mortal finitude. One of the ways by which religion, including religious traditions, intervenes in the conditions of finitude is by arranging relations and communities via partitions that demarcate morality from immorality, purity from pollution, trespass from belonging, godly from demonic, sacred from profane. Far from abstract and immaterial, these functionally sacred demarcations *take and make place* in quite concrete ways, ordering the relational and material worlds that we inhabit. The eurochristian racial capitalist settler colonial state's political work of maintaining the borders of whiteness and property is also, at the same time, a manifestation of the religious work of partitioning the world between sacred and profane. Contrary to the widely held presumption of modern secularization, the religious and the political cannot be fully extricated from each other; they intersect, complement, and coconstitute each other both conceptually and materially in a multitude of ways. At the most elementary level, as a means of navigating the conditions of finitude, religion is inherently concerned with the dynamics of shared life, which is to say, the political. While all religion is political, some of its manifestations are so absolutely fused with the maintenance of political order that some scholars identify them as instances of so-called political religion. A cousin of what scholars call "secular" or "civil" religion, political religion describes powers and practices that draw from and adapt the meaning-making myths, rituals, and practices of a given religious tradition to a political or social order, thereby sacralizing that order and the boundaries that mark it.[166]

As I have shown at length, patriarchal whiteness and private property constitute phenomena that are, at their foundations, religious. Emerging from eurochristian capitalist and colonial order, and mimicking and aspiring to embody the godlike power to transcend, manage, and possess the world, whiteness and property generate and come to depend—for their existence and their godlike power—on the dispossession, criminalization, and elimination of their enemies. There is no godlike whiteness without the construction and elimination of demonic Blackness, no sacred private property without the violence of dispossession. Moreover, there is no sacred whiteness or property without police, no capitalist and colonial heaven for a few without carceral hell for many. Police power, like the pseudo-godlike whiteness and property that it helps create, redeem, and sustain, deifies by destroying, which is to say, by criminalizing—defining, capturing, and eliminating—the enemies of sacred social order.

From the origins of the police power of criminalization to its present, it has constituted a political religion that embodies the political theologies of eurochristian tradition. Foremost among the theologies that police and carceral power put into practice is the political soteriology of subjection according to which sin and criminality are states of corruption characterized by the refusal to be properly subject to divine and political authority and according to which salvation entails a sovereign-satisfying return to life-giving subjection. From the early modern dispossessed masterless people whose refusal to be subject to capital the state used to legitimize the expansion of police power to the penitentiary that saved by subjecting the disobedient to labor and solitude to the centuries-long state practice of deploying police to eliminate those who are deemed out of place in a world made for whiteness and property, police and carceral power have always claimed and embodied the godlike power to maintain the hierarchies integral to sacred social order.

The notion that carceral captivity amounts to a kind of hell on Earth is not hyperbolic. Scores of writers, including incarcerated and formerly incarcerated writers, have long characterized the experience of prison and jail as a hellish one. Likewise, many theological and literary conceptions of hell over the course of centuries have characterized hell as a kind of prison. Hell is a kind of prison, and prison is a kind of hell. The likeness is no accident. As Hannah Bowman outlines, in predominant Christian theologies, hell is figured as either the place of the dead or a place of divine punishment.[167] The same can be said of the spaces of carceral exile both inside and outside the walls of jail and prison. Carceral confinement is a space of living death and torment designed to resemble the isolation and separation that characterizes predominant conceptions of hell. Even those who are impacted by police power who never wear physical chains or see the inside of a cage are often exiled to the hell of a life dispossessed of the means of life, a life, therefore, of unfreedom, a life vulnerable to premature death. The crucial point is that exiling millions of people to the hell of dispossession and subjection under conditions of confinement is not a randomly occurring phenomenon but a necessary component of the work of creating, protecting, and sustaining an order based on the godlike powers of patriarchal whiteness and private property.

Whiteness and property, founded on the elimination or exploitation of all who fall outside their gates, demand sacrifice not in the sense of an arbitrary cosmic arithmetic but because whiteness and property can only exist as godlike when all nonwhite and propertyless peoples are rendered disposable, deserving of elimination and death. This is the zero-sum oppositionality inherent to colonial racial capitalism. For some to be gods, others must be put in chains, made into corpses. In this way, the dispossession, capture, and caging that constitutes mass criminalization in a racial capitalist order constitutes a mass sacrifice—life-giving death—that satisfies in the sense of reaffirming and reinforcing the godlike power of white propertied "ownership of the earth forever and ever, Amen!" Police and carceral power save sacred order and deify whiteness and property by either returning the enemies of God and order to salvific subjection or eliminating them altogether. In an order in which to return to proper subjection, to one's proper place within functionally sacred hierarchies, is salvific, those who refuse sacred chains are understood to destine themselves for premature death. When someone dies at the hands of a cop or in the clutch of a cage, the mythology goes, they effectively will their own death, which is to say, they deserved it. After all, when violence workers kill, they are only doing their (divinely ordained) job.

Mass criminalization constitutes a religion not only in the sense that it mimics the godlike power to make heaven and hell on Earth but because, by offering assurance of a supposed safety that amounts to a kind of social salvation from the moral threat of the dangerous classes, criminalization elicits mass devotion not only from those who seem to benefit from it but even from those who, though they do not benefit from it, have been tricked into believing that there is no other source of security in a world riddled with demons. Most people today are so deeply devoted to cops and cages and would do anything to ensure their continued existence because the capitalist and colonial state has convinced us that without damnation to hell for those who "deserve" it, there can be no heavenly salvation for the rest of us, that without the salvation that cops and cages secure, we will all be damned. The reality, however, is that mass devotion to mass criminalization already damns us all by basing its illusory sense of safety on human elimination, which, besides facilitating a kind of spiritual death for those who are seemingly protected, inhibits the kinds of relations and allocation of resources that would actually ensure abundance—and thus safety and perhaps even real *save*-ty—for all. Mass "commitment to [the] collective values" of the resolutely hierarchical order in which we live, David Garland, channeling Émile Durkheim, writes, "has the character of a deeply held religious attachment," a kind of collective devotion.[168] Religion makes meaning of the conditions of finitude and mediates transcendence or transformation of it. The police power to criminalize constitutes a religious power because it frames reality in terms of existential danger from which only a god—mortal and immortal alike—can save us. If the criminality of the disorderly, dangerous classes of racialized and propertyless classes desecrates sacred order, then cops and cages, manifestations of the mortal God of the modern state, save it.

Considering, however, that the salvation that mass criminalization secures is in fact a kind of damnation not only for those who are held in chains and made into corpses but for all of us, we should understand the religion of mass criminalization as a religion of death, a *necroreligion*. Achille Mbembe theorizes "necropolitics" or "necropower" as the various means of "subjugating life to the power of death." Necropower, Mbembe and Christophe Ringer argue, preserves life for some, sacrificing and subjecting many to "death-worlds": "forms of social existence in which vast populations are subjected to living conditions that confer upon them the status of the *living dead*."[169] Deifying some by demonizing and dealing death to others, creating heaven for a few by criminalizing and exiling many to living and dying hell, the political necroreligion of mass criminalization elicits mass devotion to cops and cages by convincing us that safety, security, and salvation are obtainable only through chains and corpses. The power that creates, saves, and sustains the functionally sacred hierarchies of racial capitalist settler colonial order is the power of the mortal God, the police, that army of racial class warriors engaged in a holy war to "stifle the fountains of evil."[170] In a world structured by religiously and racially conceived fear of disorder and disorderly people, the illusory and deadly promise that cops and cages keep us safe from all harm soothes so deeply—so existentially—that it feels like salvation, even as it damns not only those who are rendered the polluting, monstrous, demonic objects of fear but all of us. Why do we still see "chains on black flesh"? Why did the police murder and then leave Michael Brown's body face down in the street for four and a half hours? Because the sacred order of whiteness and property measures its safety—its salvation—in chains and corpses.

Conclusion

The Religion of Abolition

If the story ended with chains and corpses, despair, like death, would be inevitable. But the story does not end there. Nor does it begin there. As Minneapolis-based Anishinaabe organizer Arriana Nason put it during the George Floyd rebellion, "there was a time before police and there will be a time after," which is also to say, there was a time before racial capitalism and settler colonialism, and there will be a time after.[1] What *is* now, in other words, is not all that has been or will be.[2] As the Zapatistas of Chiapas and a whole generation of radical social movements have put it, "another world is possible." The proclamation that another world is possible is, in some sense, a proclamation of faith—"faith" not necessarily in the sense of doctrinal belief but in the sense of the embodied conviction that there is life beyond the present order of exploitation, dispossession, and death. The order of chains and corpses is so deeply entrenched, so seemingly all-pervasive, that a world freed from it seems almost otherworldly or, better yet, *anotherworldly*. Anotherworldly faith orients toward that which is present in part but not yet in full—it leaps with others toward the beyond in our midst. More than mere intellectual assent, faith in the realizability of another world is faith that works with others to bring that world into being.

Rooted in a vision of a world of safety and abundance without cops and cages and enfleshed by political practices that build that world brick by brick, the movement for "abolition" is likewise a movement of faith. To say that abolition is a movement of faith is not to claim that all who pursue abolition identify as people of faith—while many do, many others do not, and for good reason: religion, and eurochristianity in particular, is a primary source of the problems against which we struggle. And yet, the fact that a particular manifestation of religion lies at the root of mass criminalization does not necessarily mean that building a world without criminalization demands a resolute atheism. Just as religion undergirded both chattel slavery and the struggle to abolish it, so religion is, has been, and will continue to be a feature of the struggle to abolish carceral, capitalist, and colonial order. As I have posited throughout this book, religion, broadly conceived, consists of the practices and orientations by which peoples seek to transcend, transform, and make meaning of the conditions of mortal finitude. Understanding religion, in this way, beyond formal religious affiliation alone enables us to discern instances of the meaning-making work of transcendence and transformation beyond the limits of institutional religion, including in the realm of political practices that seek to transcend the world that is by transforming it into what it could be.

Prison industrial complex abolition is precisely such a political vision and practice. While the term "abolition" seems to connote a tearing down or negation of some kind, police and prison abolitionists including Angela Davis and Ruth Wilson Gilmore argue that abolition is, at its root, a creative process. Just as cops and cages are manifestations of racial capitalist settler colonial order, so building a world beyond cops and cages means building a world beyond racial capitalist settler colonial order. As Gilmore puts it, "Abolition requires that we change one thing, which is everything. Contemporary prison abolitionists have made this argument for more than two decades. Abolition is not absence, it is presence. What the world will become already exists in fragments and pieces, experiments and possibilities. So those who feel in their gut deep anxiety that abolition means knock it all down, scorch the earth and start something new, let that go. Abolition is building the future from the present, in all of the ways we can."[3]

Building the future from the present makes the future present, which is to say, it makes the transcendence of "another world" immanent. Anthropologists of religion argue that, as much or more than religion is a matter of abstract belief, it is a matter of the embodied, material practices that *mediate* the presence of the divine here and now, making the intangible tangible and the immaterial materially present in our midst.[4] Abolition can likewise be understood as a set of practices through which people mediate the felt emergence of another reality at the interstices of our own. It is in this sense that abolition might be understood as an inherently religious practice, which is to say, a practice by which people meaningfully transcend this world by transforming it into another, bringing that other world into being even if only in part and not yet in full.

What kind of world, exactly, do abolitionists seek to build? To begin with, in contrast to the racial capitalist, settler colonial, and carceral world, abolition is the building of a world structured around abundance, reciprocity, collective care, and freedom—a world, in short, that guarantees that all people's basic life-sustaining needs are met, which is to say, a world in which humans, all creatures, and the natural world thrive. As I have narrated over the course of this book, colonial racial capitalist order is built on the privatization of that which is otherwise shared in common, a process that requires the forced dispossession of masses of people from the means of life, an act that itself requires the power of police to enforce. For the managers and enforcers of capitalist-colonial order, privatization reflects the will of God, which means that the partitions that generate and mark it are sacred and therefore must be defended at all costs. For abolitionists, the enclosures, partitions, and cages that constitute modern order are not sacred but means of profaning a world that would otherwise be shared—and, as shared, sacred—without them. In this sense, abolitionism is a sacred vision and practice based in the kind of reciprocity with the world and its peoples that Indigenous peoples have long inhabited and that colonial racial capitalism has sought to eradicate for centuries. Intertwined as cops and cages are with the fences, gates, walls, and borders that constitute our world, the vision of a world without cops and cages, Gilmore posits, "is a vision for undoing partition . . . in its many manifestations across time-space."[5] Or, as Mariame Kaba and Andrea Ritchie, drawing on the work of Brendan McQuade, put it, abolition "is about building a new world centered around 'the commons.'"[6] The exclusive abundance that belongs only to a godlike few under colonial racial capitalism, in an abolitionist future, belongs to all, including the Earth itself.

There are many ways to forge reciprocal relations with people and planet and to meet people's basic human needs, and most of them, on the surface, seem to have nothing whatsoever to do with police or prisons. But if cops and cages are manifestations of the broader social order from which they emerge, then abolishing cops and cages is also a matter of remaking the broader social order into one in which everyone has what they need to be well. If abolition is really about changing everything, then those who are creating conditions of reciprocal and just relations in which people's most basic needs are being met without resorting to state coercion or violence—administrative or physical—are contributing, whether they realize it or not, to the work of abolition.[7] The ruling class claims that mass precarity is natural and thus inevitable. But conditions of abundance for a few and scarcity for many are anything but natural. As such, the premise of abolition is that it does not have to be this way: the ruling class created this world, and we can create another.

At the same time that police and prisons control or eliminate those who are dispossessed by the capitalist-colonial state, they also claim to establish justice and safety in the name of the survivors of harm and violence. But carceral systems, like the systemically violent order of which they are a part, are themselves inherently violent and thus can only respond to the harm and violence that the state makes inevitable with more of the same by eliminating, isolating, and controlling people accused of harm rather than addressing and doing something about the conditions that produced that harm in the first place. Harming people who have harmed people neither facilitates accountability nor brings about healing or repair for those who have been hurt, especially when we recognize that harm and violence derive precisely from the fact that masses of people are struggling to survive without being able to meet their most basic human needs. Indeed, capturing and caging was never really meant to prevent all forms of harm or respond effectively to them. The function of police and prisons is not to keep us safe but to manage the outcomes of inequality, which is why cops and cages cannot be reformed: they are working exactly as designed, doing their job in service of a deliberately inequitable system that is, for those who benefit from it, sacred, and thus worthy of protection, no matter how much abandonment and violence it takes.

As I argue in the introduction, ensuring that all people's basic human needs are met by restoring the commons would itself drastically reduce the interpersonal violence and harm that our current order of mass precarity makes inevitable. And yet, abolition does not mean the total end of violence and harm. Rather, it means an entirely different and more life-sustaining way of responding to and navigating harm, including in its most severe forms. In other words, a world beyond cops and cages is a world built on the proliferation of the skills necessary to navigate conflict and harm with tools that transform the conditions that create harm in the first place and that facilitate authentic accountability and repair in its wake—what abolitionists call transformative justice. Developed largely by Black feminist survivors of violence, transformative justice is, in the words of Kaba, "a framework and vision for preventing, intervening in, and transforming harm—including the harms caused by the prison industrial complex itself—through nonpunitive accountability."[8] Police and prisons abstract instances of harm from the social conditions that help produce them and then extract the individuals who cause harm from all social relations. In so doing, police and prisons fail to disrupt— and even reinforce—the cycles of dispossession and isolation that give rise to harm, making us all less safe in the process. Transformative justice, on the other hand, deals directly with the complex individual and systemic origins of a given harm, takes seriously that harm's impact, and works with survivors and community members to make space for those who have committed harm to participate in a voluntary process of accountability that can facilitate healing or recompense for those whom they have hurt. Unlike police and prisons that claim to support survivors of harm but in fact systematically impede pathways to genuine healing, recompense, or repair, transformative justice disrupts harm in ways that enable the possibility of transformation for all involved, as well as the transformation of a society that generates so much harm to begin with.

It is common for people to respond to all-encompassing critiques of criminal punishment systems with a question such as, "What do you propose instead?" Embedded in such a question is the presumption that there must, by definition, be a single institution or practice with which we can replace police and prisons to adequately deal with a multitude of social problems. What people often fail to recognize is that this is exactly the rationale that helps produce and situate police and prisons as a one-size-fits-all response to acts of violation between people in the first place. But the reality of harm is complex, which means that there can be no one single fix for it. Instead, we need a multitude of interventions that forge new, more life-giving ways of navigating situations of violence and harm—interventions that are already being practiced around the US and beyond.[9] Transformative justice is one of those interventions. At the end of the day, abolition is a vision in which transformative justice—along with other practices guided by principles of life-preserving reciprocity, accountability, abundance, and care—becomes a new orientation for a majority of people and for the institutions we make and inhabit. Carceral societies outsource the work of navigating human conflict and violation to violence workers. Transformative justice seeks to return that work to all of us—in the name of greater safety and well-being for all.

Insofar as abolition is a vision of a world in which people live in reciprocal relation, have what they need to thrive, and navigate conflict and violation without enacting more violence, abolition constitutes a "religious" vision and practice, even in the more traditional sense of the term. Whether in sacred text, theology, or tradition, most formal "religions" include some sacred vision of a world in which all people have what they need to live full lives, as well as an ethical frame that invites reciprocal relation and shared abundance with others as a way of embodying one's devotion to and/or manifesting deep connection with the divine or sacred. Indeed, for multiple religious traditions, showing hospitality, generosity, and fairness to friends and strangers alike is often understood as a practice that mediates the presence of the divine among us—one that extends into ways of navigating conflict that preserve life for all involved. If abolition is about abundance, safety, reciprocity, and the transformation of harm, then religious traditions that are oriented toward visions and practices of abundance, reciprocity, and life-giving accountability already contain the seeds of abolition within them. Even Christianity, which, in its European iterations, has wrought so much suffering and death, is at the same time filled to the brim with scripture, traditions within the tradition, and ethical imperatives that declare the sacredness of release from captivity, freedom from oppression, and the healing of infirmities, each of which it develops out of the Jewish traditions that preceded it. Islam, Hinduism, Buddhism, traditional African spiritual systems, Indigenous traditions, and other spiritual and religious traditions bear within them the kinds of ways of being, doing, and knowing together that prison industrial complex abolitionists also envision and build toward.

Central to my argument over the course of this book is that the mass criminalization of Black people, Indigenous people, other people of color, and propertyless and dispossessed peoples of all races fulfills a religious, even pseudo-salvific function for those who benefit or think that they benefit from it. Contrary to predominant presumptions, however, the reality is that cops and cages do not keep us safe, which is to say, they cannot *save* us—socially or spiritually. Indeed, more than failing to create safety, mass faith in the pseudo-saving power of the mortal God of police and prisons ultimately damns and endangers us all. In the end, despite what detractors say, abolition is an expression of the desire for *more* safety than our system of capture and caging offers, not less.[10]

In a time of increasingly routine state violence, burgeoning fascism, climate crisis, deepening inequality, and mass vulnerability to premature death, the task of building a world of safety and abundance for all without cops and cages feels especially daunting. And yet, the legitimacy of cops, cages, and colonial racial capitalist order more broadly has never been so contested, just as faith in the possibility and urgent necessity of another world has never been so expansive. Building that world, I believe, requires us to understand police and carceral power in terms of the inherently religious function they fulfill for those who put their faith in them to make safe—to *save*. If we fail to understand and act in light of this understanding, our interventions will inevitably fail to either disrupt or transform the existential power that police and prisons wield over our imaginations, our spirits, and our lives. Likewise, and perhaps even more importantly, I believe that building a world beyond cops and cages requires us to elaborate and embody new meaning-making modes of collective transcendence and transformation, new mythologies, religiosities, and spiritualities that may in fact derive from very old mythologies, religiosities, and spiritualities. Just as mass criminalization fulfills a religious function, so must abolition embrace and deepen its faith—whether traditionally "religious" or "spiritual" or not—in the realizability of another world. Animated by such faith, the multitude of social, cultural, and political practices that constitute abolitionist organizing and healing work become functionally religious practices in the sense that they bear the power to mediate the emergence of that other world for which we struggle and toward which we leap.

May it be so.
Amen.

ACKNOWLEDGMENTS

This book is the fruit of more than a decade of intellectual and other forms of labor. Though it bears my name on the cover, I could never have conceived of, struggled over, written, or revised it over and over without so many different kinds of support from so many different people. Lindsey, you know better than anyone just how much support I needed to complete this thing. It took what felt to both of us like forever, and you accompanied me at every step, stepping in to shoulder extra life and family tasks to help me reach every finish line, including this final one. More than that, our shared life, love, spirituality, and movement labors were the ground that nourished this book into being. Thank you for your leadership, your love, your listening ear, your curiosity, your enduring patience, and your steady accompaniment. You sacrificed a great deal to make this possible. I love you. Among the other labors you carried out to help realize this book, you also brought our children into the world as I wrote this book, as a tornado destroyed our home, as we navigated a pandemic, as we rebuilt our home, and as the world caught fire after the police murders of George Floyd and Breonna Taylor. What a time. Larkin and Cayden, I have always wanted to be your dad. It is one of the great joys of my life that I am. Whether you ever read all the pages of this book or not, I want you to know that I wrote it because I want you and all the people you will ever know and love to know, in your lifetimes, the safety and abundance that we all deserve. Shortly after you started saying "no mo po po," Larkin, you learned how to say "homes for all!" Dear God, may you and Cayden live to see the day.

Mom and Dad, in addition to the gift of making space for me to ask the kinds of questions I was asking as a kid and a teenager and then being willing to keep learning with me all these years later, you, too, made this book possible by spending more hours than we will ever know loving and caring for our kids as I disappeared into my office to keep on writing. Thank you. Thank you, too, to George and Susan, and Selina, for this same indispensable support. I could not have written this without you all.

Members of my dissertation committee deserve special acknowledgment. Ellen Armour, thank you for helping to provide so much of the theoretical foundation on which this book stands and, more importantly, for guiding me through my writing in its early stages. I am grateful to continue to be in intellectual community with you. Thank you, Bruce Morrill, for taking such personal and academic interest in my project, and Paul DeHart, for inviting me, with both seriousness and humor, to the kind of theological rigor that my project required. Lisa Guenther, thank you for modeling the kind of scholarship and activism that I aspired to as a graduate student and for your multifaceted camaraderie over the years. And thank you, Dr. Stacey Floyd-Thomas, for making space for my intellectual curiosities and intuitions and for believing in my project for a full decade now. My deepest gratitude to you and Anthony Pinn for adding this book to such an excellent series.

I do not think I have ever interacted with someone in a professional capacity with as much patience, endurance, and thoughtfulness as my excellent editor at NYU Press, Jennifer Hammer. Thank you for reaching out in early 2020 and for sticking with me through more than three years of writing and revising. Your feedback helped sharpen this book in palpable ways. Many thanks, too, to Andrew Katz and Alexia Traganas for your excellent copyediting support and to Veronica Knutson and all the folks at NYU Press who have helped bring this book into the world.

Special thanks are also due to the Louisville Institute, which awarded me a Dissertation Fellowship from 2017 to 2018, making it possible to complete my dissertation. Special thanks to the staff of the Louisville Institute during that time and to A. G. Miller, Cheryl Townsend Gilkes, Courtney Bryant, Leo Guardado, Melanie Jones, Daniel Castillo, Randall Balmer, Nathan Jérémie-Brink, and Candi Cann, who provided valuable feedback during our seminar.

To Vincent Lloyd, Laura McTighe, Bryson White, Nikia Robert, Rachelle Green, Nathaniel Grimes, Alex Chambers, Christophe Ringer, Aaron Griffith, Hunter Bragg, Laura Simpson, Ed Vogel, and Pai Masavisut, thank you for being intellectual conversation partners, for affirming and making space for my work, and for producing your own important work at the intersection of religion, carcerality, and abolition from which I have learned much and hope to continue to learn. Kyle Lambelet, Aaron Stauffer, Tristan Call, Allyn Maxfield-Steele, Austin Sauerbrei, and Michael Verla, thank you for being, variously, writing partners, intellectual conversation partners, conference buddies, comrades, and dear soul friends—and, too, Peter Capretto, Amaryah Armstrong, Hilary Scarsella, Jason Smith, and others with whom I journeyed through the trenches of dissertation writing and academic study in the Graduate Department of Religion at Vanderbilt between 2013 and 2019. To Richard Goode, Lee Camp, Dana Carpenter, Matt Hearn, Scott Owings, and other dear teachers and spiritual guides who have become dear friends, your mentorship, starting nearly twenty years ago, and your friendship today continue to mean the world to me and made it possible for me to pursue the paths that led to this book. Thank you, Richard, for first inviting me behind the walls of a prison fifteen years ago. My life has taken the direction it has because you did. I continue to be so grateful to you, and to Janet Wolf, for your many decades of quiet commitment to a world beyond prisons and for always opening your doors—and prison doors—to me. The work you have both undertaken building educational and spiritual community in prison, together with Harmon Wray, made a road that I and many others are still walking. Graham Reside, thank you for affirming my work and for giving me space to carry it out with you. And Jeannie Alexander, thank you for making a way where there was no way to forge so much community between the inside and the outside. You helped weaken the walls.

To all of my brothers and friends on Unit 6, Unit 5, and Unit 2 at Riverbend Maximum Security Institution and to my fellow outsiders whom I have been on pilgrimage with there for more than a decade, our spiritual community and collective study has shaped me immensely. To the guys on the inside in particular, in addition to impacting me personally, the way you have shared life with me across the walls has generated intellectual and spiritual questions that gave rise to many of the questions I explore in this book. Thank you. I am also grateful to the students of "Life on Death Row" (Fall 2022)—both students from Vanderbilt and students on the inside at Riverbend—who participated with me in a full semester of sacred conversation and art-making. Spending every Monday afternoon with you all for a few months helped ground me in important ways as I finished this book. To my dear friend Donna McCoy, and to others with whom I have shared community at the former Tennessee Prison for Women, thank you for your wisdom and your friendship, even as years go by between our conversations. This project also would not have been possible without the dozens of criminalized people who have entrusted me with the pain of their stories of injustice at the hands of police, jails, prisons, and detention centers as part of my work researching and writing multiple public reports about the harms that these institutions proliferate. I long for the day that the power of your endurance under conditions of death is enough to bring the walls down. I pray that we—and if not us, then our children—may live to see the day.

To my comrades and fellow freedom fighters at the Nashville People's Budget Coalition—past and present—and other people and organizations helping to build a world of safety and abundance beyond cops and cages and surveillance in Nashville, across the South, and across the US, despite all the odds, I still believe in us, and that "us" will one day be a lot more of us. Our shared struggle informs this book at every turn. To Theeda, Melissa, gert, Drost, Lydia, Ed, Lindsey, and other friends practicing abolition spiritualities together, let's keep discerning paths of personal and social transformation. I think a lot might depend on it. And finally, to the Black radical feminists and abolitionists whose organizing and intellectual labor have provided so much of the groundwork for the arguments I make and the future I imagine in these pages, particularly Mariame Kaba, Andrea Ritchie, Ruth Wilson Gilmore, and Angela Y. Davis, thank you for making new worlds and inviting us to join you in that work. I am finding freedom I did not know I could find here.

NOTES

PREFACE

1 I outline the origins and meaning of broken windows policing in chapter 5.
2 The synthesis of "European" and "Christian" as "eurochristian" comes from Native American theologian Tink Tinker. Tink Tinker, "What Are We Going to Do with White People?," *New Polis*, December 17, 2019, https://thenewpolis.com. Tinker intentionally leaves the *e* in "eurochristian" lower case. For Tinker, combining "European" and "Christian" into "eurochristian" clarifies the religious and political fusion at the heart of European colonialism's violence. I likewise deploy the term throughout the book to convey as precisely as possible the religio-political nature of the colonial, capitalist, and carceral realities that the book explores and to convey their inseparability. I also occasionally deploy the formulation "European Christian" in some places, which I understand to be synonymous with "eurochristian."
3 I work with the concepts of "organized abandonment" and "organized violence" throughout the book. These concepts were first developed by Ruth Wilson Gilmore, building on the work of David Harvey. Ruth Wilson Gilmore (with Craig Gilmore), "Beyond Bratton," in *Abolition Geography: Essays towards Liberation* (Brooklyn, NY: Verso Books, 2022), 303–313; David Harvey, *The Limits to Capital* (London: Verso Books, 2006).

INTRODUCTION

1 The term "police" derives from the Greek term *polis*, referring to an assembled community, nation, state, or city. The term "cop" derives from the Latin *capere* and French *caper*, meaning "to seize" or "to take," which later evolved into English, conveying the act of "capture or arrest." Rachel Herzing, Mariame Kaba, and Andrea Ritchie point out that the term "officer" in "police officer" derives from "official," which implies a degree of "reverence and deference" that, when uncontested, can quite literally be deadly. Mariame Kaba and Andrea Ritchie, *No More Police: A Case for Abolition* (New York: New Press, 2022), 185. A core purpose of this book is to problematize and contest that reverence, which is why I opt for a combination of colloquial and formal references to police. While "cop" is more colloquial, it is also arguably more concretely descriptive—police power is the power to capture. Likewise, following rhetoric I first encountered in relationship with imprisoned people, I use the terms "cage," "caged," and "caging" throughout

the book to refer to prisons and jails and the practice of holding people captive within them. Perhaps even more so than "cop," "cage" terminology breaks through the layers of imprisonment's normalization, confronting the reader with the stark reality of an inherently dehumanizing practice that so many assume to be natural or inevitable.

2   Some of the most important texts that emerge from Black radical, Black feminist, Marxist, anarchist, Indigenous, anticolonial, critical race, critical criminologist, and abolitionist discourse and movements and that give critical insight into the fundamental nature and purpose of police and prisons, include Mumia Abu-Jamal, *Live from Death Row* (Reading, MA: Addison-Wesley, 1995); Angela Y. Davis, ed., *If They Come in the Morning . . . : Voices of Resistance* (London: Verso, 2016); Angela Y. Davis, *Are Prisons Obsolete?* (New York: Seven Stories, 2003); Angela Y. Davis, *Abolition Democracy: Beyond Empire, Prisons, and Torture* (New York: Seven Stories, 2005); Angela Y. Davis, *Angela Davis: An Autobiography* (New York: International, 1988); Angela Y. Davis, Gina Dent, Erica R. Meiners, and Beth E. Richie, *Abolition. Feminism. Now.* (Chicago: Haymarket Books, 2022); Assata Shakur, *Assata: An Autobiography* (Chicago: Lawrence Hill Books, 2001); George Jackson, *Soledad Brother: The Prison Letters of George Jackson* (Chicago: Lawrence Hill Books, 1994); George L. Jackson, *Blood in My Eye* (Baltimore: Black Classic, 1990); Stuart Hall et al., *Policing the Crisis: Mugging, the State and Law and Order*, 35th anniversary ed. (London: Red Globe, 2013); Mariame Kaba, *We Do This 'til We Free Us: Abolitionist Organizing and Transforming Justice* (Chicago: Haymarket Books, 2021); Kaba and Ritchie, *No More Police*; Mark Neocleous, *A Critical Theory of Police Power* (Brooklyn, NY: Verso Books, 2021); Dario Melossi and Massimo Pavarini, *The Prison and the Factory: Origins of the Penitentiary System*, 40th anniversary ed. (London: Palgrave, 2018); Ruth Wilson Gilmore, *Golden Gulag: Prisons, Surplus, Crisis, and Opposition in Globalizing California* (Berkeley: University of California Press, 2007); Gilmore, *Abolition Geography*; The CR10 Publications Collective, *Abolition Now! Ten Years of Strategy and Struggle against the Prison Industrial Complex* (Oakland, CA: AK, 2008); Critical Resistance and INCITE! Women of Color against Violence, "The Critical Resistance INCITE! Statement on Gender Violence and the Prison Industrial Complex," in *Color of Violence: The INCITE! Anthology*, ed. INCITE! Women of Color against Violence (Durham, NC: Duke University Press, 2016), 15–29; Andrea J. Ritchie, *Invisible No More: Police Violence against Black Women and Women of Color* (Boston: Beacon, 2017); William C. Anderson, *The Nation on No Map: Black Anarchism and Abolition* (Oakland, CA: AK, 2021); Michel Foucault, *Abnormal: Lectures at the Collège de France, 1974–1975*, trans. Graham Burchell (New York: Picador, 2003); Michel Foucault, *Discipline and Punish: The Birth of the Prison*, trans. Alan Sheridan (New York: Vintage Books); Alex Vitale, *The End of Policing* (New York: Verso, 2017); Loïc Wacquant, *Punishing the Poor: The Neoliberal Government of Social Insecurity* (Durham, NC: Duke University Press, 2009); David Correia and Tyler Wall, *Police: A Field Guide* (Brooklyn, NY: Verso, 2018); David Correia and Tyler

Wall, eds., *Violent Order: Essays on the Nature of Police* (Chicago: Haymarket Books, 2021); Kelly Lytle Hernández, *City of Inmates: Conquest, Rebellion, and the Rise of Human Caging in Los Angeles, 1771–1965* (Chapel Hill: University of North Carolina Press, 2017); Michelle Alexander, *The New Jim Crow: Mass Incarceration in the Age of Colorblindness* (New York: New Press, 2012); Maya Schenwar, Joe Macaré, and Alana Yu-lan Price, eds., *Who Do You Serve, Who Do You Protect? Police Violence and Resistance in the United States* (Chicago: Haymarket Books, 2016); Jordan T. Camp and Christina Heatherton, eds., *Policing the Planet: Why the Policing Crisis Led to Black Lives Matter* (Brooklyn, NY: Verso, 2016); Jordan T. Camp, *Incarcerating the Crisis: Freedom Struggles and the Rise of the Neoliberal State* (Oakland: University of California Press, 2016); Joy James, ed., *The New Abolitionists: (Neo)Slave Writings and Contemporary Prison Narratives* (Albany: State University of New York, 2005); Joy James, ed., *Warfare in the American Homeland: Policing and Prisons in a Penal Democracy* (Durham, NC: Duke University Press, 2007); Bernard E. Harcourt, *Illusion of Order: The False Promise of Broken Windows Policing* (Cambridge, MA: Harvard University Press, 2001); Russell Maroon Shoatz, *Maroon the Implacable: The Collected Writings of Russell Maroon Shoatz*, ed. Fred Ho and Quincy Saul (Oakland, CA: PM, 2013); Douglas Hay, Peter Linebaugh, John G. Rule, Cal Winslow, and E. P. Thompson, *Albion's Fatal Tree: Crime and Society in Eighteenth Century England* (London: Verso Books, 2011); Malcolm X and Alex Haley, *The Autobiography of Malcolm X* (New York: Ballantine Books, 1999); James Baldwin, "A Report from Occupied Territory," *Nation*, July 11, 1966; Huey Newton, *To Die for the People: The Writings of Huey Newton*, ed. Toni Morrison (San Francisco: City Lights Books, 2009); Kahlil Gibran Muhammad, *The Condemnation of Blackness: Race, Crime, and the Making of Modern Urban America* (Cambridge, MA: Harvard University Press, 2010); Kristian Williams, *Our Enemies in Blue: Police and Power in America* (Oakland, CA: AK, 2015); Randall G. Shelden, *Controlling the Dangerous Classes: A History of Criminal Justice in America*, 2nd ed. (Boston: Pearson Allyn and Bacon, 2008); Jeffrey Reiman and Paul Leighton, *The Rich Get Richer and the Poor Get Prison: Ideology, Class, and Criminal Justice*, 10th ed. (New York: Routledge, 2016); Sidney L. Harring, *Policing a Class Society: The Experience of American Cities, 1865–1915*, 2nd ed. (Chicago: Haymarket Books, 2017); Elizabeth Hinton, *From the War on Poverty to the War on Crime: The Making of Mass Incarceration in America* (Cambridge, MA: Harvard University Press, 2016); Elizabeth Hinton and DeAnza Cook, "The Mass Criminalization of Black Americans: A Historical Overview," *Annual Review of Criminology* 4 (2021): 261–286; Silvia Federici, *Caliban and the Witch: Women, the Body and Primitive Accumulation* (New York: Autonomedia, 2014); Peter Linebaugh, *The London Hanged: Crime and Civil Society in the Eighteenth Century*, 2nd ed. (London: Verso, 2006); Geo Maher, *A World without Police: How Strong Communities Make Cops Obsolete* (Brooklyn, NY: Verso Books, 2021); Eric A. Stanley and Nat Smith, eds., *Captive Genders: Trans Embodiment and the Prison Industrial Complex*, exp. 2nd ed. (Oakland, CA: AK, 2015); Nick

Estes, *Our History Is the Future: Standing Rock versus the Dakota Pipeline, and the Long Tradition of Indigenous Resistance* (Brooklyn, NY: Verso Books, 2019); Robyn Maynard and Leanne Betasamosake Simpson, *Rehearsals for Living* (Chicago: Haymarket Books, 2022); Kimberlé Williams Crenshaw and Neil Gotanda, eds., *Critical Race Theory: The Key Writings That Formed the Movement* (New York: New Press, 1995).

3 Kaba and Ritchie, *No More Police*, 177.
4 David H. Bayley, *Police for the Future* (Oxford: Oxford University Press, 1994), 3. Bayley goes on to write, "Repeated analysis has consistently failed to find any connection between the number of police and crime rates. Second, the primary strategies adopted by modern police have been shown to have little or no effect on crime" (3). An abundance of sociological research demonstrates that there is no identifiable correlation between policing and rates of crime, which is to say, no correlation between policing and general public safety. See John Jay College Research Advisory Group on Preventing and Reducing Community Violence, *Reducing Violence without Police: A Review of Research Evidence* (New York: Research and Evaluation Center, John Jay College of Criminal Justice, City University of New York, 2020); Kenneth Novak, Gary Cordner, Brad Smith, and Roy Roberg, *Police & Society*, 7th ed. (Oxford: Oxford University Press, 2016); Aya Gruber, "Crime Rates Rise and Fall. Police Mostly Having Nothing to Do with It," Garrison Project, October 26, 2021, https://thegarrisonproject.org; Alec Karakastanis, "Why 'Crime' Isn't the Question and Police Aren't the Answer," *Current Affairs*, August 10, 2020, www.currentaffairs.org. Regarding the incompleteness of "crime" and "crime rates" as reflections of harms actually being committed, see Kaba and Ritchie, *No More Police*, 49–53. Police power is, at its most basic level, the racial capitalist state's discretionary power to use legitimate force as needed to uphold racial capitalist order, which is why, as Kaba and Ritchie write, "crime rates are better understood as reflections of cops' perceptions of the proper order of things rather than harms people are actually experiencing" (50–51).
5 Danielle Sered, *Until We Reckon: Violence, Mass Incarceration, and a Road to Repair* (New York: New Press, 2019), 7.
6 The notion that police "serve and protect" is in fact a fairly recent invention, first coined in 1963 by the Los Angeles Police Department under the leadership of police chief William Parker, an "avowed white supremacist." Maher, *World without Police*, 62.
7 Stafford Beer, "What Is Cybernetics?," *Kybernetes* 31, no. 2 (2002): 209–219.
8 Kaba and Ritchie, *No More Police*, 41–70; Victoria Law, *"Prisons Make Us Safer" and 20 Other Myths about Mass Incarceration* (Boston: Beacon, 2021), 17–24; Vitale, *End of Policing*, 31–54; Amanda Alexander and Danielle Sered, "Making Communities Safer, without the Police," *Boston Review*, November 1, 2021, www.bostonreview.net; Jeff Asher and Ben Horwitz, "How Do the Police Actually Spend Their Time?," *New York Times*, June 19, 2020, www.nytimes.com; Mariame

Kaba and Eva Nagoa, *What about the Rapists? An Abolitionist FAQ Series from Interrupting Criminalization*, Interrupting Criminalization, 2021, www.interruptingcriminalization.com; John Jay College Research Advisory Group on Preventing and Reducing Community Violence, *Reducing Violence without Police*; Novak et al., *Police & Society*; Gruber, "Crime Rates Rise and Fall"; Karakastanis, "Why 'Crime' Isn't the Question."

9 Societies have used various forms of captivity for judicial purposes for millennia, primarily as a temporary holding place prior to some corporal or other form of punishment, but it was not until the seventeenth century in England that extended captivity became a form of punishment in itself, thereby giving birth to the "prison" in its modern iteration. This is the sense of the "prison" with which this book is primarily concerned. Regarding police, as I outline in chapter 3, multiple scattered forms of state and militia power fulfilling various functions preceded and subsequently lent themselves to the formal consolidation and institutionalization of uniformed police starting in the early nineteenth century. Regarding the use of the term "colonial racial capitalism," building on the work of Cedric Robinson and others, Susan Koshy, Lisa Marie Cacho, Jodi A. Byrd, and Brian Jordan Jefferson develop the notion of "colonial racial capitalism"—a term I deploy throughout this book—to attend more specifically to the inseparability of the racial regimes of colonialism and capitalism. Susan Koshy, Lisa Marie Cacho, Jodi A. Byrd, and Brian Jordan Jefferson, eds., *Colonial Racial Capitalism* (Durham, NC: Duke University Press, 2022). On the innate connection between policing and colonial racial capitalism, see Lisa Marie Cacho and Jodi Melamed, "'Don't Arrest Me, Arrest the Police': Policing as the Street Administration of Colonial Racial Capitalist Orders," in Koshy et al., *Colonial Racial Capitalism*, 159–205.

10 Vitale, *End of Policing*, 34, 51–52.

11 Gilmore, "Beyond Bratton." I follow Black radical feminist and abolitionist writers who prefer the term "mass criminalization" over "mass incarceration." I prefer "mass criminalization" because it casts a wider net than "mass incarceration," which technically refers just to the fact of people's imprisonment, whereas "mass criminalization" can refer to the determination of what constitutes criminality and who counts as criminal, as well as police surveillance, pursuit, harassment, assault, capture, arrest, imprisonment in jail, all that takes place in a courtroom, and imprisonment in prison. I also prefer "mass criminalization" because this book focuses on police as much as, if not more than, imprisonment.

12 I use the phrase "vulnerable to premature death," a concept developed by Ruth Wilson Gilmore, throughout the book. What I appreciate about this phrase is the fact that it speaks plainly about the deadly impact that forms of oppression have on people's lives. The original source of this phrase is Gilmore's definition of racism: "the state-sanctioned or extralegal production and exploitation of group-differentiated vulnerability to premature death" (*Golden Gulag*, 28).

13 Mariame Kaba, "The System Isn't Broken," in *We Do This 'til We Free Us*, 6–13; Alexander, *New Jim Crow*, 224–225.

14 Kelly Hayes, referencing the work of John Jost in his book *Left and Right*, says, "a lot of people find the inevitability of something bad easier to process than uncertainty." Hayes, "Let This Conversation with Mariame Kaba Radicalize You," *Truthout*, April 20, 2023, https://truthout.org.

15 On racial, class, and other disparities in incarceration, see Wendy Sawyer and Peter Wagner, *Mass Incarceration: The Whole Pie 2023* (Prison Policy Initiative, March 14, 2023), www.prisonpolicy.org. The state also captures and cages queer, trans, and gender-nonconforming people, especially queer, trans, and gender-nonconforming people of color, at disproportionately high rates. For data surrounding the disproportionate incarceration of queer and trans people, see Prison Policy Initiative, "LGBTQ," accessed July 1, 2023, www.prisonpolicy.org. For more on the criminalization of Black women and Black queer, trans, and gender-nonconforming people and other women, queer, trans, and gender-nonconforming people of color, see Ritchie, *Invisible No More*.

16 Kaba and Ritchie, *No More Police*, 41–70; Sered, *Until We Reckon*.

17 Sered, *Until We Reckon*, 3–4.

18 On the construction of the distinction between legitimate and illegitimate violence in the making of the US carceral state, see Naomi Murakawa, *The First Civil Right: How Liberals Built Prison America* (Oxford: Oxford University Press, 2014), 40–44.

19 Kelly Hayes, "Copaganda Arrests Our Imaginations," *Truthout*, November 3, 2022, https://truthout.org. On "capitalist realism," see Mark Fisher, *Capitalist Realism: Is There No Alternative?*, 2nd ed. (Hampshire, UK: Zero Books, 2022); on "carceral realism," see Oly Durose, "Carceral Realism: Is There No Alternative?," *Red Pepper*, May 28, 2022, www.redpepper.org.uk.

20 On prisons (and police) as solutions to social problems, see Gilmore, *Golden Gulag*, 5, 26. On how people are making safety without police and prisons, see Alexander and Sered, "Making Communities Safer, without Police." From credible messenger violence interruption programs to mutual aid networks to nonpolice mental health and crisis response and much more, people are making safety without police and prisons a reality across the US and beyond. For a database of community-based experiments in creating safer communities based primarily in the US, see One Million Experiments, a project of Interrupting Criminalization: www.millionexperiments.com. Two of the main traditions that more people are engaging these days in pursuit of safety without police and prisons are transformative justice and healing justice. On transformative justice, see Ejeris Dixon and Leah Lakshmi Piepzna-Samarasinha, eds., *Beyond Survival: Strategies and Stories from the Transformative Justice Movement* (Oakland, CA: AK, 2020); and Transform Harm, www.transformharm.org. For an account and history of healing justice, see Cara Page and Erica Woodland, *Healing Justice Lineages: Dreaming at the Crossroads of Liberation, Collective Care, and Safety* (Berkeley, CA: North Atlantic Books, 2023).

21 Vitale, *End of Policing*, 51.

22 Crime control *is* social control because "crime" is itself a social and political construction that reflects not a neutrally defined set of law-breaking instances of harm but the racial capitalist state's perception of what disrupts social order. For more on the construction of crime and the police manipulation of "crime rates," see Kaba and Ritchie, *No More Police*, 44–53.
23 On the distinction between a "negative peace" that is merely the "absence of tension" and a "positive peace" that is "the presence of justice," see Martin Luther King Jr., "Letter from Birmingham City Jail," in *A Testament of Hope: The Essential Writings and Speeches of Martin Luther King Jr.*, ed. James M. Washington (New York: HarperCollins, 1986), 289–302.
24 Danielle Sered, "To Produce Safety, We Must Understand Violence," *Common Justice*, July 8, 2020, https://blog.commonjustice.org.
25 See Transform Harm, www.transformharm.org; and One Million Experiments, www.millionexperiments.com. A highly practical resource on restorative and transformative justice and community accountability is the *Creative Interventions Toolkit*, which is available for free download at www.creative-interventions.org.
26 Sered, *Until We Reckon*.
27 Quoted by Andrea Ritchie in Hayes, "Copaganda Arrests Our Imaginations."
28 It is also unreasonable to expect of people conducting experiments in making safety without police and prisons a standard of proof of effectiveness prior to full development of a new practice or program, a standard that is not currently applied to police or prisons, which are highly ineffective at producing genuine safety.
29 Jonathan Z. Smith, "Religion, Religions, Religious," in *Critical Terms for Religious Studies*, ed. Mark C. Taylor (Chicago: University of Chicago Press, 1998), 269–284.
30 Tomoko Masuzawa, *The Invention of World Religions: Or, How European Universalism Was Preserved in the Language of Pluralism* (Chicago: University of Chicago Press, 2005); David Chidester, *Empire of Religion: Imperialism and Comparative Religion* (Chicago: University of Chicago Press, 2014).
31 This characterization of religion synthesizes Charles Long's definition of religion as "orientation in the ultimate sense" and David Chidester's characterization of religion as "a terrain in which human beings engage in meaningful and powerful ways with the material constraints and animations of matter, the interplay of sacralizing and desecrating, the labor of producing space and time, and the myriad ways in which incongruity, the material effect of the collision of incommensurables, can be transposed into moments, perhaps fleeting moments, of congruence." Charles H. Long, *Significations: Signs, Symbols, and Images in the Interpretation of Religion* (Aurora, CO: Davies, 1995), 7; David Chidester, *Religion: Material Dynamics* (Oakland: University of California Press, 2018), 2–3.
32 Long, *Significations*, 7.
33 Karl Marx critiques religion as an entirely understandable but unfortunate means by which the powers that be provide the promise of future comfort to oppressed peoples in such a way that it keeps them from challenging the systems that

oppress them. See Karl Marx, *Marx on Religion*, ed. John Raines (Philadelphia: Temple University Press, 2002). Sigmund Freud critiques religion as an illusory form of wish-fulfillment. See Sigmund Freud, *The Future of an Illusion*, trans. and ed. James Strachey (New York: Norton, 1989). Ludwig Feuerbach argues that religion and theology are essentially means by which humans project themselves onto the heavens. Ludwig Feuerbach, *The Essence of Christianity*, trans. George Eliot (Amherst, NY: Prometheus Books, 1989). Though I do not align fully with the conclusions at which each of these theorists arrive, their core critiques of religion as a phenomenon particularly vulnerable to self-projecting illusions that abet structural injustice inform this book throughout.

34 This process of naturalization is also captured in part by Marxist theorization of "ideology." As historian Patrick Wolfe writes, "As used by Marx and Engels, who did not define the concept formally, ideologies represent ruling groups' dominance as given in nature rather than as historically imposed and contingent. Attributing suzerainty to natural processes is a particularly powerful mode of legitimation, since it renders the situation seemingly eternal and unchangeable." Patrick Wolfe, *Traces of History: Elementary Structures of Race* (London: Verso, 2016), 7–8n16. For more on "ideology," see Louis Althusser, *On the Reproduction of Capitalism: Ideology and Ideological State Apparatuses*, trans. G. M. Goshgarian (London: Verso, 2014). For more on the naturalization and erasure of the formation of race, see Falguni A. Sheth, *Toward a Political Philosophy of Race* (Albany: State University of New York Press, 2009).

35 As Joel Olson puts it, race "is a constructed but socially significant category." Joel Olson, *The Abolition of White Democracy* (Minneapolis: University of Minnesota Press, 2004), 9. Or, as Michael Omi and Howard Winant write, "While it may not be 'real' in a biological sense, race is indeed real as a social category with definite social consequences." Michael Omi and Howard Winant, *Racial Formation in the United States*, 3rd ed. (New York: Routledge, 2015), 110. Beyond race's function as a negative descriptor, for Black, Indigenous, and other people of color, it has also long been a strategically and culturally reclaimed site and means of claiming power and dignity over against white oppressors. See also Gary Peller, "Race-Consciousness," in Crenshaw et al., *Critical Race Theory*, 127–158; and Neil Gotanda, "A Critique of 'Our Constitution Is Color-Blind,'" in Crenshaw et al., *Critical Race Theory*, 257–275. On the social construction and performativity of gender, see Judith Butler, *Gender Trouble* (New York: Routledge, 1990).

36 KODX Seattle, "Robin D. G. Kelley—What Is Racial Capitalism and Why Does It Matter?," recorded November 7, 2017, University of Washington, Seattle, WA, YouTube, November 18, 2017, www.youtube.com/watch?v=--gim7W_jQQ.

37 The violence through which whiteness entered the world centuries ago has endured in a multitude of forms, as whiteness—together with property—has reproduced itself over and over again ever since, permeating our literal and figurative air, water, and soil with toxicities that have shortened people's lives, and the life of the earth, for centuries up to the present. In addition to, and set in motion by, the

violent acts that founded it, rigorously—and indeed religiously—held claims to whiteness have led directly to countless harms over the course of three centuries. I offer here an incomplete litany of these harms, focused particularly on whiteness as embodied in the United States, in order to convey the scope of the violence of whiteness across the world. In addition to and contained within the overarching phenomena of racial capitalism, chattel slavery, and settler colonialism, the violence of whiteness has included large-scale acts of deadly white mob terror and destruction against Black communities, including homes and businesses, in response to gains in Black economic and political power, such as in Wilmington, North Carolina, in 1898, East St. Louis in 1917, in more than fifty cities and towns across the US during the "Red Summer" of 1919, and in Tulsa, Oklahoma, in 1921; more than four thousand instances of white terror in the form of public lynchings of Black people between 1865 and 1950; the rise, fall, and resurgence of white supremacist and white nationalist organizations and militias from Reconstruction to the present that have assaulted and killed Black people, other people of color, Jewish people, and even white people accused of being race traitors; thousands of instances of white settler violence, including sexual violence, torture, and the destruction of villages and crops, against Indigenous tribes who stood in the path of the territorial expansions of Manifest Destiny; European and American imperialism that imposed white military and police occupation and exploited nonwhite peoples to forge white American wealth and exercise geopolitical control in Central and South America and East Asia throughout the late nineteenth and twentieth centuries; the colonial and imperial fabrication of borders that disrupted the livelihoods of entire populations of nonwhite peoples, rendering them noncitizen outsider threats on the lands they called home; the mass exploitation and destruction of the earth through various forms of mining and pollution that have created and continue to create irreversible climate change that causes catastrophes that most severely impact those who are already most impacted by exploitation; racialized property laws from Reconstruction to well into the second half of the twentieth century that prevented or severely limited Black land and home ownership, thereby creating massive disparities in generational wealth between white and Black Americans that remain in effect to this day, leading to disparate access to resources, quality education, food, housing, health care, transportation, and all that contributes to people's overall well-being; disparate physical and mental health outcomes derived from centuries of anti-Black medical practice and the outright withholding of quality medical care; Jim Crow conditions of de jure and de facto discrimination that led to the Great Migration of Black people from the South to the Midwest and North, where they encountered still more violence at the hands of both working-class and ruling-class white people; redlining; white violence and federal laws explicitly discriminating against immigrants from Europe, Central and South America, and Asia; regimes of deportation; the federal surveillance, arrest, and assassination of Black, Indigenous, and Latinx leaders struggling against the forces of racial capitalism and settler colonialism; racialized neoliberal and finance capitalism that accumulates capital for fewer and fewer people by privatizing or withdrawing social goods from more and more people, thereby creating mass housing insecurity and homelessness while catalyzing gentrification and displacement; and, the focus of this book, carceral institutions including police, jail, and prisons that came into existence for the purpose of securing a racial capitalist settler colonial social order by criminalizing the personhood and agency of Black and poor people, resulting in the slow destruction of generations of entire communities through a system of so-called public safety that operates on the basis of human caging and disposal. The purpose of this litany is not to induce guilt in the inheritors of whiteness but to invite critical consciousness that catalyzes personal and collective intentionality, accountability, and repair.

38 As a manifestation of the political and religious agency of propertied men of European descent, "whiteness" is, in large part, a term that describes the agency and orientation of white people in general and white propertied men in particular. And yet, three centuries on from its initial formation, whiteness also functions and shapes the world beyond the localizable agency of individual white people. Indeed, while patriarchal and possessive whiteness is a positionality of godlike power and invulnerability, it is also the case that not all white people enjoy the full scope of such power, including especially those without property, those who disrupt norms of gender, sexuality, and ability, and white people who actively refuse allegiance to and seek to abolish its power. Moreover, some nonwhite people can obtain some degree of the godlike power of whiteness by participating in the antagonisms it wages against nonwhite and even dispossessed white peoples, including through the violence work of cops and cages, and can enjoy some of its benefits, as in the case of so-called honorary whites. Whiteness is a positionality that people can inhabit and a power that people can possess, both to varying degrees.

39 W. E. B. Du Bois, *Darkwater: Voices from within the Veil* (New York: Verso, 2016), 18.

40 Cheryl I. Harris, "Whiteness as Property," *Harvard Law Review* 106, no. 8 (June 1993): 1707–1791.

41 Mary Douglas, *Purity and Danger: An Analysis of the Concept of Pollution and Taboo* (New York: Routledge, 2002).

42 On the "white world" and the "dark world," see W. E. B. Du Bois, *Dusk of Dawn: An Essay toward an Autobiography of a Race Concept* (New Brunswick, NJ: Transaction, 2011); and Du Bois, *Darkwater*. On the "color line," see W. E. B. Du Bois, *The Souls of Black Folk* (New York: Dover, 1994). For more on Du Bois's idea that whiteness produces oppositional worlds, see Olson, *Abolition of White Democracy*, 17–30, 131–133; and Charles Mills, *The Racial Contract* (Ithaca, NY: Cornell University Press, 1997), 12–13, 21, 57.

43 Joel Michael Reynolds, "Disability and White Supremacy," *Critical Philosophy of Race* 10, no. 1 (2022): 48–70; David Roediger, *Seizing Freedom: Slave Emancipation and Liberty for All* (Brooklyn, NY: Verso Books, 2015), 67–103.

44 James Baldwin, "This Far and No Further," in *The Cross of Redemption: Uncollected Writings*, ed. Randall Kenan (New York: Vintage International, 2011), 162.
45 This encapsulation of criminalization is deeply informed by the definition of criminalization provided by Beth E. Richie and Andrea Ritchie, who write that criminalization is "the social and political process by which society determines which actions or behaviors—and by who—will be punished by the state. At the most basic level, it involves passage and enforcement of criminal laws. While framed as neutral, decisions about what kinds of conduct to punish, how, and how much are very much a choice, guided by existing structures of economic and social inequality based on race, gender, sexuality, disability, and poverty, among others." Quoted in Kaba and Ritchie, *No More Police*, 29. The quote comes from Andrea J. Ritchie and Beth E. Richie, "The Crisis of Criminalization: A Call for a Comprehensive Philanthropic Response" (Barnard Center for Research on Women, 2017). Kaba and Ritchie also provide a more concise definition that builds on Richie and Ritchie's when they write that "criminalization is a social and political process that determines whose actions will be subject to surveillance, policing, and punishment in service of maintaining and reinforcing existing relations of power" (186).
46 Kaba and Ritchie, 142–148; Brendan McQuade and Mark Neocleous, "Beware Medical Police," *Radical Philosophy* 2, no. 8 (2020): 3–9; Neocleous, *Critical Theory of Police Power*; Markus Dirk Dubber, *The Police Power: Patriarchy and the Foundations of American Government* (New York: Columbia University Press, 2005).
47 This is an allusion to W. E. B. Du Bois's definition of whiteness, which frames chapter 2 and which I summarize later in the Introduction.
48 James Baldwin credits a Muslim minister with this phrase in his book *The Fire Next Time*. James Baldwin, "Down at the Cross: Letter from a Region in My Mind," in *The Fire Next Time* (New York: Vintage, 1993), 45. Public Enemy, "White Heaven/Black Hell," on *Muse Sick-n-Hour Mess Age* (Def Jam, 1994).
49 As I outline in chapter 3, for the Christian tradition, divine-human hierarchy is understood as the arrangement that corresponds with a loving God's will, a God who is understood as the source of all life. For the carceral practice that shares origins with and draws from this Christian soteriological tradition, the restoration of hierarchy, though it is cast as a benefit to people at the bottom of social hierarchies, provides no inherent benefit to them. The only benefit—the only real salvation—I argue in chapter 5, belongs to the functionally sacred order that restores whiteness and property to godlike status by exiling others to carceral hell on earth.
50 For more on homologous relations between concepts and practices across time, see Devin Singh, *Divine Currency: The Theological Power of Money in the West* (Stanford, CA: Stanford University Press, 2018), 1–25.
51 James Baldwin, "An Open Letter to My Sister Angela Y. Davis," in *Cross of Redemption*, 255–260.

CHAPTER 1. PATRIARCHAL WHITENESS AND PRIVATE PROPERTY

1. Tinker, "What Are We Going to Do with White People?"
2. Willie James Jennings, *The Christian Imagination: Theology and the Origins of Race* (New Haven, CT: Yale University Press, 2010), 6–8.
3. Jennings, 23–24. Jennings locates the origins of "whiteness" as a clear, established, and coherent category earlier than my analysis does. While the germination of what would become whiteness certainly takes place in and through late medieval colonialism, it is arguably not until the late seventeenth or early eighteenth century that the notion of "whiteness" comes into existence as a coherent and functioning category. Thus, in striving for historical precision, what Jennings calls at this late medieval junction a matter of "whiteness" I call a matter of "what would come to be recognized as whiteness."
4. Jennings, 43.
5. Tinker, "What Are We Going to Do with White People?" For more on the relationship between religion and colonialism, see Chidester, *Religion*, 104–115.
6. Quoted in Neocleous, *Critical Theory of Police Power*, 128. The original source is Patrick Colquhoun, *A Treatise on Indigence, Etc.* (London: J. Hatchard, 1806).
7. Quoted in Neocleous, *Critical Theory of Police Power*, 153.
8. Karl Marx, *Capital, Volume 1: A Critique of Political Economy*, trans. Ben Fowkes (London: Penguin Books, 1990), 873.
9. William Graham Sumner, "William Graham Sumner on Social Darwinism," in *Voices of Freedom: A Documentary History*, 5th ed., ed. Eric Foner, vol. 2 (New York: Norton, 2017), 38–39.
10. Premised on the violence of forced displacement and the subjugations of forced dependence, capital comes into the world, Marx writes, "dripping from head to foot, from every pore, with blood and dirt" (*Capital, Volume 1*, 926).
11. A few of the many written histories documenting anticapitalist movements throughout capitalism's history include Ian Angus, *The War against the Commons: Dispossession and Resistance in the Making of Capitalism* (New York: Monthly Review Press, 2023); Silvia Federici, *Re-enchanting the World: Feminism and the Politics of the Commons* (Oakland, CA: PM, 2019); Cedric J. Robinson, *Black Marxism: The Making of the Black Radical Tradition* (Chapel Hill: University of North Carolina Press, 2000); Jeremy Brecher, *Strike!*, 50th anniversary ed. (Oakland, CA: PM, 2020); Brandon Weber, *Class War, U.S.A.: Dispatches from Workers' Struggles in American History* (Chicago: Haymarket Books, 2018); Robin D. G. Kelley, *Hammer and Hoe: Alabama Communists during the Great Depression*, 25th anniversary ed. (Chapel Hill: University of North Carolina Press, 2015).
12. In the words of Robin D. G. Kelley, there is "no such thing as non-racial capitalism" (KODX Seattle, "Robin D. G. Kelley"). The flagship text of this scholarship is Robinson, *Black Marxism*. The term "racial capitalism" was first used by intellectuals in the anti-apartheid movement in South Africa. Robinson elaborated the term into an analytic frame for understanding the shape of capitalism in a more

thoroughly global sense. For more on Robinson's work on racial capitalism, see Robin D. G. Kelley, introduction to *Boston Review: Race Capitalism Justice (Forum 1)*, ed. Walter Johnson and Robin D. G. Kelley (Boston: Boston Review, 2017). For more on the global histories of racial capitalism, see Destin Jenkins and Justin Leroy, eds., *Histories of Racial Capitalism* (New York: Columbia University Press, 2021). For more on the relationship between colonialism and racial capitalism, see Koshy et al., *Colonial Racial Capitalism*. The concept of "accumulation by dispossession" comes from Marxist geographer David Harvey. He uses the term to describe the dynamic of primitive accumulation under neoliberal capitalism, but it is also a fitting summation of the original primitive accumulation of early agrarian capitalism. David Harvey, *The New Imperialism* (Oxford: Oxford University Press, 2005).

13 Robinson, *Black Marxism*, 2, 28.
14 Gilmore, "Abolition Geography and the Problem of Innocence" in *Abolition Geography*, 471–472.
15 Gilmore, 495.
16 Gabriel L. Negretto, "Hobbes' Leviathan: The Irresistible Power of a Mortal God," *Analisi e diritto* (2001): 179–192.
17 Negretto, 179.
18 Roland Boer and Christina Petterson, *Idols of Nations: Biblical Myth at the Origins of Capitalism* (Minneapolis, MN: Fortress, 2014); Devin Singh, *Economy and Modern Christian Thought* (Boston: Brill, 2022), 14; Paul Oslington, ed., *Adam Smith as Theologian* (New York: Routledge, 2011); Paul Oslington, *Political Economy as Natural Theology: Smith, Malthus and Their Followers* (New York: Routledge, 2018). The theologian Harvey Cox also outlines the many ways that the capitalist market mimics and functions as a kind of secular God. Harvey Cox, *The Market as God* (Cambridge, MA: Harvard University Press, 2016).
19 Boer and Petterson, *Idols of Nations*.
20 Walter Benjamin, "Capitalism as Religion," trans. Chad Kautzer, in *The Frankfurt School on Religion: Key Writings by the Major Thinkers*, ed. Eduardo Mendieta (New York: Routledge, 2005), 259.
21 Benjamin, 261.
22 Cedric J. Robinson, *Terms of Order: Political Science and the Myth of Leadership* (Chapel Hill: University of North Carolina Press, 1980), 125. Robinson writes, "political society is no less a Salvationist or redemptionist paradigm than those theologic paradigms out of which it emerged and with which it has had a most constant existential and historical simultaneity." My formulation—that modern liberal racial order is a modality through which salvation is lived—borrows structurally from Stuart Hall's famous formulation, explored later in this chapter, that race is a modality through which class is lived. Stuart Hall, "Race, Articulation and Societies Structured in Dominance," in *Sociological Theories: Race and Colonialism* (Paris: UNESCO, 1980), 341. For more on how Cedric Robinson's work enables us to perceive the relationship between Christian order

and racial order, see Amaryah Shaye Armstrong, "Christian Order and Racial Order: What Cedric Robinson Can Teach Us Today," *The Bias*, June 3, 2020, https://christiansocialism.com.

23 Ancient and medieval peoples on the continent of Europe also enslaved other Europeans. See Robinson, *Black Marxism*, 9–28. As the early twentieth-century Black radical scholar and activist W. E. B. Du Bois writes, "The using of men for the benefit of masters is no new invention of modern Europe. It is quite as old as the world. But Europe proposed to apply it on a scale and with an elaborateness of detail of which no former world ever dreamed. The imperial width of the thing,— the heaven-defying audacity—makes its modern newness." Du Bois, *Darkwater*, 24. Historians estimate that European and European-American colonizers shipped approximately 12.4 million African people across the Atlantic between the late fifteenth and the late nineteenth centuries. Approximately 1.8 million Africans died in the "Middle Passage," and many millions more died early deaths as a result of the many forms of violence that European and European-American colonizers inflicted on them. Marcus Rediker, *The Slave Ship: A Human History* (New York: Penguin, 2007), 5.

24 Hugh Thomas, *The Slave Trade: The Story of the Atlantic Slave Trade: 1440–1870* (New York: Simon and Schuster, 1997); Robin Blackburn, *The American Crucible: Slavery, Emancipation and Human Rights* (London: Verso, 2013). European peoples' enslavement and global trade of African peoples quite literally transformed the world by depleting African nations of people, power, and resources and transforming them into means of the economic and political empowerment of European and European-American peoples and nations. Walter Rodney, *How Europe Underdeveloped Africa* (New York: Verso Books, 2018).

25 As the historian Walter Johnson writes, "The history of capitalism makes no sense separate from the history of the slave trade and its aftermath. There was no such thing as capitalism without slavery." Walter Johnson, "To Remake the World: Slavery, Racial Capitalism, and Justice," in Johnson and Kelley, *Boston Review: Race Capitalism Justice (Forum 1)*, 25. For more on the relationship between capitalism and chattel slavery, see Edward E. Baptist, *The Half Has Never Been Told: Slavery and the Making of American Capitalism* (New York: Basic Books, 2016); Walter Johnson, *River of Dark Dreams: Slavery and Empire in the Cotton Kingdom* (Cambridge, MA: Harvard University Press, 2017); Eric Williams, *Capitalism and Slavery* (Chapel Hill: University of North Carolina Press, 1994); Robinson, *Black Marxism*. On the intercontinental connections that colonialism and slavery formed, see Lisa Lowe, *The Intimacies of Four Continents* (Durham, NC: Duke University Press, 2015).

26 Patrick Wolfe, "Settler Colonialism and the Elimination of the Native," *Journal of Genocide Research* 8, no. 4 (December 2006): 388.

27 Historians estimate that more than one hundred million Indigenous peoples in North America alone died early deaths as a result of European settler violence in all its forms over the course of four centuries. In North America, centuries

of destruction wrought by European settler colonialism included thousands of outright violent attacks against and massacres of Indigenous tribes, the introduction of infectious diseases, innumerable acts of torture and sexual violence against Indigenous peoples, and tens of thousands of instances of child abduction and murder. But it also included, among other things, manipulative or altogether violated land treaties that reduced native title to native occupancy and eventually to displacement; forced relocation, including the 1831 forced displacement of Cherokee tribes from the southeastern United States, followed by the burning of their villages; criminalization and forced relocation through "dumping" at the hands of colonial police; religious conversion; and resocialization through forced assimilation, the goal of which was, in the words of Richard Pratt, the founder of the Carlisle boarding school, to "kill the Indian" in order to "save the man." Wolfe, 397.

28 James A. Morone, *Hellfire Nation: The Politics of Sin in American History* (New Haven, CT: Yale University Press, 2003), 169–182.
29 Albert J. Raboteau, *Slave Religion: The "Invisible Institution" in the Antebellum South*, updated ed. (Oxford: Oxford University Press, 2004), 213, 295.
30 Richard Furman, "Exposition of the Views of the Baptists Relative to the Coloured Population of the United States in Communication to the Governor of South Carolina" (Charleston, 1823), reprinted in James A. Rogers, *Richard Furman: Life and Legacy* (Macon, GA: Mercer University Press, 1985), § 7.
31 Before slave owners permitted enslaved people to become Christians, the idea of their becoming Christians through baptism was a threat to the solidity of plantation capitalism and the Christianity of which it was a part, which is why, when enslaved African peoples were permitted to become Christians, it was only as resolutely inferior subjects whose inferiority was articulated in theological terms. For more on this history, see M. Shawn Copeland, *Enfleshing Freedom: Body, Race, and Being* (Minneapolis, MN: Fortress, 2010); Raboteau, *Slave Religion*; Katharine Gerbner, *Christian Slavery: Conversion and Race in the Protestant Atlantic World* (Philadelphia: University of Pennsylvania Press, 2018).
32 Quoted in Dwight N. Hopkins, *Down, Up, and Over: Slave Religion and Black Theology* (Minneapolis, MN: Fortress, 2000), 90. See also Morone, *Hellfire Nation*.
33 Quoted in Hopkins, *Down, Up, and Over*, 91.
34 As Hopkins writes, "this catechism syncretized God, the Devil, and human labor" and in so doing established that "the immediate, long-term, divine, and ultimate purpose of black humanity (that is, its theological anthropology) was to work for the masters' wealth" (91).
35 Peter Linebaugh and Marcus Rediker, *The Many-Headed Hydra: Sailors, Slaves, Commoners, and the Hidden History of the Revolutionary Atlantic* (Boston: Beacon, 2003); Marx, *Capital, Volume 1*, 896–904.
36 Quoted in Linebaugh and Rediker, *Many-Headed Hydra*, 15.
37 Linebaugh and Rediker, 15.

38 Quoted in Linebaugh and Rediker, 16. Historian William Carroll notes that "swarm" was a common metaphor widely used to depict dispossessed peoples in the early modern period. William C. Carroll, "'The Nursery of Beggary': Enclosure, Vagrancy, and Sedition in the Tudor-Stuart Period," in *Enclosure Acts: Sexuality, Property, and Culture in Early Modern England*, ed. Richard Burt and John Michael Archer (Ithaca, NY: Cornell University Press, 1994), 39.
39 Quoted in Linebaugh and Rediker, *Many-Headed Hydra*, 20.
40 Nancy Isenberg, *White Trash: The 400-Year Untold History of Class in America* (New York: Penguin, 2016), 21.
41 Edmund S. Morgan, *American Slavery, American Freedom: The Ordeal of Colonial Virginia* (New York: Norton, 2003), 295–315.
42 Alexander, *New Jim Crow*, 23. See also David Roediger, *How Race Survived U.S. History: From Settlement and Slavery to the Obama Phenomenon* (London: Verso, 2010); Linebaugh and Rediker, *Many-Headed Hydra*; E. Morgan, *American Slavery, American Freedom*.
43 Linebaugh and Rediker, *Many-Headed Hydra*, 8–35.
44 In spite of the fact that an initial basis of the rebellion was Governor Berkeley's refusal to equip Bacon with a militia to further dispossess Native Americans and settle their territories, the interests of many of those who participated transcended these concerns, making it a significant event not only for its peculiar unifications but for the reverberations it would set off in colonial America and indeed around the world. For more, see Roediger, *How Race Survived U.S. History*, 5–10, 19–21; Linebaugh and Rediker, *Many-Headed Hydra*, 136–137.
45 Linebaugh and Rediker, *Many-Headed Hydra*, 136–137; Roediger, *How Race Survived U.S. History*, 5–10, 19–21; Alexander, *New Jim Crow*, 24–25; Ladelle McWhorter, *Racism and Sexual Oppression in Anglo-America: A Genealogy* (Bloomington: Indiana University Press, 2009), 66–77.
46 Linebaugh and Rediker, *Many-Headed Hydra*, 135–139.
47 Theodore Allen, *The Invention of the White Race: The Origin of Racial Oppression* (Brooklyn, NY: Verso, 2021); E. Morgan, *American Slavery, American Freedom*; Roediger, *How Race Survived U.S. History*.
48 Roediger, *How Race Survived U.S. History*, 5.
49 Alexander, *New Jim Crow*, 25.
50 People groups discerned and treated other people groups as different well before the eighteenth century, but, as Patrick Wolfe observes, "the mere fact that people have differentiated between human collectivities does not mean that they have been imbued with the discursive formation that today we call 'race'" (*Traces of History*, 7).
51 McWhorter, *Racism and Sexual Oppression*, 59.
52 McWhorter, 73.
53 Wolfe, *Traces of History*, 7.
54 Wolfe, 7.

55 As Du Bois shows in his classic text *Black Reconstruction*, this same dynamic solidified racial distinction after the formal end of chattel slavery when white workers once again chose whiteness over what they shared with regard to class solidarity with formerly enslaved Africans, thereby helping to guarantee that the "color line" would indeed become the problem of the twentieth century, as he earlier prophesied in his *Souls of Black Folk*. W. E. B. Du Bois, *Black Reconstruction in America: 1860–1880* (New York: Free Press, 1998). For more on this dynamic, see Olson, *Abolition of White Democracy*.
56 Robinson, *Black Marxism*, 26; David R. Roediger, *Class, Race, and Marxism* (New York: Verso, 2017); KODX Seattle, "Robin D. G. Kelley"; Nikhil Pal Singh, *Race and America's Long War* (Oakland: University of California Press, 2017).
57 Kelly Brown Douglas, *Stand Your Ground: Black Bodies and the Justice of God* (Maryknoll, NY: Orbis Books, 2015), 8–18.
58 As McWhorter writes, "in 1705 Virginians did not as yet refer simply to 'white people'; they resorted to a religious category—'Christian'—and a list of disjuncts—not negro, not mulatto, not Indian" (*Racism and Sexual Oppression*, 74).
59 Federici, *Caliban and the Witch*, 107.
60 Hopkins, *Down, Up, and Over*, 52, 93.
61 Robert Birt, "The Bad Faith of Whiteness," in *What White Looks Like: African-American Philosophers on the Whiteness Question*, ed. George Yancy (New York: Routledge, 2004), 61–62.
62 Roediger, *How Race Survived U.S. History*, 81.
63 Jennings, *Christian Imagination*; J. Kameron Carter, *Race: A Theological Account* (Oxford: Oxford University Press, 2008).
64 For a breakdown of the history of Christian and scientific rationales undergirding white supremacy, see Terence Keel, *Divine Variations: How Christian Thought Became Racial Science* (Stanford, CA: Stanford University Press, 2018).
65 McWhorter, *Racism and Sexual Oppression*, 77–79.
66 McWhorter, 80.
67 McWhorter, 96–97.
68 McWhorter, 96.
69 McWhorter, 115.
70 McWhorter, 119–120.
71 Roediger, *How Race Survived U.S. History*, 85–87. According to Roediger, the work of Cartwright and others like him shows how the imperatives of "mastering" and "improving" enslaved people meshed in the form of the industry enterprises of "race management."
72 Roediger, 95. McWhorter, *Racism and Sexual Oppression*, 119–120.
73 Nell Irvin Painter, *The History of White People* (New York: Norton, 2011), 256–290.
74 For more on the role of European settler colonialism in implementing the gender binary, see Andrea Smith, *Conquest: Sexual Violence and American Indian Genocide* (Durham, NC: Duke University Press, 2015).

75 In the absence of the commons that the enclosures of capitalism transferred into the hands of private landowners, Federici writes, "proletarian women became for male workers the substitute for the land lost to the enclosures, their most basic means of reproduction, and a communal good anyone could appropriate and use at will." Indeed, *"women themselves became the commons,"* Federici writes, "as their work was defined as a natural resource, laying outside the sphere of market relations" (*Caliban and the Witch*, 97).

76 Black feminist and womanist scholars clarify that it is not racism alone, sexism alone, or classism alone but all three together that create the multidimensional oppressions that Black women experience. Black trans and gender-nonconforming people, inhabiting gender and race in ways that disrupt the normative binaries of white supremacist cis-heterosexist culture, are also subject to a multitude of compounding forms of violence.

77 Katie G. Cannon, *Black Womanist Ethics* (Atlanta: Scholars, 1988), 31–34; Angela Y. Davis, *Women, Race and Class* (New York: Vintage Books, 1983). As bell hooks writes, "the black male slave was primarily exploited as a laborer in the fields; the black female was exploited as a laborer in the fields, a worker in the domestic household, a breeder, and as an object of white male sexual assault." Quoted in Cannon, *Black Womanist Ethics*, 37; bell hooks, *Ain't I a Woman? Black Women and Feminism*, 2nd ed. (New York: Routledge, 2015), 22.

78 As Robin Kelley puts it, extending Stuart Hall's formulation, "race and gender are modalities in which class is lived" (KODX Seattle, "Robin D. G. Kelley"). For Stuart Hall's original formulation—that race is a modality in which class is lived—see Hall, "Race, Articulation and Societies Structured in Dominance."

79 Quoted in Roediger, *How Race Survived U.S. History*, 28.

80 Roediger, 29.

81 For more on the relationships between race, gender, and reproduction in the context of chattel slavery and racial capitalism, see Saidiya Hartman, "The Belly of the World: A Note on Black Women's Labors," *Souls: A Critical Journal of Black Politics, Culture, and Society* 18, no. 1 (2016): 166–173; Jennifer L. Morgan, *Laboring Women: Reproduction and Gender in New World Slavery* (Philadelphia: University of Pennsylvania Press, 2004); Alys Eve Weinbaum, *The Afterlife of Reproductive Slavery: Biocapitalism and Black Feminism's Philosophy of History* (Durham, NC: Duke University Press, 2019).

82 Kimberlé Crenshaw, "Mapping the Margins: Intersectionality, Identity Politics, and Violence against Women of Color," in Crenshaw et al., *Critical Race Theory*, 367–370. For an exploration of the myth of Black women as unrapeable, see Lisa A. Crooms, "Speaking Partial Truths and Preserving Power: Deconstructing White Supremacy, Patriarchy, and the Rape Corroboration Rule in the Interest of Black Liberation," *Howard Law Journal* 40, no. 2 (1997): 459–512.

83 J. Morgan, *Laboring Women*, 42.

84 J. Morgan, 49.

85 Dana D. Nelson, *National Manhood: Capitalist Citizenship and the Imagined Fraternity of White Men* (Durham, NC: Duke University Press, 1998), 10–11.
86 Aileen Moreton-Robinson, *The White Possessive: Property, Power, and Indigenous Sovereignty* (Minneapolis: University of Minnesota Press, 2015).
87 Isenberg, *White Trash*, 41.
88 As Robin Kelley puts it, "Race and gender are not incidental or accidental features of the global capitalist order; they are constitutive. Capitalism emerged as a racial and gendered regime" (KODX Seattle, "Robin D. G. Kelley").
89 On how race is not "prepolitical," see Olson, *Abolition of White Democracy*, 30. On race as a "strategic" political tool, see Michael Omi and Howard Winant, *Racial Formation in the United States*, 3rd ed. (New York: Routledge, 2015), 111.
90 Wolfe, *Traces of History*, 10; KODX Seattle, "Robin D. G. Kelley."
91 Omi and Winant, *Racial Formation in the United States*, 105–112.
92 Baldwin, *Fire Next Time*, 104.
93 Gilmore, *Golden Gulag*, 28.
94 While people of European descent are the primary inheritors of, and those who aspire most to, the powers of patriarchal and possessive whiteness, nonwhite people can and do also aspire to proximity to or partial habitation within the bounds of whiteness.
95 Roediger, *How Race Survived U.S. History*, 22.
96 Saidiya Hartman, *Lose Your Mother: A Journey along the Atlantic Slave Route* (New York: Farrar, Straus, and Giroux, 2007), 6.
97 M. Douglas Meeks, *God the Economist: The Doctrine of God and Political Economy* (Minneapolis, MN: Fortress, 1989), 100.
98 Frank S. Alexander, "Property and Christian Theology," in *Christianity and Law: An Introduction*, ed. John Witte and Frank S. Alexander (Cambridge: Cambridge University Press, 2008), 208, 216.
99 Henry Campbell Black, *A Dictionary of Law* (Clark, NJ: Lawbook Exchange, 1991), 955.
100 F. Alexander, "Property and Christian Theology"; Christopher Pierson, *Just Property: A History in the Latin West*, vol. 1, *Wealth, Virtue, and the Law* (Oxford: Oxford University Press, 2013); C. B. Macpherson, ed., *Property: Mainstream and Critical Positions* (Toronto: University of Toronto Press, 1978).
101 As theologian Douglas Meeks writes, "The prevailing model or paradigm of property will often reflect the prevailing perception of God and vice versa. The history of property is the history of human power and authority and thus in many ways the history of the way human beings have conceived and worshiped divine power and authority" (*God the Economist*, 99).
102 The details and many streams of thought comprising those variations are beyond the scope of this work. For a robust treatment of evolutions in thinking on property through John Locke, see Pierson, *Just Property*, vol. 1.
103 See Roediger, *How Race Survived U.S. History*, 8–12; Tink Tinker, "John Locke on Property," in *Beyond the Pale: Reading Ethics from the Margins*, ed. Stacey M.

Floyd-Thomas and Miguel A. De La Torre (Louisville, KY: Westminster John Knox, 2011), 49–59; Pierson, *Just Property*, vol. 1, 208–245.

104 C. B. Macpherson, "The Meaning of Property," in Macpherson, *Property*, 13.

105 For more on liberal conceptions of "liberty" as a matter of the security of property, see Neocleous, *Critical Theory of Police Power*, 114.

106 Neocleous, 114. Roediger, *How Race Survived U.S. History*, 44.

107 Pierson, *Just Property*, vol. 1, 208–254.

108 John Locke, *Second Treatise of Government*, in *Two Treatises of Government*, ed. Peter Laslett (Cambridge: Cambridge University Press, 1988), § 32.

109 Locke, §§ 27–35.

110 Onur Ulas Ince, "Enclosing in God's Name, Accumulating for Mankind: Money, Morality, and Accumulation in John Locke's Theory of Property," *Review of Politics* 73, no.1 (2011): 29.

111 C. B. Macpherson, *The Political Theory of Possessive Individualism: Hobbes to Locke* (Oxford: Oxford University Press, 1962), 263–264. A number of commentators have challenged Macpherson's interpretation of Locke as an unabashed purveyor of capitalist political economy and private property, including James Tulley. Without ascribing to Locke total responsibility for establishing and absolutizing private property relations in the West, it is nevertheless apparent that the overwhelming thrust of Locke's argument, not to mention the legacy of political thought on property that his work subsequently puts into motion, favors private property as the best form of human interaction with the material world. See Pierson, *Just Property*, vol. 1; and Allan Greer, "Commons and Enclosure in the Colonization of North America," *American Historical Review* 117, no. 2 (2012): 365–386.

112 Locke, *Second Treatise of Government*, § 27.

113 Macpherson, "Meaning of Property."

114 Étienne Balibar, *Identity and Difference: John Locke and the Invention of Consciousness* (Brooklyn, NY: Verso Books, 2013), 71–72.

115 Balibar, 97–99.

116 Locke, *Second Treatise of Government*, § 34; Roediger, *How Race Survived U.S. History*, 11–12.

117 Crenshaw, "Mapping the Margins," 373. For more on the relation of women to property in feudalism and capitalism, see Federici, *Caliban and the Witch*. On the relationship between "owning" and "being" property in the context of the European colonial dispossession of Indigenous peoples, see Moreton-Robinson, *White Possessive*.

118 Crenshaw, "Mapping the Margins," 373.

119 Crenshaw, 373; Roediger, *How Race Survived U.S. History*, 24–25.

120 Locke, *Second Treatise of Government*.

121 Locke, §§4, 124–131. See also Linebaugh, *London Hanged*; Andrew Dilts, *Punishment and Inclusion: Race, Membership, and the Limits of American Liberalism* (New York: Fordham University Press, 2014).

122 As Nancy Isenberg writes, "Locke was a founding member and third-largest stockholder of the Royal African Company, which secured a monopoly over the British slave trade" (*White Trash*, 43). See also David Armitage, "John Locke, Carolina, and the *Two Treatises of Government*," *Political Theory* 32, no. 5 (October 2004): 602–627; Tinker, "John Locke on Property," 54–56; Isenberg, *White Trash*, 43–63; Roediger, *How Race Survived U.S. History*, 17.
123 Linebaugh and Rediker, *Many-Headed Hydra*; Peter Linebaugh, *Stop, Thief! The Commons, Enclosures and Resistance* (Oakland, CA: PM, 2014); Marx, *Capital, Volume 1*.
124 Harris, "Whiteness as Property," 1720.
125 Harris, 1720. See also J. Morgan, *Laboring Women*; Federici, *Caliban and the Witch*.
126 Harris, "Whiteness as Property."
127 Robinson, *Black Marxism*.
128 For more on the racial character of English conquest of Ireland and Scotland, see Robinson, 36–43; Roediger, *How Race Survived U.S. History*, 18; Allen, *Invention of the White Race*, 52–70.
129 Iain MacKinnon and Andrew Mackillop, "Plantation Slavery and Landownership in the West Highlands and Islands: Legacies and Lessons," discussion paper (Community Land Scotland, November 2020), www.communitylandscotland.org.uk. After abolishing slavery in 1833, the British Empire reimbursed former slave owners enormous sums of money for the loss of their enslaved "property." Many former slave owners used those funds to expand their claims to landownership, displacing hundreds and thousands of commoners in the process. For a summary of this research, see Nora McGreevy, "How Profits from Slavery Changed the Landscape of the Scottish Highlands," *Smithsonian Magazine*, November 17, 2020, www.smithsonianmag.com.
130 J. M. Neeson, *Commoners: Common Right, Enclosure and Social Change in England, 1700–1820* (Cambridge: Cambridge University Press, 1996), 32.
131 Harris, "Whiteness as Property," 1716. Malcolm X, Speech at the Militant Labor Forum, New York, NY, May 29, 1964, in *Malcolm X Speaks: Selected Speeches and Statements*, ed. George Breitman (New York: Grove, 1965), 69. For a similar take from a similar trajectory within the Black freedom movement, see Fred Hampton, "It's a Class Struggle Goddammit!," speech delivered at Northern Illinois University, DeKalb, IL, September 1969 (accessed at Lfk(s) Collectif, www.lfks.net).
132 Harris, "Whiteness as Property," 1722.
133 Harris, 1715, 1721.
134 Brenna Bhandar, *Colonial Lives of Property: Law, Land, and Racial Regimes of Ownership* (Durham, NC: Duke University Press, 2018), 5–8.
135 Harris, "Whiteness as Property," 1721, 1731. As one example, influenced by the racial logic of whiteness as property and the "improving" function of accumulation by dispossession, Andrew Carnegie argued in 1896 that, though the seizure

of Indigenous land was unfortunate, "upon the whole the management of the land acquired by our race has been for the higher interests of humanity" and that "civilization" made "the acquisition of land necessary." Quoted in Roediger, *How Race Survived U.S. History*, 89.

136 Harris, "Whiteness as Property," 1724–1725; Macpherson, "Meaning of Property."
137 Harris, "Whiteness as Property," 1721, 1744; Roediger, *How Race Survived U.S. History*, 68.
138 Roediger, *How Race Survived U.S. History*, 12.
139 Tinker, "John Locke on Property," 50. Tinker intentionally does not capitalize "european."
140 Roediger, *How Race Survived U.S. History*, 11–12; George Lipsitz, *The Possessive Investment in Whiteness: How White People Profit from Identity Politics*, rev. and exp. ed. (Philadelphia: Temple University Press, 2006).
141 Roediger, *How Race Survived U.S. History*, 24.
142 Roediger. See also Isenberg, *White Trash*; Nelson, *National Manhood*. On the consolations of whiteness for poor white people, see Du Bois, *Black Reconstruction in America*; David R. Roediger, *The Wages of Whiteness: Race and the Making of the American Working Class*, rev. ed. (London: Verso, 2007).
143 Harris, "Whiteness as Property," 1721, 1744.
144 Harris, 1714–1721, 1734.
145 Bhandar, *Colonial Lives of Property*.
146 Jennings, *Christian Imagination*, 59.
147 Wolfe, *Traces of History*, 17.
148 As Ruth Wilson Gilmore puts it, "we cannot have capitalism without capitalism saving capitalism from capitalism." Daniel Denvir, "The Prison-Industrial Complex Goes Beyond Cops and Jails. It's All Around Us: An Interview with Ruth Wilson Gilmore, Alberto Toscano, and Brenna Bhandar," *Jacobin*, August 2, 2022, https://jacobin.com. See also Gilmore, "Beyond Bratton."

CHAPTER 2. "OWNERSHIP OF THE EARTH FOREVER AND EVER, AMEN!"

1 Émile Durkheim, *The Elementary Forms of Religious Life*, trans., Carol Cosman (New York: Oxford University Press, 2001), 171.
2 M. Douglas, *Purity and Danger*, 44; Sigmund Freud, "Character and Anal Eroticism," in *The Standard Edition of the Complete Psychological Works of Sigmund Freud*, vol. 9 (London: Hogarth, 1959), 172.
3 M. Douglas, *Purity and Danger*, 2–3.
4 M. Douglas, 140. As Douglas argues, designations of "dirt" only occur within—because they are a "by-product" of—a context characterized by "systematic ordering and classification" (44).
5 According to David Chidester, "Structured oppositions . . . are important features of the production of meaningful and powerful religious space. Perhaps derived from the left-right axis of the human body, the primary space of religious production, structural oppositions—inside and outside, up and down—are deployed

in producing spatial orientations of religious purity and power: religious purity through rituals of exclusion and religious power through rituals of subordination, subjection, and extraction of human and material resources" (*Religion*, 45).

6 Gilmore, *Golden Gulag*, 28.
7 For Du Bois on the political economy of global and plantation capitalism, see Du Bois, *Black Reconstruction in America*. For Du Bois's most sustained reflection on religion as a means of freedom for oppressed Black people, see Du Bois, *Souls of Black Folk*.
8 Du Bois, *Souls of Black Folk*, 1.
9 Du Bois, *Darkwater*, 17–18. To avoid confusion in relation to what I argue in chapter 1, I have omitted from this quote Du Bois's claim that whiteness originates in the nineteenth and twentieth centuries. While it is arguably the case that "personal whiteness" solidifies during these centuries, scholars who elaborate on Du Bois's work convincingly argue, as I do in chapter 1, that whiteness first takes coherent shape in the early eighteenth century and goes through periods of reproduction and reconstitution thereafter.
10 James Baldwin traces a similar dynamic regarding the inherent relation between white empowerment and Black disempowerment and dehumanization. See, for example, James Baldwin, "The Nigger We Invent," in *Cross of Redemption*, 116.
11 Du Bois, *Souls of Black Folk*, 1.
12 Baldwin also attends to the embarrassment and shame inherent in whiteness. See, for example, Baldwin, "On Being White . . . and Other Lies," in *Cross of Redemption*, 166–170.
13 Du Bois, *Darkwater*, 28, 18.
14 Du Bois, 18, 20, 27. For more on the doctrine of discovery, see Robert J. Miller, Jacinta Ruru, Larissa Behrendt, and Tracey Lindberg, *Discovering Indigenous Lands: The Doctrine of Discovery in the English Colonies* (Oxford: Oxford University Press, 2010).
15 Du Bois, *Darkwater*, 19.
16 Emanuel AME Church is the congregation from which cofounder Denmark Vesey preached an early iteration of Black liberation theology based primarily in the Exodus account of Israel and from which he and others plotted what would have been, had it not been foiled, the largest enslaved people's uprising in US history. Vesey and others were executed in Charleston in 1822. The white supremacist Dylann Roof murdered nine Black churchgoers during a Bible study at Emanuel AME on June 17, 2015, three days after the 193rd anniversary of the planned date of Vesey's uprising. James H. Cone, *Risks of Faith: The Emergence of a Black Theology of Liberation, 1968–1998* (Boston: Beacon, 1999), 42–45, 127.
17 David Walker, *David Walker's Appeal to the Coloured Citizens of the World*, ed. Peter P. Hinks (University Park: Pennsylvania State University Press, 2000), 21, 43; Morone, *Hellfire Nation*, 169–182; Richard Furman, "Exposition of the Views of the Baptists Relative to the Coloured Population of the United States in Communication to the Governor of South Carolina" (Charleston, 1823), reprinted in

James A. Rogers, *Richard Furman: Life and Legacy* (Macon, GA: Mercer University Press, 1985), 274–286; Raboteau, *Slave Religion*, 213, 295.
18 Walker, *David Walker's Appeal*, 19.
19 Baldwin, "On Being White . . . and Other Lies," 167–169.
20 James H. Cone, *A Black Theology of Liberation*, 40th anniversary ed (Maryknoll, NY: Orbis Books, 2010), 114–115.
21 Cone, 12.
22 Cone, 8.
23 K. Douglas, *Stand Your Ground*, 42.
24 K. Douglas, 42–43.
25 Jennings, *Christian Imagination*, 60.
26 Jennings, 60, 37, 31. Counterintuitive as it may seem, the boundarylessness of whiteness depends on the creation of boundaries against which the presence of all nonwhite others registers as threatening embodiments of impurity or trespass.
27 Jennings, 143.
28 Carter, *Race*, 35.
29 Jennings, *Christian Imagination*, 59, 43.
30 For more on the relationship between whiteness and possession, see Lipsitz, *Possessive Investment in Whiteness*. See also Moreton-Robinson, *White Possessive*.
31 Mills, *Racial Contract*, 42–43; Du Bois, *Darkwater*, 17.
32 Mills, *Racial Contract*, 46.
33 Armstrong, "Christian Order and Racial Order."
34 Mills, *Racial Contract*, 16, 48.
35 Mills, 53.
36 Wendy Brown, *Walled States, Waning Sovereignty* (Brooklyn, NY: Zone Books, 2010), 55.
37 Brown, 58. For the full explanation of this idea, see Brown, 55–59.
38 Eugene McCarraher, *The Enchantments of Mammon: How Capitalism Became the Religion of Modernity* (Cambridge, MA: Harvard University Press, 2019), 39.
39 As Nancy Isenberg writes, "Locke was a founding member and third-largest stockholder of the Royal African Company, which secured a monopoly over the British slave trade" (*White Trash*, 43). See also Armitage, "John Locke, Carolina, and the *Two Treatises of Government*." On Locke's role in the Caroline colonies, see Isenberg, *White Trash*, 43–63. On Locke's stake in the enclosure movement, see Roediger, *How Race Survived U.S. History*, 17; and Tinker, "John Locke on Property," 54–56. As Wendy Brown points out, even when Locke is not speaking explicitly about actual mechanisms of enclosure, "fences, titles, and enclosures are among Locke's most fecund and ubiquitous metaphors in the *Second Treatise*" (*Walled States, Waning Sovereignty*, 56).
40 Marx, *Capital, Volume 1*, 873–895; Linebaugh and Rediker, *Many-Headed Hydra*, 17.
41 Linebaugh and Rediker, *Many-Headed Hydra*, 17.
42 Linebaugh, *Stop, Thief!*, 144.

43 Linebaugh and Rediker, *Many-Headed Hydra*; Linebaugh, *Stop, Thief!*; Marx, *Capital, Volume 1*.
44 Linebaugh and Rediker, *Many-Headed Hydra*, 16.
45 Marx, *Capital, Volume 1*, 895–897; Christopher Hill, *The World Turned Upside Down: Radical Ideas during the English Revolution* (London: Penguin Books, 1991), 53.
46 Marx, *Capital, Volume 1*, 784–805; Linebaugh and Rediker, *Many-Headed Hydra*; KODX Seattle, "Robin D. G. Kelley."
47 Andrew McRae, *God Speed the Plough: The Representation of Agrarian England, 1500–1660* (Cambridge: Cambridge University Press, 1996), 140–142.
48 John Worlidge, *Systema Agriculturae* (1669), 13.
49 Quoted in Carroll, "Nursery of Beggary," 38.
50 Nicholas Blomley, "Making Private Property: Enclosure, Common Right and the Work of Hedges," *Rural History* 18, no. 1 (2007): 6.
51 Blomley, 12, 20n9.
52 Blomley, 5, 9.
53 Quoted in Blomley, 9.
54 Isenberg, *White Trash*, 46.
55 Isenberg, 51–52.
56 E. P. Thompson, *The Making of the English Working Class* (New York: Vintage Books, 1966), 61.
57 J. M. Neeson, "The Opponents of Enclosure in Eighteenth-Century Northamptonshire," *Past & Present*, no. 105 (November 1984): 114–139.
58 Quoted in McRae, *God Speed the Plough*, 51.
59 Linebaugh, *Stop, Thief!*, 2.
60 Neeson, *Commoners*, 278.
61 Rev. James Tyley, "Inclosure of Open Fields in Northamptonshire" (1823), *Northamptonshire Past and Present* 1, no. 4 (1948): 35–41.
62 Notably, this poem is dated 1823, only two decades after theorist of police power Patrick Colquhoun, Henry and John Fielding, and others began to forge institutionalized police power for the express purpose of criminalizing working-class practices of gleaning from the products of their labor, as I outline in chapter 4. In this sense, Tyley articulates a political theology of the police power to criminalize dispossessed peoples. I develop this argument further in the chapters that follow.
63 Mills, *Racial Contract*, 54.
64 The early (ancient) purpose of theologizing about the divine attributes as a means of characterizing the nature of God was not primarily to make philosophical abstractions but to provide guidance in Christian disciples' practice of imitating God as revealed in Christ, to clarify the distinctively monotheistic nature of Christian faith, and to elaborate Christians' understanding of God's triunity, all of which was, in the ancient Christian church, inseparable from the life of Christian faith, including prayer, communal worship, and mutually supportive life together.

Ysabel de Andia, "Attributes, Divine," in *Encyclopedia of Christian Theology*, 3 vols., ed. Jean-Yves Lacoste (New York: Routledge, 2005), 1:113.

65 Baldwin, "On Being White . . . and Other Lies," in *Cross of Redemption*, 167.
66 Parts of this subsection draw from arguments I make in Andrew Krinks, "The Color of Transcendence: Whiteness, Sovereignty, and the Theologico-Political," *Political Theology* 19, no. 2 (2018): 137–156.
67 God, the seventh-century theologian Maximus Confessor writes, "does not fall within any limit." Quoted in Antoine Coté, "Infinite," in Lacoste, *Encyclopedia of Christian Theology*, 2:778.
68 Coté, 2:778.
69 The Latin phrase is "*Si comprehendis, non est Deus*." Augustine, Sermon 117, in *The Works of Saint Augustine: Sermons*, vol. 4, *94A–147A* (Brooklyn, NY: New City, 1991).
70 Cyrille Michon, "Omnipresence, Divine," in Lacoste, *Encyclopedia of Christian Theology*, 2:1153.
71 As Augustine writes, "[God] is wholly present in all of [the world] in such wise as to be wholly in heaven and wholly in earth alone and wholly in earth and heaven together; not confined in any place, but wholly in himself everywhere." Augustine, *Letter 187 (to Dardanus)*, chap. 7, "On the Presence of God," in *Saint Augustine Letters*, vols. 3–4, *The Fathers of the Church*, trans. W. Parsons (New York: Fathers of the Church, 1953), 221.
72 Lipsitz, *Possessive Investment in Whiteness*, 1.
73 For more on racial inequities in wealth and access to resources, see George Lipsitz, *How Racism Takes Place* (Philadelphia: Temple University Press, 2011); Roediger, *How Race Survived U.S. History*, 70–71. Roediger shows the differences between white and Black property possession throughout US history, which has stayed inequitable at roughly the same rate from the period of late chattel slavery to today.
74 Lipsitz, *Possessive Investment in Whiteness*, 1.
75 Jennings, *Christian Imagination*, 25.
76 Carter, *Race*, 82–96.
77 George Yancy, *Black Bodies, White Gazes: The Continuing Significance of Race* (Lanham, MD: Rowman and Littlefield, 2008), 49. See also Birt, "Bad Faith of Whiteness"; Stacey M. Floyd-Thomas, "Plato on Reason," in Floyd-Thomas and De La Torre, *Beyond the Pale*, 3–13.
78 Floyd-Thomas, "Plato on Reason."
79 Yancy, *Black Bodies, White Gazes*, 46.
80 Jennings, *Christian Imagination*, 59.
81 Jennings, 7–8.
82 Nelson, *National Manhood*, 10. For more on the role of human classification in European colonialism, see Edward W. Said, *Orientalism* (New York: Vintage Books, 1979).

83 Nelson, *National Manhood*, 10–11.
84 Derrida cites a passage in a work by Anatole France in which the character Polyphilos posits that metaphysicians are like "knife-grinders" that efface inscriptions on coins that signify their value and origin. In so doing, metaphysicians carry out the multivalent work implied in the word "usure": both erasing and producing surplus value—two "indistinguishable" parts of the same process. Freed "from all limits of time and space," Polyphilos and Derrida suggest, the coins—the language—of metaphysics are reinscribed with "an inestimable value," an "exchange value extended indefinitely." Jacques Derrida, "White Mythology: Metaphor in the Text of Philosophy," in *Margins of Philosophy* (Chicago: University of Chicago Press, 1982), 210.
85 Derrida, 211.
86 Derrida, 213.
87 For more on the white mythologies that constitute the "rhetoric of modernity," see Barnor Hesse, "Racialized Modernity: An Analytics of White Mythologies," *Ethnic and Racial Studies* 30, no. 4 (2007): 643–663.
88 Michael Naas, *Derrida from Now On* (New York: Fordham University Press, 2008), 203. Derrida theorizes phantasm largely in terms of sovereignty, but I believe that it is a concept that provides critical insight beyond strictly sovereign political configurations.
89 Jacques Derrida, *Paper Machine* (Stanford, CA: Stanford University Press, 2005), 106; Naas, *Derrida from Now On*, 195.
90 Jacques Derrida, *The Death Penalty*, trans. Peggy Kamuf, vol. 1 (Chicago: University of Chicago Press, 2014), 258.
91 Jacques Derrida, "Racism's Last Word," in *Signature Derrida*, ed. Jay Williams (Chicago: University of Chicago Press, 2013), 57. By theorizing racism as a phantasmatic pursuit of purity, Derrida aligns somewhat with Foucault, who understands (biopolitical) racism as the means by which societies purify themselves of perceived abnormalities. Michel Foucault, *Society Must Be Defended: Lectures at the Collège de France, 1975–76*, trans. David Macey (New York: Picador, 2003), 255.
92 Naas, *Derrida from Now On*, 191.
93 uchrivideo, "April 2003 tRACES Day 1: Jacques Derrida Keynote Response to Etienne Balibar," tRACEs: Race, Deconstruction, and Critical Theory Conference, University of California Research Institute, April 10, 2003, YouTube, October 1, 2013, www.youtube.com/watch?v=LfXdYefgKjw.
94 Derrida argues that, if Carl Schmitt is right that every instance of the political is also an instance of the theological-political, then "every racism *as* political is theological-political through and through" (uchrivideo). See also Jacques Derrida, "But, Beyond . . . (Open Letter to Anne McClintock and Rob Nixon)," in *Signature Derrida*, 74, in which he insists that "the history of apartheid . . . would have been impossible . . . without Judeo-Christian ideology."
95 Derrida, "White Mythology," 210.

96 Derrida, *Death Penalty*, 258.
97 Kathryn Tanner, *Jesus, Humanity and the Trinity: A Brief Systematic Theology* (Minneapolis, MN: Fortress, 2001), 4, 11, 13. Some philosophical theologians even argue that God "is" beyond the category of "being" altogether. See, for one example, Jean-Luc Marion, *God without Being: Hors-Texte*, 2nd ed. (Chicago: University of Chicago Press, 2012).
98 Tanner, *Jesus, Humanity and the Trinity*, 2.
99 Birt, "Bad Faith of Whiteness," 58.
100 Birt, 58.
101 As George Yancy writes, "Whiteness is true transcendence, an ecstatic mode of being; blackness, however, in its ontological structure, is true immanence, a thing unable to be other than what it was born to be, a thing closed upon itself, locked into an ontological realm where things exist not 'for-themselves' but 'in-themselves,' waiting to be ordered by some external, subjugating purposive (white) consciousness." George Yancy, "Introduction: Fragments of a Social Ontology of Whiteness," in Yancy, *What White Looks Like*, 11.
102 David Roediger, *Towards the Abolition of Whiteness: Essays on Race, Politics, and Working Class History* (New York: Verso, 1994), 13.
103 Hayden White, quoted in Mills, *Racial Contract*, 43. See also Eric A. Weed, *The Religion of White Supremacy in the United States* (Lanham, MD: Lexington Books, 2017).
104 Olivier Boulnois, "Omnipotence, Divine," in Lacoste, *Encyclopedia of Christian Theology*, 2:1150–1151. Christian theologies throughout the tradition have also explored the implications of such limitless power: Does omnipotence *actually* mean that God can will *anything*, including even evil? Most Christian theologies answer that God's will, on the one hand, and God's goodness and love, on the other, are two sides of the same coin, which is why God cannot, properly speaking, will evil or injustice. As Boulnois writes, "Omnipotence should be seen not as an isolated attribute but as that of the good God, who would cease to be himself if he ceased to be good" (1151). Or, as Augustine writes, "If God can be what he does not want to be [namely, evil], he is not omnipotent" (quoted in Boulnois, 1151).
105 "Aseity" comes from the Latin *a*, "from," and *se*, "self."
106 Thomas Aquinas, *Summa Theologica*, Ia, Question 3.
107 Quoted in Coloman Viola, "Aseity," in Lacoste, *Encyclopedia of Christian Theology*, 1:102.
108 Dorothee Soelle, *Suffering* (Philadelphia: Fortress, 1986), 36.
109 John Milbank, "Immutability/Impassibility," in Lacoste, *Encyclopedia of Christian Theology*, 2:760–761. See also Soelle, *Suffering*, 36–45.
110 Catherine Keller, *From a Broken Web: Separation, Sexism, and Self* (Boston: Beacon, 1988), 36.
111 Lipsitz, *How Racism Takes Place*, 28–29.
112 Quoted in Lipsitz, 40.
113 M. Douglas, *Purity and Danger*, 44.

114 Harris, "Whiteness as Property."
115 Naas, *Derrida from Now On*, 203.
116 Douglas Hay, "Property, Authority and Criminal Law," in Hay et al., *Albion's Fatal Tree*, 19.
117 Neocleous, *Critical Theory of Police Power*, 40.
118 McRae, *God Speed the Plough*; Linebaugh, *London Hanged*; Hay, "Property, Authority and Criminal Law"; David Graeber, "Manners, Deference, and Private Property: Or, Elements for a General Theory of Hierarchy," in *Possibilities: Essays on Hierarchy, Rebellion, and Desire* (Oakland, CA: AK, 2007), 13–55.
119 Lipsitz, *How Racism Takes Place*, 29; Locke, *Second Treatise of Government*, § 32; Ince, "Enclosing in God's Name, Accumulating for Mankind," 52–53.
120 Jennings, *Christian Imagination*, 60.
121 Cornel West, *Prophesy Deliverance! An Afro-American Revolutionary Christianity* (Louisville, KY: Westminster John Knox, 1982), 53–61.
122 On the notion of the "dark world," see Du Bois, *Dusk of Dawn*; and Olson, *Abolition of White Democracy*, 19–25.
123 Yancy, *Black Bodies, White Gazes*, 229. On the "self-deception" of whiteness, see Mills, *Racial Contract*, 18.
124 Biko Mandela Gray, Stephen C. Finley, and Lori Latrice Martin, "'The Souls of White Folk': Race, Affect, and Religion in the Religion of White Rage," in *The Religion of White Rage: White Workers, Religious Fervor, and the Myth of Black Racial Progress*, ed. Stephen C. Finley, Biko Mandela Gray, and Lori Latrice Martin (Edinburgh: Edinburgh University Press, 2020), 5–10. The authors point to the raging defensiveness of Judge Brett Kavanaugh in the face of accusations of sexual violence during his Supreme Court appointment hearings as a prime example of what they call the "religion of white rage."
125 On the religiosity of lynching, see Donald G. Matthews, *At the Altar of Lynching: Burning Sam Hose in the American South* (New York: Cambridge University Press, 2018).
126 Gray, Finley, and Martin, 7.
127 Long, *Significations*, 7.
128 Gray, Finley, and Martin, 11–12.
129 Gray, Finley, and Martin, 8.
130 Milbank, "Immutability/Impassibility, Divine"; Viola, "Aseitas."
131 Roediger, *How Race Survived U.S. History*, 79–80.
132 Ellen Armour, engaging and elaborating on Michel Foucault's "archaeological" and "genealogical" accounts of modernity, describes the formation of the modern subject of "Man" as a formation that occurred alongside significant shifts in ways of "knowing, doing, and being." Ellen T. Armour, *Signs and Wonders: Theology after Modernity* (New York: Columbia University Press, 2016).
133 Nelson, *National Manhood*. See also Roediger, *How Race Survived U.S. History*, 54–59. Still today, research shows the continued predominance of the idea that

whiteness and Christian faith are central to popular understandings—especially among white Christian nationalists—of what constitutes an "American." See, for example, Andrew L. Whitehead and Samuel L. Perry, *Taking America Back for God: Christian Nationalism in the United States* (Oxford: Oxford University Press, 2020), 89–119.

134 Derrida, "White Mythology," 210.
135 For more on the theological problem of patriarchy grounded in notions of separable, absolutely independent personhood, see Keller, *From a Broken Web*. See also Cannon, *Black Womanist Ethics*, 31–57; Copeland, *Enfleshing Freedom*, 33–34; Floyd-Thomas, "Plato on Reason," 3–13.
136 Armour, *Signs and Wonders*, 18–22.
137 Armour, 47.
138 Armour, 2–3. As outlined earlier, James Cone describes whiteness in a similar way: "Whiteness characterizes the activity of deranged individuals intrigued by their own image of themselves" (*Black Theology of Liberation*, 8).
139 Armour, *Signs and Wonders*, 47.
140 While this is especially a trait of white patriarchy, Black men and other men of color can also embody this quest for retrieving a sense of mastery. See Angela P. Harris, "Gender, Violence, Race, and Criminal Justice," *Stanford Law Review* 52 (1999–2000): 780.
141 For a treatment of the idea that the fear of death itself proliferates more death, see Ernest Becker, *The Denial of Death* (New York: Free Press, 1973). Becker develops his argument in part through engagement with the work of Sigmund Freud.
142 Mircea Eliade, *The Sacred and the Profane: The Nature of Religion*, trans. Willard R. Trask (San Diego: Harcourt Brace Jovanovich, 1987), 25–26
143 Eliade, 29.
144 David Chidester and Edward T. Linenthal, introduction to *American Sacred Space*, ed. David Chidester and Edward T. Linenthal (Bloomington: Indiana University Press, 1995), 1–42; Joseph R. Winters, "The Sacred Gone Astray: Eliade, Fanon, Wynter, and the Terror of Colonial Settlement," in *Beyond Man: Race, Coloniality, and the Philosophy of Religion*, ed. An Yountae and Eleanor Craig (Durham, NC: Duke University Press, 2021), 245–268.
145 Eliade, *Sacred and the Profane*, 34.
146 Eliade, 47.
147 Eliade, 39, 65.
148 Eliade, 47–48.
149 Eliade, 47–49.
150 Eliade, 48.
151 Neocleous, *Critical Theory of Police Power*, 10.
152 Neocleous, 10.
153 Weed, *Religion of White Supremacy in the United States*, xxvii–xxviii.
154 Cone, *Black Theology of Liberation*, 11–12.
155 Du Bois, *Darkwater*, 28, 18.

156 Whiteness was deceptive in its origins: the privileges afforded to poor Europeans in colonial America at the founding of "whiteness" were limited by design and ultimately served European elites above anyone else, including poor and criminalized people of European descent. See E. Morgan, *American Slavery, American Freedom*; Allen, *Invention of the White Race*; Roediger, *How Race Survived U.S. History*.

157 James Baldwin, "Black English: A Dishonest Argument," in *Cross of Redemption*, 159.

158 Baldwin, "On Being White . . . and Other Lies," 169.

159 Baldwin, "Down at the Cross," 16.

160 Baldwin, "Open Letter to My Sister Angela Y. Davis," 258–259. The notion of whiteness as a "genocidal" lie is found in Baldwin, "On Being White . . . and Other Lies," 167–169.

161 For one recent account of how the aspiration to whiteness harms white people as well, see Jonathan M. Metzl, *Dying of Whiteness: How the Politics of Racial Resentment Is Killing America's Heartland* (New York: Basic Books, 2019).

CHAPTER 3. THE MORTAL GOD OF POLICE POWER

1 Adam Looney and Nicholas Turner, "Work and Opportunity before and after Incarceration," Brookings Institution, March 2018, www.brookings.edu; Christopher Ingram, "Where America's Future Prisoners Are Born," *Washington Post*, March 14, 2018, www.washingtonpost.com.

2 On the history of the interstate highway project that intentionally avoided white and wealthy areas and instead destroyed much of predominantly Black North Nashville, see Benjamin Houston, *The Nashville Way: Racial Etiquette and the Struggle for Social Justice in a Southern City* (Athens: University of Georgia Press, 2012), 202–234. For a recent journalistic and narrative-driven account of the history of divestment, policing, incarceration, and gentrification in North Nashville, see Steven Hale, "History Repeats Itself in North Nashville," *Nashville Scene*, June 7, 2018, www.nashvillescene.com.

3 As manifestations of the hierarchies inherent in racial capitalism and settler colonialism, the disruptive and displacing forces of gentrification impact people of different racial, class, and gender positionalities in different ways. While my wife and I were displaced by gentrification from one neighborhood, the fact that we are white people born into white, upper-middle-class, property-owning households—and are thus inheritors of some degree of wealth, good credit, and all the other properties that accompany whiteness—enabled us to access relatively affordable housing in another gentrifying neighborhood in ways that people of other positionalities could not. Impacted both negatively and positively by gentrification, and convinced that benefits that require the suffering of others are ultimately detrimental to us all, we navigate the contradictions of these dynamics as best we can through commitments to and active participation in local movements for racial and economic justice, affordable housing, and abolition, as well

as commitments to building mutual relationship with neighbors and eventually transitioning our home in a way that contributes to affordability rather than displacement. While the forces that create gentrification and displacement precede and exceed the agency we exercised in buying an affordable home in North Nashville, we nevertheless strive to take responsibility to dwell here with as much justice as possible in a world structured by the forces of racial capital.

4 As outlined in chapter 2, George Lipsitz describes this white settler orientation in relation to the world around it as an expression of a "white spatial imaginary" that engages in the violence work of "frontier defense." Lipsitz, *How Racism Takes Place*, 13.

5 Neil Smith, *The New Urban Frontier: Gentrification and the Revanchist City* (New York: Routledge, 1996).

6 On the notion of police as violence workers, see Micol Seigel, *Violence Work: State Power and the Limits of Police* (Durham, NC: Duke University Press, 2018).

7 Dubber, *Police Power*, 136. "The point of police," Dubber writes, is "not to punish wrongdoing, and thereby to redress wrong. Instead, it [is] to identify and eliminate threats."

8 Tyler Wall argues that police mythology amounts to a "police invention of humanity." Tyler Wall, "Inventing Humanity, or the Thin Blue Line as 'Patronizing Shit,'" in Correia and Wall, *Violent Order*, 23–29.

9 Harris, "Whiteness as Property," 1721, 1744.

10 Neocleous, *Critical Theory of Police Power*; Linebaugh, *London Hanged*, 434–435. Linebaugh writes, "The eighteenth-century view regarded the police function as not so much to defend private property (though this of course was included) as to create and then to sustain the class relations in the production of private property" (434–435).

11 Many Protestant Christian denominations in the US utilize the liturgical language of "creator, redeemer, and sustainer" as another way of talking about the trinitarian God: Father, Son, and Holy Spirit. I use this and similar language throughout to describe the creative, saving, and maintaining function that police perform in relation to colonial racial capitalist order.

12 Mark Neocleous, *The Universal Adversary: Security, Capital, and "The Enemies of All Mankind"* (New York: Routledge, 2016), 90.

13 George Browning, *The Domestic and Financial Condition of Great Britain* (London: Longman, Rees, Orme, Brown, Green, and Longman, 1834), 294.

14 Linebaugh and Rediker, *Many-Headed Hydra*; Sonja Schillings, *Enemies of All Humankind: Fictions of Legitimate Violence* (Lebanon, NH: Dartmouth College Press, 2017); Neocleous, *Universal Adversary*; Foucault, *Discipline and Punish*, 101, 299–300.

15 Quoted in Jennifer Graber, *The Furnace of Affliction: Prisons and Religion in Antebellum America* (Chapel Hill: University of North Carolina Press, 2014), 120.

16 Christophe Ringer, *Necropolitics: The Religious Crisis of Mass Incarceration in America* (Lanham, MD: Lexington Books, 2021), 39–60, 103.

17 Baldwin, "This Far and No Further," 162.
18 In Durkheim's words, punishment "maintain[s] social cohesion intact." Quoted in David Garland, *Punishment and Modern Society: A Study in Social Theory* (Chicago: University of Chicago Press, 1990), 33–34. Similarly, the philosopher George Herbert Mead argued that "without the criminal, the cohesiveness of society would disappear." Quoted in Garland, 77.
19 Garland, 30. Garland, channeling Durkheim, writes, "our commitment to [our] collective values has the character of a deeply held religious attachment." The notion of orientation toward the ultimate channels Charles Long's characterization of religion as "orientation in the ultimate sense." Long, *Significations*, 7.
20 Quoted in Garland, *Punishment and Modern Society*, 42.
21 Emile Durkheim, *The Division of Labor in Society*, trans. W. D. Halls (New York: Free Press, 2014); Garland, *Punishment and Modern Society*, 23–46.
22 God is referred to as "Lord" thousands of times throughout scripture. The realm of God is figured as a "kingdom" throughout all of scripture and especially in the New Testament. As for God as just judge or lawmaker, a few of many examples include Genesis 16:5; Judges 11:27; Psalm 72:2; Psalm 75:7; Isaiah 33:22; Micah 4:3; Hebrews 12:23; James 4:12; Revelation 6:15–17.
23 Timothy Gorringe, *God's Just Vengeance: Crime, Violence, and the Rhetoric of Salvation* (Cambridge: Cambridge University Press, 1996), 22. During this period, Gorringe writes, "Theology drew on legal notions and legal discussion, . . . and law turned to theology for metaphysical justification."
24 John Witte, *God's Joust, God's Justice: Law and Religion in the Western Tradition* (Grand Rapids, MI: Eerdmans, 2006), 287.
25 Witte, 286–287.
26 Thomas Hobbes, *Leviathan* (New York: Oxford University Press, 1996), 114.
27 Mark Neocleous, "The Monster and the Police: Dexter to Hobbes," in Correia and Wall, *Violent Order*, 141–157.
28 Neocleous, *Universal Adversary*, 95.
29 Quoted in Dubber, *Police Power*, 116.
30 Melossi and Pavarini, *Prison and the Factory*; Caleb Smith, *The Prison and the American Imagination* (New Haven, CT: Yale University Press, 2011); Graber, *Furnace of Affliction*; Foucault, *Discipline and Punish*. My argument is that the relationship between police power and the power of salvation is homologous: they resemble each other because they share common conceptual and practical origins. For more on homologous relations in the history of politics and theology, see D. Singh, *Divine Currency*, 1–25.
31 Another, sometimes overlapping trajectory of Christian soteriological thought that I do not explore in this book conceptualizes sin not strictly as a state of guilt or indebtedness but as an ailment that needs the divine healing of salvation.
32 Augustine, *Confessions*, trans. Henry Chadwick (Oxford: Oxford University Press, 2008), 22–23. Augustine understands this pride to lead to the enjoyment of sin for

its own sake, in the sense of the pleasure it brings: sin becomes its own end, which he defines in terms of a kind of wanton criminality (31–33).

33 Augustine, 32.
34 Augustine, "Enchiridion," in *Basic Writings of Saint Augustine*, ed. Whitney J. Oates, vol. 1 (New York: Random House, 1948), 673. Sin, for Augustine, is inherited hereditarily after Adam, so that humans are born into a state of condemnation and depend absolutely on God for deliverance from it.
35 Augustine, *Confessions*, 24.
36 Augustine, 47–48. God also does not technically choose to deliver prideful humanity to the Devil; rather, because God is just, the human refusal to be subject leads as a consequence to human subjection to evil, which is why it is essentially humans that deliver themselves to the Devil.
37 For example, Psalm 7:14–16; Psalm 9:15–16.
38 Augustine, *Confessions*, 25.
39 Anselm of Canterbury, *Why God Became Man*, in *The Major Works*, ed. Brian Davies and G. R. Evans (Oxford: Oxford University Press, 2008), 269.
40 Anselm, 283.
41 Anselm, 287.
42 Anselm, 288.
43 Anselm, 283.
44 Anselm, 287.
45 Anselm, 269.
46 Anselm, 301–303, 314.
47 Anselm, 301–303.
48 Anselm, 283.
49 John Calvin, *Institutes of the Christian Religion*, trans. Henry Beveridge (Peabody, MA: Hendrickson, 2008).
50 Calvin, 162, 180.
51 Calvin, 181.
52 Calvin, 154.
53 Calvin, 152.
54 F. W. Dillistone, "Redemption," in *The Westminster Dictionary of Christian Theology*, ed. Alan Richardson and John Stephen Bowden (Philadelphia: Westminster, 1983), 487–488.
55 Augustine, *On the Trinity, Books 8–15*, ed. Gareth B. Matthews (Cambridge: Cambridge University Press, 2002), 124.
56 Anselm, *Why God Became Man*, 268. In Jewish and Christian scripture, the notions of propitiation and expiation for sin share a common etymological and conceptual ancestry with the idea of "satisfaction," which is itself associated with notions of cleansing. As Timothy Gorringe writes, "The Hebrew word group translated by 'propitiate,' 'expiate,' or even occasionally 'atone' is grouped around the noun *kopher*—what would later be called satisfaction, or *wergild*—and the verb *kipper*. The verb is . . . a denominative meaning 'to

perform an expiatory ceremony,' and is closely associated with 'to be clean' or 'to cleanse' (*taher*).'' Likewise, in Jewish religion and culture, the concept of atonement—"at-one-ment"—is understood to be a means of restoring order in the wake of the moral pollution of sin. Gorringe, *God's Just Vengeance*, 36–37.

57 Anselm, *Why God Became Man*, 352–353.
58 Anselm, 304.
59 Anselm, 287–288.
60 Calvin, *Institutes of the Christian Religion*, 184.
61 Calvin, 328.
62 Calvin, 184.
63 Calvin, 341.
64 Calvin, 329.
65 Calvin, 328.
66 Calvin, 325.
67 This corresponds to the predominant conceptions of the place of private property in divine and social order outlined in chapter 1.
68 Calvin, *Institutes of the Christian Religion*, 975.
69 Calvin, 971.
70 Calvin, 976.
71 Calvin, 974. Calvin argues that disobedience is only warranted when government clearly and fundamentally ceases to perform the role God set out for it.
72 Jean-Jacques Rousseau, *The Social Contract, and Discourses*, trans. G. D. H. Cole (London: Everyman Paperbacks, 1993), 207; Derrida, *Death Penalty*, vol. 1: "In other words, the citizen receives his life from the state, and therefore has no right over his life" (15n20).
73 Augustine, "Enchiridion," 672–673.
74 Rousseau, *Social Contract*, 209.
75 Gilmore, *Golden Gulag*, 12. See also Angela Y. Davis, *The Meaning of Freedom* (San Francisco: City Lights Books, 2012), 67–68.
76 Quoted in Neocleous, *Critical Theory of Police Power*, 112; Adam Smith, *An Inquiry into the Nature and Causes of the Wealth of Nations*, ed. R. H. Campbell and A. S. Skinner (Oxford: Oxford University Press, 1976), 775.
77 M. Douglas, *Purity and Danger*, 44
78 "Trespass," *Online Etymology Dictionary*, accessed July 1, 2023, www.etymonline.com. For more on the etymology and theology of "trespass," see David Wilton, "Trespass/Sin/Debt," wordorigins.org, accessed July 2, 2023, www.wordorigins.org; Tom Banbury, "The Ancient Roots of Trespass," *Tribune Magazine*, January 28, 2021, https://tribunemag.co.uk.
79 Marcia Pally, "'Forgive Us Our Debts': The Economics of the Lord's Prayer," *ABC Religion & Ethics*, July 16, 2019, www.abc.net.au.
80 The restored relation that the Christian soteriology of subjection seeks may be a hierarchical one between a sovereign God and human subjects, but it is a benefi-

cent and loving relation nonetheless, whereas carceral obligation has nothing to do with beneficence at all.
81 Foucault, *Discipline and Punish*, 100, 251.
82 Gorringe, *God's Just Vengeance*, 27.
83 More than just analogous, soteriological powers of subjection and police and carceral powers of the state are homologous, sharing both family origins and functions. For more on homologous relations between concepts and practices across time, see D. Singh, *Divine Currency*, 1–25.

CHAPTER 4. CRIMINALIZATION AND DEIFICATION

1 Marx notes that, as part of the process of forcibly creating "a class of free and rightless proletarians" and wage laborers, the state deployed "police methods to accelerate the accumulation of capital" by increasing exploitation (*Capital, Volume 1*, 905).
2 Marx, 896–904.
3 Quoted in Linebaugh, *Stop, Thief!*, 1.
4 Hill, *World Turned Upside Down*, 43.
5 "God is the God of order" is from a pro-enclosure pamphlet from the mid-seventeenth century, previously referenced in chapter 2. Quoted in Carroll, "Nursery of Beggary," 38.
6 A. L. Beier, "'A New Serfdom': Labor Laws, Vagrancy Statutes, and Labor Discipline in England, 1350–1800," in *Cast Out: Vagrancy and Homelessness in Global and Historical Perspective*, ed. A. L. Beier and Paul R. Ocobock (Athens: Ohio University Press, 2008); Marx, *Capital, Volume 1*, 895. On popular resistance to compulsory labor laws and the enclosure movements that preceded them, see Linebaugh and Rediker, *Many-Headed Hydra*; Linebaugh, *Stop, Thief!*; Roger B. Manning, *Village Revolts: Social Protest and Popular Disturbances in England, 1509–1640* (Oxford: Oxford University Press, 1988); Neeson, *Commoners*; A. W. Ager, *Crime and Poverty in 19th Century England: The Economy of Makeshifts* (London: Bloomsbury, 2014); George F. E. Rudé, *Paris and London in the Eighteenth Century: Studies in Popular Protest* (New York: Viking, 1973).
7 Marx, *Capital, Volume 1*, 896–904; Leonard C. Feldman, *Citizens without Shelter: Homelessness, Democracy, and Political Exclusion* (Ithaca, NY: Cornell University Press, 2004), 27–56; Matthew Beaumont, *Nightwalking: A Nocturnal History of London* (London: Verso, 2016), 15–72. By the sixteenth century in England, the very status of vagrancy, which was interpreted as an immoral opting out of available "poor relief" and exploitative labor and which was viewed as an inherent disposition to criminality, came to be considered a crime in itself and was penalized as such. Even when the details of the law eventually shifted to focus less explicitly on the status of vagrancy and more on the specific acts and behaviors that tended to accompany it, it remained—and remains—the case that police power criminalized the status of economic dispossession itself and not just the acts associated with it. For more on the distinction between status and act in vagrancy law, see

Correia and Wall, *Police*, 86, 200; Margaret K. Rosenheim, "Vagrancy Concepts in Welfare Law," *California Law Review* 54, no. 2 (1966): 512–517; Risa Goluboff, *Vagrant Nation: Police Power, Constitutional Change, and the Making of the 1960s* (Oxford: Oxford University Press, 2016); Dubber, *Police Power*.

8 Beaumont, *Nightwalking*, 33, 65.
9 Blackstone quoted in Feldman, *Citizens without Shelter*, 32; Beaumont, *Nightwalking*, 65.
10 As Linebaugh writes, "Idleness meant the refusal of discipline, subordination or obedience" (*London Hanged*, 14).
11 Quoted in Browning, *Domestic and Financial Condition of Great Britain*, 294.
12 "An Act for the Punishing of Vagabonds," 1 Edward VI, c 3.
13 Quoted in Beaumont, *Nightwalking*, 64.
14 Quoted in Beaumont, 34.
15 Melossi and Pavarini, *Prison and the Factory*, 27–82; Beaumont, *Nightwalking*, 69; Beier, "New Serfdom," 54.
16 Melossi and Pavarini, *Prison and the Factory*, 30–32.
17 Adam Jay Hirsch, *The Rise of the Penitentiary: Prisons and Punishment in Early America* (New Haven, CT: Yale University Press, 1992), 13, 16.
18 Linebaugh, *London Hanged*, 12–14.
19 Neocleous, *Critical Theory of Police Power*, 132 (emphasis in original).
20 Correia and Wall, *Police*, 201.
21 Melossi and Pavarini, *Prison and the Factory*, 38. The discipline of production is also central to the liberal notion of *homo economicus*. See Foucault, *Discipline and Punish*, 122–123; Beier, "New Serfdom," 54.
22 Georg Rusche and Otto Kirchheimer, *Punishment and Social Structure* (New York: Routledge, 2017), 45.
23 Quoted in Rusche and Kirchheimer, 45.
24 As Massachusetts minister Charles Chauncey wrote in 1752, "Who are so much noted for the moral Disorder of *Lying* and *Stealing*, as those who have settled into the Habits of Laziness? Their Laziness . . . reduces them to Straits and Difficulties; and these, as the readiest and easiest Way to supply their wants put them upon . . . robbing [persons] of their Money, and their Goods." Quoted in Hirsch, *Rise of the Penitentiary*, 27.
25 Quoted in Linebaugh, *London Hanged*, 14. See also Christopher Hill, *Puritanism and Revolution: Studies in Interpretation of the English Revolution of the 17th Century* (Harmondsworth, UK: Penguin Books, 1990), 218.
26 Henry Mayhew, *London Labour and the London Poor* (London: Penguin Books, 1985). The original subtitle of Mayhew's text was "The Condition and Earnings of Those That Will Work, Cannot Work, and Will Not Work." For more, see Neocleous, *Critical Theory of Police Power*, 164.
27 Melossi and Pavarini, *Prison and the Factory*, 224. As Melossi and Pavarini write, "the propertyless is the same as the criminal—the criminal is the same as the prisoner—the prisoner is the same as the proletarian."

28 Witte, *God's Joust, God's Justice*, 273.
29 Hirsch, *Rise of the Penitentiary*, 9.
30 Graber, *Furnace of Affliction*, 9.
31 Ringer, *Necropolitics*, 21–33.
32 Ringer, 23–24.
33 Quoted in Ringer, 26.
34 Cotton Mather, *Tremenda. The Dreadful Sound with Which the Wicked Are to Be Thunderstruck. In a Sermon Delivered unto a Great Assembly, in Which Was Present, a Miserable African, Just Going to Be Executed for a Most Inhumane and Uncommon Murder* (Boston: B. Gray and J. Edwards, 1721), 33–36.
35 Ringer, *Necropolitics*, 26.
36 Ringer, 27.
37 Hirsch, *Rise of the Penitentiary*, 3–31; Mark Colvin, *Penitentiaries, Reformatories, and Chain Gangs: Social Theory and the History of Punishment in Nineteenth-Century America* (New York: St. Martin's, 1997), 47–53. Regarding the ineffectiveness of public punishment, see Colvin, *Penitentiaries*, 36. Regarding the desire for effectiveness and humane treatment, see Colvin, *Penitentiaries*, 29; and C. Smith, *Prison and the American Imagination*, 17. It is important to note that there were two predominant models of the penitentiary in early American: Auburn and Pennsylvania. While they were distinct in important ways, they also held more in common than not.
38 Hirsch, *Rise of the Penitentiary*, 19.
39 Hirsch, 19.
40 C. Smith, *Prison and the American Imagination*, 6.
41 C. Smith, 28.
42 C. Smith, 12.
43 C. Smith, 13.
44 C. Smith, 37–38.
45 Quoted in C. Smith, 39.
46 C. Smith, 41.
47 Quoted in C. Smith, 38.
48 Quoted in C. Smith, 27.
49 This resonates with Augustine's notion, explored in chapter 3, of merciful punishment: "For you were always with me, mercifully punishing me, touching with a bitter taste all my illicit pleasures. . . . You 'fashion pain to be a lesson' (Ps. 93:20 LXX), you 'strike to heal,' you bring death upon us so that we should not die apart from you (Deut. 32:39) (*Confessions*, 25).
50 Graber, *Furnace of Affliction*, 54.
51 Quoted in Dominique DuBois Gilliard, *Rethinking Incarceration: Advocating for Justice That Restores* (Downers Grove, IL: IVP Books, 2018), 123.
52 Gilliard, 123.
53 Melossi and Pavarini, *Prison and the Factory*, 209.
54 Melossi and Pavarini, 211.

55 Colvin, *Penitentiaries*, 51; Graber, *Furnace of Affliction*, 12.
56 Foucault, *Discipline and Punish*, 123.
57 Melossi and Pavarini, *Prison and the Factory*, 214–215.
58 Mark E. Kann, *Punishment, Prisons, and Patriarchy: Liberty and Power in the Early American Republic* (New York: New York University Press, 2005), 210–211.
59 Gilliard, *Rethinking Incarceration*, 123–124; Graber, *Furnace of Affliction*, 113.
60 Quoted in Gilliard, *Rethinking Incarceration*, 134; Graber, *Furnace of Affliction*, 123.
61 Shelden, *Controlling the Dangerous Classes*, 72–73; K. Williams, *Our Enemies in Blue*, 56.
62 K. Williams, *Our Enemies in Blue*, 56–57.
63 K. Williams, 57. See also Beaumont, *Nightwalking*.
64 Beaumont, *Nightwalking*, 39.
65 K. Williams, *Our Enemies in Blue*, 58.
66 Michael Andrew Žmolek, *Rethinking the Industrial Revolution: Five Centuries of Transition from Agrarian to Industrial Capitalism in England* (Leiden: Brill, 2013), 526–528.
67 Neocleous, *Critical Theory of Police Power*, 154–159; Shelden, *Controlling the Dangerous Classes*, 74.
68 Quoted in Witte, *God's Joust, God's Justice*, 282.
69 Patrick Colquhoun, *Treatise on the Police of the Metropolis; Containing a Detail of the Various Crimes and Misdemeanors by Which Public and Private Property and Security Are, at Present, Injured and Endangered: and Suggesting Remedies for Their Prevention*, 6th ed. (London: H. Baldwin and Son, 1800).
70 Neocleous, *Critical Theory of Police Power*, 156; Jason Ditton, "Perks, Pilferage, and the Fiddle: The Historical Structure of Invisible Wages," *Theory and Society* 4 (1978): 39–71. On the irreligiosity of what Colquhoun called the "lower classes," see Colquhoun, *Treatise on the Police of the Metropolis*; and Francis Dodsworth, "Police and the Prevention of Crime: Commerce, Temptation and the Corruption of the Body Politic, from Fielding to Colquhoun," *British Journal of Criminology* 47 (2007): 439–454.
71 K. Williams, *Our Enemies in Blue*, 58–59.
72 Vitale, *End of Policing*, 35–36.
73 Vitale, 36.
74 Vitale, 36–37.
75 Quoted in K. Williams, *Our Enemies in Blue*, 176.
76 Vitale, *End of Policing*, 37–39. For an account of how working-class European immigrants became "white," see Noel Ignatiev, *How the Irish Became White* (New York: Routledge, 1995); David R. Roediger, *Working toward Whiteness: How America's Immigrants Became White* (New York: Basic Books, 2005); Matthew Frye Jacobson, *Whiteness of a Different Color: European Immigrants and the Alchemy of Race* (Cambridge, MA: Harvard University Press, 1998).
77 As Sidney Harring writes, "In one day of killing in 1877, the Chicago police secured for themselves the respect of the ruling class and their allies and secured for

the police institution a place in the complex arena of community power as a well-trusted, coercive weapon of the bourgeoisie" (*Policing a Class Society*, 108–109).
78. Morone, *Hellfire Nation*, 169–182.
79. Gerbner, *Christian Slavery*; Chris L. De Wet, *Preaching Bondage: John Chrysostom and the Discourse of Slavery in Early Christianity* (Oakland: University of California Press, 2015), 46–51.
80. Sally E. Hadden, *Slave Patrols: Law and Violence in Virginia and the Carolinas* (Cambridge, MA: Harvard University Press, 2003), 11.
81. Hadden, 11–12.
82. Hadden, 17.
83. Most narratives of the formation of modern police cite 1829 London as the birthplace of a form of professional policing that subsequently proliferated throughout the northern US, giving us police as we know them today. But decades before Sir Robert Peel organized English state "police" power into a formal institution tasked with using violence to reproduce the social order by defending it against threats of working-class rebellion, cities like New Orleans, Savannah, and Charleston already had salaried, armed, uniformed, municipal-run police forces whose central purpose was controlling people of African descent, as well as indentured servants, vagrants, and debtors of European descent and Native Americans, all of whom colonists and owners viewed as inherently untrustworthy and inclined to disrupt an order built on the dispossession, exploitation, or outright eradication of all who were not white property owners. It is thus arguably southern US cities, and Charleston in particular, not London, that gives us the first modern professional police force. See Vitale, *End of Policing*, 45–46; K. Williams, *Our Enemies in Blue*, 67–68, 74–78.
84. Quoted in K. Williams, *Our Enemies in Blue*, 69.
85. Quoted in K. Williams, 77.
86. Vitale, *End of Policing*, 47; K. Williams, *Our Enemies in Blue*, 65–70; Hadden, *Slave Patrols*, 83.
87. Quoted in Hadden, *Slave Patrols*, 71.
88. Joy James, "Introduction: Democracy and Captivity," in James, *New Abolitionists*, xxii; US Constitution, Amendment 13 (emphasis mine).
89. Du Bois, *Black Reconstruction in America*, 30.
90. South Carolina's Black Code, for example, passed shortly after abolition in 1865, required that Black workers would be called "servants" and that they should refer to their employer as "master." Like the slave codes that preceded them only months prior, Black workers were required to carry a pass from their "master" whenever leaving the plantation. Brian Sawyers, "Race and Property after the Civil War: Creating the Right to Exclude," *Mississippi Law Journal* 87, no. 5 (2018): 721.
91. As Angela Davis writes, "vagrancy was coded as a black crime, one punishable by incarceration and forced labor, sometimes on the very plantations that previously had thrived on slave labor" (*Are Prisons Obsolete?*, 29).

92 Quoted in K. Douglas, *Stand Your Ground*, 78.
93 Quoted in K. Douglas, 78.
94 Sawyers, "Race and Property after the Civil War," 735. In addition to vagrancy laws, other statutes reconstituted enslavement-like arrangements, including enticement laws that prohibited Black workers from changing jobs, as well as apprenticeship laws that gave former enslavers priority to "employ" those whom they previously enslaved. In some states, people convicted of petty property crimes were forced to labor to pay their debts and fines, and in some cases, planters were allowed to pay a convicted Black person's fines in exchange for months of their labor. Sawyers, 736–738; Alex Lichtenstein, *Twice the Work of Free Labor: The Political Economy of Convict Labor in the New South* (London: Verso Books, 1996), 29.
95 Quoted in M. Alexander, *New Jim Crow*, 28.
96 Lichtenstein, *Twice the Work of Free Labor*, 19.
97 Vitale, *End of Policing*, 47. For a wealth of detail on these systems and the impact they had on people's lives, see Douglas A. Blackmon, *Slavery by Another Name: The Re-enslavement of Black Americans from the Civil War to World War II* (New York: Anchor Books, 2009); David M. Oshinsky, *"Worse than Slavery": Parchman Farm and the Ordeal of Jim Crow Justice* (New York: Free Press, 1997). As Alex Lichtenstein summarizes, multiple systems of convict labor existed in the decades following the Civil War that forced imprisoned people to labor for someone else's profit, including various forms of prison-factories in which caged peoples manufactured products for industry (*Twice the Work of Free Labor*, 18–19). See also Davis, *Are Prisons Obsolete?* 29.
98 Blackmon, *Slavery by Another Name*; Lichtenstein, *Twice the Work of Free Labor*.
99 M. Alexander, *New Jim Crow*, 32. For more on extended prison sentences for Black Americans as a punishment for petty crimes during the postslavery era, see Lichtenstein, *Twice the Work of Free Labor*, 37–72.
100 Muhammad, *Condemnation of Blackness*.
101 Du Bois, "Souls of White Folk," 20.
102 Du Bois, *Souls of Black Folk*, 107–108.
103 Davis, *Are Prisons Obsolete?*, 29–30; Bryan Stevenson, "A Presumption of Guilt: The Legacy of America's History of Racial Injustice," in *Policing the Black Man*, ed. Angela J. Davis (New York: Pantheon Books, 2017), 12.
104 Ritchie, *Invisible No More*, 31. As historians including Sarah Haley and Kali Gross show, the late nineteenth- and early twentieth-century criminalization of Black life across the US was fueled by the criminalization of Black women in particular, whom the white ruling class constructed as inherently deviant threats to social order. Sarah Haley, *No Mercy Here: Gender, Punishment, and the Making of Jim Crow Modernity* (Chapel Hill: University of North Carolina Press, 2016), 3. While the Jim Crow South was a central site of the germination of the new forms of carcerality and exploitation that replaced chattel slavery, these institutions were not manifestations of the southern United States alone, as seen, for example, in

historian Kali Gross's study of the racialized, gendered, and sexualized criminalization of Black women during the late nineteenth and early twentieth centuries in Philadelphia. Kali N. Gross, *Colored Amazons: Crime, Violence, and Black Women in the City of Brotherly Love, 1880–1910* (Durham, NC: Duke University Press, 2006).

105 Interrupting Criminalization, *Shrouded in Silence: Police Sexual Violence: What We Know and What We Can Do about It* (2021), www.interruptingcriminalization.com.
106 Ritchie, *Invisible No More*, 36.
107 Survived and Punished, *No Selves to Defend: A Legacy of Criminalizing Women of Color for Self-Defense* (September 2016), https://noselves2defend.files.wordpress.com.
108 On the notion of "abolition democracy," see Du Bois, *Black Reconstruction*; and Davis, *Abolition Democracy*.
109 On the religiosity of lynching, see Matthews, *At the Altar of Lynching*, 127. On the Ku Klux Klan and its connection to policing, see K. Williams, *Our Enemies in Blue*, 121–173; Vitale, *End of Policing*, 47–48.
110 On the migration of Black people from the South, see Isabelle Wilkerson, *The Warmth of Other Suns: The Epic Story of America's Great Migration* (New York: Vintage Books, 2011). On the brutal police power that received Black migrants in places like Chicago, see Simon Balto, *Occupied Territory: Policing Black Chicago from Red Summer to Black Power* (Chapel Hill: University of North Carolina Press, 2019), 22.
111 These new ways include, among many others, interstate highway construction and redlining, both of which geographically and materially fractured and disenfranchised Black communities on a staggering scale.
112 Baldwin, "Report from Occupied Territory."
113 James Baldwin, "To Crush a Serpent," in *Cross of Redemption*, 199–200.
114 Aaron Griffith, *God's Law and Order: The Politics of Punishment in Evangelical America* (Cambridge, MA: Harvard University Press, 2020), 120.
115 Quoted in Aaron Griffith, "'Policing Is a Profession of the Heart': Evangelicalism and Modern American Policing," *Religions* 12, no. 194 (2021): 5.
116 Ritchie, *Invisible No More*.
117 Davis, *Are Prisons Obsolete?*, 68.
118 Kann, *Punishment, Prisons, and Patriarchy*, 6–7. On the inherently patriarchal nature of police power, see Dubber, *Police Power*.
119 Kann, *Punishment, Prisons, and Patriarchy*, 65. See also Nelson, *National Manhood*, 13.
120 Kann, *Punishment, Prisons, and Patriarchy*, 207, 65.
121 Hernández, *City of Inmates*, 47, 14.
122 Quoted in Hernández, 45.
123 Kann, *Punishment, Prisons, and Patriarchy*, 64.
124 N. Singh, *Race and America's Long War*, 46; Neal Shirley and Saralee Stafford, "Where Do the Police Come From?," *Scalawag*, September 7, 2016, https://scalawagmagazine.org.

125 Frank B. Wilderson III, "The Prison Slave as Hegemony's (Silent) Scandal," in James, *Warfare in the American Homeland*, 26.
126 Locke, *Second Treatise of Government*, § 85; Adam Smith, *Inquiry into the Nature and Causes of the Wealth of Nations*, 775.
127 Locke, *Second Treatise of Government*, § 11. As Nikhil Pal Singh summarizes, Locke "framed crimes against property, including those that did not threaten physical harm, as warranting punishment up to and including homicide," because "theft of property de facto entered the criminal, outlaw, or thief into 'a state of war' that threatened the natural rights of the individual and the basis of civil government" (*Race and America's Long War*, 43).
128 This aspect of Locke's liberal social contract theory shows its connections to Hobbes, who came before him, and Rousseau, for whom he helps pave the way after him.
129 Locke, *Second Treatise of Government*, § 8. For more on the notion of trespass against the species, see Sinja Graf, "'A Trespass against the Whole Species': Universal Crime and Sovereign Founding in Locke's *Second Treatise of Government*," *Political Theory* 46, no. 4 (2018): 560–585.
130 As Colquhoun puts it, "all depredations on property are public wrongs, in the suppression of which every member of the community is called upon to lend his assistance" (quoted in Neocleous, *Critical Theory of Police Power*, 133).
131 Locke, *Second Treatise of Government*, § 8; Dilts, *Punishment and Inclusion*, 88, 104–108.
132 Hay, "Property, Authority and Criminal Law," 18; Hirsch, *Rise of the Penitentiary*, 43; Foucault, *Discipline and Punish*, 107; Colvin, *Penitentiaries*, 35–36.
133 Quoted in Neocleous, *Critical Theory of Police Power*, 40.
134 Hay, "Property, Authority and Criminal Law," 19.
135 Linebaugh, *London Hanged*, 78–79.
136 Linebaugh, xxii.
137 As Hirsch explains, in early America, "the problem faced by authorities was not crime in general but *property* crime, committed in the main by indigent transients" whose "criminal" tendencies allegedly found their "impetus," as explained earlier, in "idleness" (*Rise of the Penitentiary*, 43).
138 As Correia and Wall write, police "are central to both race-making and place-making." David Correia and Tyler Wall, "Introduction: On the Nature of Police," in Correia and Wall, *Violent Order*, 1.
139 N. Singh, *Race and America's Long War*, 36–38.
140 Sawyers, "Race and Property after the Civil War," 713, 740–741.
141 Sawyers, 741.
142 Sawyers, 741–744.
143 Steven Hahn, "Hunting, Fishing, and Foraging: Common Rights and Class Relations in the Postbellum South," *Radical History Review* 26 (1982): 46; Sawyers, "Race and Property after the Civil War," 745.
144 Charles L. Flynn Jr., *White Land, Black Labor: Caste and Class in Late Nineteenth-Century Georgia* (Baton Rouge: Louisiana State University Press, 1983), 115. It is

important to note that these laws also negatively impacted landless white workers, who, though they had whiteness, did not always have the access to capital and land that whiteness was supposed to guarantee them, which itself clarifies the lie on which whiteness stands, as explored earlier in the book.

145 Lichtenstein, *Twice the Work of Free Labor*, 59.
146 Colquhoun, *Treatise on the Police of the Metropolis*, 218.
147 Some police forces developed during the eighteenth and nineteenth centuries specifically as a means of accomplishing Indigenous elimination. The St. Louis police, for example, formed in 1808 in order to "protect" the city's residents from Native Americans, and some cities used police forces to enforce pass systems and vagrancy laws that deliberately targeted Indigenous peoples. Ritchie, *Invisible No More*, 24.
148 Isenberg, *White Trash*, 17–42; Sherene H. Razack, *Dying from Improvement: Inquests and Inquiries into Indigenous Deaths in Custody* (Toronto: University of Toronto Press, 2015), 170.
149 Razack, *Dying from Improvement*, 168–170; Nick Estes, Melanie K. Yazzie, Jennifer Nez Denetdale, and David Correia, *Red Nation Rising: From Bordertown Violence to Native Liberation* (Oakland, CA: PM, 2021), 61.
150 Ritchie, *Invisible No More*, 23.
151 Razack, *Dying from Improvement*, 165.
152 Razack, 161.
153 Eliade, *Sacred and the Profane*, 29.
154 Razack, *Dying from Improvement*, 161.
155 Harsha Walia, *Border and Rule: Global Migration, Capitalism, and the Rise of Racist Nationalism* (Chicago: Haymarket Books, 2021), 21.
156 Walia, 32.
157 Walia, 29, 32.
158 Walia, 33. As Walia notes, the same year that the federal government created the US Border Patrol, forty thousand Klansmen marched for the passage of the Johnson-Reed Immigration Act, which "barred all Asian immigration and imposed a national origins quota" (34).
159 Clarifying the innate connections between the border and boundary formations of property and police power, the Texas Ranger Hall of Fame and Museum in Waco, Texas, features an exhibit showing the history of the Rangers and the history of land surveyors during the Anglo settlement of Texas as a "linked tradition." City of Waco Productions, "Texas Ranger Hall of Fame and Museum—Rangers and Surveyors," Vimeo, 2015, video, https://vimeo.com/145323237.
160 N. Singh, *Race and America's Long War*, 49. Catalyzed by President McKinley's racial and religious rhetoric, popular US media at that time regularly depicted the Filipino people in exaggerated, caricatured, and explicitly anti-Black and anti-Indigenous ways as wild savages who needed either conquering or Americanizing and Christianizing, which is to say whitening. Late nineteenth-century

issues of the periodicals *Puck* and *Judge* contained many of these racist cartoons. One image in particular depicts President McKinley washing a young Filipino child, who is wearing traditional Indigenous accessories and holding a spear. The brush is labeled "Education," and the body of water is labeled "Civilization." Grant Hamilton, "The Filipino's First Bath," *Judge*, June 10, 1899.

161 General James Rusling, "Interview with President William McKinley," *Christian Advocate*, January 22, 1903, 17, reprinted in *The Philippines Reader*, ed. Daniel Schirmer and Stephen Shalom (Boston: South End, 1987), 22–23.

162 N. Singh, *Race and America's Long War*, 49. On the relationship between US imperial and colonial policing and domestic policing in the US, see Stuart Schrader, *Badges without Borders: How Global Counterinsurgency Transformed American Policing* (Oakland: University of California Press, 2019); Julian Go, "The Imperial Origins of Policing: Militarization and Imperial Feedback in the Early 20th Century," *American Journal of Sociology* 125, no. 5 (March 2020): 1193–1254.

163 Vitale, *End of Policing*, 41.

164 Vitale, 42–43.

165 Schrader, *Badges without Borders*. Included in the imperial internationalism of twentieth- and twenty-first-century policing is the relationship between police in the US and Israel, which has entailed multiple "exchanges" in which US police train with Israeli police and vice versa. The practical result of this cross-pollination in police practice is that the same brutal tactics that Israeli police use as part of Israel's decades-long settler colonial apartheid occupation of Palestine are, in many cases, the same tactics that US police use to suppress mass protests against racial injustice and anti-Black police violence at home. More importantly, just as police in the US and Israel coordinate, so Black activists in the US and Palestinians have formed networks of international solidarity with one another not only over the past decade but since at least the 1960s. For more on these phenomena, see Khury Petersen-Smith, "Cops Here, Bombs There: Black-Palestinian Solidarity," in *Palestine: A Socialist Introduction*, ed. Sumaya Awad and brian bean (Chicago: Haymarket Books, 2020): 169–183.

166 N. Singh, *Race and America's Long War*, 73.

167 Baldwin, "Report from Occupied Territory"; Baldwin, "To Crush a Serpent."

168 Correia and Wall, *Police*, 82.

169 As Kelly Lytle Hernández, writes, "Mass incarceration is mass elimination" (*City of Inmates*, 1).

170 Friedrich Engels, *The Condition of the Working Class in England* (Oxford: Oxford University Press, 2009), 234–235.

CHAPTER 5. MEASURING SALVATION IN "CHAINS AND CORPSES"

1 Baldwin, "Open Letter to My Sister Angela Y. Davis," 255.
2 Baldwin, 254–260.
3 Baldwin, 260.

4   Du Bois also refers to the experience of prison as the experience of hell. See Julian Bond's foreword to *If They Come in the Morning . . . : Voices of Resistance*, ed. Angela Y. Davis (London: Verso, 2016), xi.
5   James Baldwin, "The Fire This Time: Letter to the Bishop," in *Cross of Redemption*, 265.
6   Baldwin, "On Being White . . . and Other Lies," 169.
7   Baldwin, 167–169.
8   Neocleous, *Critical Theory of Police Power*, 9–10.
9   Baldwin, "Open Letter to My Sister Angela Y. Davis," 258–259.
10 Achille Mbembe, *Necropolitics*, trans. Steven Corcoran (Durham, NC: Duke University Press, 2019), 72.
11 Neocleous, *Critical Theory of Police Power*; Mark Neocleous and George S. Rigakos, eds., *Anti-Security* (Ottawa: Red Quill Books, 2011); Kelly Hayes, "Abolition Means Reclaiming the Commons and Rejecting Securitization" (interview with Brendan McQuade), *Truthout*, February 3, 2022, https://truthout.org.
12 Mark Neocleous, *Critical Theory of Police Power*, 10.
13 Neocleous, 34. Neocleous and Rigakos, *Anti-Security*.
14 On the idea of "manufactured consent," see Edward S. Herman and Noam Chomsky, *Manufacturing Consent: The Political Economy of Mass Media* (New York: Pantheon Books, 2002).
15 Long, *Significations*, 7.
16 Baldwin, "Down at the Cross," 16.
17 The Greek *soteria*, conveying the same thing, is the source of the term "soteriology," signifying a doctrine of salvation.
18 Calvin, *Institutes of the Christian Religion*, 325.
19 René Girard, *Violence and the Sacred*, trans. Patrick Gregory (Baltimore: John Hopkins University Press, 1977).
20 Timothy Malone, "The Carceral Death Machine: Savagery, Contamination and Sacrifice in the Contemporary Prison" (PhD diss., Claremont Graduate University, 2022), 306, 418.
21 The notion of "sacrificable" peoples as an integral component of racial capitalism comes from Ruth Wilson Gilmore, in Abraham Paulos, Ruth Wilson Gilmore, and Mariame Kaba, "The Hard Road to Abolition // Strategies to Win," *Abolitionist: A Publication of Critical Resistance*, no. 28 (Winter 2018): 8.
22 Joseph Henninger, "Sacrifice [First Edition]," trans. Matthew J. O'Connell, in *Encyclopedia of Religion*, ed. Lindsay Jones, 2nd ed., vol. 12 (Detroit: Macmillan Reference, 2005), 7997. See also Chidester, *Religion*, 34.
23 Henninger, "Sacrifice," 8004.
24 The "paradox" lies in the fact that "redemption" literally refers to release from subjection. For carceral soteriology, salvation is release *from* subjection to the Devil and release *for* subjection to God.
25 Dubber, *Police Power*, 58–59.
26 Dubber, 131.

27 Dubber, 131–132 (emphasis mine).
28 Estes et al., *Red Nation Rising*, 61.
29 For example, in 2022, in Tennessee, where I live, the state legislature passed a law making unapproved camping on any public property a felony offense. Police and sheriffs who advocated for the law's passage dubiously suggested that criminalization benefited unhoused people by giving them an opportunity to be connected to social services and housing resources, despite the fact that the law contained no such provision. I have heard such remarks many times over the past fifteen years.
30 Mariah Timms, "Tennessee Deputy Groped Woman, Forced Her into 'Baptism' in Frigid Lake Waters, Lawsuit Claims," *Tennessean*, October 3, 2019, www.tennessean.com.
31 WTVC, "Lawsuit Finds Soddy-Daisy Woman at Center of Deputy Baptism Lawsuit Died of Overdose," April 14, 2022, https://newschannel9.com.
32 Sam Peña, "Hamilton County Spent Thousands in Defense of Former Sheriff Deputy over Last 3 Years," WTVC, November 15, 2022, https://newschannel9.com.
33 Foucault, *Discipline and Punish*, 123.
34 Ringer, *Necropolitics*; Judith Vasquez, "On the Verge of Hell," in *Hell Is a Very Small Place: Voices from Solitary Confinement*, ed. Jean Casella, James Ridgeway, and Sarah Shourd (New York: New Press, 2016); Hannah Bowman, "The Abolition of Hell: Abolitionist Interpretations of Jesus' Descent into Hell," in *Spirituality and Abolition*, ed. Ashon Crawley, Roberto Sirvent, and Abolition Collective (Brooklyn, NY: Common Notions, 2023).
35 Griffith, *God's Law and Order*, 52.
36 Quoted in Griffith, "Policing Is a Profession of the Heart," 6.
37 Quoted in Griffith, *God's Law and Order*, 161.
38 Quoted in Griffith, 164.
39 Quoted in Griffith, "Policing Is a Profession of the Heart," 7.
40 Quoted in Griffith, 12.
41 The plaque was paid for by the Nashville Fraternal Order of Police, which is based out of the Andrew Jackson Lodge, named for the famous enslaver of Africans and killer of Indigenous peoples.
42 Peter K. Manning, *Police Work: The Social Organization of Policing*, 2nd ed. (Prospect Heights, IL: Waveland, 1997), 106.
43 P. Manning, 279.
44 P. Manning, 279–280.
45 P. Manning, 267. Manning also notes that the more crime is articulated as a threat, the stronger the myth of police power tends to be: "The myth of police power tends to escalate as the threat of crime is seen as growing apace" (280).
46 Camp, *Incarcerating the Crisis*, 5–6.
47 Gilmore, "Beyond Bratton," 303–313. On the road to mass incarceration beginning in the 1940s, see Murakawa, *First Civil Right*.
48 On the racial constitution of neoliberalism via notions of "culture" and "civilization," see Arun Kundnani, "The Racial Constitution of Neoliberalism," *Race and*

Class 63, no. 1 (2021): 51–69. On the "eurochristian" character of neoliberalism, see Roger Kurt Green, "Neoliberalism and eurochristianity," *Religions* 12, no. 688 (2021): 1–25.

49 For more on the fundamental dynamics of neoliberal racial capitalism, including how it constitutes an act of counterinsurgency, see Camp, *Incarcerating the Crisis*. On criminalization as class war, see Gilmore, "Beyond Bratton."
50 Gilmore, *Golden Gulag*.
51 Hinton, *From the War on Poverty to the War on Crime*; Murakawa, *First Civil Right*.
52 Gilmore, *Golden Gulag*; Camp, *Incarcerating the Crisis*.
53 Wacquant, *Punishing the Poor*, xxii. Angela Davis similarly writes, "The prison has become a black hole into which the detritus of contemporary capitalism is deposited" (*Are Prisons Obsolete?*, 16).
54 Whereas Wacquant views insurgent uprisings of the long freedom movement as a less significant factor in the rise of the carceral state, Camp argues that such movements posed specific crises of legitimacy in relation to which neoliberal security and austerity were posed as solutions, which is why one cannot fully understand the rise of the carceral state apart from them. See Camp, *Incarcerating the Crisis*, 6–8, for his engagement with Wacquant's work. Alex Vitale makes a similar argument in *End of Policing*, 50.
55 Camp, *Incarcerating the Crisis*, 5. As Ruth Wilson Gilmore writes, "the dominant explanation for prison growth" in the late twentieth century is that "crime went up; we cracked down; crime came down." The reality, however, she argues, is that "crime went up; crime came down; we cracked down" (*Golden Gulag*, 17, 20).
56 Gilmore, "Beyond Bratton," 306; Denvir, "Prison-Industrial Complex."
57 Luca Mavelli, "Neoliberalism as Religion: Sacralization of the Market and Post-truth Politics," *International Political Sociology* 14 (2020): 57–76.
58 Mavelli. For more on the religious qualities and dimensions of neoliberalism, see D. Singh, *Economy and Modern Christian Thought*, 55–57; Joshua Ramey, *Politics of Divination: Neoliberal Endgame and the Religion of Contingency* (Lanham, MD: Rowman and Littlefield, 2016); Adam Kotsko, *Neoliberalism's Demons: On the Political Theology of Late Capital* (Stanford, CA: Stanford University Press, 2018).
59 On the production of enemies and "demons" within neoliberalism, see Kotsko, *Neoliberalism's Demons*.
60 Dubber, *Police Power*.
61 Bryan Wagner, *Disturbing the Peace: Black Culture and the Police Power After Slavery* (Cambridge, MA: Harvard University Press, 2009), 10.
62 Dubber, *Police Power*; Wagner, *Disturbing the Peace*.
63 Wagner, *Disturbing the Peace*, 10–11. This resonates with Tyler Wall's notion of a "police conception of history," which derives from Hobbes's account of sovereign state and police power as the power of a mortal God that creates, defends, and sustains the hierarchies of sacred social order ("Inventing Humanity").

64 Dubber, *Police Power*; Goluboff, *Vagrant Nation*.
65 Goluboff, *Vagrant Nation*; Christopher Lowen Agee, "From the Vagrancy Law Regime to the Carceral State," *Law & Social Inquiry* 43, no. 4 (Fall 2018): 1658–1668.
66 For more on the *Terry* decision and its impacts, see Goluboff, *Vagrant Nation*, 186–220; M. Alexander, *New Jim Crow*, 63.
67 George L. Kelling and James Q. Wilson, "Broken Windows: The Police and Neighborhood Safety," *Atlantic*, March 1982.
68 Quoted in Loïc Wacquant, *Prisons of Poverty*, exp. ed. (Minneapolis: University of Minnesota Press, 2009), 23. George H. W. Bush also said in 1989, "We must raise our voices to correct an insidious tendency—the tendency to blame crime on society rather than on the criminal. . . . I, like most Americans, believe that we can start building a safer society by first agreeing that society itself doesn't cause the crime—criminals cause the crime." George H. W. Bush, "Remarks at a Briefing on Law Enforcement for United States Attorneys," June 16, 1989, American Presidency Project, www.presidency.ucsb.edu.
69 Wacquant, *Punishing the Poor*, xxii.
70 In a 1994 speech to the Heritage Foundation, Bratton, speaking specifically about "squeegee men," said, "In New York, we know who the enemy is" (quoted in Ringer, *Necropolitics*, 103).
71 Quoted in Issa Kohler-Hausmann, *Misdemeanorland: Criminal Courts and Social Control in an Age of Broken Windows Policing* (Princeton, NJ: Princeton University Press, 2018), 26–27.
72 Quoted in Aya Gruber, "Policing and 'Bluelining,'" *Houston Law Review* 58, no. 867 (2021): 896.
73 Wacquant, *Prisons of Poverty*, 14–16.
74 Quoted in Ritchie, *Invisible No More*, 54.
75 K. Babe Howell, "The Costs of Broken Windows Policing: Twenty Years and Counting," *Cardoza Law Review* 37, no. 3 (2016): 1059–1073.
76 Kohler-Hausmann, *Misdemeanorland*, 2.
77 Kohler-Hausmann, 4.
78 Kelling and Wilson, "Broken Windows."
79 Giuliani and Bratton proclaimed that the purpose of the broken windows approach was to restore New York City to a "society of civility." Kohler-Hausmann, *Misdemeanorland*, 26.
80 Harcourt, *Illusion of Order*, 25.
81 Harcourt, 30–31, citing Edward C. Banfield, *The Unheavenly City Revisited* (Boston: Little, Brown, 1974). *The Unheavenly City Revisited* is a revised version of Banfield's prior book, *The Unheavenly City: The Nature and the Future of Our Urban Crisis* (Boston: Little, Brown, 1970).
82 Wall, "Inventing Humanity."
83 Charles Colson, "Cleanliness Is Next to Crimelessness," *Christianity Today*, January 6, 1997, www.christianitytoday.com.

84 Colson.

85 Marybeth Shinn and Jill Khadduri, *In the Midst of Plenty: Homelessness and What to Do about It* (Hoboken, NJ: Wiley Blackwell, 2020).

86 Alice Speri, "Police Make More than 10 Million Arrests a Year, but That Doesn't Mean They're Solving Crimes," *Intercept*, January 31, 2019, https://theintercept.com. For the Vera Institute's tool to explore arrest trends in the US, see https://arresttrends.vera.org.

87 National Law Center on Homelessness and Poverty, *Housing Not Handcuffs: Ending the Criminalization of Homelessness in U.S. Cities* (2019), https://homelesslaw.org.

88 National Law Center on Homelessness and Poverty.

89 Andrew Krinks, "Criminal: When Existing in Public Becomes Illegal," *Contributor* 7, no. 11 (July 11, 2013): 1.

90 Krinks, 10.

91 K. Williams, *Our Enemies in Blue*, 179. On the use of obstruction and other quality-of-life laws, including trespass and loitering, during the Black freedom movement of the 1960s, see Goluboff, *Vagrant Nation*, 118–119.

92 Krinks, "Criminal," 11.

93 Krinks, 9.

94 Krinks, 8.

95 Krinks, 12.

96 Quoted in Katherine Beckett and Steve Herbert, *Banished: The New Social Control in Urban America* (Oxford: Oxford University Press, 2009), 6.

97 Michel Foucault, "Truth and Power," in *Power/Knowledge: Selected Interviews and Other Writings, 1972–1977*, ed. Colin Gordon (New York: Pantheon Books, 1980), 119. In an interview on Prentis Hemphill's podcast *Finding Our Way*, Mariame Kaba explores the idea that imprisonment brings about pleasure for people living in a carceral society. Prentis Hemphill, "Harm, Punishment, and Abolition with Mariame Kaba," *Finding Our Way* (podcast), July 5, 2021. On the pleasures of punishment, engaging with the thought of Sigmund Freud, see Garland, *Punishment and Modern Society*. On the pleasures of enslavement for enslavers, see Saidiya V. Hartman, *Scenes of Subjection: Terror, Slavery, and Self-Making in Nineteenth-Century America* (Oxford: Oxford University Press, 1997), 3–48.

98 Kelling and Wilson, "Broken Windows." In deploying the term "improve" as part of a theoretical argument about purifying space of threatening people, Kelling and Wilson reveal the continuity of their thought with Lockean liberal political philosophy and the legacy of white racial capitalist settler colonial thought of which it is a part: according to Locke and countless other commentators throughout the early modern period, "improvement"—as in the "improvement" of commons and Indigenous lands that enclosure and settlement catalyzed—constituted an inherently sacred political good. Locke, *Second Treatise*, § 37. On the political theology of improvement, see McCarraher, *Enchantments of Mammon*, 23–47.

99   Speri, "Police Make More than 10 Million Arrests a Year."
100 Quoted in Davis, *Are Prisons Obsolete?*, 30.
101 On anti-Black criminalization as purification, see Rima Vesely-Flad, *Racial Purity and Dangerous Bodies: Moral Pollution, Black Lives, and the Struggle for Justice* (Minneapolis, MN: Fortress, 2017).
102 On the impacts of broken windows policing, see Gaurav Jashnani, Priscilla Bustamente, Brett G. Stoudt, "Dispossession by Accumulation: The Impacts of Discretionary Arrests in New York City," *Race and Justice* 10, no. 3 (2020): 269–296; Jan Haldipur, *No Place on the Corner: The Costs of Aggressive Policing* (New York: New York University Press, 2019); Gideon's Army, *Driving while Black: A Report on Racial Profiling in Metro Nashville Police Department Traffic Stops* (2016), 70–88, https://drivingwhileblacknashville.wordpress.com.
103 Editors of the *Nation*, "You Can't Fix 'Broken Windows,' So End It Now," *Nation*, June 17, 2015, www.thenation.com.
104 Jordan T. Camp and Christina Heatherton, "Introduction: Policing the Planet," in Camp and Heatherton, *Policing the Planet*, 1.
105 The idea of police as the muscle of racial capitalism comes from Alyxandra Goodwin. Kaba and Ritchie, *No More Police*, 28.
106 Correia and Wall, "Introduction," 1.
107 Wall, "Inventing Humanity," 13–29.
108 Neocleous, "Monster and the Police," 149–156; Wall, "Inventing Humanity," 23–25.
109 Correia and Wall, "Introduction," 3.
110 Correia and Wall; Wall, "Inventing Humanity," 21, 16.
111 Maurice Chammah and Cary Aspinwall, "The Short, Fraught History of the 'Thin Blue Line' Flag," Marshall Project, June 8, 2020, www.themarshallproject.org. As noted in the book's introduction, Parker is also largely responsible for the development and proliferation of the notion that police "serve and protect" communities. Maher, *World without Police*, 62.
112 Wall, "Inventing Humanity," 13–15; Correia and Wall, *Police*, 122.
113 Correia and Wall, *Police*, 120; Wall, "Inventing Humanity," 16.
114 Ronald Reagan, "Remarks at the Annual Meeting of the International Association of Chiefs of Police," New Orleans, Louisiana, September 28, 1981, www.reaganlibrary.gov.
115 Kelling and Wilson, "Broken Windows."
116 Wall, "Inventing Humanity," 18.
117 Ritchie, *Invisible No More*, 56–57.
118 Hinton, *From the War on Poverty to the War on Crime*, 286–291.
119 On defensible space, see Oscar Newman, *Defensible Space: Crime Prevention through Urban Design* (New York: Macmillan, 1972); Oscar Newman, *Creating Defensible Space* (Washington, DC: US Department of Housing and Urban Development, Office of Policy Development and Research, April 1996); H. G. Cisnernos, *Defensible Space: Deterring Crime and Building Community* (Washington, DC: US Department of Housing and Urban Development, 1995). On crime prevention

through environmental design (CPTED), see C. Ray Jeffery, *Crime Prevention through Environmental Design*, rev. ed. (Beverly Hills, CA: Sage, 1977); Timothy D. Crowe, *Crime Prevention through Environmental Design*, 3rd ed., rev. Lawrence J. Fennelly (Amsterdam: Elsevier, 2013).

120 Sylvia Chenery, "Neighborhood Watch," in *Oxford Research Encyclopedias: Criminology and Criminal Justice*, ed. Henry N. Pontell (Oxford: Oxford University Press, 2017); Sidi Salah Zehour and Aiche Messaoud, "From Urban Security to Residentialization: Historical Milestones and Evolution," *International Journal of Innovative Studies in Sociology and Humanities* 8, no. 1 (2023): 491.

121 Sarah Schindler, "Architectural Exclusion: Discrimination and Segregation through Physical Design of the Built Environment," *Yale Law Journal* 124, no. 6 (2015): 1934–2024.

122 By signing the form, signees are agreeing to the following: "I, ___, the owner or person having the authority of the owner, do hereby give members of the Metropolitan Nashville Police Department permission to act as my agents in enforcing Tennessee Code Annotated § 39-14-405, Criminal Trespass, and prosecuting person(s) for trespassing on my property.... The purpose of this authorization is to assist the Metropolitan Nashville Police Department in their efforts to prevent crime in Nashville." MNPD Form 188, rev. February 2019.

123 Gruber, "Policing and 'Bluelining,'" 891–892.

124 Gruber, 896.

125 Wacquant, *Prisons of Poverty*, 14. According to political theorist Leonard Feldman, antihomeless law enforcement practices strive to protect the literal flow of a middle-class consuming public, which is accomplished by moving those "physical blockages [that prevent] the achievement of a unified public space in which consumer goods and consumers move unobstructed" (*Citizens without Shelter*, 44). I argue, however, that the problem posed by underclass people's presence is not simply being an impediment to consumption but being trespassers within a landscape oriented around racialized "accumulation by dispossession."

126 Randall Amster, "Patterns of Exclusion: Sanitizing Space, Criminalizing Homelessness," *Social Justice* 30, no. 1 (2003): 206.

127 Amster.

128 N. Smith, *New Urban Frontier*.

129 Brenden Beck, "The Role of Police in Gentrification," *Appeal*, August 4, 2020; Stop LAPD Spying Coalition, *Automating Banishment: The Surveillance and Policing of Looted Land*, accessed May 1, 2022, https://automatingbanishment.org.

130 For more on the connection between police and gentrification, see Correia and Wall, *Police*, 193–195.

131 P. Manning, *Police Work*, 106.

132 Linebaugh, *London Hanged*, 428; Colquhoun, *Treatise on the Police of the Metropolis*.

133 Dubber, *Police Power*, 139–140.

134 Neocleous, *Critical Theory of Police Power*, 175–177; Neocleous, "Monster and the Police," 145.
135 Quoted in Ringer, *Necropolitics*, 13.
136 Quoted in Ringer, 103.
137 Vesely-Flad, *Racial Purity and Dangerous Bodies*, 3.
138 Vesely-Flad, 3.
139 Vesely-Flad, 31–32.
140 Amster, "Patterns of Exclusion," 197–199.
141 M. Douglas, *Purity and Danger*, 44.
142 As quoted earlier, Dr. John, reflecting on his experience of criminalization at the hands of police, said, "It's nothing you can do. You're never right. You're always wrong."
143 M. Douglas, *Purity and Danger*, 140.
144 Beckett and Herbert, *Banished*. See also Stop LAPD Spying Coalition, *Automating Banishment*.
145 Amster, "Patterns of Exclusion," 199. Amster is quoting Jeff Ferrell, "Remapping the City: Public Identity, Cultural Space, and Social Justice," *Contemporary Justice Review* 4, no. 2 (2001): 161–180. For more on policing and spatiality, see Steve Herbert, "Territoriality and the Police," *Professional Geographer* 49, no. 1 (1997): 86–94.
146 Likewise, with regard to carceral power, David Garland notes that prisons are often framed as quarantine zones. David Garland, *Culture of Control: Crime and Social Order in Contemporary Society* (Oxford: Oxford University Press, 2001), 178.
147 Wall, "Inventing Humanity," 21.
148 Neocleous, "Monster and the Police," 154.
149 Foucault, *Discipline and Punish*, 101. See also Foucault, *Abnormal*, 55–79.
150 Quoted in Neocleous, "Monster and the Police," 154–155.
151 Wall, "Inventing Humanity," 27.
152 Stephanie Rogish and Dave Grossman, *Sheepdogs: Meet Our Nation's Warriors* (Jackson, WI: Delta Defense, 2013), 29.
153 Rogish and Grossman, 28.
154 Lori Beth Way and Ryan Patten, *Hunting for "Dirtbags": Why Cops Over-Police the Poor and Racial Minorities* (Boston: Northeastern University Press, 2013).
155 Quoted in Wall, "Inventing Humanity," 28–29.
156 US Department of Justice, Civil Rights Division, "Investigation of the Ferguson Police Department," March 4, 2015.
157 Quoted in "State of Missouri v. Darren Wilson: Grand Jury Volume V" (September 16, 2014), 212.
158 Quoted in "State of Missouri v. Darren Wilson," 224–225 (emphasis mine).
159 Linebaugh and Rediker, *Many-Headed Hydra*.
160 S. Jonathon O'Donnell, *Passing Orders: Demonology and Sovereignty in American Spiritual Warfare* (New York: Fordham University Press, 2021), 5.

161 O'Donnell, 163n21.
162 O'Donnell, 7. See also Kotsko, *Neoliberalism's Demons*.
163 Neocleous, *Universal Adversary*, 7, 81. On the criminalization of dispossessed peoples cast as "folk devils," see Hall et al., *Policing the Crisis*.
164 Neocleous, *Universal Adversary*, 7. O'Donnell similarly argues that sustaining the enclosure of paradise is "inextricable from articulations of security, sovereignty, and the stability . . . of states and selves" (*Passing Orders*, 5).
165 Quoted in K. Williams, *Our Enemies in Blue*, 41.
166 For accounts of "political religion," see Emilio Gentile, *Politics as Religion*, trans. George Staunton (Princeton, NJ: Princeton University Press, 2006); and Joost Augusteijn, Patrick G. C. Dassen, and Marrtje J. Janse, eds., *Political Religion beyond Totalitarianism: The Sacralization of Politics in the Age of Democracy* (New York: Palgrave Macmillan, 2013).
167 Bowman, "Abolition of Hell."
168 Garland, *Punishment and Modern Society*, 30.
169 Mbembe, *Necropolitics*, 92; Ringer, *Necropolitics*.
170 Dubber, *Police Power*, 153.

CONCLUSION

1 Arianna Nason and Ricardo Levins Morales, "Planting the Seeds of Abolition," *Forge*, June 13, 2020, https://forgeorganizing.org.
2 For further exploration of the dynamics of abolitionist time, faith, struggle, and imagination, see Andrew Krinks, "Is, Was, and Is to Come: Freedom Dreamworld Dispatches," in Crawley, Sirvent, and Abolition Collective, *Spirituality and Abolition*.
3 Ruth Wilson Gilmore, "Making Abolition Geography in California's Central Valley," conversation with Léopold Lambert, *Funambulist*, December 20, 2018, https://thefunambulist.net.
4 Birgit Meyer, "Religion as Mediation," *Entangled Religions* 11, no. 3 (2020): 1–21.
5 Free Library of Philadelphia Author Events, "Ruth Wilson Gilmore | Abolition Geography: Essays towards Liberation," conversation with Chenjerai Kumanyika, Philadelphia, PA, September 22, 2022, YouTube, September 27, 2022, www.youtube.com/watch?v=-rocfvvcyZs&t=648s.
6 Kaba and Ritchie, *No More Police*, 215.
7 Ruth Wilson Gilmore makes this point in multiple venues.
8 Mariame Kaba, "Connecting the Dots: Issue 2—Transformative Justice at Interrupting Criminalization," email newsletter, Interrupting Criminalization, July 7, 2023. For more on Kaba's framework for understanding transformative justice, see Mariame Kaba, *Transformative Justice: Processes and Practices* (2018), https://drive.google.com. For a broader introduction to transformative justice, see Dixon and Piepzna-Samarasinha, *Beyond Survival*. For transformative justice resources for practitioners, see the *Creative Interventions Toolkit*, which is available for free download at www.creative-interventions.

org. For a digital repository of resources that explore the theory and practice of transformative justice and other nonpunitive forms of accountability, see Transform Harm, www.transformharm.org.
9 See One Million Experiments, a project of Interrupting Criminalization: www.millionexperiments.com.
10 This resonates with Erin Miles Cloud's remark, quoted in the book's introduction: "Everyone cares about someone's safety, somewhere, some of the time. Abolitionists care about everyone's safety, everywhere, all of the time." Quoted by Andrea Ritchie in Hayes, "Copaganda Arrests Our Imaginations."

INDEX

abolition, xii, 1–2, 9, 14–15, 31, 37, 78–79, 166, 174, 194, 202, 211, 213, 235–241; and abundance, 7, 9, 11, 31, 37, 233, 235, 237–38, 240–41; anotherworldliness of, 235; and care, 7, 9, 111, 113, 205, 223, 237, 240; as mode of creation, 7, 31, 236; and reciprocity, 237, 239–40; and repair, xiii, 8–9, 238–39; and safety without police and prisons, 252n20
Alexander, Michelle, 165
Amster, Randall, 220
Anselm of Canterbury, 26, 125–33, 139, 186, 224
Aquinas, Thomas, 96
Armour, Ellen, 104–5
Augustine, 26, 91, 125–28, 130–34, 139, 186, 204, 228

Bacon's Rebellion, 44–45, 262n44
Baldwin, James, 21, 29, 54, 79, 111–12, 119, 167–68, 179, 181–85, 196
Balibar, Étienne, 60
Banfield, Edward, 203–4
Barbados, 161–162, 177, 184
Bayley, David, 2
Beaumont, Matthew, 143
Beer, Stafford, 2
Benjamin, Walter, 39
Bhandar, Brenna, 65, 67
Bible, x, 26, 38–39, 41, 69, 75, 84, 88, 125, 130, 137, 192
Birt, Robert, 48, 95
Blackness: as "out of place," 67–68, 152; and anti-Blackness, 35, 54, 92, 94, 102, 167, 174, 177, 196, 223; and Cain, 41; Eurocolonial constructions of, 16, 19, 41–42, 44–47, 50–52, 55-56, 61, 63–66, 124, 148–49, 160–62, 64–65, 174, 176, 188–89; Eurocolonial constructions of animality of, 102, 160, 213, 225, 228; eurochristian constructions of depravity and immorality of, 16, 28, 42, 48, 50, 76, 79, 88, 124, 160–161, 164, 166, 168, 176, 216, 222, 228; as inherently criminal, 100, 148, 161, 165–66, 171, 211; as means of collective power and life, 55–56; as proximity to death, 56, 79; as outlaw, 171; as trespass, 18–19, 98, 116, 210
Blackstone, William, 59, 143
Blomley, Nicholas, 85
borders, 71, 81, 107, 152, 177, 214–19, 229–230, 237. *See also* partition
boundaries, 18, 20, 24, 29, 36, 40, 52, 64, 67, 70–72, 80, 82, 91, 98, 100, 107, 109, 118, 152, 154, 171, 173–74, 176, 185, 193–94, 214, 216, 218–219, 221, 231. *See also* partition
Bowman, Hannah, 232
Bratton, William, 200–201, 204, 217, 222
Bridewell, 144–45, 149
Browder, Kalief, 212
Brown, Michael, 226–30, 234
Brown, Wendy, 82, 108

Calvin, John, 26, 123, 125–26, 128–29, 131–33, 139, 186, 224
capitalism. *See* racial capitalism

carcerality, 23, 27, 29, 39, 67, 95, 110, 113, 116, 118–21, 124–25, 129, 133–40, 142–43, 145, 147–53, 162–63, 165, 167, 169–70, 174–75, 181, 184, 186–88, 190, 194–95, 201, 203, 210, 213–14, 219, 222–23, 225, 228, 231–232, 238, 241; bondage and, 16, 23, 91, 101, 127, 130, 147–48, 181–82; caging and, xii–xiii, 1–6, 9–11, 15, 22–25, 27, 29–31, 33, 43, 73, 116, 120–21, 135, 137, 145–47, 153–154, 163, 167, 170, 184–86, 196–97, 223, 225, 232–38, 241; 247–48n1; captivity and, 6, 23, 27–28, 40, 67, 95, 120, 122, 125–27, 129–32, 134–37, 161, 165, 181–82, 190, 231, 240; capture and, 1–2, 4, 6, 11, 21–23, 28, 33–34, 38–42, 46, 52, 67, 99–101, 118–21, 135, 142, 145–47, 151–52, 154–55, 158, 161–62, 165, 167, 170–71, 178, 181, 188, 195–96, 211, 226, 231–32, 238, 241; constructed naturalness of, 135; rehabilitation to subjection inherent to, 149, 151, 153–54

Carter, J. Kameron, 80

Cartwright, Samuel, 50

chaos, 11, 26, 38, 57–59, 62, 70–71, 81, 89, 99–100, 108–9, 117, 133–34, 139, 185, 193–94, 203, 214–15, 225–26, 228–29

Christianity, 13, 35, 39, 111, 122, 168, 240

civilization, 30, 35, 37, 40–41, 50, 61, 153, 165, 172, 178, 192, 195–96, 203, 214–17, 221, 225; and the construction of "uncivilized" peoples, 16, 38, 160, 171, 174, 195, 225

Cloud, Erin Miles, 9

colonialism, 15–16, 18–19, 24, 34–48, 50–56, 58, 60, 62–65, 67–68, 80–84, 86, 92–93; Eurocolonialism, 46, 105; notion of wilderness and, 82, 225; occupation and, 107–8, 156–57, 177–79; settler colonialism, 40, 108, 116–17, 170, 175–78, 189, 203, 216, 220, 222, 225

Colquhoun, Patrick, 35, 155–57, 173, 175, 222

Colson, Charles, 204

commons, the, 8, 28, 35–36, 38, 42–43, 45, 47–48, 56–58, 60, 62, 64, 66, 82–89, 99–100, 103, 119, 124, 137, 141, 143–44, 156, 161, 175–76, 210, 219, 222, 237–38

condemnation, 26–27, 122, 125–26, 128–29, 132, 138, 143–144, 160, 165, 168, 186, 224

Cone, James, 79, 110

Correia, David, 145, 214–16

crime, 2, 6, 8, 116, 121, 135, 140, 146–47, 149–50, 154–57, 163, 165–66, 173, 175, 184, 191–92, 195–96, 198–201, 203–4, 206, 209, 211–12, 216, 218, 222; crime control in relation to social control, 6, 253n22; etymology of, 20–21; relation of rates of crime and policing, 250n4; relation of rates of crime and incarceration, 294n55

Crime Prevention Through Environmental Design, 218

criminality, constructions of, ix, xi–xii, 3, 5, 7–9, 20–23, 27–28, 30, 43, 98, 100, 113, 119–21, 123–24, 126, 133–36, 138–40, 142–43, 146–50, 152–53, 155–56, 158–59, 165–66, 170–75, 185, 187, 190–91, 193, 200–206, 208–9, 211, 216, 218, 222, 224–27, 229, 231, 233, 239

criminalization, 2–3, 6, 10–11, 22–23, 28–30, 68, 72, 86, 118–20, 136, 141, 147, 159, 169; "mass criminalization," 3, 8, 10, 23, 29, 31, 72, 194–214, 227, 232–34, 251n11; banishment and, 35–36, 224; of beasts, 30, 78, 166, 172, 224–29; of beggars, 144–45; of behaviors, 21–22, 158, 169, 199–200, 203, 219; of Blackness, 210–14; centrality of antivagrancy to, 199, 210, 218; definition of, 22–23, 257n45; of homelessness, 205–10; in the form of Black Codes, 164–65, 211, 286n90; irredeemability of people targeted by, 154, 186; irreligiosity of people targeted by, 86, 156; religion of, 11, 29, 137, 189–94, 230–34; the role of the terry stop in, 198, 208, 212

Davis, Angela Y., 29, 31, 169, 181, 183, 236
death: broken windows policing and, 212–13, 226–28; carceral death, 150–51, 232; Christian understanding of, 96; in exchange for life, 11, 110, 130–32, 134, 183, 186–87, 227, 232; death penalties, 94, 173; fear of, 106, 109, 111, 183, 234; sacrificial death, 11, 140, 187; social death, 45; spiritual death, 233; vulnerability to premature death, 3, 22, 30, 37, 54–55, 72, 194, 202, 211, 251n12
debt, 27, 121–22, 128–32, 137–38, 186–87; and indebtedness, 26–27, 125–28, 131, 137–38, 209; the concept of owing as it relates to, 127–28, 130–31, 138; release from, 137
Defensible Space, 218
deification and destruction, 25, 28, 107–12, 180, 190, 217
demons and demonization, 30, 48, 70, 88, 108, 124, 214, 224–31, 233–34
Derrida, Jacques, 93–94
Devil, 42, 109, 124, 126, 130–32, 143, 229
dirt, 70, 204, 221–24
discipline, 145–47, 149, 153, 188, 218
dispossessed peoples: as enemies of order, 119, 124, 136, 138, 141, 200–201, 214, 222; as immoral, 28, 85–89, 99, 143–44, 146, 153–54, 156, 164, 176, 190–91, 200, 203, 206, 222, 223–24, 282n6, 283n24; as threatening swarm, 43, 262n38
dispossession, 33, 35–36, 38, 43, 54, 62–65, 73, 81, 84, 86–87, 101, 104–5, 110–11, 141, 164–67, 173, 183–84; criminalization and, 141–46, 150, 154–60, 168–69, 174–76, 190, 194–199, 202, 205, 211–12, 217, 223, 232; eurochristian legitimation of, 59–62, 84–85, 99, 110, 118, 124, 146, 150, 231; landlessness and, 86–87, 289–290n144.
divine attributes, 90–107, 271–272n64, 274n104; aseity, 96–97; impassibility, 97, 103–4; incomprehensibility, 91; justice, 122, 127, 130, 132; omnipotence, 95–96, 100, 274n104; omnipresence, 91, 95; omniscience, 95; transcendence, 91, 94–95, 106
Douglas, Kelly Brown, 79–80
Douglas, Mary, 70–71, 99, 173, 204, 221, 224
Douglass, Frederick, 211
Du Bois, W. E. B., 16, 18, 25, 47, 73, 75–78, 81, 97, 99, 110–11, 163, 165
Dubber, Markus, 188
Durkheim, Émile, 70, 120–21, 204, 233

Eliade, Mircea, 107–109, 176
enclosure, 23, 28, 35, 38, 43, 60, 62–64, 67, 82–89, 98–99, 108–9, 137, 141–42, 144, 146, 156, 160, 172–73, 209–10, 229, 237
enemies, 21–23, 25, 108–10, 118–20, 124, 134, 136, 139, 142–44, 146–147, 152, 154, 159, 167, 172, 184–185, 187, 192, 196–97, 201, 214–18, 222–32
Engels, Friedrich, 179–180
eurochristianity, xiii, 13–14, 16–19, 21, 24, 28, 30, 34, 36, 38–39, 41–42, 45–48, 51–54, 56, 58, 60, 62–63, 65, 67, 70–73, 80–82, 89, 108, 117, 121, 148, 160, 164, 166–67, 176, 181, 191, 195–96, 216, 230–31, 235
evangelicalism, Christian, 75, 80, 168, 191–93, 204

fear, ix–x, xiii, 2, 4, 23, 38, 106, 109, 111–12, 161, 183, 185, 192, 217, 234
Federici, Silvia, 61
finitude, 13–14, 25, 31, 34, 57–59, 62, 69, 71–72, 76–77, 79, 89, 91, 93–99, 103–6, 109, 111–12, 130–31, 139, 182–83, 195, 214, 228, 230, 233, 236
Finley, Stephen C., 101, 103
Floyd, George, xii, 201, 213, 235
Foucault, Michel, 153, 210, 225
frontier, 113, 117, 177, 179, 220, 225
Furman, Richard, 41

Garland, David, 233
Garner, Eric, 201, 212–13
gender, 15, 19, 24, 51–53, 61, 63–64, 66–67, 73, 77, 104–5, 152, 154–55, 166, 169, 176, 195, 202, 207, 211, 224
gentrification, 99, 113–14, 117, 220, 277–278n3
geography, 30, 49, 81, 99–100, 120, 174, 229
Gilmore, Ruth Wilson, 31, 37, 54, 136, 194, 196, 236–37
Girard, René, 186–87
Giuliani, Rudy, 200, 204, 217, 222
Gorringe, Timothy, 140
Graber, Jennifer, 148, 152
Gray, Biko Mandela, 101
Griffith, Aaron, 191
Grossman, Dave, 225
Gruber, Aya, 219

Hadden, Sally, 162
Hakluyt, Richard, 43
Hamer, Fannie Lou, xiii
Hanno, Joseph, 148–149
Harcourt, Bernard, 203
Harris, Angela, 105
Harris, Cheryl, 16, 63–66
Hartman, Saidiya, 55–56
Harvey, David, 194
Hay, Douglas, 99, 173
Hayek, Friedrich, 196
hell, ix–x, xiii, 9–10, 13, 22–23, 25, 29–30, 55, 71–72, 78, 90, 100, 107, 110, 112, 118, 139, 181–82, 190, 194, 219, 230–34
Hernández, Kelly Lytle, 170
Hill, Christopher, 84, 146
Hirsch, Adam, 144, 148
Hobbes, Thomas, 26, 38–39, 60, 82, 123–24, 134, 215
homelessness, 205–10
homology, 27, 279n30, 282n83
Howell, Babe, 201
human elimination, 3, 7–8, 18, 21–26, 30, 33, 40–42, 45, 54, 68, 70, 81–82, 84, 89, 109–10, 117–21, 124, 134–36, 139, 142–43, 145–47, 154, 159, 169–73, 175–77, 179, 182–84, 186–88, 192, 194–95, 197–200, 202–6, 211, 214–15, 217–18, 221–24, 226–28, 230–33, 238

idleness, 43, 85, 119, 143–145, 150, 152, 158, 164, 200
imperialism, 12, 35, 62, 75–76, 78, 81, 99, 117, 130, 175, 177–79, 194, 216
improvement, colonial-capitalist-carceral concept of, 83–85, 296n98
Ince, Onur Ulas, 60
Indigenous peoples, xiii, 1, 3–4, 18–20, 24, 29–30, 33, 38, 40–43, 46–48, 53–54, 59, 61, 63–66, 77, 82, 92, 100–101, 104, 106, 111, 116–17, 119–120, 124, 136, 139, 160, 166, 169, 174, 176–77, 182, 201, 209, 211, 213, 215–16, 221–22, 224–25, 237, 240, 260–61n27, 290–91n160
Irvin, Dale, 137
Isenberg, Nancy, 43, 53, 86

Jackson, George, 98, 151
jail, xii, 2, 4, 6, 8, 22–23, 113, 140, 144, 154, 189, 195–96, 202, 207–9, 211–12, 216, 219, 231–32
Jennings, Willie James, 34, 67, 80–81, 92
Jesus Christ, 129–33, 140, 186
Jim Crow, 167, 196, 211
justice, 135, 138–40, 173, 186, 197, 201, 204, 213, 216, 238–40

Kaba, Mariame, 1–2, 9, 237, 239
Kelley, Robin D. G., 15, 54
Kelling, George, 199–200, 203–4, 216–17
Kirchheimer, Otto, 145
Kohler-Hausmann, Issa, 202
Ku Klux Klan, 164, 167, 177

labor: forced, 40–41, 43, 142, 144–45, 149–50, 161, 165; reproductive, 45, 50–52, 61, 63, 169; strikes, 157–59, 171, 178, 208;

wage, 35, 37, 44, 47, 84–85, 141–42, 146, 153, 155, 157, 160–61, 196
land, 17, 22, 28, 33–35, 37–38, 40–41, 43, 46, 53, 59, 62–65, 67, 80–81, 83–85, 87, 100, 108, 113, 116–17, 123, 137, 141, 146, 149, 160–61, 170, 172–76, 179, 192, 210, 221–22, 225. *See also* property
law: Blackness and, 171; criminalization and, 121, 123, 141, 147, 161–62, 179–80, 192, 206; divine, 128, 134, 146–47, 168, 179–80, 192; labor law, 141–42, 144, 282n6, 287n94; law and order, 21–22, 128, 136–37, 168, 179–80, 191, 195, 197, 199, 206, 215–16; lawbreaking, 86, 140, 148, 168, 196; natural law, 36, 59, 160, 168; property law, 64, 83, 155; vagrancy law, 28, 43, 142–47, 157–58, 164–65, 188, 190, 198, 210–11, 218
liberalism, 26, 36, 38–39, 41, 59, 109, 117, 133–34, 138, 143, 160, 172, 183; centrality of security and social contract to, 123, 134, 138–39, 151, 183; liberty, 59, 134, 151, 170, 172;
Linebaugh, Peter, 83–84, 87, 145, 174
Linnaeus, Carolus, 49
Lipsitz, George, 66, 91, 97–99
Locke, John, 38–39, 58–62, 65–66, 82–86, 89, 99, 134, 172–73, 175–76, 222
Long, Charles, 13, 102, 185
Luther, Martin, 123
lynching, 102, 166–67

MacArthur, John, 192
Macpherson, C. B., 60
Malcolm X, 64
Malone, Timothy, 187
manifest destiny, 35, 78, 117, 177
Manning, Peter, 193
Marx, Karl, 84
masculinity, 52, 66, 105, 170, 176
masterless people, 28, 146, 215, 231
Mather, Cotton, 148–49
Mbembe, Achille, 183, 233
McCarraher, Eugene, 83

McKinley, William, 178–79
McQuade, Brendan, 237
McWhorter, Ladelle, 46, 49
mediation (religious), 31, 233, 236, 240–41
Mills, Charles, 81, 88
monstrosity, 21, 30, 52, 112, 141, 166, 183, 203, 214, 224–29, 234
Moreton-Robinson, Aileen, 53
Morgan, Jennifer, 52
Morton, Samuel George, 50
myth, 2, 10–11, 26–27, 30–31, 33, 36–39, 52, 76, 93, 134, 140, 143, 150–51, 172, 183, 190, 193, 196, 203, 214–17, 224–26, 229–30, 232, 241

Naas, Michael, 94
Nason, Arriana, 235
Native Americans, 13, 19, 65, 162, 170, 175–76, 189. *See also* Indigenous peoples
natural law, 36, 59, 160
natural order, 42, 58, 60, 75, 132, 168
necropolitics, 183, 233
necroreligion, 233–34
Neeson, J. M., 64, 87
Nelson, Dana, 53, 93
Neocleous, Mark, 99, 109, 124, 145, 183–84, 229
neoliberalism, 3, 17, 23, 29–30, 62, 191, 194–203, 205, 209, 211–13, 217–20, 222–23

obedience, 26, 38, 41–42, 60, 83, 125, 129–34, 145, 148, 152–53, 186, 188, 192, 196, 203
obligation, 26, 127–28, 130–31, 137–38, 148
Omi, Michael, 54
oppositionality, 18, 21, 23, 25, 54, 120–121, 232; antagonism and, 19–20, 55, 100, 134, 174, 187, 225; inherent to criminalization, 28, 121; inherent to modern racial capitalist state and order, 21–22, 120; inherent to patriarchal and possessive whiteness, 18, 23–25, 67, 78, 86, 92, 95, 109, 152, 181, 232; inherent to religion, 14, 71, 268–69n5

order: disorder, 3, 11, 14, 18–20, 26–27, 29–30, 70–71, 85, 99, 108, 117, 121, 124, 126–127, 135–36, 139, 141–44, 146–47, 152–54, 156, 158–59, 168, 178, 185–87, 191, 195, 199–201, 203–4, 206, 214, 217, 220–21, 223, 229, 233–34; maintenance of order, 22, 55, 69, 136, 138, 201–2, 230; restoration of hierarchical order, 27, 121, 135, 140, 143, 148, 153, 161, 186–87, 201; sacred social order, 10–11, 20–21, 25–26, 29, 119–21, 124, 128, 134–35, 139, 145–46, 148–49, 153–54, 184, 187–88, 191, 196, 228, 231

organized abandonment, xiii, 3, 191, 194–96, 201, 205, 211–12, 217, 220, 222, 238

ownership. *See* possession; property

partition, 14, 17–18, 20, 23, 29–30, 37, 81–82, 120, 144, 152, 163, 172–73, 194, 204, 214, 220, 229–30, 237

Pasquino, Pasquale, 222

patriarchy, 19, 105, 166; security and, 105

Pavarini, Massimo, 152

Peel, Sir Robert, 156–157, 177

penitentiary, 28, 119, 145, 147, 149–51, 153, 174, 190, 223, 231. *See also* prison

Philippines, 178–179

police: badged, 1, 21, 215; bluelining and, 219; Bow Street Runners, 155; broken windows policing, 30, 189, 199–214; centrality of discretion to, 117, 136, 150, 155, 189, 197–98, 206, 209, 220; Charleston Guard and Watch, 162–63; as civic father, 117, 169; constable, 144, 155, 157, 162, 178; copaganda, 9; cops, etymology of, 247–48n1; as counterinsurgent power, 178, 196–97; early militia forms of, 162, 177; etymology of, 247–48n1; first modern police department, 286n83; as garbagemen, 222; as guided by mission to "serve and protect," 2, 250n6; internationalism of, 177–79, 291n165; as law enforcement, 22, 33, 215–16; as managers of the outcomes of dispossession, 5, 29, 142, 144, 184, 196, 212, 238; as mortal God, 4, 10, 13, 26, 28, 38, 69, 72, 106, 123–24, 127, 134–35, 137–38, 140, 146–47, 152–54, 159, 161, 168, 171, 173–75, 177, 179–80, 182–83, 187, 193, 196, 198, 202, 213–14, 217, 224–28, 230, 233–34, 236, 241; as muscle of racial capitalism, 213; London Metropolitan Police, 157; Metro Nashville Police Department, xi, xii, 193; military and, x, 157, 178, 225; New York Police Department, 200, 212, 217; ordained violence of, 10, 117, 159, 193, 216, 221, 227; order-maintenance and, 30, 111, 139, 147, 159, 199, 201–2; order-sustaining power of, 10, 22, 26, 68, 104–5, 118, 134, 159, 171, 180, 193–94, 202, 209, 214, 220, 231–32, 234, 238; as paternal force, 188; patriarchal dimensions of (police), 26, 117, 143, 153–55, 166, 169–71, 188–190, 197, 203; Philippine Constabulary, 178; police power and, 21–22; police power as godlike, to create, redeem, and sustain order, 10, 22, 26, 68, 118, 121, 134, 159, 171, 180, 193, 202, 214, 220, 231–32, 234, 278n11; policeman, 168, 180, 192; *policies* and, 21; policing, xi, 7, 28, 30, 47, 67, 113, 118, 136, 155, 157, 159, 163, 167, 169, 177–79, 189, 191–93, 197–206, 210–12, 217–18, 222, 226; preservation of order and, 2, 24, 71, 102–3, 133, 136, 141, 155, 157, 185–86; preservation of property and, 62, 133–34, 136, 138–39, 146, 157–58, 172–73; relationship between settler colonial land surveyors and, 290n159; Royal Irish Constabulary, 157; security as objective of, 3, 6, 24–25, 82, 120–21, 161, 171, 175–77, 179, 183–84, 197; as sheepdogs, 225; sheriffs and, 155, 165, 168, 189; slave patrols and, 161–64, 171, 177, 184, 190; strikebreaking and, 157–59, 171, 178, 208; Texas Rangers and, 177; Thames River Police, 156–157; thin blue line, 1, 20, 30, 192, 215–16, 218–21,

225, 228–30; uniformed, 1, 21, 117, 162, 215, 222

pollution, 28, 70–72, 89, 121, 129, 149, 185, 214, 221–24, 230, 234; moral, 149, 223, 280–81n56

possession, 16–20, 24–25, 28–29, 35–36, 38, 40, 46–48, 53–67, 73, 76–78, 80–84, 86, 89, 91, 96–106, 108–12, 115–18, 128, 138–39, 142, 159, 166, 169–77, 179, 183, 190, 197, 217, 219–21, 231; concept of "having," 61

prison, 1–11, 14, 22–23, 31, 43, 126, 138, 140, 142, 144, 150–54, 165, 170, 175, 184, 187–88, 195–96, 202, 204–5, 211, 216, 231–32, 236–41; as burial, 151; as living tomb, 150; mortification within, 28, 147, 150–51, 153, 188; prison cell, 23, 113, 151, 207, 219; solitary confinement within, 150–51, 212

profane, 14, 20, 25, 70–72, 107–8, 116, 120–21, 185, 193, 195, 214, 216–17, 221, 230, 237

property: absolutely exclusive private property, 17, 36, 56–62, 82–83; constructed naturalness of, 59, 64, 110; crimes against, 149–50, 152–53, 155–57, 173–75, 289n137; displacement and, 18, 20, 24, 113–20, 141–42; etymology of, 56; landowning and, 35, 44, 62, 83–84, 87, 89, 141–142, 161, 175; nonpropertied or unpropertied people, 48, 98, 100, 109, 224; political theology of, 57–60, 62–63, 67–68, 82–90, 98–100, 106–12, 120, 124, 128, 131, 133, 146, 159, 171–75, 179–80, 183, 214–22, 229, 265n101; propertylessness and, xii–xiii, 15, 19–20, 24, 28–29, 33, 35, 47, 66, 83, 89–90, 120, 135–36, 139, 153, 162, 164, 170, 174, 182, 200, 213, 220–21, 232–33, 240; public property, 206–7, 219–20; race and, 51–53, 62–68, 113–20; reclamation of, 83, 116, 216–17, 220; in relation to paradise, 229–30; security and, 136,

138–39, 155–56, 206; sin and, 57–59, 62, 89; waste and, 30, 43, 60, 64, 100, 154, 176, 210, 222, 225

punishment, 4–5, 8–9, 21, 27, 43, 62, 70, 120–23, 126–29, 131–35, 137, 139–40, 142–43, 146–50, 153, 156, 163, 166, 169, 173–75, 186–88, 191–92, 196, 198, 202, 206, 211, 223–25, 232, 239; and social cohesion, 120, 279n18

Puritans, 28, 147–49

purity, 14, 20, 50, 70–72, 89, 94–95, 102, 121, 128–29, 149, 185 203–4, 214, 221, 223–224, 230; cleanliness and, 30, 131–32, 204, 221–24; contagion and, 23, 88–89, 98, 102, 110, 128, 154, 170, 176, 188, 222, 224; impurity and, 14, 70–71, 94, 127–128, 132, 155, 204, 222, 224; preservation of, 11, 71, 188, 233; purification, 112, 116–17, 129, 149, 176, 189, 204, 206, 211, 218, 224, 226, 228

race: and abnormality, concept of, 19, 49, 75; absolute racial differentiation, 46–47, 54–55; as anthropological essence, 38, 40, 46, 49–51, 54, 60, 122, 126, 139, 145, 151, 168, 221–22; biological, 45–46, 49–50, 134; blood and, 102; constructed naturalness of hierarchies based on, 15, 42, 46, 50, 54, 76, 161, 254n35; irrationality and, 14, 51, 89, 92, 210, 225; jungle and, 30, 168, 203, 216–17; as means of definition and differentiation, 30, 34, 37, 39, 47, 52, 54–55, 81, 88, 175, 211; morphological conceptions of, 47–49; oppositionality inherent to modern race, 54; phenotypical, 55; preservation of racial purity, 102; pseudoscientific, 48–50; racialism and, 37–38, 49, 64; racialization and, 3, 19, 50, 52, 55–56, 61, 80–81, 101, 148, 154, 158, 161, 168, 176, 204, 216, 222, 233; racism and, 5, 37, 49–50, 54, 64, 94, 98, 114, 165, 168; skin color and, 49, 55, 76; sterilization and, 50 racial capitalism, 35–39, 116, 141–42, 154, 156, 160, 183–184; accumulation and, 19, 35–38, 40, 45, 47, 51, 84–86, 99, 101, 104, 111, 142, 159, 174, 195, 215; appropriation and, 53, 60–61, 65, 83; capital and, 17, 28, 37–38, 40, 42–43, 45, 47, 51, 53, 83–84, 99, 141–44, 146–147, 149, 155–56, 163, 171, 174, 180, 184, 195, 205, 213, 217, 219–21, 223, 231; chattel slavery's role in producing and expanding, 41, 44, 260n25; colonial racial capitalism, 251n9; constructed naturalness of, 36, 39, 146, 254n34; gender and, 265n88; expropriation and, 41, 44, 46, 84; necessity of poverty to, 35–36, 54; neoliberal, 3, 23, 194–97, 213; patriarchal dimensions of, 51, 143, 155, 169–171, 203; patriarchal structure of, 51–53; religious structure of, 38–39, 99, 223; security and, 7, 18–20, 22, 33, 46, 50, 71, 161, 183–84, 187, 215, 219; self-generated crises of, 30, 34, 68, 196, 202

racial class war, 22, 179, 195–96, 216, 234

Razack, Sherene, 176, 189

Reagan, Ronald, 216–17

Rediker, Marcus, 83–84

refusal to be subject, 26–28, 125–30, 134, 138–39, 142–48, 152, 154, 161–63, 166, 186, 188, 228–29, 231

religion: as concerned with a "beyond," 13, 16, 55, 69, 77, 93–94, 103, 108–9, 120, 229, 235–236, 241; critiques of, 253–54n33; meaning of, 12–15, 34–35, 69–73, 253n31; as orientation, 6, 13–14, 34, 70, 73, 102, 108, 139, 183, 185, 240, 253n31; self-deification and, 70, 180

restorative justice, 7–8

revanchism, 3, 195–97, 220

Ringer, Christophe, 148–49, 233

Ritchie, Andrea, 1–2, 166, 237

Robinson, Cedric, 37, 39, 53, 63

Roediger, David, 48, 51, 66, 95

Rousseau, Jean-Jacques, 82, 134, 228

Rusche, Georg, 145

sacrifice, 6, 11, 80, 111, 130, 140, 151, 186–87, 193, 197, 210, 227, 232–33

safety, ix, xii–xiii, 1–9, 11, 22, 25, 29–31, 33, 65, 98–99, 111–12, 121, 133, 161, 168, 172, 181–86, 190, 193, 196–97, 209, 214, 226–27, 230, 233–35, 238–41; absolute safety, 182–84; illusion of, 14, 25, 30–31, 54, 66, 73, 75–76, 78, 90, 93–94, 104–6, 182–84, 190, 205, 233–34; security and, 33, 112, 183–85; transcendent safety, 185, 190

salvation: etymology of, 186; security and, 22, 24, 77, 94, 185–87, 210, 229, 233–34. *See also* safety; soteriology of subjection

Sered, Danielle, 2, 5, 7–8

sexual violence, 45, 51–52, 66, 102, 105, 166, 169, 189–90, 212

Singh, Nikhil Pal, 178–79

Slave Codes, 161–162, 164

slavery, 24, 37–42, 44–45, 47–51, 56, 59, 63–65, 78–79, 84, 86, 122, 124, 126–29, 142–44, 148, 151, 160–65, 166–67, 171, 174–77, 181, 184, 188, 190, 192, 210–11, 228, 236; indentured servitude and, 40, 42, 44–45, 47; constructed naturalness of, 41, 52; plantation and, 40–41, 43–49, 51, 62–63, 73, 151, 161, 163–65, 174–75, 177, 211; Redemption (southern) and, 166–67, 197; reenslavement, 44, 163

Smith, Adam, 39, 59, 136, 172, 222

Smith, Caleb, 150–151

soteriology of subjection, 26–27, 125, 127–29, 131–34, 137–40, 143, 145, 147–48, 152–53, 186, 196, 224, 228, 231; Anselm's pearl in mud and, 128, 224; atonement and, 126, 131–32; bondage and, 129–31, 137; chains and, 127, 135; corruption and, 21, 26–27, 125–26, 129, 131–32, 138, 154, 156, 188, 224, 231;

dishonor and, 129, 132; disobedience and, 27, 29, 38, 83, 125–26, 128–32, 134–35, 146–49, 168, 187–89, 228; etymology of soteriology, 292n17; expiation and, 132, 148–49, 280–81n56; guilt and, 26–27, 115, 126–27, 129, 131, 137, 202; humans' state of ruination and, 125, 127–29; merciful punishment and, 284n49; offense and, 18, 21, 38, 80, 121, 128, 137–38, 148, 155, 164, 188, 204–7, 212; payment of debt and, 27, 128–31, 138, 18687; propitiation and, 130, 132, 280–81n56; ransom theory of atonement as expression of, 129–30, 132; recompense and, 8, 27, 127–29, 131, 239; redemptive state violence and, 150, 152, 167, 189; restoration to subjection to God and, 129, 131, 186, 190; retributivism and, 126, 129, 132; satisfaction and, 27, 44, 122, 126–32, 137–38, 140, 144, 149, 186, 231–32, 280–81n56; security and, 33, 112, 183–85; sin and the state in, 133, 138–39; sin in, 26–27, 124–33, 140, 152, 186; sin of pride in, 38, 123, 126–28, 130; substitution in, 126, 132–133, 186

sovereignty, 18, 26, 30, 82, 96, 122, 127–28, 131, 133–34, 145, 147, 174, 186, 197, 215, 229, 231

spatiality, 14, 16–17, 23–25, 30, 34, 51, 56, 67, 69–71, 77, 81–82, 89, 91, 93–94, 97–100, 107–10, 116, 120, 128, 137, 144, 150, 152, 170, 175–78, 206, 208–10, 213–14, 217–20, 223–24, 229, 232, 239

subduing, 38, 60, 64, 82, 99, 132, 145, 155, 157

subjection, 8, 10–11, 18, 22, 26–30, 40–41, 51, 55, 60, 73, 104–5, 123–36, 138–40, 142–54, 156, 160–63, 166–67, 171, 178, 184, 186–90, 196, 198, 214–15, 219, 225, 228–29, 231–34

subjugation, 52, 73, 76, 162, 164–67, 189–90, 197, 211, 233

submission, 37, 41, 87, 123, 130, 133–34, 141–42, 145–47, 166, 195

subordination, 50, 64, 127–29, 138, 161, 164

surplus peoples, 43, 186, 195–96, 205, 217

surveillance, 22, 33, 47, 100, 135, 155, 157–58, 161, 164, 171, 175, 195, 219

Tanner, Kathryn, 94
Taylor, Breonna, xii, 221
theo-carcerality, 29, 149, 162, 186
thieves, 172, 199
Thirteenth Amendment (US Constitution), 163
Thompson, E. P., 86, 173
Tinker, Tink, 13, 35, 66
Tocqueville, Alexis de, 119
transcendence: abolitionist transcendence, 14, 31, 236–237, 241; Black transcendence, 56; divine transcendence, 91, 94–95, 106; religion as transcendence and transformation, 13–14, 25, 31, 69, 71, 230, 233, 236; transcendent nature of police power of the state, 121, 135, 197; transcendent power of capital, 196; transcendent power of whiteness and property, 16, 19, 25, 31, 34, 48, 72–73, 75, 77–79, 91–99, 101, 103–8, 111, 117–18, 181–83, 185, 214, 229, 231, 274n101

transformative justice, 7–8, 239
trespass, xi–xii, 12, 17–18, 20–21, 23–24, 28–29, 62, 67–68, 71, 77, 86, 89, 98–99, 102, 110, 113, 116, 118, 120, 124, 135, 137, 139, 141, 152, 161, 171–73, 175–76, 206–10, 213, 217–21, 229–30; matter and people "out of place" and, 18–19, 25, 29, 67–70, 94–98, 121, 136–37, 139, 141, 144, 152, 154, 161, 172–73, 176, 187, 198–208, 213, 221, 224, 231; sin and, 18, 137

Tyley, James, 87–89

unhoused, x–xi, 30, 189, 199–201, 205–10, 218–21, 223

vagrancy, 28, 43, 85–87, 119, 142–47, 149, 157–58, 164–65, 170, 188, 190, 198, 203–4, 206, 210–11, 218, 222, 282–83n7, 286n91. *See also* idleness
Vesely-Flad, Rima, 223
Vesey, Denmark, 79
Vitale, Alex, 6, 157
Vollmer, August, 178
vulnerability, xiii, 3, 11, 16, 22, 25, 37, 55, 72, 77, 93–94, 97–98, 103–4, 106, 111, 166, 175, 182–84, 199, 202–3, 213, 232, 241

Wacquant, Loïc, 195
Wadsworth, Benjamin, 148
Wagner, Bryan, 197
Walia, Harsha, 177
Walker, David, 78–79
Wall, Tyler, 145, 214–16, 225–26
white manhood, 53, 66, 92–93, 103, 105, 115, 160, 223
whiteness, 15–20, 23–25, 29, 33–56, 62–82, 89–120, 135, 138–39, 157–71, 174–83, 185, 189–90, 194, 197, 203, 208–14, 217–18, 220–21, 223–24, 228, 230–32; Anglo identity and, 47–48, 79, 123, 170, 203; antagonism inherent to, 55, 159; anxiety of, 72, 76–77, 105–16, 111, 166, 217, 223, 236; apatheia and, 97; apotheosis of, 73, 193; aseity os, 96–98, 103–4; aspiration to, 6, 16, 21, 71, 73, 77–82, 91, 93–95, 97–98, 103–5, 110, 117, 145, 159, 161, 181–83, 214, 220; authority of, 55, 77, 80, 99–104, 115, 160, 171; deceptiveness of, 277n156; deputization of, 161, 171; Europeanization and, 81; Europeanness and, 16, 34, 80, 161; as genocidal lie, 6, 18, 34, 79, 90, 182; infinitude of patriarchal and possessive whiteness, 18, 23, 77, 80, 82, 89, 91, 93, 95, 97, 109, 149, 176–77, 181–82, 196–98; as inherently threatened, 109; insecurity of, 76, 106, 109, 183–84; immutability of, 49, 97; impassibility of, 97–98, 103–4; invulnerability of, 25, 72, 95, 97–98, 103–4, 181–82; mastery and, 93–94, 103–6, 170; as means of dispossession, 67; as phantasm, 78, 93–94, 104, 229; metaphysics and, 70, 90–91, 93, 95, 106; moral innocence of, 101–2; nonwhiteness and, 4, 8, 18–20, 24, 48–50, 54, 79, 81–82, 89–90, 92–93, 95, 98, 100, 103–4, 109, 116–17, 135, 139, 160, 169, 195, 211, 216, 220, 232; normative gaze of, 53, 93, 100, 115; omnipotence of, 93, 95–96, 100, 117–18, 143, 159, 181, 215, 220; omnipresence of, 91, 95–96; patriarchal nature of, 16, 19, 25, 50–53, 93, 101, 103–6, 166; pseudo-divine attributes of, 48, 90–91, 96–97, 104, 106, 133; in relation to "white people," 256n38; security and, 65–66, 92, 104, 111; security and property and, 59, 65, 73, 76, 89, 98, 100, 106, 108–9, 171, 175, 182–83, 213; violence of, 254–256n37
Wilderson III, Frank, 171
Williams, Kristian, 155
Wilson, James Q., 199
Winant, Howard, 54
Witte, John Jr., 123
Wolfe, Patrick, 18, 40, 46, 54
womanhood: and the commons, 264n75; Black womanhood, 45, 51–53, 61, 65, 92, 104, 166; white womanhood, 51, 53, 66, 92, 102–4, 155, 169
workhouse, 43, 145, 149, 174, 188

Yancy, George, 92, 101

Zapatistas, 235

ABOUT THE AUTHOR

ANDREW KRINKS is an independent scholar, educator, and movement builder based in Nashville, Tennessee. His writing on religion and abolition has appeared in multiple journals and edited volumes. He teaches courses on religion, theology, and carceral studies. He organizes and educates as part of the movement for a world of safety and abundance beyond police and prisons.

www.ingramcontent.com/pod-product-compliance
Lightning Source LLC
Chambersburg PA
CBHW020354080526
44584CB00014B/1009